T0150403

TWO SOCIETIES IN OPPOSITION

STUDIES IN ECONOMIC, SOCIAL, AND POLITICAL CHANGE:
THE REPUBLIC OF CHINA
Ramon H. Myers, General Editor

Understanding Communist China:
Communist China Studies in the United States
and the Republic of China, 1949–1978
    Tai-chün Kuo and Ramon H. Myers, editors

Phoenix and the Lame Lion:
Modernization in Taiwan and Mainland China
    Alan P. Liu

The Great Transition:
Political and Social Change
in the Republic of China
    Hung-mao Tien

A Unique Relationship:
The United States and the Republic of China
under the Taiwan Relations Act
    Ramon H. Myers, editor

The Foreign Factor:
The Multinational Corporation's Contribution to
the Economic Modernization of the Republic of China
    Chi Schive

Two Societies in Opposition:
The Republic of China and the
People's Republic of China after Forty Years
    Ramon H. Myers, editor

All Under Heaven ...:
Sun Yat-sen and His Revolutionary Thought
    Sidney H. Chang and Leonard H.D. Gordon

OF RELATED INTEREST:

Last Chance in Manchuria: The Diary of Chang Kia-ngau
    Hoover Archival Documentary
    Donald G. Gillin and Ramon H. Myers, editors
    Dolores Zen, translator

TWO SOCIETIES IN OPPOSITION

THE REPUBLIC OF CHINA AND THE PEOPLE'S REPUBLIC OF CHINA AFTER FORTY YEARS

EDITED BY
Ramon H. Myers

HOOVER INSTITUTION PRESS
Stanford University
Stanford, California

Hoover Press Publication 401
Copright 1991 by the Board of Trustees of the
    Leland Stanford Junior University

First printing, 1991
96 95 94 93 92 91   9 8 7 6 5 4 3 2 1
Simultaneous first paperback printing, 1991
96 95 94 93 92 91   9 8 7 6 5 4 3 2 1

Manufactured in the United States of America
Printed on acid-free paper

Library of Congress Cataloging-in-Publication Data

Two societies in opposition : the Republic of China and the People's
Republic of China after forty years / Ramon H. Myers, editor.
        p.   cm. — (Studies in economic, social, and political change,
the Republic of China)
    Includes bibliographical references and index.
    ISBN 0-8179-9091-7. — ISBN 0-8179-9092-5 (pbk.)
    1. Taiwan—Economic conditions—1945-   2. Taiwan—Social
conditions—1945-   3. Taiwan—Politics and government—1945-
4. China—Economic conditions—1949-   5. China—Social
conditions—1949-   6. China—Politics and government—1949-
I. Myers, Ramon Hawley, 1929-   . II. Series.
HC430.5.T88   1991   90-49364
951.05′9—dc20   CIP

Contents

Contributors

Thomas A. Metzger is a Senior Fellow at the Hoover Institution and professor emeritus at the University of California at San Diego. He received his Ph.D. from Harvard University in history and Far Eastern languages. In 1982–1983 and 1984–1985 he was Visiting Research Professor at National Taiwan Normal University. The author of numerous papers and articles, his books are entitled *The Internal Organization of Ch'ing Bureaucracy: Legal, Normative, and Communication Aspects* and *Escape from Predicament: Neo-Confucianism and China's Evolving Political Culture.*

Ramon H. Myers is a Senior Fellow and Curator-Scholar of East Asian Studies at the Hoover Institution. He is the coauthor, with Tai-chün Kuo, of *Understanding Communist China* (1986), coeditor, with Donald G. Gillin, of *Last Chance in Manchuria: The Diary of Chang Kia-ngau* (1989), and editor of *A Unique Relationship: The United States and the Republic of China Under the Taiwan Relations Act* (1989).

Paul A. Cohen teaches at Wellesley College and is affiliated with the Fairbank Center for East Asian Research, Harvard University. He writes on both nineteenth- and twentieth-century China. His latest book is *Discovering History in China: American Historical Writing on the Recent Chinese Past* (1984).

Yü Yü-lin is an associate Research Fellow at the Institute of International Relations, National Chengchih University.

Hongda Harry Wu first came under suspicion and investigation by Chinese authorities in 1957, when he was a twenty-year-old university student, after he openly disagreed with the suppression by Soviet forces of the Hungarian revolution of 1956. In 1960, he was sentenced to a labor reform camp for nineteen years. In 1985 he came to the United States as a visiting scholar to the civil engineering department of the University of California at Berkeley. From 1987 to the present, he has been a visiting scholar doing research and study at Hoover Institution.

John C. H. Fei is a professor of economics at Yale University. He is a member of Academia Sinica of the Republic of China. He has done research and teaching on economic development in China.

Lü Ya-li earned his B.A. degree at National Taiwan University and his Ph.D. from Indiana University. Since 1972 he has served as an associate professor and professor of political science at National Taiwan University. He also served as a Senior Fellow at the Atlantic Council, Washington, D.C., in 1984. He has published books and papers in Chinese and English.

Hsin-huang Michael Hsiao is a Fellow at the Institute of Ethnology, Academia Sinica, and a professor of sociology at National Taiwan University.

Hu Chang is an associate Research Fellow at the Institute of International Relations at National Chengchih University.

Thomas B. Gold is chair of the Center for Chinese Studies and associate professor of sociology at the University of California at Berkeley. In 1988–1989 he was a National Fellow at the Hoover Institution.

Nicholas R. Lardy is a professor at the Henry M. Jackson School of International Studies, University of Washington at Seattle. He received his Ph.D. from the University of Michigan in 1975. His most recent publication is *China's Entry into the World Economy* (1987).

Joseph Fewsmith is an analyst at the Foreign Broadcast Information Service in Washington, D.C. He received his Ph.D. from the University of Chicago in political science and has published numerous articles on contemporary Chinese political and economic affairs. His latest book is *Party, State, and Local Elites in Republican China*. He is currently working on a book about the political economy of reform in the Dengist period.

An-chia Wu received his Ph.D. from National Chengchih University. He is a Research Fellow and convener of the Mainland Research Group, Institute of International Relations, National Chengchih University. His major publications are *Chinese Historiography since 1976, Change and Continuity of*

CCP's Ideology, A Study of the Controversies over the Societal History of China, and "Mainland China in Forty Years: a Retrospect and Prospect" (editorial).

Edward I-hsin Chen is an associate professor in the Department of History, Bowling Green State University, Ohio. Born in Taiwan, he received his B.A. from National Taiwan University and his Ph.D. from the University of Pennsylvania. Professor Chen's specialty is Japanese history, particularly Japanese colonialism in Taiwan and Korea, and most of his publications have been in this area. Five years ago he branched into the study of legal education in Japan. His latest publication is "A Foreigner's Views on the Japanese Legal Education System" (translated Japanese title), *Juristo,* January 1991.

Stanley Rosen is an associate professor at the University of Southern California in the Department of Political Science. He received his Ph.D. from the University of California at Los Angeles in 1979. Professor Rosen has written and edited a number of books on China including *Red Guard Factionalism and the Cultural Revolution in Guangzhou* and *Survey Research in the People's Republic of China* (coauthored with David Chu).

Harry Harding is a Senior Fellow in the Foreign Policy Studies Program at the Brookings Institution in Washington, D.C. He received his undergraduate education at Princeton University and his graduate training in political science at Stanford University. He is the editor of *China's Foreign Relations in the 1980s* (1984) and *Sino-American Relations, 1945–1955: A Joint Reassessment of a Critical Decade* (1989). He is also the author of *Organizing China: The Problem of Bureaucracy, 1949–1976* (1981), *China's Second Revolution: Reform after Mao* (1987), *China and Northeast Asia: The Political Dimension* (1988), and many other works on Chinese domestic affairs, foreign policy, and U.S.-China relations. He taught for one year at Swarthmore College and twelve years at Stanford University before assuming his present position in the fall of 1983.

Andrew G. Walder is a professor of sociology at Harvard University, where he is also an associate of the Fairbank Center for East Asian Research. He is the author of *Communist Neo-Traditionalism: Work and Authority in Chinese Industry* (1986) and *Chang Ch'un-ch'iao and Shanghai's January Revolution* (1978).

Preface

On June 8–11, 1989, the Hoover Institution on War, Revolution and Peace hosted the eighteenth Sino-American Conference on China Mainland Affairs. In this series of conferences prominent experts from the United States and the Republic of China have met annually to present their research findings on problems and developments in the People's Republic of China (PRC). The first conference was convened in 1971 in Taipei and hosted by the Institute of International Relations and other research and academic organizations in the Republic of China (ROC). The second conference was held in 1972 in San Francisco and was hosted by the Hoover Institution. In subsequent years, this conference has rotated between Taipei and various institutes and universities in the United States.

For the 1989 conference, Dr. Chang King-yuh, director of the Institute of International Relations, and his staff played an important role by helping to identify scholars and assist in the planning of that meeting. We warmly acknowledge their moral support and assistance.

Mrs. Maxine Douglas, secretary to Dr. Ramon H. Myers, assisted in coordinating the conference and arranging for distribution of conference papers. Ms. Teresa Terry handled the logistics and management of the conference. The Hoover Institution sponsored the conference and received funding assistance from the American cosponsoring institutions that have supported these conferences in previous years.

Both Pinyin and Wade–Giles romanizations were used in the conference papers, according to each author's preference. *Beijing* has been used instead of *Peking* to identify the capital of the People's Republic of China.

The editor gratefully acknowledges the assistance of the Hoover Institution.

Thomas A. Metzger and Ramon H. Myers

Introduction

Two Diverging Societies

Differences of Kind or of Degree?

The Chinese Communist Party (CCP) and the Nationalists (Kuomintang; KMT) have been locked in a titanic struggle since 1927, when the KMT carried out a bloody purge of Communists in Shanghai and elsewhere. With some interruptions, armed conflict continued until 1949, when the CCP forced the KMT off the mainland onto Taiwan and five sets of islets, including Kinmen and Matsu. Each group then set about in its part of China to organize society as it saw fit.

Four decades later, there is a glaring contrast, which few scholars predicted, between the economic-political successes of the Republic of China (ROC) under the KMT and the failures of the People's Republic of China (PRC) under the CCP. While the PRC remains economically backward, the ROC is the envy of the developing world.[1] We were off by only a year or two when we predicted in 1983 that by 1985 praise of the ROC's political

---

[1] See the articles in this book by John C.H. Fei and Nicholas R. Lardy. Their findings are essentially uncontroversial. See, *e.g.,* Ramon H. Myers, "How Can We Evaluate Communist China's Economic Development Performance?" *Issues & Studies,* vol. 23, no. 2 (Feb. 1987):122–55. For interactions between the state and the private sector, see Danny K. K. Lam, "Independent Economic Sectors and Economic Growth in Hong Kong and Taiwan," *International Studies Notes,* vol. 15, no. 1 (Winter 1990): 28–34.

development would match praise of its economic progress.[2] Today, even strong critics of the KMT, such as the Legislator Chu Kao-cheng, say that the era of dictatorship is in the past. Full democratization is imminent. When an important opposition party, the Democratic-Progressive Party (DPP), was legalized in 1989, China for the first time in its history institutionalized a form of social coalescence that was legal, political, and independent of the chain of command under the head of state.[3] In the 1980s, however, political liberalization in the PRC turned out to be abortive. On the night of June 3– 4, 1989, the People's Liberation Army crushed the students demonstrating in Tien-an-men Square for democracy.[4] Thereafter the PRC reverted to an overtly coercive mode it had begun to leave behind after the death of Mao Tse-tung in 1976.

To what extent has this contrast been due not only to recent events and trends going back to the 1970s, but also to systemic ideological and insti-tutional differences between the two societies as the CCP and the KMT had respectively shaped them by the 1960s or even the 1950s?

To a large extent, we think. The contributors to this symposium, how-ever, do not all necessarily agree with us. Each of the articles in this volume stands on its own, and the views in some of them are in tension with the argument we shall try to develop in this introduction.

Much in tension with it is the common Chinese view that the only systemically important political distinction is between "democracy" (*min-chu*) and "dictatorship" (*chuan-chih*). From this standpoint, because CCP and KMT rule were both dictatorial, differences between them were only a matter of degree. Similarly, in this book, Lü Ya-li identifies as a single category all cases in which "the state is very powerful and makes all major decisions for the society."

A major Western outlook is similar. Using a term that could as well apply to the KMT, Harry Harding's article holds that "the first defining feature of the Chinese Communist politics has been its tutelary quality." In 1988, Paul A. Cohen developed a similar perspective. He granted that the

---

[2]Amy A. Wilson, Sidney L. Greenblatt, and Richard W. Wilson, eds., *Methodological Issues in Chinese Studies* (New York: Praeger Publishers, 1983), p. 49.

[3]An abortive period of political pluralism occurred in 1911–1913. The comment by Chu Kao-cheng is in *Shih-chieh jih-pao*, April 29, 1990. On democratization in the ROC, see the articles below by Lü Ya-li and Hsin-huang Michael Hsiao; also Hung-mao Tien, *The Great Transition* (Stanford, Calif.: Hoover Institution Press, 1989).

[4]See Chu-yuan Cheng, *Behind the Tiananmen Massacre: Social, Political, and Economic Ferment in China* (Boulder, Colo.: Westview Press, 1990), and Geremie Barmé, "Confession, Redemption and Death: Lu Xiaobo and the Protest Movement of 1989" (unpublished, so far as we know).

ROC's policies have "achieved a substantial measure of success," while the PRC's "polity as presently constituted confronts a profound dilemma," which can be resolved only through the "restructuring of the state-society relationship."[5] Yet he did not consider whether the ROC had succeeded because it had from the outset structured the state-society relation in a way different from that of the PRC.

In his eyes, the Taiwan case has been distinguished only by situational factors, such as "the island's small scale, the positive legacy of a half century of Japanese colonial rule, a high per capita level of U.S. aid."[6] With regard to institutional factors, Cohen depicts a broad mainstream including not only Taiwan but also the late Ch'ing "self-strengthening" movement, the Empress Dowager's policies at the turn of the century, Yuan Shih-k'ai's and Chiang K'ai-shek's policies during the Republican period (1912–1949), PRC reforms after 1976, and, to some extent, Mao's policies after 1949.

In all these cases, Chinese pursued a "national agenda . . . transcending parochial political and ideological commitments." That agenda was centered on the "quest for wealth and power." The emphasis was on power[7] and "authoritarian" "state building."[8] That is, all these cases displayed "great antipathy . . . to any and all forms of power sharing. . . . an abiding aversion . . . to pluralism in the political realm, in the sense of constitutionally safeguarded opposition and dissent."[9] Pursuing "authoritarian moderniza- tion,"[10] leaders in all these cases used reforms to enhance the power of the state over society, to effect economic, military, and educational moderniza- tion, to wrestle with the bureaucratic problems of "factionalism and pa- tronage," and to learn from the West without succumbing to imperialism.[11]

To conceptualize differences within this institutional mainstream, Cohen uses two concepts: "oscillation between centralization and decentralization," and "different modalities of reform."[12] These notions are indeed useful for discussion of the differences between the PRC and the ROC. Cohen, how- ever, uses them mainly to clarify contrasts between modes of PRC governance.

Thus, with regard to the crucial issue of centralization, he sees no

---

[5]Paul A. Cohen, "The Post-Mao Reforms in Historical Perspective," *The Journal of Asian Studies,* vol. 17, no. 3 (Aug. 1988):536–37.
[6]Ibid., p. 536.
[7]Ibid., p. 534.
[8]Ibid., p. 519.
[9]Ibid., pp. 531, 533.
[10]Ibid., p. 535.
[11]Ibid., pp. 529–31.
[12]Ibid., pp. 525–27, 532.

contrast between PRC and ROC institutions. True, referring to KMT efforts in the period 1928–1949 "to gather as much power as possible into the hands of the central government," "[to maximize] the state's control over society's resources," and to "extend the reach of the state as deeply as possible into society,"[13] he notes that these efforts were undermined by local elites. He does not, however, mention any decentralization due to the KMT's own goals and policies.

Similarly, Cohen no doubt grants that ROC and PRC "modalities of reform" differed, but he emphasizes differences between PRC modalities, namely those of Mao and Teng. Thus he depicts a spectrum not unlike ours, set out below, distinguishing between more "conservative" reforms and those trying to create a "new social order" by destroying the power of old elites and pursuing "planned social transformation."[14] He then puts Mao at the latter pole and grants that Teng was closer to it than Chiang. His key point, however, is that both Teng and Chiang belong to the more "conservative" "mainstream" going back to the nineteenth century.[15]

Yet there is much evidence undiscussed by Cohen suggesting that contrasts between KMT governance and even Teng Hsiao-p'ing's policies constituted a difference of kind, not of degree.

An Analytical Framework

Thinking about societies comparatively, one cannot avoid some distinction between differences of kind and of degree. Yet especially because the typological, often Parsonian way of distinguishing between different kinds of "social systems" has come under fire,[16] how to establish a difference of kind is a controversial issue that cannot be settled by applying any scientific rule. All one can do is appeal to the reader's judgment by adducing tendencies that suggest persistently different cognitive, institutional, and behavioral patterns.

What organizing concepts are available to describe such differences? There are, to begin with, normative approaches, civic guidelines, such as the official doctrine of the ROC (Sunism; the Three Principles of the People)

---

[13]Ibid., pp. 523, 530–532.

[14]Ibid., pp. 532–33.

[15]Ibid., pp. 535–36.

[16]See, *e.g.,* Randall Collins, "A Comparative Approach to Political Sociology," in Reinhard Bendix, ed., *State and Society: A Reader in Comparative Political Sociology* (Boston, Mass.: Little, Brown and Company, 1968), pp. 42–67.

or Maoism. We happen to think that the former contributed to the ROC's successes, and that the latter contributed to the failures of the PRC. Whatever their effects, however, the actual nature of each is an empirical problem, study of which requires a descriptive analytical approach, not normative guidelines.[17]

Admittedly, such a descriptive framework cannot stray far from Cohen's two categories: degree of centralization and modality of reform. This is clear from a survey of the available methodologies. Some terminological adjustments, however, can facilitate induction and analysis.

One approach would be to use the distinction between "totalitarian" and "authoritarian" political systems, a distinction pertaining to the issue of centralization and developed by Gabriel A. Almond and G. Bingham Powell, Jr.[18] True, this famous distinction is implicitly rejected by some scholars, such as Paul Cohen, Harry Harding, and, perhaps, Lü Ya-li. Certainly "totalitarianism" is linguistically infelicitous, since no leader has ever controlled a society totally. Moreover, these categories are too general, each denoting actually very disparate cases. Yet this problem of generalness is hardly alleviated by subsuming the PRC and the ROC under one general category, "authoritarian rule," instead of two.

Moreover, we think it is hard not to use some kind of distinction such as the one Almond and Powell made. Again, the issue, as Cohen suggests, is very much that of the state-society relation. To be a bit clearer, however, we shall make use of Edward A. Shils' concept of a political "center."[19] Simplifying his approach, we define a "political center" as the legally most powerful roles and collectivities in a society, along with their subordinates and centripetal elites. We want to focus on the structural relationship between this center and the rest of society.

This relationship, we argue, can vary in ways greatly affecting issues that matter deeply to many people, such as freedom, equality, and living standards. One version of this relationship uses a system of relatively free elections to subordinate the center to political demands arising out of both the center and the rest of society. This is Millsian, Schumpeterian democracy,

---

[17]For Sun Yat-sen's doctrine, see Chu-yuan Cheng, ed., *Sun Yat-sen's Doctrine in the Modern World* (Boulder, Colo.: Westview Press, 1989); for Mao's, see Stuart R. Schram, *The Political Thought of Mao Tse-Tung* (New York: Praeger Publishers, 1969).

[18]Gabriel A. Almond and G. Bingham Powell, Jr., *Comparative Politics: A Developmental Approach* (Boston, Mass.: Little, Brown and Company, 1966), pp. 272–73.

[19]Edward A. Shils, *Center and Periphery: Essays in Macrosociology* (Chicago, Ill.: University of Chicago Press, 1975).

whether or not a "civil society" is constituted in the full normative sense of that term.[20] We call it a "subordinated center." In another case, there is no such subordination of the center to society's political demands, but the center does not control many of the society's resources, and it gives much leeway to other loci of decisionmaking, such as "self-propelled adults" using their own judgment rather than following state commands to decide where to reside, how to pursue education, what intellectual and moral choices to make, what occupation to enter, what business deals to make, and what political cause to support. We call this an "inhibited center." A third kind of center minimizes such leeway and maximizes centralization. We call this an "uninhibited center."

With regard to Cohen's other variable, modality of reform, many scholars, including Cohen, have suggested distinctions similar to ours between "transformative" and "accommodative" policies.[21] John C.H. Fei's article, for instance, distinguishes between the PRC's "politicized, revolutionary approach" to economic development and the ROC's "pragmatic, evolutionary" approach.

Few would dispute, however, that all such categories are very general and should be supplemented by what Robert K. Merton called "middle-range" categories.[22] We use ten of these:

1. each center's autocratic core;
2. its ideological or cognitive modes;
3. the internal organization of the ruling party;
4. governmental structure;

---

[20]To appreciate that "civil society" is a fundamentally normative term, not a simply descriptive one such as "center," see John Keane, *Democracy and Civil Society* (London: Verso, 1988). A descriptive term to match "center" is thus hard to find, since "periphery" does not do justice to some of the important social contours involved.

[21]We used the transformative-accommodative distinction in our "Sinological Shadows: The State of Modern China Studies in the United States," *The Washington Quarterly*, vol. 3, no. 2 (Spring 1980):110–13. That traditional Confucian thought involved a dichotomy of this sort is a point now basic to a good deal of research, especially that of Max K.W. Huang (Huang K'o-wu) on Ch'ing statecraft thought. The dichotomy was set forth in Thomas A. Metzger, *The Internal Organization of Ch'ing Bureaucracy* (Cambridge, Mass.: Harvard University Press, 1973), pp.74–79, and discussed also in his later writings.

[22]Robert K. Merton, *Social Theory and Social Structure* (Glencoe, Ill.: The Free Press, 1959).

5. the kind of control exerted by the ruling party over its auxiliary organizations;
6. the society's economic and social structure;
7. the main sanction pattern used by the center to control the rest of society (we use Amitai Etzioni's typology, distinguishing between normative, remunerative, and coercive sanctions);[23]
8. the extent of state-directed mobilization of the population;
9. some leadership characteristics, such as success in dealing with the problems of stability and gerontocracy; and
10. basic relationships with the international community.

Using these ten categories to sort out the facts, we can make clear many specific contrasts between the two Chinese societies as they were constituted by the 1950s. We also can show that the main trends in the case of each society tended to form a coherent whole made up of patterns reinforcing each other in a logical and practical way. Each society, in other words, included a basic "package" of symbolic-institutional tendencies mutually displaying elective affinity, to use S. N. Eisenstadt's term. The two "packages" were different in kind, and each displayed what Douglass North calls "path dependency," that is, inertia.[24]

The distinctiveness of each "package," moreover, is suggested by evidence that each differed from the other in terms of its relation with the traditional civilization. To be sure, this is a controversial subject. Some scholars describe such a contrast by accepting the CCP's claim that it tried to break completely with China's "feudal" past, and that the KMT perpetuated much of the latter. At the very least, this view fails to take into account connections with the past that are not consciously formulated. Another approach, close to Cohen's, rejects such a contrast and instead posits a traditional authoritarianism or other "poisons of feudalism" that influenced both the KMT and the CCP. This approach, however, suffers from a shortcoming also affecting the first one: it does not sufficiently consider all the different aspects of the tradition. Moreover, emphasizing Chinese practices, such as foot-binding, that are repulsive by modern stan-

---

[23] Amitai Etzioni, *A Comparative Analysis of Complex Organizations* (New York: Free Press of Glencoe, 1961).

[24] The "package" concept was worked out by S. N. Eisenstadt in some recent writing so far unpublished so far as we know. "Path dependency" is a concept, credit for which Douglass C. North gives to Brian Arthur and Paul David. See North's "Economic Development in Historical Perspective: The Western World" (paper for the Conference on the Wealth of Nations, Hoover Institution, March 7–8, 1990).

dards, it suggests that in the Chinese case, authoritarian and inhumane practices were more important than in the Western. Western horror stories, in other words, do not reveal the Western essence, but the dark side of Chinese civilization was its main side. Thus Mao was a typical product of Chinese civilization, but Hitler and Stalin were not typical of the West. This kind of disparagement, however, is no way to study cultures, even though it has often been subtly used to excuse the regimentation and repression inflicted by the CCP on mainland Chinese.

At least three major aspects of the Chinese traditional base line should be considered when analyzing Chinese modernization. First, research has established that Confucian thought had both a transformative side, calling for the total elimination of selfishness in society, and an accommodative one, accepting the persistence of some evil while promoting gradual, piece-meal reforms. Mao's policies were largely transformative; KMT policies, accommodative.

Second, this tranformative approach in Confucianism included the ideal of an uninhibited center, one ruled by a sage with whose absolutely moral insight all activities in society uniformly accord. At the same time, the actual monarchy in late imperial times was an inhibited center, one failing to control many of the society's activities and resources, giving much freedom or leeway to people so long as they did not politically challenge it, and perceived as morally inadequate government. While the CCP developed an uninhibited center based on utopian moral claims, and to that extent evoked the Confucian ideal of the uninhibited center, the KMT inherited the actual monarchy's inhibited center.

Third, the tradition included a popular culture made up especially of Confucian familism, a Taoist-Buddhist religion, and a competitive market economy. The CCP sought to abolish this popular culture, while the KMT largely endorsed it.[25]

In noting the KMT's endorsement of Confucian culture, moreover, one has to take into account the specific feelings and values this endorsement promoted. A generic concept of tradition is of no use. Again, however, we encounter controversy. One school of thought sees Confucian values as authoritarian, another emphasizes their "humanistic" way of nurturing moral autonomy. The latter interpretation, which we follow, and which is fol-

---

[25]This approach to the question of the traditional base line in China has been carried further in Thomas A. Metzger, "Confucian Culture and Economic Modernization: An Historical Approach," in *Conference on Confucianism and Economic Development in East Asia* (Taipei: Chung-Hua Institution for Economic Research, Conference series #13, 1989, pp. 141–95).

lowed also by scholars such as Chang Hao, Yü Ying-shih, Tu Wei-ming, and Wm. Theodore de Bary, not to mention T'ang Chün-i, Hsu Fu-kuan, and Mou Tsung-san, further heightens the contrast between life in the PRC and the ROC. It suggests that propagation of Confucian values facilitated organization of society around the "self-propelled adult."[26]

The contrast between the two political centers is heightened also if one agrees that economic modernization requires a social structure with decentralized, pluralistic loci of decisionmaking. Without such decentralization, the instrumental rationality Max Weber emphasized cannot be easily cultivated. F. A. Hayek demonstrated the cognitive impossibility of centrally planning a complex, large economy in a way maximizing economic incentives and minimizing transaction costs; Karl W. Deutsch pointed out that a modernizing society requires pluralistic communication channels open to the global flow of information and diverse ideas; and the Millsian tradition has maintained that some degree of political pluralism is indispensable to prevent the state from expanding as an organ of corruption, exploitation, and inefficiency.[27] If one accepts these premises, an inhibited center is better suited to encouraging economic modernization than an uninhibited one because it gives more leeway to "the self-propelled adult" and to local, private groups.

In other words, there is plenty of evidence to hypothesize that as a cognitive-institutional "package" mixing the goal of modernization with the establishment of an uninhibited center, with a transformative way of thinking also similar to an aspect of the Confucian tradition, and with a determination to eradicate the traditional popular culture, the CCP's mode of governance was incompatible with the kinds of decentralization and pluralism economic modernization requires. Conversely, as a cognitive-institutional "package" mixing the goal of modernization with China's inherited inhibited center, with an accommodative way of thinking similar to one wing of Confucian thought, and with endorsement of the traditional culture (popular and elite), the KMT's mode of governance was much more

---

[26]For these two schools of thought, see Thomas A. Metzger, "Continuities between Modern and Premodern China: Some Neglected Methodological and Substantive Issues," in Paul A. Cohen and Merle Goldman, eds., *Ideas across Cultures* (Cambridge, Mass.: Council on East Asian Studies, Harvard University, 1990), pp. 263–92.

[27]See F. A. Hayek, *The Fatal Conceit: The Errors of Socialism,* ed. W. W. Bartley, III, vol. 1 in *The Collected Works of F. A. Hayek* (Chicago, Ill.: University of Chicago Press, 1988); and Karl W. Deutsch, *The Nerves of Government* (New York: Free Press, 1966). On the Millsian tradition, see David Held, *Models of Democracy* (Stanford, Calif.: Stanford University Press, 1987).

compatible with the kinds of decentralization and pluralism required by economic modernization.

The systemic contrasts between the two centers can also be seen in the kinds of crises they engendered. The key crises in the PRC over the years clearly stemmed from its failure to cope with the problem of economic modernization. This is abundantly clear from the accounts of the PRC policy debates described in this book by Yü Yü-lin, Joseph Fewsmith, Wu An-chia, and Edward I-hsin Chen. True, the moral legitimacy of the CCP was challenged, especially after 1976. Yet this was not a dominant issue for many years, since many intellectuals accepted the CCP's uninhibited center as representing the "will of the people." In the ROC, the crisis pattern was different. It stemmed hardly at all from failures to deal with the problem of economic modernization. The key problem was the inhibited center, para-doxically harder to legitimize in the modern Chinese cultural arena than the uninhibited one.[28] The ROC's legitimacy was challenged as intellectuals cited either its undemocratic character, its inability to continue ruling the mainland, or Taiwan's alleged destiny as an independent nation.

The systemic contrasts between the two political centers thus have a complex nature that did not become clear to scholars until some years ago and that indeed is still not taken seriously by many scholars. Yet while these contrasts were important enough as they had crystallized by the 1950s or 1960s, the contrasts today between these two societies are the result also of the trends that occurred in each society during the 1970s and 1980s, and that in turn seem to have had a causative relation to the structures laid down by the 1960s. Most important were the economic growth that occurred in the ROC and the process of social-political change that was interwoven with economic growth. The absence of any matching trends in the PRC widened the gulf between the two societies.

To be sure, definitive corroboration that such causative linkages oc-curred is hard to come by in the study of history. What we do insist on is that the evidence indicating these early systemic contrasts and their seeming consequences be fully sorted out and pondered.

Why? First, the principle of studying societies inductively and compar-atively requires no less. Second, if a systemic cognitive-institutional pattern was vital to the only case of successful Chinese modernization on a provincial

---

[28]For a culture area in modern times where authoritarian regimes or "inhibited centers" have been much less challenged by popular or intellectual movements demanding democracy, see Ira M. Lapidus, "Islam and the Middle East: Historic Cultures and Modern States" (paper for the Conference on Culture and Polity in the Developing World since World War Two, Hoover Institution, April 1990).

scale, this is worth knowing. By understanding what this pattern was and not just crediting situational factors, people in Taiwan can identify institutions or policies they might want to preserve as they deal with the rising flood of mainland influences, instead of assuming without careful discussion that Taiwan's way of life and that of the mainland can easily merge to everyone's benefit. Conversely, by knowing what systemic patterns Taiwan's success may have depended on, mainlanders can look into the possibility that these patterns could serve as helpful guidelines for them. Looking for such guidelines, many Chinese intellectuals still prefer to carry on purely theoretical or philosophical discussions, debating Neo-Confucianism, hermeneutics, Aristotle, Hegel, and Max Weber. Why not instead formulate practicable guidelines by examining an empirical, historical case of economic-political success?[29]

Third, there is the question of defining "modern China." Books are still being written about "modern China" that ignore what happened on Taiwan. Yet, even if one prefers to see Taiwan as a separate political entity, it still is part of China culturally and historically. Therefore, to understand the main ways in which China has developed in modern times requires studying the Taiwan experience and comparing it to what happened in the rest of China. "Modern China," moreover, is not just a historical term; it is also a normative one, as illustrated by the title of Jonathan Spence's recent book, *The Search for Modern China*. Such a title refers not to an actual, historical society, but to a normal, desirable, practicable way for Chinese to live in the modern era. Yet how can this standard of normality be defined? By tolerating without demur those painful limits imposed by Maoism or by the kind of hybrid governance Maoism led to?[30] By dilating on that transformative, utopian ideal of a society free of selfishness going back to T'an Ssu-t'ung and earlier? Or by empirically studying practicable alternatives? Fourth, if plans for reunification are to succeed, will they not have to take into account the extent to which the two societies differ?

---

[29]This criticism of a major contemporary Chinese intellectual trend is developed a bit in the article by Metzger referred to in note 25.

[30]For a Chinese protest against Theodore White's then widely shared opinion that Americans should sympathize with the CCP's view of what is normal and reasonable for China, see the article by Ku Ying (also known as Min Hung-k'uei, David S. Min) in *Chung-yang jih-pao,* January 3, 4, 5, and 6, 1984. Mr. Min here criticized an article by White very sympathetic to the Teng regime that had been published in *Time,* September 26, 1983. Mr. Min's far more accurate picture of the Teng regime was thus published more than five years before the Tien-an-men incident, but efforts in the United States to publish an English translation of this Chinese *cri du coeur* were fruitless.

Systemic Differences Clear by the 1960s

1. If, using the ten categories listed above, we look at the PRC's political center as an uninhibited one that up to 1976 was often transformative and the ROC's political center as an inhibited, accommodative one, we should first recognize that both had a core of autocracy embodied in a party organization. In each case, the party hierarchy was unified on the basis of Lenin's principle of democratic centralism; party members occupied the most powerful positions in the government and in a vast network of auxiliary organizations; and the party used the government and this network to mobilize support and weaken or destroy political opposition, greatly relying on a nationwide system of propaganda and political education.[31]

2. The contrast between these two centers can be seen, first of all, in the symbol systems or cognitive modes they promoted. It is true that, in both cases, the extent to which any prominent ideological pattern was taken seriously by various sectors of the population remains in doubt. Stanley Rosen, for instance, adduces opinion surveys carried out in 1987 by Chinese investigators showing that youths in Beijing were mostly interested in their own career opportunities and other nonideological issues. Metzger notes that many people in Taiwan had complex, ambivalent feelings about political issues or were not interested in political matters except as they affected the economic climate. Nevertheless, in both societies there was a flow of public argument about how to shape the polity, and we cannot assess the importance of this flow without analyzing it.

Again, many political scientists use the "rational choice model" to analyze such arguments, seeing political ideas as just expressing the desire to retain or obtain universal forms of egotistic gratification, such as freedom, knowledge, prestige, power, and wealth. Especially in Chinese circles, this viewpoint often merges into the view that political thinking *should* become completely "rational" and discard all "ideology." In this context, "reason" is often correlated to "morality," not only to egotistic gratification. Following a Weberian tradition developed by Talcott Parsons, Robert N. Bellah, and S. N. Eisenstadt, however, we see "rational" orientations in any society as interwoven with culturally disparate ways of defining moral-sacred values, a "moral language," which may or may not accord with morality in some universal sense. Any modernizing society thus faces the problem of

---

[31]On these aspects of the PRC, see the articles by Hongda Harry Wu, An-chia Wu, Harry Harding, and Andrew G. Walder. This aspect of the ROC is well covered in Hung-mao Tien, *The Great Transition* cited in note 3 above.

combining its sacred-moral values with the quest for modernization, especially economic modernization.[32] This challenge is often called "secularization."

In the Chinese case, Metzger argues, sacred-moral values basic to public political discourse took the form of a widely shared, eightfold teleological vision that had arisen at the turn of the century. (The distribution of its intellectual roots in Confucian and Western thought still is a matter of debate.) This vision was a logically and cognitively unified one revolving around an ascetic morality implied by reason and demanded by the movement of history.

It called for turning China into an "ideal" society "free of any economic inequalities that were morally unjustified, free of confusing intellectual competition blocking grasp of right doctrine, free of any power structure out of accord with the true will of the people (*min-i*), and free of any competition between selfishly inclined interest groups."[33]

It was hard, therefore, to reconcile this vision with the goal of modernization, if that goal required private property and free enterprise, an eclectic intellectual marketplace open to the global flow of ideas and information, tolerance of controversy about whether the government adequately expresses "the will of the people," and acceptance of interest groups or political parties competing with each other by pursuing legal but selfish ends.

In trying to effect this reconciliation between their cherished ideals and the goal of modernization, Chinese intellectuals at the turn of the century, Metzger argues, had to select out possibilities from, on the one hand, the Millsian-Marxist problematique they were importing from the West and, on the other, the variety of transformative and accommodative perspectives they had inherited from their own tradition. Even before the Revolution of 1911, many of them, including even Sun Yat-sen and his group, articulated the teleological vision noted above by adopting a highly transformative, morally puristic, utopian approach and by inclining toward socialistic, Rousseauistic concepts of democracy (if not to anarchism) rather than Millsian ones. This has been made clear especially by Chang Hao's study of the influential T'an Ssu-t'ung (1865–1898) and by Chu Hung-yuan's study of the thought of Sun Yat-sen's and Chang T'ai-yen's party, the T'ung-meng-hui, on the eve of the 1911 Revolution.[34]

---

[32]For a definition of economic modernization, see R. H. Myers' article in *Issues & Studies* mentioned in note 1 above.

[33]See Metzger's article herein, p. 3.

[34]Chang Hao, *Lieh-shih ching-sheng yü p'i-p'an i-shih: T'an Ssu-t'ung ssu-hsiang-te fen-hsi* (The spirit of heroism and radical moral criticism: An analysis of T'an Ssu-t'ung's thought) (Taipei: Lien-ching ch'u-pan shih-yeh kung-ssu, 1988); Chang Hao *Chinese*

By the early 1920s, when the CCP was created (1921) and Sun Yat-sen recognized the KMT (1923–1924), four main ideological outlooks had been formed, Sunism, Chinese Marxism, Chinese liberalism, and modern Confucian humanism. The CCP chose Marxism and largely adhered to this choice, as made clear by Wu An-chia, Edward I-hsin Chen, Harry Harding, and Yü Yü-lin. Even during the reform period of 1978–1989, adherence to the "Four Basic Principles" (socialism, the dictatorship of the proletariat, rule by the CCP, and Marxism-Leninism, along with the thought of Mao) remained fundamental to the CCP's political program.

Wu An-chia also speaks of Mao's "transformative" policies, while Harding notes their "utopian cast." Transformation was based on a definition of evil and the passion to do away with evil. The CCP's definition identified evil not only with the "feudal" past but also with precisely those kinds of economic, intellectual, and political pluralism noted above as seemingly needed for modernization: "private property," "material interests," "selfish interests," "capitalism," "bourgeois liberalism," and the "spiritual pollution" created by an open marketplace of ideas. The CCP's opposition to intellectual diversity is illustrated also by its insistence on using a "line" to control the thinking of its members and the rest of society, as discussed by Yü Yü-lin.

True, there were periods when control was relaxed, especially the Hundred Flowers Period in 1956–1957 and the recent reform period, 1978–1989. Even in the latter period, however, many objections, not only within the CCP, arose against those "evil" tendencies Maoism had denounced, as discussed below.

While identifying the hateful, "bad," "selfish" aspects of society with capitalism as well as "feudalism," the CCP defined itself as "the central force" leading the revolution, one cultivating a "spirit utterly free of the slightest selfishness."[35] Thus the CCP elegantly justified vastly expanding its centralized political structure in order to substitute morality for the evils of traditional familism, of the Taoist-Buddhist religion, of the market sector, and of all anti-Marxist ways of thinking, and to effect a closure of the mainland's economic and intellectual world, cutting it off from the evil circles centered in the capitalistic West. The CCP's definition of evil also

---

Intellectuals in Crisis: Search for Order and Meaning (1890–1911) (Berkeley, Calif.: University of California Press, 1987); Chu Hung-yuan, *T'ung-meng-hui-te ko-ming li-lun: Min-pao ko-an yen-chiu* (The *T'ung-meng-hui's* theory of revolution: A case study based on the magazine *Min-pao*) (Taipei: Institute of Modern History, Academia Sinica, 1985).

[35] *Mao chu-hsi yü-lu* (Sayings of Chairman Mao) (Beijing: Hsin-hua shu-tien, 1967), pp. 1, 146–47.

justified what Andrew G. Walder refers to as three decades of "discrimination and abuse" directed against those with specialized education in the Western sense.

During the 1980s, many a Western scholar argued that this whole ideological position had been superseded by a new commitment to "pragmatism," but ROC scholars never made this mistake, and neither did Stuart R. Schram.[36] In fact, this ideological stance not only rationalized the vested interests of the CCP but also evoked that moral-sacred, teleological vision which had arisen at the turn of the century. The CCP could adjust this ideological stance in favor of pragmatic thinking, but the CCP could not have discarded it without adopting a different ideological mode reconciling such pragmatic thinking with the old moral-sacred vision. This vision, in other words, had to be evoked somehow.

Metzger argues that reconciliation of this vision with a commitment to the pluralism required by modernization was realized by the ideological situation that evolved in Taiwan under KMT rule. He sees a mix there of five main outlooks: Sunism (the KMT doctrine), a "petty bourgeois" outlook, modern Confucian humanism, Chinese liberalism, and a version of the latter aiming to establish Taiwan as an independent nation. Though much of this mix evoked the moral-sacred vision, the overall emphasis was on accommodative, not transformative, change.

Evil was identified by Sunism not so much with "feudalism" and capitalism as with the CCP. (Marx himself was partly respected.) Sun had long before rejected the May Fourth Movement's wholesale denunciation of traditional Chinese civilization. By defining evil in a way very different from the CCP's, the KMT necessarily adopted a different concept of the state-society relation. Determined, like the CCP, to expand its power as needed to extirpate evil, the KMT lacked any moral mandate to expand its power to the point of uprooting the traditional popular culture and replacing with its own centralized organization the traditional private sector made up of Confucian familism, the Taoist-Buddhist religion, and a vast market economy. Instead, it participated in a broad consensus either endorsing or tolerating the traditional culture, capitalism, a diverse intellectual marketplace sensitive to Western educational standards, the promise, at least, of Millsian democracy, and varied contacts with the Western capitalistic world. Thus, in contrast with conditions in the CCP, a major tool for climbing the ladder of power in the ROC has long been a Western, usually American, Ph.D.,

---

[36]Stuart R. Schram, *Ideology and Policy in China Since the Third Plenum, 1978–1984* (London: Contemporary China Institute, School of Oriental and African Studies, University of London, Research Notes and Studies no. 6, 1984), pp. 74, 79–80.

as illustrated by the current president of the ROC, Lee Teng-hui, who holds a doctorate in agricultural economics from Cornell University.

While the sense of living in a selfish, intellectually vacuous, and disoriented society can be often found today in Taiwan as well as on the mainland, this feeling in Taiwan has not been mobilized to form a political movement determined to transform society by severely limiting capitalism, intellectual diversity, and political pluralism. Instead, such pluralism has been increasingly accepted, if not embraced, even while the "selfishness" and "confusion" (*fen-yun*) it has bred have been deplored. Thus in both societies, Metzger argues, this tendency to identify with evil the pluralism needed for modernization reflected the continuing influence of a moral-sacred vision with which China entered the modern age, but in Taiwan cognitive modes were nevertheless cultivated that fundamentally accommodated this morally suspect pluralism.

3. There is also a contrast between the internal organization of the CCP and that of the KMT. The Leninist principle of democratic centralism was never implemented by the KMT as vigorously as it was by the CCP. This point was already made by A. Doak Barnett in 1967.[37] Lü Ya-li makes the same point, noting that the KMT differed from other Leninist parties also in lacking emphasis on any ideological "line" and in rarely effecting disciplinary expulsions, not to mention purges. The KMT asked that members avoid public behavior embarrassing the Party, not necessarily private thoughts or conversations at odds with the leadership's views. Many KMT members, in fact, have had ambivalent political feelings, sympathizing with the KMT's critics, even those calling for the independence of Taiwan. Discretion was always the key demand, not any process of self-examination and group criticism seeking to generate total loyalty to any party line. Another point of contrast with the CCP is suggested by Harding's comment that before 1976 the CCP was run largely without any bureaucratic system of rules.

4. With regard to governmental structure, apart from formal differences, the key issue is the relation to Millsian ideals and the actual process of competitive elections. The CCP ideologically rejected Millsian democracy, and its governance included what Harding describes as a "weak legislative system, featuring noncompetitive, indirect elections to powerless representative bodies." It is true that in the ROC, vigorous competition between KMT and non-KMT candidates did not begin until 1977. Moreover, even then, the KMT reserved for itself many organizational advantages; serious opposition parties were not legalized until 1989; and even in 1990 voters

---

[37]A. Doak Barnett, *Cadres, Bureaucracy, and Political Power in China* (New York: Columbia University Press, 1967), p. 436.

only partly determined the composition of the most powerful representative bodies. Yet, as Tien Hung-mao says, the KMT all along was "committed to progressive change from dictatorship to constitutional democracy."[38] Its critics cite the influence of Lenin while ignoring its eclectic ideology, which has a Millsian component. Moreover, regular elections to local and provincial offices have been held in Taiwan since 1946. These occurred about every four years. They were used to select the members of the Provincial Assembly of Taiwan and of the city councils of Taipei and Kaohsiung, as well as the mayors or executive heads of 21 cities and counties and many other local officials. Popular interest in the elections was always intense—in 1946, 30,000 candidates ran for 8,000 positions—and in 1978, Ralph N. Clough took the view that "Up to the present . . . the workings of the electoral process seem to have met fairly well the demands for political participation on the part of the mass of people in Taiwan.[39] The key point, however, is that as these demands increased from the 1970s on, the state's ideological and institutional commitment to fairly free, regular elections was already in place and could be utilized by liberals demanding democracy. Not surprisingly, therefore, the book published in 1978 by two dissidents, Lin Cheng-chieh and Chang Fu-chung, about the Chung-li incident of 1977 was called *Hsuan-chü wan-sui!* (Hurray for elections!).[40] The institutionalization of an election system thus paralleled the institutionalization of an eclectic intellectual marketplace. Each had momentum on its own and in interaction with the other.

    5. Both the CCP and the KMT reinforced their control of the government with control of a vast network of auxiliary organizations, such as the PRC's Young Communist League, Young Pioneers, General Labor Union, and Women's Federation, and the ROC's Chinese Youth Anti-Communist League, farmers' associations, irrigation associations, trade unions, and commercial and industrial associations. It is true that from the start the KMT decisively penetrated and monitored this network, running it in what Tien Hung-mao calls a "corporatist" way. Only the Council of Presbyterian Churches, with strong roots in the community going back to the late nineteenth century, showed some independence. Moreover, what Tien calls

---

[38]Hung-mao Tien, *Great Transition*, p. 1.

[39]Ralph N. Clough, *Island China* (Cambridge, Mass.: Harvard University Press, 1978), p. 57. On the 1946 elections, see Lai Tse-han, Ramon H. Myers, and Wei Wou, *A Tragic Beginning: The February 28, 1947 Uprising in Taiwan* (Stanford, Calif.: Stanford University Press, in press).

[40](Taipei: Kuei-kuan t'u-shu kung-ssu, 1978).

"limited pluralism" developed as a characteristic of this network only as part of the social-political changes beginning in the 1970s.

Nevertheless, it is clear that, as in the case of the KMT's internal organization, this network, too, was not the vehicle for those kinds of intensely centralized forms of political mobilization typical of Maoist China. In the ROC, this network functioned more to serve KMT patronage needs, to articulate local interests, and to abort local political impulses that might embarrass the KMT.

The relative decentralization of this network in the ROC is also indicated by the fact that, except for the Chinese Youth Anti-Communist League, this network was made up of a very large number of organizations leaving out up to 75 percent or so of the population. In 1952, about 2,560 registered associations had about 1.3 million members. Taiwan's population then was perhaps 8 million. In 1987, there were "nearly 11,306 [registered associations] with about 8.3 million members." Population then was around 19 million.

The expansion of this network, moreover, did not mean increasing KMT control over the population, since the expansion largely coincided with what Tien calls the shift from "authoritarian corporatism" to "limited pluralism" in the KMT's relation with this network.[41]

6. The much greater decentralization of society in the ROC is especially evident from a look at social-economic structure. To be sure, decentralization was an important theme in the whole structure designed by the CCP. Harding notes that despite shifts to more centralization in the mid-1950s and the early 1960s, the Maoist state was a "relatively decentralized political system, with substantial power delegated to, or arrogated by, provincial and regional units of governance." He also notes that since 1978 there has been still more emphasis on the decentralization of government.

Centralized or decentralized, however, the political structure controlled by Mao to a large extent collectivized economic facilities, directed economic activities, and controlled a good deal of the population's noneconomic life. Whether this political structure is regarded as totalitarian or clientelistic, it largely replaced the private organization of the economy, if not the society.

True, re-emergence of some private business was occasionally permitted in the PRC after periods of upheaval, such as the Great Leap of 1958–1960, and, after 1978, a considerable expansion of the market sector occurred. As Wu An-chia notes, however, by 1956 the socialist sector "constituted 85.6 percent of the economy." Andrew G. Walder says that "In both rural and urban areas, local communities and workplaces under Mao were noteworthy for their tightly controlled boundaries and extensive corporate organiza-

---

[41]Hung-mao Tien, *Great Transition*, pp. 43–45.

tion." Nicholas R. Lardy holds that "in its allocation of capital and particularly of labor, China appears, even after a decade of reform, to be far less market-oriented than other socialist states." Harding and Walder both emphasize the "cellular" nature of the local economies under Mao, which was complemented by his emphasis on autarky, discussed by Lardy. Thus, both internationally and domestically, Mao minimized the play of the free market as a way to effect the principle of comparative advantage. By contrast, despite a large state sector, the economy in Taiwan was largely privatized, and it was opened to the global market economy especially after the shift from import substitution to export growth around 1962. As John C.H. Fei has written, "The economic miracle of the four dragons (including Taiwan) was primarily a story of the success of a competitive market system."[42]

7. There is also a major contrast between the CCP's use and the KMT's use of what Amitai Etzioni has called the three types of sanctions: normative, remunerative, and coercive. The fundamental reliance of Mao on ideological persuasion (normative sanctions) and the use of coercive, terroristic sanctions is well known.[43] Hongda Harry Wu, like Jean Pasqualini (Bao Ruo-wang), bases his knowledge of PRC prison camps on personal experience and inquiries, though also using some published documents. Describing the Labor-Reform Camps (*Lao-kai-tui*), which were set up during the 1950s, he notes that they were based on Mao's concept of waging a "class struggle" against "the enemies of the people" and always emphasized both the political reform of the prisoners and the creation of wealth for the state. Run by a police force of about 300,000 in 1986, these labor camps were scattered throughout the country. There were about 5,000 to 6,000 in 1989, when the total number of inmates was about twenty million. By this time, however, most inmates, Wu holds, were common criminals, not political prisoners. Obviously, since June 4, 1989, more political prisoners have been added.

As for the ROC, the use of terror was not always absent. During the months after the uprising of February 28, 1947, KMT forces killed thousands (8–10,000 is the figure given in a recent monograph, but some have claimed 25,000).[44] Tien Hung-mao estimates that 10,000 cases involving "civilians

---

[42]John C.H. Fei, "The Taiwan Economy in the Seventies" (paper for the Conference on Chiang Ching-kuo's Leadership in the Development of the Republic of China on Taiwan, Miller Center of Public Affairs, University of Virginia, March 16–18, 1990).

[43]See the article by Hongda Harry Wu herein; Bao Ruo-wang (Jean Pasqualini) and Rudolph Chelminski, *Prisoner of Mao* (New York: Penguin Books, 1976); reports published by Amnesty International Publications; and Fox Butterfield, *China: Alive in the Bitter Sea* (New York: Times Books, 1982). Also see Andrew J. Nathan, "A Culture of Cruelty," *The New Republic,* July 30 and August 6, 1990, pp. 30–35.

[44]See Lai, Myers, and Wei, *A Tragic Beginning.*

were decided in military court trials from 1950 to 1985."[45] Other coercive measures were important also, especially censorship.

Mainly, however, the KMT tried to build political support by combining propaganda and administrative as well as electoral tactics with remunerative sanctions, that is, by promoting economic prosperity. Its bloodless land reform, carried out in 1949–1953, not only destroyed the landlord class as a rural political elite hostile to the KMT, but also was "highly popular" with the bulk of the rural population, as Lü Ya-li notes. With one administrative stroke, in other words, the KMT won over the bulk of the population. (Taiwan then was only 20 percent urbanized.) Similarly, it is clear that the KMT's consistent ability to win some 60 to 70 percent of the votes in all the many elections from 1946 through 1990 has been due not only to its organizational advantages, but also to its ability to take credit for improving economic conditions, which are of supreme concern to the majority of the voters.

8. There is a further contrast created by the far greater emphasis in the PRC on what Harding calls "mobilizational politics," the use of the Party, the government, and the whole auxiliary network since the 1950s in time-consuming, tiring, and often violent educational or economic campaigns, such as the collectivization movements of the 1950s, the Great Leap of 1958–60, and the Cultural Revolution, which began by 1966. Had the PRC merely established a state-controlled society as described under point 6 above, the contrast with the ROC would have been strong enough. The contrast was heightened, however, by the unusually dynamic and often terroristic way in which the CCP used this whole organizational system.[46] To be sure, in 1978–1989, this particular contrast between the two societies faded, but we are speaking here mainly of patterns that had crystallized by the 1960s.

9. Another contrast lies in what Harding refers to as the PRC's "frequent struggle among factions." In the early 1950s, Kao Kang and Jao Shu-shih were purged. Later, Mao successively turned on P'eng Te-huai, Liu Shao-ch'i, Lin Piao, and Teng Hsiao-p'ing. After Mao's death in 1976, Hua Kuo-feng turned on the Gang of Four; Teng Hsiao-p'ing overturned Hua Kuo-feng by 1978; and during the 1980s there was a struggle especially between Li P'eng's faction and the one headed by Hu Yao-pang and Chao Tzu-yang, who fell from power in 1987 and 1988, respectively.

---

[45]Hung-mao Tien, *Great Transition*, p. 111.
[46]For a focus on the work unit, the system of class labels, and the political campaign as a distinctive institutional combination of Mao's China, see Lynn T. White III, *Policies of Chaos: The Organizational Causes of Violence in China's Cultural Revolution* (Princeton, N.J.: Princeton University Press, 1990).

Yü Yü-lin analyzes the factional struggles after 1976 as one between protégés of Party elders, whose prestige went back to the days of the civil war, while the struggles in Mao's time were more between the members of this victorious generation itself. Yü Yü-lin also notes how the continuing prestige of this victorious generation eventually gave the PRC the problem of gerontocracy: in 1989, the Party was controlled by eight elders, all of whom were more than 81 years old.

All in all, then, this leadership situation undermined the need for predictability and stability, what some political scientists call the "durability" of policy decisions, and compromised the effort to meet the need for vigorous leadership able to overcome the inertia of vested interests.[47] The situation in the ROC was markedly different, since from 1948 through 1990, there was a smooth succession of four presidents, and gerontocracy, at least eventually, was less of a problem. In 1988, the average age of the 31 members of the KMT Central Standing Committee was 63.7 years.[48]

What accounts for the distinctive inability of the CCP to realize policy "durability" and a stable leadership regularly replenished by younger blood? Certainly, the personality traits of Mao and others have to be considered, but are there any systemic causes? Harding emphasizes the inability to solve the problem of succession. One could also consider how relations between leaders affected the PRC's attempt to combine modernization with sacred-moral values by setting up an uninhibited political center often pursuing transformative policies. This way of pursuing modernization created great political crises because it repeatedly and drastically failed to solve the problem of economic modernization. The severity of the chronic economic crisis could not but exacerbate frictions within the leadership. Indeed just about all the factional debates analyzed by Yü Yü-lin consisted of criticisms and recriminations generated by this unending economic crisis and the popular discontent it produced. At the same time, these debates were often inflamed by the tension between the CCP's transformative version of modern China's teleological vision and more utilitarian ideas about economic and social organization.

Within the KMT, however, this tension between moral-sacred values and utilitarian policies has been mild at best, and as rising economic prosperity muted popular discontent, political stability was easier to maintain.

Thus, even though both had a core of autocracy, the CCP's and the

---

[47]On "durability," see Barry R. Weingast, "The Political Institutions of Representative Government: Legislatures," Working Papers in Political Science P-89-14, The Hoover Institution, December 1989.
[48]Hung-mao Tien, *Great Transition*, p. 77.

KMT's political centers were very different, and the disparate features of each largely meshed together in a logical and practical way to form a coherent cognitive-institutional "package." In the ROC, mutually reinforcing cognitive and institutional tendencies all gave more leeway to decisionmaking processes independent of the center's commands than did parallel tendencies in the PRC.

10. These "packages," however, cannot be described without taking into account how each was fitted into the international community. As Hsin-huang Michael Hsiao says, Taiwan was "integrated into the postwar capitalist world system." Lü Ya-li similarly says that "The importance of influence from the West, particularly the United States, for the ROC's political development cannot be overemphasized." Thus we again find a systemic mesh of patterns, the mesh between the domestic tendency toward various kinds of action independent of the center and the close connections to a society, that of the United States, emphasizing just such pluralism. We also find another major contrast with the PRC, since in the evolution of the latter's relationship with the international community, there was no integration of the domestic society with the capitalistic West, not even after 1978.

Yet the ROC's relationship with the international community has differed from the PRC's, not only because of the ROC's close connections with the capitalistic West, but also because of its asymmetrical relation with the PRC. For the PRC, this relation was just one among a number of foreign policy issues. In the ROC, however, it was interwoven with political life in a number of complex, partly contradictory ways.

While the KMT focused on the problem of military security created by the PRC, it also focused the society's definition of evil on the CCP and was strongly motivated by its competition with the CCP to turn Taiwan into an economic and political showcase. Thus the tension between the CCP and the KMT reinforced the pressures on the ROC from the United States to depoliticize the economy and to democratize.

At the same time, other feelings, unendorsed by the KMT, also arose in Taiwan with regard to the mainland. These were important after the 1960s but can be conveniently noted here. By the 1960s, an illegal movement was crystallizing that aimed to turn Taiwan into an independent nation dealing with the PRC as a friendly neighbor. Coming more into the open after the reforms of 1986, this movement had to compete with still another emerging view, the often liberal idea that because there was no systemic difference between the two governments, opposing Communism was less important than bringing all Chinese together. Still a fourth outlook arose after 1987, when the ROC largely lifted the ban on travel by its citizens to the PRC. As the article by Chang Hu shows, such travel by Taiwan's mainlanders aroused in them many ambivalent feelings, often including a desire to keep prosperous Taiwan from being dragged down into the mainland's mire of backwardness.

Given all these major contrasts between these two societies as they had crystallized by the 1950s, it is hard to see how one can view their cognitive-institutional patterns as parts of a single developmental mainstream. Paul A. Cohen's list of features that they shared is correct to a significant extent, but these similarities were not more important than differences he either did not notice or decided were not significant enough to discuss. The reader will have to decide whether these differences, described above in terms of ten variables, were or were not between firmly institutionalized patterns that pertained to aspects of life mattering deeply to human beings, such as freedom, equality, living standards, and the quest for knowledge. Yet subsequent developments on both sides of the Taiwan Straits further deepened the divergence between the two societies.

More Divergence during the 1970s and 1980s

Some of the ten categories above can be used to highlight the contrasts between what happened in the two societies after the 1960s. In the ROC, there were three related breakthroughs. Two of these pertained to category 6: the society's economic and social structure. Already decentralized to the point of institutionalizing capitalism, the economy experienced remarkable growth, which led to a social transformation: the urbanization of society and the rise of a large middle class. This social transformation in turn had some important causative connections, however hard they are to specify, with what Hung-mao Tien calls "the great transition" from the era of KMT autocracy to a more pluralistic political structure. In other words, the social transformation was associated with a political breakthrough that pertained to the ability of the KMT to maintain its autocratic position, to the governmental structure, to the KMT's control of the network of auxiliary organizations, and to the internal organization of the KMT, as well as to other politically significant matters. As of July 4, 1990, the inhibited center was well on the way to turning into a subordinated center.

Nothing comparable to these three related breakthroughs occurred in the PRC. Certainly, state-directed mobilization of the population became far less important, and the sanction pattern shifted from normative-coercive sanctions toward remunerative ones (categories 7 and 8). In the case of economic and social structure, however, instead of an economic breakthrough and a social transformation, the CCP allowed some privatization of the economy without giving the economy that basically capitalistic structure which had already existed in the ROC for many years. Similarly inconclusive adjustments were made in the case of ideology, as some intellectual diversity was allowed without fundamentally opening up the society's cognitive channels to the global flow of information and ideas. In various other ways, too, centralized political controls were relaxed in the period 1978–1989, but, as Andrew G. Walder notes, no "qualitatively new type" of political system emerged.

John C.H. Fei analyzes economic modernization in Taiwan by noting that even though Taiwan had a capitalistic structure from the start, this structure went through a process of "depoliticization." "Depoliticization" was needed, he holds, because China's "traditional political culture of paternalism" as well as the statism generated by anticolonialism since the turn of the century had furthered politicization of the economy. Depoliticization was, in his eyes, facilitated by the fact that the Chinese tradition included not only paternalism but also at least incipient values in accord with those Western ones basic to industrial capitalism and democracy. It was also facilitated, he implies, by the KMT's decision to adopt a "pragmatic evolutionary" approach to modernization rather than a "politicized revolutionary" one.

Fei then analyzes the stages through which depoliticization of the economy in Taiwan has proceeded. He criticizes the kinds of politicization that did persist, argues that Taiwan's economic success has owed more to depoliticization than to the variety of other state economic policies, and concludes that Taiwan has "almost" completed the process of economic modernization.

Hsin-huang Michael Hsiao and also Lü Ya-li analyze the societal transformation that was largely a consequence of economic modernization. The rise of the service and industrial sectors of the economy effected the urbanization of the society, and we would add that it also overcame the traditional Chinese economic, social, and even cultural split between the city and the countryside. Some scholars have identified an accompanying shift toward smaller nuclear families and more "individualism."[49] Hsiao notes growing social pluralism that includes a great increase (already mentioned) in the

---

[49]Ibid., p. 29; Yang Kuo-shu, *Chung-kuo-jen-te shui-pien* (The metamorphosis of the Chinese) (Taipei: Kuei-kuan t'u-shu ku-fen yu-hsien kung-ssu, 1988), p. 407. The table on p. 407 accurately sums up the thesis developed consistently in the book. Yang uses psychological survey data to describe personality or attitudinal changes in Taiwan during the period of industrialization.

number of registered organizations (from 2,560 in 1952 to 11,306 in 1987) and a loosening of KMT control over this organizational network.[50]

There also was a transformation of the pattern of stratification. Hsiao emphasizes a great increase in the size of the "urban working class" and of "the new middle classes," but the relation between Taiwanese and mainlanders also was transformed. Many Taiwanese raised their social status as they came to dominate the middle class and the higher rungs of business, not to mention the lower ones, while increasingly penetrating the professions, intellectual and academic life, the governmental bureaucracies, the military, the KMT, and the highest rungs of the government, not to mention electoral politics.

As Hsiao and others have made clear, however, all these changes led neither to a great increase of large corporate structures outside the state nor to a great increase in "class consciousness." On the one hand, although a few large companies like Formosa Plastics arose, Taiwan's economy, unlike South Korea's, remained dominated by vigorously competitive small and medium-sized enterprises.[51] On the other, class consciousness failed to grow much. This was partly because so many families, factional networks, and social or political movements cut across class lines.[52]

In both cases, the Chinese exhibited their traditional inclination to leave large groupings to the political world and focus their private lives on small groups and fluidly formed networks. One probably should also take into account a tradition-rooted tendency, noted by Metzger, to think about political life in complex and ambivalent, if not detached or passive ways.

Nevertheless, by the late 1970s, many members of this transformed social structure began to mount an increasing variety of social and political movements often focusing on the demand for more democracy. Beginning in 1986, the government undertook a number of reforms increasingly meeting this demand. Yet because there was no unified, politically conscious middle class demanding democratization, the causes of democratization are far from obvious. Hsiao sees this process as a change in the "dialectical" relation between state and society, and as the rise of a "participatory political culture." He describes the proliferation of social and political movements also as a "resurrection of the civil society," which the state slowly and incompletely recognized.

Our own view differs from his, since we do not feel that the state played

---

[50]Hung-mao Tien, pp. 43–45.

[51]See R. H. Myers' article in Lawrence J. Lau, pp. 54–55.

[52]For this point, see not only the article by Prof. Hsiao, but also Huang-mao Tien, pp. 164–71, 190.

such a monolithic role in this whole interactive process. We also would argue that a mediate cause of this process was the inhibited, partly Millsian political center set up by the KMT when it first came to Taiwan in the late 1940s. Thus we would analyze the ROC's democratization as based on this older set of institutions, furthered by the breakthroughs in economic growth and social structure and, finally, due to a considerable variety of proximate causes, including the social movements Hsiao analyzes; what Reinhard Bendix has called "intellectual mobilization";[53] that evolution of the KMT analyzed by Lü Ya-li; the international context; the leadership of President Chiang Ching-kuo; and the momentum inherent in the election system. Among the many significant aspects of the democratization that occurred by 1990 have been the new patterns of behavior arising in the Legislative Yuan, which Lü Ya-li describes. We think that some such multicausal account of the ROC's political breakthrough is needed, because the political scene there was distinguished neither by a monolithic state uniformly opposed to serious political reform, nor by demands for reform based mainly on "class consciousness." Nor is it obvious that Taiwan is part of an evolutionary process according to which class consciousness will necessarily increase (or should increase), not to mention methodological doubts that the concept of "class" can even be used at all, except in the roughest sense.

As already mentioned, the mainland did not experience changes like these three related breakthroughs. In the case of the economy, instead of beginning with a capitalistic structure and then depoliticizing it further, the PRC largely collectivized the economy by 1956 and then in December 1978 decided to allow market signals to play an increasing role as one way to pursue the Four Modernizations. Thomas B. Gold and Nicholas R. Lardy analyze this change, which is discussed also in the articles by Harry Harding and Andrew G. Walder.

As Gold tells us, agricultural goods and then many others were "commoditized, freeing their prices." The system of collectivized agriculture, on which so much energy and blood had been fruitlessly spent, was quickly dismantled. Private ownership of land was not restored, but a household was permitted to lease land for fifteen years or more and sell its production on the free market, except for a contractually fixed amount to be sold to the state at a fixed price. Households were permitted to switch at least partly from agriculture to ventures in the service and industrial sectors. The legal

---

[53]Reinhard Bendix, *Kings or People: Power and the Mandate to Rule* (Berkeley, Calif: University of California Press, 1978), pp. 265–72. Used by Bendix to explain the political transformation in western Europe during the early modern period, this concept is remarkably applicable to the current political transformation in Taiwan.

enforcement of business contracts was introduced, and a free labor market appeared.

By 1987, according to official estimates, the number of persons working in "individual enterprises" had risen to 21.58 million. Another 2 million or more, it was estimated, worked in "private enterprises" having eight or more employees.

Gold believes that all such official estimates are too low. He also concludes that the private sector became dominant in the field of repairs and in some retailing fields. Wealthy entrepreneurs emerged, and some political pronouncements gave them moral legitimacy. The policy of autarky was at least partly discarded, as four "Special Economic Zones" and many other places were established that offered packages of incentives for foreign investment, especially emphasizing exports. Some people switched from state to private employment. The state economic sector itself was variously adjusted to increase efficiency, especially as economic incentives were used to make state enterprises and state workers more responsible for their productivity. Whole cities or parts of them came to display the kind of economic hustle-bustle visitors are accustomed to seeing in Taiwan.

Thus the mainland, according to Gold, underwent a fundamental shift away from a rigid Stalinist-type centralized planned economy toward an economy with mixed ownership and a complex relationship between plan and market. Yet, as Gold, Lardy, and Walder all point out, the extent of that shift was severely limited. The institutional structure of the economy was never decentralized to the point of turning capitalism into the organizational foundation of the economy.[54]

The private sector remained largely dependent on the state sector for supplies and was often subject to political harassment, which in turn could be justified by cadres in terms of the persisting ideological objections to "capitalism." As Rosen and Gold observe, inflation, corruption, and economic inequality were blamed on the market sector by many people, not only cadres, and so popular resentment blended into ideological objections.

Noting the complex, often corrupt connections between private enterprises and cadres, Walder asks "whether markets will erode China's political hierarchies, or whether the political hierarchies will distort and manipulate the workings of the market."

Moreover, as Lardy observes, the decentralization within the bureau-

---

[54]For an illuminating comparison of these PRC economic reforms with those in the USSR, see Jan S. Prybyla, "Economic Changes in China and the Soviet Union: Similarities and Differences," in *The American Asian Review*, vol. 7, no. 2 (Summer 1989): 1–18.

cracy that occurred along with the rise of the market often enhanced the power of local cadres who were less interested than Beijing in promoting the market. Harry Harding refers to an "iron triangle" of provincial interests, local managers, and local workers interested in "protection against competition from other provinces." Lardy describes how local protectionism often undermined the principle of comparative advantage and specialization and expresses doubt that foreign trade has been a "source of efficiency gains in the [PRC's] economy."

Vulnerable to official corruption and the uncertainties of governmental policy, the private sector in cities, Walder says, has been "primarily a phenomenon of urban youths and a transient rural population." Gold describes how their uncomfortable institutional environment colored the thinking of these entrepreneurs, who "take a decidedly short-term view. They do not plan to expand operations or reinvest their profits." There were complaints about youths dropping out of schools to join this private sector, but Gold notes that its career opportunities were not appealing to most urban residents. In other words, the energies of the educated elite were not poured into it.

Not surprisingly, therefore, the quantitative expansion of the private sector was rather limited. Walder notes that in "urban areas, the new private sector still employs under 10 percent of urban residents" (but presumably more than 10 percent of the urban working population). Most private enterprises, it seems clear, were rural. Yet even in rural areas, the private sector was limited, since it was largely restricted to agriculture and the service sector. Rural industry, Walder notes, remained largely in the hands of cadres.

While the flow of labor, in urban areas at least, from the state to the private sector remained small, Lardy notes that labor markets within the state sector were less developed than in the USSR. All in all, he concludes, "in certain critical respects the salient characteristics of the economy have been largely untouched, suggesting the very partial character of the reform to date."

Lardy also sums up the growth history of the economy. It is true that statistics suggest an impressive 5 percent per annum growth of national income in real terms on a per capita basis from 1953 to 1987. After 1978, moreover, reported growth rates rose amazingly to surpass even those of "the newly industrialized economies of East Asia." Even though, as Jan S. Prybyla has long emphasized, much of this output was handled so inefficiently as to be useless, growth still occurred. After all, we do not know that the *rate* of wasteful production increased.

Yet, Lardy goes on to say, agricultural output in per capita terms was stagnant between 1957 and the late 1970s; "per capita consumption of food for the entire population declined" during this period; and during roughly the same period, total factor productivity either did not increase or declined.

After 1978, the picture brightened considerably, but by the mid-1980s much attention was focused on a syndrome that included stagnating agricultural production, inflation, and budget deficits. By 1988–1989 there was a growing sense that Chao Tzu-yang's reforms had failed.

There are various reasons for the mainland's failure to escape from the misery of economic backwardness. All observers agree that before 1976 Mao's transformative policies often undermined growth. More basically, as Lardy suggests, the mainland's economy is in a predicament because, on the one hand, it is too big to base growth on export growth, while, on the other hand, it suffers from relatively poor resource endowment.

Yet another basic point also is clear. The articles by Gold, Harding, Lardy, and Walder all show that, while economic hopes were pinned on the private sector, its growth was seriously limited by a political environment that has insisted on keeping this sector small, has surrounded it with an often hostile and envious population, has given the entrepreneurs in it a sense of uncertainty and fear about their economic and personal futures, has often undermined the principle of comparative advantage, has continuously and corruptly inflicted high transaction costs, and so has inhibited the entrepreneurs' long-range planning, the reinvestment of profits, and growth.

What, however, are the political tendencies that have created such a political environment so unfriendly to the private sector? Do they consist of some changeable aspects of the PRC's political structure, or are they integral to that structure itself?

Harding and Lardy both lean toward the former answer, in that both see Harding's "iron triangle" of provincial and local vested interests as inhibiting the rise of the market. As Lardy says, "economic reform in China is a curious blend of increased market forces and enhanced powers of provincial and local governments . . . many of the problems of China's current reform may be the consequence of this ultimately incompatible mix." Yet, if the enhancement of local political power were replaced by the enhancement of central political power, would there be more compatibility between political tendencies and the needs of the market? How can such compatibility be realized without fully institutionalizing private property and free enterprise and then carrying out still more depoliticization of the economy?

In any case, without an economic breakthrough like Taiwan's, there also could be no breakthrough with regard to those societal changes— especially the rise of a primarily urban society and of a large middle class— that can occur only as consequences of economic growth. Therefore, unless one is prepared to argue that such societal changes are not probable prerequisites of democratization, one cannot be surprised that the political and ideological changes accompanying the rise of the market sector on the mainland did not lead to any political breakthrough. Nor can one be surprised that these political and ideological changes were as partial and inconclusive as were those institutional changes outlined above pertaining more directly to economic activity.

These political and ideological changes are discussed in many of the articles. They agree on many points: In the 1980s, the disrupting political campaigns of the past and intensive programs of indoctrination came to an end. The emphasis on strict adherence to doctrinal correctness was attenuated. Sanctions against heterodoxy became much rarer; state control of communication declined; and intellectual freedom increased a lot. Officials in some cases broadened their circles of consultation; public-opinion polls came into fashion; and the government experimented with some contested elections at the county level and below. Cadre control of economic and residential life declined to some extent and, as Walder notes, "the early 1980s saw the elimination of the entire class of team cadres, formerly the lowest level of administration in rural areas." Such relaxation of the political center's controls was, moreover, accompanied by a shift toward "bureaucratic rationalization" and a "resurgence of bureaucratic influence" in the policy-making process, as Harding observes.

This tendency toward the relaxation and rationalization of the political center's controls was accompanied by not only the rise of the market sector, but also what Wu An-chia analyzes as a shift after 1976 from a "transformative" version of the CCP's Marxism to an "accommodative" one. By 1977, Hua Kuo-feng's insistence on strict adherence to Mao's views was challenged by Teng Hsiao-p'ing's emphasis on "practice" as the criterion of correctness. Some criticism of Mao was increasingly permitted. Teng de-emphasized the idea of class struggle. Flexibility was suggested when Teng in 1982 called for "socialism with Chinese characteristics." Other ambiguous formulas emerged, such as "socialist planned commodity economy," which came to light around 1984. In 1987, Chao Tzu-yang formulated the theory of "the initial stage of socialism" to justify those shifts toward free enterprise outlined above. Fewsmith discusses the different schools of economic theory that had arisen by that time, and that debated just what should be the scope of state planning and administrative measures in relation to the market.

As Walder points out, these ideological and policy changes had important effects on political and social behavior, though he doubts that these changes amounted to the "'rebirth of civil society.'" Overall, Walder notes, the population became less dependent on cadre decisions. With less cadre control over occupational, intellectual, and residential life, there was, as Rosen notes, some breakdown of the communication channels between the CCP and its auxiliary organizations. Walder notes that cadre-dominated clientelism became more controversial. The relations between cadres and others tended more toward a mode of informal bargaining, and this mode in turn was intertwined with corruption. Social mobility became less politicized, as education and competence became more important in the competition for higher status (as did social connections, it seems).

While the political center allowed more intellectual freedom, intellectuals using this freedom increasingly challenged the parameters with which the center sought to limit it. Edward I-hsin Chen describes the wide range of dissident voices. Many intellectuals called for democracy in a broad sense which they regarded as coinciding with socialism and the true intentions of Marx, and this mixture was then sometimes combined with an appeal to Confucian humanism, though more usually with the iconoclasm of the May Fourth Movement. In some cases, even Marxism, socialism, and the moral authority of Mao were challenged. Debates about how to rearrange the formal governmental structure arose, as some called for a multiparty system, but explicit endorsements of capitalism were rare. As already mentioned, a sense of ideological disorientation became widespread and was unrelieved by any suggestion that instead of the missing ideological guidance, China needed an open, eclectic marketplace of ideas.

This "crisis of popular confidence" in the government was fueled also by widespread complaints about inflation, about inequality in the distribution of opportunities to obtain wealth and status, and about cadre corruption. The intellectuals also felt strongly about issues materially affecting them in particular, such as irrational job assignments. Arising out of this whole syndrome of discontent, alienation, and outrage, student demonstrations occurred first in the winter of 1986–1987, recurred the next winter, and erupted once again when Hu Yao-pang died on April 15, 1989. With suppression of the demonstrations on June 4, 1989, the PRC reverted to a more overtly coercive form of governance, and another era of abortive liberalization and hope came to an end.

Even apart from this reversion, however, political and ideological change had been severely limited by the CCP. As already mentioned, the CCP was unwilling or unable to create a political environment fully releasing the energy of the market sector. None of the economic theorists discussed by Fewsmith called for an economy based on private property and free enterprise. As Walder points out, while the state sector continued to dominate the urban economy, work units within this state sector retained their "cellular and cohesive character." He also notes that, despite the rise of rural marketing, rural cadres continued to manage most rural industry, to be in charge of the rural infrastructure, and to distribute many services and benefits.

As many of the articles show, tolerance of ideological diversity did not arise, not to mention an independent press or political parties independent of the CCP. Thus the "Four Basic Principles" remained intact; Teng Hsiao-p'ing insisted that Mao's merits outweighed his faults; and reverence for Mao remained widespread, even within the prodemocracy movement of the students during the spring of 1989.

Furthermore, as the factional struggle between the reformers (such as Chao Tzu-yang) and the leftists (such as Li P'eng) continued, the state several times launched campaigns to contain or push back the tendencies toward intellectual diversity and political liberalization (the 1979 campaign against liberalism, the 1983–1984 campaign against spiritual pollution, and the 1987 campaign against bourgeois liberalization).

What the knowledgeable, soberly written articles in this collection fully document, therefore, is a strong political tendency inside and outside the CCP to resist political pluralism, ideological diversity, and any fundamentally capitalistic reorganization of the economy—the three kinds of pluralism that seem needed to realize economic modernization, not to mention democracy.

This political tendency certainly has had much to do with the vested interests of the CCP and its cadres. But it has also been based on an overall institutional structure that much of the population has become accustomed to, and on widespread cognitive modes resisting the introduction of any formlessly eclectic intellectual marketplace. Such resistance, indeed, is reflected in not only the CCP's objections to ideological pluralism but also in the widespread feeling of many outside the CCP that China now suffers from an "ideological vacuum." Yet, while different kinds of pluralism were resisted in different ways, we cannot view cognitive modes, institutional structures, and political interests as three disparate, disconnected kinds of phenomena. On the contrary, their mutual elective affinity and systemic interconnection are apparent.

It follows that as Chinese in the twentieth century adopted the goal of modernization and grappled with the problem of how to pursue it, they had to choose between rejecting or accommodating themselves to capitalism, ideological diversity, and political pluralism. Many rejected them. Why? One major reason is that these three things, for many Chinese, appeared as threatening to turn society into an uncontrolled mix of selfish impulses and disorderly, unpredictable thinking. This mix contradicted that goal of intellectual-moral-social-political unity and solidarity which modernizers had called for in China since the turn of the century. In other words, these three forms of pluralism often seemed to clash with that moral-teleological vision the early modernizers had either inherited from their past or constructed out of their encounter with the West. Whether to try nevertheless to accommodate these pluralistic forms thus became a central choice for Chinese elites in the twentieth century.

This momentous choice is what has differentiated the PRC's experience from that of the ROC. True enough, in neither of these societies was it possible easily to institutionalize any of these three kinds of pluralism. As John C.H. Fei notes, institutionalization of capitalism in the ROC led to a long and tortuous process of depoliticizing the economy. Even more obviously, resistance in the ROC to ideological diversity long remained important, and the opposition to democratization was still harder to overcome.

Yet, to an important extent, the ROC's "inhibited political center" allowed for capitalism and the play of competing ideologies; it had a Millsian component, both ideologically and institutionally; and it endorsed Confucian orientations toward the self-group relation. Thus it was different in kind, not just degree, from the PRC's "uninhibited political center," even when the latter shifted from transformative to accommodative policies.

This divergence then was deepened by developments during the past two or three decades. In the ROC, made possible by the accommodative, inhibited center, three interrelated breakthroughs occurred: the almost completed process of economic modernization, the rise of a fundamentally urbanized society with a large middle class, and a "great transition" from authoritarian rule to increasing political pluralism. In the PRC no comparable breakthroughs occurred.

If, then, this analysis is on target, the effort to bring economic modernization and democratization to the mainland will require more than angry opposition to tyranny combined with the reiteration of high ideals and subtle philosophical reflection. What is needed still more is concrete discussion about how to institutionalize on the mainland those three kinds of pluralism basic in Taiwan to the three breakthroughs that transformed the society there.

History surely has its surprises. The Three Principles of the People facilitated institutionalization of three crucial kinds of pluralism, and these three kinds of pluralism were causatively basic to the three interrelated breakthroughs that offer hope to China.

Paul A. Cohen

Response to Introduction

Situational versus Systemic Factors in Societal Evolution

I welcome the opportunity to respond to some of the points made by Professors Metzger and Myers in their introduction to this volume. Since I assume that readers of my response will have already read the introduction and are therefore familiar with the position taken by the authors with respect to my 1988 article, "The Post-Mao Reforms in Historical Perspective," there is no need for me to restate that position. For those readers who have not seen or who do not remember the original article, however, let me say a word or two about its purpose and contents.

In the article, which was originally written as a paper for a conference on the post-Mao reforms, I attempted to apply a historical perspective to these reforms "as a supplement to the more widely used systemic approach" of social science analysts.[1] It was not my intention to discredit the systemic approach but rather to suggest that a historical approach was capable of drawing attention to certain themes that the systemic approach tended to overlook. The main themes explored in the article were two processes that had been at work in China at least since the late Qing, and that continued to be of great importance in the 1980s: state building and authoritarian reform. I suggested that, although in some respects the older processes had

---

[1] Paul A. Cohen, "The Post-Mao Reforms in Historical Perspective," *Journal of Asian Studies*, vol. 47, no. 3(Aug. 1988):520.

taken new shapes in the recent period, in other respects they had shown remarkable continuities with the past. Most important in this regard was the pattern of authoritarian reform, which I described as "a kind of mainstream of Chinese reformism."[2] In making this case, I first sketched the main parameters of several earlier (that is, pre-1949) periods of Chinese reform—1898–1900 (Cixi), 1912–1916 (Yuan Shikai), and 1927–1937 (Chiang Kai-shek)—and then argued that the reforms of Deng Xiaoping in the 1980s reflected many of the same overall themes. Since during the pre-1949 periods dealt with in the article Taiwan was a Japanese colony, and when my discussion turned to the Deng reforms it was generally in the context of a historical comparison with pre-1949 reform efforts, when I referred in the article to "China" it was almost exclusively the Chinese mainland that I had in mind. In fact, the only specific reference to Taiwan in the entire piece was in a paragraph toward the end where I identified some of the situational factors that may have affected the fate of the reforms introduced there by Chiang Kai-shek after 1949.[3]

It seems clear from the introduction that the issue which really troubles Metzger and Myers is my situating Chiang and Deng in a single authoritarian reformist tradition. They would much prefer to distinguish between more and less authoritarian systems or, as they put it, systems with uninhibited and inhibited centers. Actually, I find this a quite useful distinction (much better certainly than the totalitarian-authoritarian distinction, which the authors also seem to find not altogether adequate), provided that we think of "uninhibited center," "inhibited center," and the authors' third category, "subordinated center," not as airtight systemic types but as points along a continuum. The problem I have with the Metzger-Myers analysis is that it does not directly compare the state-society arrangement that existed in China during the Nanjing decade and the arrangement that existed on the mainland after 1949, in particular during the era of the Deng reforms. Instead, in their effort to demonstrate that the differences between the PRC and the ROC are systemic differences, differences of kind rather than degree, the authors spend most of the introduction comparing the post-1949 mainland (the PRC) with post-1949 Taiwan (the ROC). In and of itself, this is a valid and useful comparison to make. But unless we are to assume that the ROC on Taiwan in the 1950s and after was not significantly different from the ROC on the mainland in the 1920s and 1930s,[4] I am puzzled about how the post-1949 ROC-PRC comparison relates to the analysis in my article.

---

[2]Ibid., p. 533.

[3]Ibid., p. 536.

[4]Metzger and Myers, unfortunately, are not clear on this point. They do not *explicitly*

Let me turn now to the post-1949 Taiwan-mainland comparison. In my brief reference to the factors contributing to the success of Chiang Kai-shek's authoritarian reform program on Taiwan after 1949, I placed overriding emphasis, as Metzger and Myers correctly state, on situational factors. I made this assertion in the context of outlining the radically changed conditions that the Communist revolution had brought about on the Chinese mainland. The conditions I specifically identified were three: the elimination of armed internal challenges and the establishment of effective control over the nation's territory; the removal of the political, economic, and psychological constraints generated by imperialism; and the destruction of the main social barrier to state-sponsored reform at the local level, the old rural elite. I then observed that "when preconditions not altogether different from the foregoing were established on Taiwan after the Guomindang's retreat there at the conclusion of the civil war, Chiang Kai-shek . . . was able to initiate a program of authoritarian reform that achieved a substantial measure of success." I added, however, we ought not to conclude from this that the Deng reforms will be crowned with comparable success. I noted that "Chiang had special advantages on Taiwan—the island's small scale, the positive legacy of a half century of Japanese colonial rule, a high per capita level of U.S. aid—that the mainland Chinese today do not enjoy," while, conversely, some of the obstacles to successful reform on the mainland, such as bureaucratism and population size, were far more serious in the late 1980s than they had been earlier in the century.[5]

Metzger and Myers do not take the position that situational factors are of no or little consequence. (In fact, they don't address the issue directly at all.) But the burden of their argument appears to be that such factors—I sometimes refer to them in my article as "historical context"—are less consequential than systemic factors. It is the latter, in their judgment, that determine the "kind" of system a country has, and it is the kind of system a country has that, in turn, plays the major role in determining the sorts of policies it is likely to pursue.

My own feeling is that the matter is more complicated than this. Cer-

---

assume that the ROC of the 1950s was not significantly different from the ROC of the 1930s. There are points in their analysis, however, where such an assumption may be implied, as, for example, where they take me to task for not considering "whether the ROC succeeded because it had all along structured the state-society relation in a way different from that of the PRC." It is not clear here whether "all along" refers to the entire period of Guomindang rule starting in the 1920s, or only to the period of Guomindang rule on Taiwan.

[5]Cohen, p. 536.

tainly, I would not deny the point that the ROC and PRC in the post-1949 era developed along different paths, initially in the ideological and economic realms and eventually in the political realm. Nor would I deny that, in some limited sense, the various components of the developmental trajectories taken by the two societies "hung together" in systemic, mutually reinforcing ways. (Metzger and Myers use the term "package" as a metaphor to describe the "fit" among the different parts of a system.) Beyond this, however, I find that there are more problems than answers.

One problem, which the authors themselves recognize, is the difficulty in establishing the distinction between a difference of degree and a difference of kind. Watermelons, cantaloupes and cranshaws are different in kind, but as members of the vegetable kingdom they differ only in degree. Similarly, as I point out in my article, with respect to the reform programs of the self-strengtheners, Cixi, Yuan Shikai, Chiang Kai-shek, and Deng Xiaoping: "There are important differences . . . and the differences become all the more conspicuous the more specific one gets. Nevertheless, at a certain level of generality, the commonalities of these reform programs—the features they share—are substantial, significant, and heretofore little noted."[6] The focus of my article was on these broad common features. Metzger and Myers, in their extended comparison of post-1949 Taiwan and the post-1949 Chinese mainland, go into greater detail, and inevitably the differences between the two societies assume greater salience. The question that remains unanswered—and perhaps unanswerable—is whether these differences add up to a difference of kind (as the authors contend) or one of degree.

A second problem relates to the component parts of a "system," more specifically the degree to which certain things fit together, almost naturally, with certain other things. Metzger and Myers see political pluralism, ideological diversity, and capitalist economic organization as "three kinds of pluralism" that have a "mutual elective affinity and systemic interconnection." They see the ROC as having been basically receptive to all three of these pluralist forms, although at different points in time and to different degrees, while the PRC has, in their view, been basically resistant to all three, although here, too, they certainly recognize differences between the Mao and Deng eras and among different sectors of societal behavior.

As I was reading this section of the introduction, I must confess to having often had the sense that what the authors describe as a glass half full, I would be more inclined to describe as a glass half empty, and vice versa. Despite their very real efforts to be both fair and honest, their preference for the ROC over the PRC is so strong that it inevitably colors the way in which

---

[6]Ibid., p. 533.

they articulate the comparison between the two. I do not have enough space to defend this contention systematically. A few isolated examples will therefore have to suffice to show that the coloring can work in the other direction as well.

First, with respect to ideological diversity, during the early 1960s, when I (and Professor Myers) lived in Taiwan, there was nothing even faintly approaching a free marketplace of ideas: the works of most major twentieth-century Chinese writers (Lu Xun, Lao She, and Shen Congwen, to name only a few) were unavailable in the bookshops, people (like Lei Zhen) were incarcerated for advocating in print policies that took issue with major political commitments of the government, and photographs of Chinese Communist figures in non-Chinese magazines such as *Time* were stamped *fei* (bandit) before being permitted on the newsstands. Conversely, on the mainland in the 1980s a very wide range of ideas (including those of Confucian humanists) came under public discussion in the context of the *wenhua re;*[7] artists, filmmakers, and writers were freer than at any other time since 1949 to experiment;[8] and Western writings of an explicitly anticommunist nature (such as the books of Karl Popper) were translated and openly circulated. The point is not that the PRC in the 1980s was as free intellectually as the contemporary ROC—certainly the newspaper press was not—but rather that, just as a considerable expansion of intellectual freedom had taken place in Taiwan between the early 1960s and the late 1980s, it was also possible, at least temporarily, for a comparable evolution to take place within the institutional environment of the PRC.

Second, I quite agree with Metzger and Myers that no real democratization took place in the political realm in the PRC during the Deng years, while a very welcome shift toward a more pluralistic political system has occurred in the ROC. My sense, nevertheless, is that the loosening up of the political system on Taiwan did not have its beginnings during the period of Chiang Kai-shek's rule, that indeed it did not really get under way until well into the rule of his son, while on the other hand, on the mainland, although no important structural changes took place during the 1980s, a significant weakening of the center, in relation to both the economy and

---

[7]For his forthcoming book on the cultural debates of the 1980s, Lin Tongqi has collected over a thousand articles embracing a wide range of different viewpoints.

[8]Note, for example, the modernist experiments of Zhang Xinxin, which Jeffrey C. Kinkley discusses in his "The Cultural Choices of Zhang Xinxin, a Young Writer of the 1980s," in Paul A. Cohen and Merle Goldman, eds., *Ideas Across Cultures: Essays on Chinese Thought in Honor of Benjamin I. Schwartz* (Cambridge, Mass.: Council on East Asian Studies, Harvard University, 1990), pp. 137–62.

society and lower levels of the administrative structure, did occur. I say this despite the events of June 1989, which suggest to me not a powerfully uninhibited center, but rather a state that was then, and remains now, simultaneously strong and weak.[9]

In the economic sphere as well, I would paint a picture that is somewhat less neatly contrastive than that offered by Metzger and Myers. Recent research by William C. Kirby, based on Guomindang and Communist archives, shows convincingly that, building on the ideas of Sun Yat-sen, central-government industrial planning was a major commitment of the Guomindang from the early 1930s on and that both post-1949 Chinese governments based themselves on pre-1949 Guomindang industrial policy, made use of Guomindang planning personnel and, at least until the late 1950s, shared certain basic industrial planning conceptions in common. Toward the end of the 1950s, substantial U.S. economic aid combined with internal economic and financial reform to promote gradually a more truly "mixed" economy in Taiwan. This was only gradual, however, and even in the late 1980s, according to Kirby, the role of the state in industrial planning remained important.[10] In the PRC also, there has been a transition to a more mixed economy, with greater emphasis on market mechanisms, profit incentives, and foreign investment. The transition did not really get under way until 1978, and its fate as of the end of the 1980s was uncertain at best. A substantial beginning, nevertheless, was made.

I draw two conclusions from this. First, the ROC, throughout the period from 1949 to the present, has been something other than a pure example of free markets and capitalist enterprise, while the PRC, since the late 1970s, has witnessed a significant extension of market mechanisms and capitalist-style incentives, most conspicuously in the agricultural sector, but in the industrial sector as well. The contrast between the two, in short, is not as clear-cut as Metzger and Myers imply; nor is it manifest that the two

---

[9]I am indebted to Vivienne Shue for the notion that "states everywhere, but especially perhaps in the third world, can be 'strong' and 'weak' at the same time." See Shue's "Powers of State and Pathologies of Dominion: China 1949–1979" (paper presented at "Four Anniversaries China Conference," Annapolis, Md., September 11–15, 1989). I am not sure exactly where a weak-strong state would fit on the subordinated center-inhibited center-uninhibited center continuum developed by Metzger and Myers.

[10]I base myself on the prepared text of a talk given by Professor Kirby at Harvard University on September 29, 1989, entitled "Continuity and Change in Modern China: Chinese Economic Planning on the Mainland and on Taiwan, 1932–1958." The talk, with some revisions, appears in *Australian Journal of Chinese Affairs,* no. 24(July 1990).

economies are, as the authors explicitly contend, moving in increasingly divergent directions.

None of this, I hasten to add, has any necessary bearing on the issue of "success." I (and presumably everybody else) would agree with Metzger and Myers that, by almost any measure, the ROC economy has been phenomenally successful, whereas the PRC economy has been beset by a range of serious problems, particularly since the mid-1980s. I am not, however, prepared to accept the view—and this brings me to my second conclusion— that the success differential between the two societies is more a consequence of systemic differences than of situational ones.

I will leave aside the matter of territorial and demographic scale (although I happen to view it as an enormously important situational variable)[11] and take up instead another conspicuous situational factor: the economic relationship between Taiwan and the United States in the postwar period. I implied in my article that high per capita U.S. aid contributed significantly to Chiang Kai-shek's reform policies in Taiwan. Kirby, as we have seen, credits U.S. economic aid with having played an important part in the development of the private sector in the ROC, beginning in the late 1950s. Even Metzger and Myers, in their lengthy discussion of early emerging systemic differences between the ROC and PRC, attach importance to the close ties Taiwan had with the capitalist world system, especially the United States, although they see pressures from the latter not as having created single-handedly a more pluralistic environment in Taiwan, but rather as having meshed with and reinforced domestic tendencies that were moving in this direction independently of U.S. influence.

The problem we are left with is, I fear, every bit as intractable as the problem of distinguishing empirically between differences of degree and differences of kind. In most historical contexts, systemic and situational factors both are operative. Sometimes it is difficult to distinguish the one from the other. Even when they can be distinguished with some measure of confidence, moreover, there is no scientific rule for establishing which sort of factor—the systemic or the situational—has greater causal weight in shaping a society's evolution. In circumstances such as this, scholars tend to fall back upon deep-seated convictions about how societies work. Professors Metzger and Myers, although not (as we have seen) denying the part played by situational factors, are prepared to go quite far in claiming that societies are best understood as systems, the component parts of which work together and in some sense belong together. I see societies as much messier

---

[11]Cohen, pp. 525, 536, 537.

than this. To the extent that they can be understood as "systems," I see the parts as fitting together only loosely and precariously at best. And, perhaps for this reason, in my efforts to understand societal evolution, I am much more drawn to causal explanations that rest heavily on contingent, contextual, and situational factors.

Part One
Systemic Aspects of the ROC and PRC

The Chinese Reconciliation of Moral-Sacred Values with Modern Pluralism

Political Discourse in the ROC, 1949–1989

Political Discourse in the Construction of the ROC's Political Center

The economic and political development of the Republic of China (ROC), which has governed Taiwan and five sets of islets since 1949, has been much praised by economists and political scientists.[1] Compared to other devel-

---

[1]This paper reflects years of discussion with Dr. Ramon H. Myers, to whom I am most grateful. It builds on arguments in Thomas A. Metzger and Ramon H. Myers, "Understanding the Taiwan Experience. An Historical Perspective," *The Pacific Review*, vol. 4, no. 2(1989):297–311 (hereafter M#1); Thomas A. Metzger, "Developmental Criteria and Indigenously Conceptualized Options: A Normative Approach to China's Modernization in Recent Times," *Issues and Studies*, vol. 23, no. 2(Feb. 1987):19–81 (hereafter M#2); my "Confucian Culture and Economic Modernization: An Historical Approach," a paper delivered at the 1989 Conference on Confucianism and Economic Development in East Asia (hereafter M#3); my "Continuities between Modern and Premodern China: Some Neglected Methodological and Substantive Issues," in Paul A. Cohen and Merle Goldman, eds., *Ideas across Cultures* (Cambridge, Mass.: Council on East Asian Studies, Harvard East Asian Monographs, no. 150, 1990), pp. 263–92 (hereafter M#4); my "Success and the

oping nations, the ROC has compiled an extraordinary economic record distinguished by the rapid growth of its gross domestic product combined with much success in containing the ills of growth, namely, inflation, unemployment, increasing inequality in the distribution of wealth, social deviancy, and political instability (ecological damage in Taiwan perhaps has been comparable to that in other industrializing societies).[2] Since the political reforms of 1986–1989, when martial law was ended and a second major, legal political party was formed, many observers have concluded that the ROC is becoming a democracy in the Western liberal sense, although undemocratic features remained in place in 1990.[3] These reforms, which began

---

Sense of Predicament: A Cultural Perspective on Modernization in the Republic of China," a paper delivered at the 1987 conference on "Dynamism in Asia: Noneconomic Elements in Economic Development" (unpublished; hereafter M#5); my "Ts'ung Yueh-han Mi-erh min-chu li-lun k'an T'ai-wan cheng-chih yen-lun (Taiwan's political discourse: A discussion from the standpoint of J. S. Mill's theory of democracy)," *Tang-tai*, vol. 24 (April 1, 1988):78–95 (hereafter M#6); and my "Lun tzu-i ching-shen yü p'ing-ku cheng-chih-te piao-chun" (On the spirit of self-doubt and the criteria of political success)," *Tang-tai*, vol. 35 (March 1989):141–48 (hereafter M#7). Some of the literature referred to in these texts will not be cited again in this paper.

[2]On this record there is a large bibliography, including notably Ramon H. Myers, "The Economic Development of the Republic of China on Taiwan, 1965–1981," in Lawrence J. Lau, ed., *Models of Development: A Comparative Study of Economic Growth in South Korea and Taiwan* (San Francisco, Calif.: ICS Press, 1986), pp. 13–64.

[3]See Ramon H. Myers, "Political Theory and Recent Political Developments in the Republic of China," *Asian Survey*, vol. 27, no. 9 (Sept. 1987):1003–22; Kuo Tai-chün and Ramon H. Myers, "The Great Transition: Political Change and the Prospects for Democracy in the Republic of China on Taiwan," *Asian Affairs*, vol. 15, no. 3 (Fall 1988):115–33; and Ts'ai Ling and Ramon H. Myers, "Winds of Democracy: The 1989 Taiwan Elections," *Asian Survey*, vol. 30, no. 4 (April 1990):360–79. See also a very useful recent study, Hung-mao Tien, *The Great Transition: Political and Social Change in the Republic of China* (Stanford, Calif.: Hoover Institution Press, 1989). Prof. Tien tries to be objective and is well-informed, but his book is flawed by an anti-KMT bias. For instance, in asking why the KMT has long enjoyed support from a majority of the voters, he grants that the KMT "now has . . . perhaps even a dominant position among the middle class" (p. 194), has drawn "heavy support . . . from . . . college professors, college students . . . professionals" (p. 191), and is likely "to hold onto a respectable majority of the popular vote" even after the full liberalization of the polity (pp. 193–94). Yet he never considers the possibility that this strong popular support is based on the rational feeling of voters that the KMT, on the whole, is the political organization best representing their interests, especially

under Pres. Chiang Ching-kuo, have also impressed mainland intellectuals, such as the famous dissident Wang Jo-wang, who in a letter to Teng Hsiao-p'ing urged him to learn from them.[4]

It is true that many intellectuals, both Chinese and non-Chinese, still do not regard the Taiwan experience as a modernization model for the rest of China.[5] The massive student movement sparked on the mainland in early 1989 by the death of Hu Yao-pang called for "democracy" as an ideal based on the May Fourth Movement, instead of turning to the Taiwan model as a concrete alternative to Marxism.[6] Yet a Princeton-educated economist born and raised on the mainland, Li Shao-min, has presented survey evidence that an increasing number of mainland intellectuals now studying in the United States and on the mainland believe that "China ought to learn from Taiwan."[7] It seems clear, moreover, that Chinese holding this view do not

---

their desire for prosperity and stability. Nor does Tien refer to well-known writings taking this point of view, such as Ku Ying, *I-ko hsiao shih-min-te hsin-sheng* (An ordinary citizen speaks out; Taipei: Chung-yang jih-pao-she, 1972). Ku Ying (also known by the names Min Hung-k'uei and David S. Min) was introduced to Taipei intellectuals by the widely respected academic and political figure Dr. Shen Chün-shan, and the common liberal claim that his book was a forgery encouraged by the KMT has long been discredited. Ku Ying speaks of a "silent majority" that gives the KMT more credit than the liberals want to give it, and my experience in Taiwan fully supports his view. Yet Prof. Tien ignores this view in asserting that the KMT's electoral success is due primarily to organizational skills and advantages (pp. 192–94). Whether or not he accepts Ku's view, it should at least be considered when weighing explanations of the KMT's electoral successes.

Another example of his bias is his unqualified statement (p. 38) that "Taiwanese fare better in low-level positions and local government administration, whereas mainlanders control the national levers of power in both the KMT and the government." Tien fails to see the contradiction between this proposition and his own account of how the chairman of the KMT and the president of the ROC wield enormous power, which increases still more when both positions are held by one person, and of how a Taiwanese, President Lee Teng-hui, came to hold both positions in 1988, a fact he himself notes (pp. 73, 113, and 114).

[4]Wang Jo-wang's letter is in *Chung-kuo shih-pao*, April 29, 1989. I am grateful to Chang Hao and Ramon H. Myers for this reference.

[5]A good example is Lao Ssu-kuang's discussion in *Chung-kuo shih-pao*, July 14, 15, and 16, 1988. I am grateful to Prof. William Tay for this reference.

[6]See Geremie Barmé, "Confession, Redemption and Death: Liu Xiaobo and the Protest Movement of 1989," and Edward I-hsin Chen, "Current Debates over Marxist Theory in Mainland China," both unpublished so far, I believe.

[7]See Li's article in *The Wall Street Journal*, May 11, 1989, and in *Orbis*, vol. 33, no. 3 (Summer 1989):327–40.

take seriously the common Western idea that, because of circumstances peculiar to Taiwan, such as its relatively small population and the economic aid given it by the United States until about 1965, the Taiwan model of development is not relevant to mainland problems.[8]

But what is the Taiwan model of Chinese modernization? Many members of the ruling party, the Kuomintang (KMT), would describe it as based on the official doctrine, the Three Principles of the People, which is today a doctrine combining the ideas of Sun Yat-sen (1866–1925), provisional president of the Republic of China when it was founded in 1911, and Chiang K'ai-shek (1887–1975), who led the Republic of China from 1928 until his death. This doctrine, long admired by some of China's most brilliant thinkers (such as Mou Tsung-san) but also dismissed as shallow by other outstanding Chinese intellectuals, was indeed vital to the ROC's success and today is receiving increasing respect from students of economic and political development.[9] Yet it does not amount to an interdisciplinary analysis of the Taiwan experience.

Such an analysis might well emphasize six factors:

1. Cultural homogeneity is taken for granted in the Chinese case, but should be kept in mind as facilitating development.

2. Taiwan's situational advantages include the fact that for about 150 years it has enjoyed much more law and order than the mainland. Like Japan but unlike the mainland, it was not devastated by great rebellions in the late nineteenth century. Then, in 1895–1945, while waves of political and economic disorder repeatedly engulfed much of the mainland, Taiwan peacefully developed under the Japanese colonial administration.

3. Other situational circumstances allowed Taiwan to obtain adequate access to natural resources. Largely lacking the latter, Taiwan could get enough of them only through export growth. Had Taiwan's population been gigantic, however, like that of the mainland, foreign markets could not have absorbed the volume of exports needed to bring back enough goods to raise greatly the living standards of such a huge population.

---

[8]This is at least implied by John K. Fairbank's minuscule discussion of the Taiwan experience in his *The Great Chinese Revolution, 1800–1985* (New York: Harper & Row, 1987) and by the utter absence of any reference to this experience in Gilbert Rozman, ed., *The Modernization of China* (New York: The Free Press, 1981).

[9]Chu-yuan Cheng, ed., *Sun Yat-sen's Doctrine in the Modern World* (Boulder, Colo.: Westview Press, 1989). Also see A. James Gregor, Maria Hsia Chang, and Andrew B. Zimmerman, *Ideology and Development: Sun Yat-sen and the Economic History of Taiwan* (Berkeley, Calif.: Center for Chinese Studies, 1981).

4. Various kinds of external help were important. Most important was the influx of foreign cognitive modes admired by Chinese modernizers since the turn of the century. Also important were conditions peculiar to Taiwan, such as the infrastructure left behind by Japanese colonialism, the transfer of much mainland administrative talent to Taiwan after 1949, and U.S. economic aid, which was important for capital formation until about 1965.
5. The familistic, partly ascetic popular culture was crucial, including its traditionally positive attitude toward competition in the economic marketplace.
6. To use Edward A. Shils' term, this popular culture was complemented by a sovereign political "center" that focused on instrumental rationality and economic growth and used the standard of instrumental rationality to revise the popular culture, nurturing asceticism and other aspects of it that facilitated modernization, while checking cognitive and social patterns dysfunctional from the standpoint of this standard.[10]

The word "sovereign" must be underlined. Many scholars point to Chinese commercial prowess in Hong Kong and Singapore to argue that it does not depend on any complex ideological-political structure such as the one erected by the KMT in Taiwan. In these cities, however, Chinese did not face the problem of themselves erecting a sovereign state capable of governing a large Chinese society, ideologically and militarily able to resist the threat of Communist domination, and simultaneously focused on the instrumental rationality needed to promote economic growth.

"Instrumental rationality," Max Weber's *Zweckrationalität*, refers to what Chinese call *kung-chü li-hsing*, the kinds of logical calculations typical of modern science and technology, as well as of managerial and political decisions aimed at realizing the widespread modern goal of increasing economic growth or "trend acceleration," while minimizing the ills of growth.

The thought of J. S. Mill, F. A. Hayek, and Karl Deutsch further suggests that a society focused on such rationality — a modern society — cannot be realized without considerable economic, intellectual, and political pluralism. History has vindicated Hayek's point that, because it is cognitively impossible for a state-planned economy to maximize economic incentives and minimize transaction costs, economic efficiency depends on instituting a free-enterprise economy (among other things). It has also vindicated Deutsch's thesis that competitiveness in the international arena depends on a great

---

[10]Edward A. Shils, *Center and Periphery: Essays in Macrosociology* (Chicago, Ill.: University of Chicago Press, 1975). (This is vol. 2 of *Selected Papers of Edward Shils*.)

degree of intellectual pluralism and openness to the global and historical flow of information and ideas.[11] It has also vindicated the Millsian view that political power unchecked by political pluralism is likely to undermine economic efficiency as well as other values.[12]

Thus I argue that basing a society on instrumental rationality means basing it on a decentralized, pluralistic way of choosing between the options basic to adult life: where to live; what to study; what profession to select; what economic deal to close; what worldview to adopt; what political cause to support, etc. These choices can be made by a state using a "line" to regiment society; by a local group, such as a family, tribe, or occupational group; by the "self-propelled adult" himself or herself applying norms imbibed through socialization, education, and other biographical experiences; or by two or more of these three. Unless these choices can be largely made by the self-propelled adult flexibly working with those personally close to him or her, it is hard to see how the members of a society can act in an economically efficient way, keep up with the global flow of information, and reduce political tendencies toward inefficiency, corruption, and exploitation.

While the idea of a decentralized, pluralistic society based on the self-propelled adult can thus be correlated to that of a society rationally pursuing economic modernization, it also coincides with less utilitarian, more ethical conceptualizations of a pluralistic, open, democratic society. This ideal has been articulated in recent years by the Taiwan psychologist Yang Kuo-shu and others (see below). Writes the young intellectual Chou Yang-shan: "The idea of a pluralistic society refers to the way that an individual, within the context of the rule of law, freedom, and democracy, acts in accord with his own interests, talents, and outlook as a moral and educated person and so does what he himself wants to do, forms the groups he himself wants to form, and freely participates in social activities."[13]

Whether or not one is willing thus to see economic, social, intellectual, and political pluralism as necessary for a society strongly focused on instrumental rationality, "instrumental rationality" can also be defined in terms of the qualities historically identified in a particular society as furthering or

---

[11]See F. A. Hayek, *The Fatal Conceit: The Errors of Socialism*, ed. W. W. Bartley, III; vol. 1 of *The Collected Works of F. A. Hayek* (Chicago, Ill.: The University of Chicago Press, 1988). For an excellent symposium on this book, see *Humane Studies Review*, vol. 6, no. 2 (Winter 1988–1989). See also Karl W. Deutsch, *The Nerves of Government* (New York: The Free Press, 1966).

[12]On Millsian thought, see David Held, *Models of Democracy* (Stanford, Calif.: Stanford University Press, 1987).

[13]Chou Yang-shan, *Tang-tai Chung-kuo yü min-chu* (Contemporary China and democracy) (Taipei: San-min shu-chü ku-fen yu-hsien kung-ssu, 1986), p. 206.

hindering "modernization." In the Chinese case, a broad consensus has developed bridging the Taiwan Straits and distinguishing between those aspects of the tradition that are functional relative to modernization and those that are not.

On the functional side, many praise the traditional norms emphasizing family cohesion, frugality and savings, hard work, respect for authority, respect for education and academic competition, competition in the economic marketplace, and certain bureaucratic skills. Some also emphasize the Confucian concept of moral autonomy.[14] On the dysfunctional side, there has been much criticism of the "ceremonial fund," the desire for many children, the great emphasis on the authority of the old and the male, and the tendency of the rich to switch from asceticism to conspicuous consumption. Particularism has been criticized for impeding a focus on the free development of the individual, equality under law, and the good of society as a whole. Many would agree with a mainland scholar, Li Tsung-kuei, who recently criticized traditional cognitive modes. His varied criticism amounts to the charge that they were insufficiently focused on instrumental rationality, neglecting logic, epistemology, the differentiation of topics, factual accuracy, practical efficacy, natural science, and the innovative acquisition and application of new information. He sees them as "intuitive" and "panmoralistic." These cognitive deficiencies were then interwoven with exploitative kinds of bureaucratic and patron-client relations.[15] Mainlanders call all these dysfunctional tendencies *feng-chien i-tu* (poisons inherited from the feudal era).[16]

Yet if we grant that Taiwan's success depended to an important extent on its having a sovereign political center focused in a rationally effective way on economic growth, cultivating the functional and trying to minimize

---

[14]See, *e.g.*, John C.H. Fei, "The Chinese Market System in Historical Perspective," in *The Second Conference on Modern Chinese Economic History* (3 vols.) (Taipei: The Institute of Economics, Academia Sinica, 1989), pp. 31–57; Yü Ying-shih, *Ts'ung chia-chih hsi-t'ung k'an Chung-kuo wen-hua-te hsien-tai i-i* (Modernization and the value system of Chinese Culture) (Taipei: Shih-pao wen-hua ch'u-pan shih-yeh yu-hsien kung-ssu, 1984); and Yü Ying-shih, "Ju-chia ssu-hsiang yü ching-chi fa-chan: Chung-kuo chin-shih tsung-chiao lun-li yü shang-jen ching-shen (Confucian thought and economic development: The religious ethic and the merchant ethos in late imperial China)," *The Chinese Intellectual*, vol. 6 (Winter 1985):3–45.

[15]See M#4 and Li Tsung-kuei, *Chung-kuo wen-hua kai-lun* (An overview of Chinese culture) (Canton: Chung-shan ta-hsueh ch'u-pan-she, 1988), pp. 264 and 271–72.

[16]Tu Wei-ming, *Ju-chia ti-san-ch'i fa-chan-te ch'ien-ching wen-t'i* (Reflections on the dawning of the third period in the evolution of the Confucian tradition) (Taipei: Lien-ching ch'u-pan shih-yeh kung-ssu, 1989).

the dysfunctional aspects of the inherited culture, we should ask to what extent this focus depended on the ideological climate in Taiwan. One answer, already mentioned, is that the official doctrine, the Three Principles of the People, indeed was the basis of governmental policy. A second approach, illustrated by Tien Hung-mao's and Robert G. Sutter's study,[17] is to ignore ideology, implying that politically important ideas in the ROC were either technocratic calculations, ideas rationalizing the KMT's vested interests, or liberal ideals in accord with human rights as universal principles. This viewpoint largely accords with the rational choice model so much used by political scientists. This model, however, cannot replace an effort to assess the importance of all major verbal patterns with which political actors expressed their motives and gave meaning to their activities.

As I have long tried to argue, such discourse includes utterances that can be identified as utterly unoriginal and uncontroversial within the context of that writer's arena of communication. By spotting these clichés and analyzing the worldview they express, we can grasp key assumptions shared within that arena and the shared agenda they imply, putting conflicting ideological claims into context.[18] Thus identifying the assumptions basic to a particular body of discourse, we can ask whether or not they include sacred-moral values that had to be reconciled with the demands of instrumental rationality. We can then also ask whether there was any "elective affinity" between a particular pattern of ideological reconciliation and the rest of the political center.

My thesis here is that, evolving only slowly, political discourse in Taiwan by the 1960s was a mix of five leading trends: the official doctrine (the Three Principles of the People); a "petty bourgeois" outlook; modern Confucian humanism; Chinese liberalism; and a version of the latter intertwined with the movement to turn Taiwan into an independent nation. I further argue that this ideological mix formed a limited consensus, rejecting Communism and to a large extent endorsing economic, social, intellectual, and political pluralism; that it largely reconciled instrumental rationality with an eightfold historical vision which had arisen in China at the turn of the century, and which had deep moral meaning for virtually all Chinese in the twentieth century trying to construct a sovereign political center; that there was an elective affinity between it and the rest of the ROC's political center; and that it was a necessary cause of effective modernization in Taiwan.

---

[17]Robert G. Sutter, *Taiwan: Entering the 21st Century* (New York: University Press of America, 1988). This volume was sponsored by The Asia Society.

[18]I first used this methodology in *Escape from Predicament* (New York: Columbia University Press, 1977).

In other words, Chinese Marxism and the ideological mix in Taiwan both evoked a moral-sacred vision of historical transformation that had arisen at the turn of the century, but they evoked it differently. Chinese Marxism pursued this vision in a puristic, utopian way, failing, even after 1976, to reconcile it with the patterns of economic, social, intellectual, and political pluralism now recognized as needed for modernization. The ideological mix in Taiwan, however, in effect sought such a reconciliation.

The Five Major Political Outlooks in the ROC

The Official Doctrine

One of the five major political outlooks in Taiwan has been made up of the ways in which different political figures or intellectuals directly or indirectly supported the official doctrine, the Three Principles of the People. It is summed up here by using two standard textbooks, that of Ting Ti (1978), which won three prizes and has been published at least six times, and that of Lin Kuei-p'u (1981), also published at least six times.[19] Because we are interested in what the official doctrine means for people in Taiwan, not in the ideas of Dr. Sun and President Chiang per se, these textbooks are appropriate source material for us.

This doctrine's starting point is not the philosophy of culture or the moral experience of the individual, but the fate of the nation. China is a "society," a "tradition," a "people" of the highest value. But China today exists in a time of utmost peril, resembling someone struggling in the midst of "deep water or a hot fire" (*shui shen huo je*). Facing this peril is a problem for "us," not the individual alone. The textbooks repeatedly refer to "we." Facing this peril, "we" want to "save the nation and save the people."

In other words, this doctrine evokes not the relation between the individual and a cosmic-moral order according with or rejected by "Chinese culture," but what Robert N. Bellah calls a "community of memory" defined as a nation in crisis. Time and again, "we" are asked by the textbooks to

---

[19]For bibliographical details, see Metzger #2, pp. 48–51. My description here of the official doctrine closely follows ibid., pp. 65–71. For the intellectual genesis of the doctrine, see Chu Hung-yuan, *T'ung-meng-hui-te ko-ming li-lun—Min-pao ko-an yen-chiu* (The revolutionary theory of the T'ung-meng-hui—A case study based on the magazine *Min-pao*) (Taipei: Institute of History, Academia Sinica, Monograph no. 50, 1985).

remember what is in fact one of the modern world's major sagas: the 1911 Revolution, the Northern Expedition, the victory over Japan, the establishment of the Constitution in 1947, the loss of the mainland to the Communists, and the subsequent achievements in Taiwan, which have "long since been noted and praised by Chinese and foreigners alike."

To bring this saga to a successful conclusion, a "great doctrine" (ta-tao) is needed, one based on universally correct moral-factual principles (ho-ch'ing ho-li ho-fa-te yuan-tse) and so able to guide action "putting to an end all difficulties" (fang-chih i-ch'ieh-te liu-pi). This doctrine already exists. It was established by a "great" man, Dr. Sun, whose "thought was a crystallization of the most valuable concepts found in all schools of thought, Chinese and foreign, old and new."[20] Therefore "we" should accept, praise, and act on his doctrine. Today, however, the textbooks continue, it is controversial, unappreciated by many. Therefore "we" need to study it and explain its true meaning to others.

Its ontological basis is the principle of "the oneness of mind and matter" (hsin wu ho-i). This condition takes the form of a cosmos "unendingly bringing things into being, unendingly progressing" (sheng-sheng pu-i, chin-pu pu-i). Exhibited by this cosmos are "the principles of mankind" (jen-lei-chih tao-li). Conceptualized by studying all human achievements, these principles accord with the "tide" of history: "the thought of our nation's father accords with the fundamental tendency of the current tide of world events" (ch'ao-liu-te ch'ü-shih).[21]

These principles call for the fullest development of all human and cosmic possibilities, especially economic ones: "every person will be able exhaustively to develop his abilities, the resources of the earth will be exhaustingly exploited, the utility of all things will be developed to the utmost, and commercial prosperity will be unqualified."[22] Such development, moreover, will coincide with the highest moral principle, "devotion to the good of all, leaving behind all selfishness" (ta-kung wu-ssu).[23]

Following this principle, the Chinese seek international peace based on equality, but must mobilize themselves and, again on the basis of equality, harmoniously cooperate with each other (t'uan-chieh, hu-chu). More specifically, to be effective, such cooperation requires realizing the "people's livelihood," "national development," and "democracy." Pursuing these Three

---

[20]Lin Kuei-p'u, Kuo-fu ssu-hsiang ching-i (The essence of the thought of our nation's father) (Taipei: Cheng-chung shu-chü, 1981), p. 5.
[21]Ibid., pp. 8, 27, 154, and 158.
[22]Ibid., p. 159.
[23]Ibid., p. 140.

Principles in a world still largely not accepting them, the Chinese must carry out a "Revolution."

To do this, the Chinese people must both retain control over their own destiny and establish a political party that will on their behalf set up an "all-efficacious government" (*wan-neng cheng-fu*).

Freedom is thus limited by the morally ultimate need to effect the Revolution. Freedom, in other words, excludes the freedom to reject "the principles of mankind": "When Chinese discuss freedom, they cannot do so to the point of departing from the thought of our nation's father."[24] Moreover, according to his thought, freedom of choice cannot supersede the principle of equality and its corollaries. True equality (as in Confucian thought) calls for hierarchy based on wisdom and morality. It also precludes the rights of the "enemies of the people," those people who do not affirm the "principles of mankind" and the Revolution based on them. This is so because rights are derived from the Revolution, not from nature.[25]

Even more, individual freedom is limited by the need for "all-efficacious government." The "freedom of the state is more important than the freedom of the individual. . . . When the state has attained complete freedom, it ought to give the people a reasonable degree of freedom." The people have to "trust" their government the way a passenger trusts the driver of a car. This is especially so during the first two stages of the Revolution, the military and the tutelage stages, which lasted until 1947.[26] After that, even after martial law was ended in 1987, limits on freedom were justified as required during the "period of mobilization for the suppression of the Communist rebellion."

According to the official doctrine, however, this "all-efficacious government" able to limit individual freedom and deal severely with "the enemies of the people" was simultaneously "government by all the people" (*ch'üan-min cheng-chih*). It had only administrative authority derived from them (*chih-chüan*), while they retained sovereign authority over it (*cheng-ch'üan*). Their sovereign authority took the form of the Four Rights: initiative, referendum, election, and recall. These rights were exercised by the National Assembly, to be elected by all the people. The Control Yuan could impeach anyone by addressing its impeachments to the National Assembly.

The official doctrine thus posits a political structure the feasibility of which depends on leadership actually true to cosmic principles of morality.

---

[24]Ting Ti, *Kuo-fu ssu-hsiang yen-chiu* (A study of the thought of our nation's father) (Taipei: P'a-mi-erh shu-tien, 1978), p. 187.

[25]Lin Kuei-p'u, pp. 69, 120.

[26]Ibid., p. 70; Ting Ti, pp. 187, 189, 192, and 261.

To be sure, it also allows for the fallibility of this leadership. In providing mechanisms to deal with this fallibility, however, the Three Principles of the People relied more on the impeachment power of a governmental organ than on either checks and balances between the executive, judicial, and legislative branches, or on free electoral competition between two or more political parties.

Dr. Sun himself believed competition between political parties should be restricted to "good political parties" (*liang cheng tang*), those affirming the Revolution, and should exclude "selfish competition" between interest groups not committed to the public good.[27] Thus he implied the need for a kind of political authority somehow representing "the people" in a complete way and umpiring political competition by expelling from it any group that was selfishly motivated. The textbooks made a similar point, before the reforms of the late 1980s, in explaining why the Republic of China should not use a two-party system: this system can be "established only in a country where the political experience of the people is profound and where the morality of parties is on a high level. Only then can this system work without breaking down. If it is set up without these conditions, it easily leads to an extreme state of conflict and mutual opposition."[28]

Sun and his followers believed that by thus conceptualizing a powerful, unified government that is one with the moral will of the people, they brilliantly avoided two Western problems: the excesses of individual freedom and control of the state by special interest groups, as opposed to "the people as a whole." Their project, however, depended on the practicability of forming a political party that could simultaneously amass great political

---

[27]Cited in Ch'en Yü-ch'ing, "Chung-shan hsien-sheng-te cheng-chih ssu-hsiang yü hsien-shih cheng-chih wen-t'i" (The political thought of Sun Yat-sen and practical political problems), pp. 17–18. This paper was presented at the "Symposium on the Thought of Sun Yat-sen and the Modern World," June 12–16, 1988, sponsored by the Pacific Cultural Foundation and the Dr. Sun Yat-sen Institute. The proceedings have recently been published. In the section of his book entitled "The Concept of a Political Party Developed by Chinese at the End of the Ch'ing and the Beginning of the Republican Period," Chang Yü-fa shows that political thought then did not even touch on the possibility that parties or interest groups pursuing selfish but legal ends are a normal part of democracy; see Chang Yü-fa, *Min-kuo ch'u-nien-te cheng-tang* (Political parties during the first years of the republic) (Taipei: Chung-yang yen-chiu-yuan, Chin-tai-shih yen-chiu-so, 1985), pp. 10–15. Similarly, Chu Hung-yuan shows that the T'ung-meng-hui felt far more at home with Rousseau's than with J. S. Mill's vision of democracy. See note 19.

[28]Lin Kuei-p'u, p. 468.

power, stay true to universal moral principles, and freely use its power to limit the freedom of citizens to oppose it.

Yet in depending on this vision of a powerful organization guiding the nation by truly following objective, uncontroversial moral principles, Sun was criticized by Chinese little if at all. Chinese saw nothing impractical or utopian about this vision. They just criticized the KMT's failure to realize it. It was, after all, the same concept of unselfish political power Mao invoked, and it had much in common with repeated proposals on the part of liberals and humanists to solve China's problems by just putting government in the hands of "good persons" who transcend selfish, particular political interests (see below).

The same belief in the practicability and imminence of totally moral leadership is basic also to the work of Hu Ch'iu-yuan, a highly nationalistic follower of Sun Yat-sen who has vigorously tried in Taiwan to develop Sun's views. Hu sets forth a philosophy enabling Chinese to decide their future by depending only on their own will and reason and so "transcending" all other intellectual content, whether Chinese or foreign (*ch'ao-yueh ch'ien-chin-lun*). After this collective act of transcendence, Chinese will be able autonomously to decide what theories or traditions suit their needs. Hu holds that once all Chinese grasp the rationality of his ideas, they will end all their intellectual and political disagreements, leave behind the disastrous eclecticism of a confused intellectual marketplace dominated by the unthinking acceptance of foreign as well as traditional doctrines, unify China, establish an economic-political system free of all unfair privilege and selfish interests, and turn China into the equal of either superpower. Emphasizing geopolitical issues, his thought expresses in an especially acute way the widespread feeling that China's currently secondary position in the international order is an intolerable aberration. It also expresses well the common view that Taiwan is very far from being a model of Chinese modernization. Anything accomplished there has been insignificant, Hu is sure, compared to what Chinese can achieve. Hu has been criticized for being too nationalistic or conservative, but his commonplace belief in the need for a collective, unified, purely rational, purely autonomous, objectively moral Chinese will has aroused little if any comment.[29]

There are also more liberal supporters of the official doctrine. Unusual in avoiding Hu's radically critical and pessimistic way of looking at the ROC, the widely respected KMT figure T'ao Pai-ch'uan has long held to a

---

[29]Hu Ch'iu-yuan, *I-pai-san-shih-nien-lai Chung-kuo ssu-hsiang shih-kang* (An outline history of Chinese thought during the last one hundred and thirty years) (Taipei: Hsueh-shu ch'u-pan-she, 1980).

vision of liberal reform within the KMT framework. Since 1986, the KMT mainstream has moved close to his views. One of his chief arguments has been the common liberal claim in China that the more democratization there is, the more will the moral-political unity (*t'uan-chieh*) of the nation grow.[30]

There is also a prominent tendency to vindicate the development of the ROC by using American modernization theory. Leading examples are the Hong Kong sociologist Chin Yao-chi (who also uses the name Ambrose Y.C. King) and the high official Wei Yung, both prolific and much-read writers.[31] These scholars thus greatly differ from Hu Ch'iu-yuan in their development of the interdisciplinary thesis that Taiwan has become a model of Chinese modernization.

The "Petty Bourgeois" Outlook

Apart from such ways of supporting the official doctrine, a second major outlook is that of the many voters who support the KMT at the ballot box but do not explicitly or intellectually identify themselves with its ideology. Probably their thinking was accurately described by Min Hung-k'uei (also known both as Ku Ying and as David S. Min) in a book he published in 1972, and in which he called them "the silent majority": *I-ko hsiao-shih-min-te hsin-sheng* (An ordinary citizen speaks out). Ku Ying is the closest thing yet in the ROC to a cross between George F. Will and Patrick J. Buchanan. I would label his outlook "petty bourgeois," a term the pejorative connotations of which would amuse him. He mixes together criticism of the Sun-Chiang doctrine, admiration for Milton Friedman's concept of the free market, a Buddhist-Confucian sense of morality, and a feeling that by so greatly improving the material lot of the masses, "crafty" KMT politicians met high political standards, whatever their shortcomings.[32] From the standpoint of liberal critics like Ho Huai-shuo, however, Ku Ying merely expresses the materialistic, self-serving attitudes of the masses and does not

---

[30]See, *e.g.*, T'ao Pai-ch'uan, *T'ai-wan hai neng keng hao ma?* (Can Taiwan become still better?) (Taipei: Ching-shih shu-chü, 1980).

[31]See, *e.g*, Wei Yung, *K'o-hsueh, jen-ts'ai, yü hsien-tai-hua* (Science, the development and use of human resources, and modernization) (T'ai-wan hsueh-sheng shu-chü, 1985).

[32]For a description of Ku Ying's thought, see Thomas A. Metzger, "Chinese Communism and the Evolution of China's Political Culture," in *Proceedings of the Eighth Sino-American Conference on Mainland China* (Institute of International Studies, University of South Carolina, 1979), pp. 71–75. See note 3.

deserve to be called "a true intellectual," one who puts aside all bias and self-interest to devote himself in a completely objective way to the public good.[33]

Modern Confucian Humanism

A third major category of political thinking is a moderate tendency often connected to what we can call modern Confucian humanism, the belief that China's successful modernization depends on reaffirming the ethical ideals of Confucius. In contrast to the views Ku Ying expresses, this moderate tendency is propagated for the most part by professional scholars, persons trying seriously to resolve central problems in the theory of history, culture, and modernization, particularly the question of the relation between Confucian values and modern ones. While generally approving the KMT's direction, these people often agree it should speed up the process of democratization. Their perspective differs from that of the official doctrine in that their intellectual starting point is not the nationalist saga of China's travails during the last century but rather the nature of "Chinese culture." Defending it against the attacks of the May Fourth Movement, they see it not as authoritarian or collectivistic but as coinciding with the modern quest for individual moral autonomy.[34]

This group is most prominently represented by the metaphysical "New Confucians," especially the great scholars T'ang Chün-i, Mou Tsung-san, and Hsu Fu-kuan, three of the signers of the famous manifesto of 1958.[35] It also includes a variety of scholars in at least partial disagreement with the New Confucians, such as University Professor Yü Ying-shih of Princeton, whose famous book on Chinese modernization, published in 1984 in Taipei, adopted a more historical, interdisciplinary approach to Chinese culture than that of the New Confucians. He agreed with them, however, in emphasizing great compatibility between Confucian values and modern ones, including not only the Confucian emphasis on moral autonomy but also its attitude

---

[33]See the article by Ho Huai-shuo in *Chung-kuo shih-pao,* April 20 and 21, 1987, especially the opening of article of April 20, which attacks Ting Pang-hsin by comparing him to Ku Ying.

[34]For more evidence supporting their view of the historical Confucian emphasis on moral autonomy, see Thomas A. Metzger, "Confucian Thought and the Modern Chinese Quest for Moral Autonomy," *Jen-wen chi she-hui k'o-hsueh chi-k'an (San-min chu-i yen-chiu-so, Chung-yang yen-chiu-yuan),* vol. 1, no. 1 (Nov. 1988):297–358.

[35]Chang Hao, "New Confucianism and the Intellectual Crisis of Contemporary China," in Charlotte Furth, ed., *The Limits of Change* (Cambridge, Mass.: Harvard University Press, 1976), p. 276.

toward existential concerns, its rationality, and its legitimization of a market-oriented economic life.[36]

Other humanists have also seen an affinity between free enterprise and Confucianism, contradicting the common modern Chinese leaning to socialism and thus returning to that affirmation of capitalism more common in China at the turn of the century, as illustrated by the later views of Liang Ch'i-ch'ao. Prof. John C.H. Fei of Yale unqualifiedly endorses the free play of market forces as ensuring both economic efficiency and "distributional justice." He then links Confucius to capitalism by emphasizing all the Confucian values, such as moral autonomy and self-reliance, that mesh with the values of the entrepreneur. For him, these Confucian values somehow superseded Confucian ideas, such as the ideal of the well-field system (*ching-t'ien*), implying limits on the play of the market, not to mention on the selfish desire for material gain.[37]

There are also many humanists who theorize little about modernization but take for granted the value of their Confucian heritage, which they study in a highly detailed way reflecting the influence of both German historiography and the Ch'ing "textual research" movement (*Han-hsueh*).[38] Some Confucian humanists, like the great historian Ch'ien Mu, who publicly endorsed Chiang K'ai-shek's rule in Taiwan, have sought a middle course between textual studies and theory. Some are practical, unintellectual men, often officials who say with great conviction "I am a Confucian," simply referring to personal ethical ideals. Some, like Ch'en Chien-fu, are not part of the academic community, can be viewed as part of the grass-roots culture, and yet see themselves as the truest vehicles of Confucian philosophy in the modern age.[39] The extremely vigorous and academically respected group around the journal *O-hu yueh-k'an* should be mentioned as illustrating the influence of the New Confucians in Taiwan, which is also illustrated by the writings of the Harvard professor Tu Wei-ming, board chairman of *Tang-tai,* a famous literary and intellectual periodical in Taipei.[40]

---

[36]See Yü's article mentioned in note 14; for a description of his position, see M#2, pp. 51–52, 62–63.

[37]See Fei's article cited in note 14.

[38]Chou Yang-shan, p. 208.

[39]See, *e.g.*, Ch'en Chien-fu, *Hsin-ju-hsueh: yu-ming hsin shih-chieh-te ssu-hsiang* (The new Confucian philosophy—Also known as The Thought of the World's New Age) (Taipei: T'ai-wan wen-yuan shu-chü yu-hsien kung-ssu, 1966). This was the sixth printing. The book is presented as "fusing together" all the best learning of the world, old and new, Chinese and Western.

[40]See Tu's book cited in note 16.

All in all, this mix of Confucian humanists has greatly affected the mass media and the cultural climate. Moreover, the fact that Taiwan has been so successful economically has convinced many that Confucian values facilitate modernization. There are still complaints in Taiwan about the "unscientific," "feudal" character of inherited popular values, but when intellectuals in Taiwan today criticize their society, they seldom focus on "the evils inherited from feudalism" (*feng-chien i-tu*) to the extent that their colleagues on the mainland do.

Modern Confucian humanism, however, does not simply exalt traditional values. It affirms them only within the context of the modern commitment to science and democracy. Exactly how to revise these values has thus become the central problem for the humanists. They worry especially about how to criticize while still revering them, much as Neo-Confucians for hundreds of years worried about how to extirpate selfish desires while nurturing confidence in the goodness of human nature. Indeed, in modern Chinese thought generally, not only modern Confucian humanism, "Chinese culture" has replaced "human nature" as the key ontological given that must be understood in order to pursue the right way to live.

Modern Confucian humanism has offered a multiplicity of views. T'ang Chün-i, Yü Ying-shih, and others have emphasized confidence in the overall goodness of the inherited culture. Tu Wei-ming tries to combine exaltation and criticism of it. Chang Hao has emphasized the traditional culture's lack of a sufficiently "transcendent" basis for evaluating and thinking beyond the status quo, and of a sufficiently strong awareness of the moral weaknesses of human nature and their implications for political life (*yu-an i-shih*).[41] Lao Ssu-kuang has emphasized using "reason" to identify and discard traditional values out of accord with modernity.

A philosopher at the Chinese University of Hong Kong, Lao Ssu-kuang is one of the most respected thinkers in the Chinese world. He moved from Taiwan to Hong Kong in 1955, seeking freedom. In 1981, he published a major history of Chinese philosophy as well as a famous book on Chinese modernization, *Chung-kuo-chih lu-hsiang* (The direction of China's development). In 1988, encouraged by the political reform in Taiwan, he came back for a visit, and his most recent thoughts about modernization appeared in two articles printed in three issues of one of Taiwan's two most important,

---

[41]Chang Hao, *Yu-an i-shih yü min-chu ch'uan-t'ung* (Awareness of the dark side of life and the democratic tradition) (Taipei: Lien-ching ch'u-pan shih-yeh kung-ssu, 1989). In 1989, this book was chosen as "one of the year's ten best" by the mass circulation *Chung-kuo shih-pao*.

mass-circulation dailies (*Chung-kuo shih-pao*). Adulatory remarks by the reporter interviewing him framed his views.

For Lao, as for many other humanists, that great doctrine Sun Yat-sen claimed to have found has in fact not yet been found, not to mention any claim that the KMT truly follows such a doctrine. Like Sun, however, he believes that finding such a doctrine is the indispensable tool needed to solve China's whole political-economic problem of modernization.

Lao therefore seeks to establish a global theory of cultural development distinguishing normative from undesirable cultural change. He sees a "culture" as an "integrated" "system" based on a set of central values. "History" is also a highly determinate process, one consisting of "stages" that evolve in a "spiral-like" fashion. New stages present a culture with new challenges, and a culture should be evaluated by looking at how it has met these challenges. Those values useful for only one stage are "closed," but any "universal" values can be used to meet challenges during later stages as well. Which values are "closed" and therefore should be discarded can be fully determined through "reason." "Reason" also indicates the need for economically and politically practicable goals, for long-term goals, and for a grasp of the difference between indigenously initiated cultural change and change based on the "imitation" of foreign cultures (as in the case of modern China).

If people grasp these principles, they can "control" (*chu-tsai-hsing-te i-i*) the development of their culture and society. If not, they will just confusedly and passively react to events (*meng-lung-kan*) and fall victim to vested interests blocking needed reforms.

These principles of normative cultural change apply to China's current historical stage, for which "modernization" is the main challenge. Like "culture" and "history," "modernization" for Lao is a highly determinate process. According to its "intrinsic nature," it focuses on "instrumental rationality," "the natural, bodily human impulses," and society as a "contractual" system with "rules of the game." It also leads to "postmodern" problems of environmental pollution, etc.

Lao then emphasizes that Western culture was inherently more suited to modernization than Chinese. Instead of "instrumental reason," "the East" has emphasized a "rational will" oriented to morality. Instead of "natural desires," the East has emphasized the "moral transformation of life." Instead of contractual norms, the East has based society on the individual's "moral character." These Eastern tendencies may be useful for dealing with "postmodern" problems, he holds, but they left the East inferior in developing logic, differentiating political from other moral norms, and grasping the nature of democracy.

Hampered by this systemic incongruence between modernity and their traditional culture, Chinese intellectuals since the nineteenth century have failed to grasp the principles of normative cultural change and apply them to China, which thus lost its "sense of direction" and so lurched from disaster to disaster. Lao's focus on this evolutionary disaster allows him simultaneously to praise Taiwan's economic-political development and to brush it aside.

The problem for him is not mainly Taiwan's small size or other such situational factors emphasized by Western scholars as making the Taiwan model irrelevant to the mainland. For Lao, Chinese in Taiwan and elsewhere could attain a much higher level of modernization than Taiwan has reached were they to adopt the correct theory of cultural change, which, he suspects, is his.

Refuting the theories of the iconoclasts and the New Confucians by claiming to adduce the most authoritative Western ideas (especially those of Aristotle, Hegel, and Max Weber), he sets forth the "rational" principles of cultural change noted above, and he holds that Chinese efforts to modernize will not succeed until Chinese learn to "treat the Confucian tradition as a fact, not a norm." That is, grasping the need for China's continuing cultural identity as a civilization that can modernize by "imitating" others, Chinese should retain much of their civilization as the simply factual basis of their continuing cultural identity, instead of retaining it because they revere it as a normative order with universal value.

True, since maintaining cultural identity is actually a process of continuing to honor inherited norms, Lao's seems like a distinction without a difference. Determined to distance himself from the New Confucians, however, Lao insists his rationale for honoring tradition accords with "reason," in contrast to their "religious sense of loyalty" to Confucianism. "Reason" is crucial, he feels, because eventually, after a period of imitating the West while retaining many traditional ways, Chinese will have to "bring about the reconstruction of society on the basis of universally significant values," making possible the eventual "merging of Chinese and Western values."[42]

---

[42]Lao Ssu-kuang's recent views were published in *Chung-kuo shih-pao,* July 14, 15, and 16, 1988. I am greatly indebted for this reference and many others to Prof. William Tay (Cheng Shu-sen). See also Lao Ssu-kuang, *Chung-kuo-chih lu-hsiang* (The direction of China's development) (Hong Kong: Shang-chih ch'u-pan-she, 1981). For Lao's criticism of T'ang Chün-i, see not only the above articles, but also Feng Ai-ch'ün, ed., *T'ang Chün-i hsien-sheng chi-nien-chi* (Essays in memory of T'ang Chün-i) (Taipei: T'ai-wan hsueh-sheng shu-chü, 1979), pp. 266–67. This criticism, however, is badly thought out. Lao says that T'ang Chün-i merely emphasized the valid aspects of Confucianism and did not also "make clear the reasons for the decline" of Confucianism. In fact, both T'ang and Lao give reasons for the decline of Con-

Chinese Liberalism

Besides viewpoints clustering around the official doctrine, a widespread "petty bourgeois" outlook, and modern Confucian humanism, the ideological landscape of Taiwan includes Chinese liberalism. Much of the latter's intellectual foundation overlaps that of modern Confucian humanism, as illustrated by the thought of Lao Ssu-kuang or—most movingly—Hsu Fu-kuan. Yet Chinese liberalism has still more been associated with May Fourth iconoclasm. Particularly important have been Hu Shih; the philosopher Yin Hai-kuang, whose 1966 *Chung-kuo wen-hua-te chan-wang* (An appraisal of Chinese culture and its prospects) used Western social science to make a major iconoclastic and liberal statement; and the psychologist Yang Kuo-shu, whose optimistic belief in the "open, pluralistic society" well expresses much liberal thinking in Taiwan today.

Most significant is the teleological theory of history in which Prof. Yang has grounded his optimism. The fact that this theory has aroused little if any controversy demonstrates that it expresses a widespread orientation. According to him, the various psychological and social aspects of a society are largely based on its ecotype. He thus analyzes Taiwan as currently moving out of a "traditional, agricultural" stage into a "modern, industrial" one. In other words, it is leaving behind a past that was "agricultural," "collectivistic," "hierarchical," "monistic," "authoritarian," "particularistic," "closed," unscientific, and undemocratic and moving into an era that will be increasingly "industrialized," "individualistic," "egalitarian," "pluralistic," "universalistic," "open," scientific, and "democratic." A clearer way of deriving "ought" not from "is" but from "was" or from "about to be" could hardly be imagined.

At the same time, most Chinese today do not understand what history is doing. Yang Kuo-shu regards Taiwan's thought and value orientations as still mired in the obsolete culture of the "traditional, agricultural" period: "First of all, we see that in Taiwan and Hong Kong, a new modern Chinese society has already emerged, and in these new Chinese societies, a new, modern kind of Chinese has gradually appeared, but the Chinese who live

---

fucianism in modern times, and Lao should have formulated this problem by comparing his reasons with T'ang's. Lao's reasons include the idea that Confucian values were inherently out of accord with the "intrinsic" values of modernity. T'ang instead suggests that the effective development of Confucian ideas was undermined by mistaken intellectual trends since the seventeenth century, ranging from the Han Learning movement to naturalism and Marxism. This argument indeed is one of his most basic themes, woven into several of his books. His own philosophy is an effort to correct these perceived mistakes.

in these Chinese societies lack experience with this new kind of Chinese society and lack the slightest understanding of this new type of Chinese person."[43]

Given his definite though qualified iconoclasm, Yang Kuo-shu regards the heavy emphasis in Taiwan on Confucian values as a refusal to affirm the values of the emerging "modern, industrial society." Thus he disagrees with New Confucians or thinkers like Lao Ssu-kuang or Yü Ying-shih, who call for more Chinese identification with Confucian values. Yet he agrees with them that most Chinese today live in a state of fundamental intellectual confusion, that this confusion is the prime cause for China's predicament, and that the key to clearing it up is achieving a highly precise, scholarly, if not scientific understanding of the extent to which Confucian values accord with the modern values that Chinese today should embrace.

The shared image is that of two determinate entities—"Chinese culture" and "modernization"—each of which must be precisely described in the one and only correct way in order to form a seamless whole (which will include parts of Chinese culture to the extent that they are consistent with modern values). Whether this image is an accurate description of what Chinese are doing or can reasonably be expected to do is, of course, another question. What is clear is that this viewpoint calls for democratization while emphasizing a deep gulf between the way most citizens think and the way they would think were they properly to understand history and its objectively moral implications. The purpose of democratization is to put those who think correctly into the political center. Thus, as clearly indicated, "democracy" in liberal Chinese eyes cannot be reduced to just a purely procedural or constitutional system that distributes power by counting votes. Instead, it is *also* seen as what I would call *hsien-jen cheng-fu* (rule by the moral-intellectual elite).[44] Conversely, "the people" in "rule by the people" (*min-chu*) does not denote the actual desires of the majority so much as a normative group following the wisdom of the enlightened.

A recent example of this notion of *hsien-jen cheng-fu* can be found in an essay, published in April 1990, by Chu Kao-cheng, a famous Legislator (*Li-fa wei-yuan*) who is a member of the main opposition party, the Democratic Progressive Party (DPP). He wrote that even though Taiwan had a "brilliant" economic record and had left "the system of dictatorship" (*chuan-chih*

---

[43]Yang Kuo-shu, *Chung-kuo-jen-te shui-pien* (The metamorphosis of the Chinese) (Taipei: Kuei-kuan t'u-shu kung-ssu, 1988), pp. i–ii, 407. Prof. Yang's many political writings include *K'ai-fang-te to-yuan she-hui* (The open, pluralistic society) (Taipei: Tung-ta t'u-shu yu-hsien kung-ssu, 1982).
[44]See Metzger, #2, pp. 44–47.

t'i-chih) in its past, it was in a "state of political crisis": "democratic government is parliamentary government. Yet we now have representatives whose
training and education are so poor that parliamentary discussion is paralyzed.
This in turn undermines administrative efficiency. An ineffectual democracy
amounts to a dead and buried democracy. . . . The people's representatives
are supposed to represent the desires of the people, but where are the desires
of the people? The interests pursued by the type of representative who is
opportunistic are just his own interests. The ideals pursued by the idealists
are just their own ideals. . . . The representative assemblies that are supposed
to nurture political talent are a source of dismay and are unable to represent
the desires of the people [*min-i*]." The cause for this disaster is the lack of
"good party politics. . . . Because each of the leading parties was from its
very start structured in a bad way, neither is able to carry out its responsibilities well. On the contrary, both corrupt the very substance of party
politics." This degeneration has in turn been due to the fact that "Taiwan's
democratization has merely inflated the consciousness of political rights, it
has not improved the civic culture [*kung-min wen-hua*]. This is mainly because
society's elite have not taken responsibility for public affairs." Chu Kao-
cheng thus hoped to found a new political party, one that would finally put
"society's elite" in charge of the government.

"Elite" was thus used by Chu in a normative, not a sociologically
descriptive way. He did not define the term as referring to all persons with
either power, prestige, or wealth. Such people, after all, already were in
power. He had in mind an elite currently lacking at least power and wealth
and distinguished by outstanding ability. A "robust democracy" (*chien-ch'üan
min-chu*) depended on putting the latter into the political center.[45]

Yang Kuo-shu is a bit unusual among Taiwan liberals in having given
credit to the KMT and in having spoken proudly of the ROC's success in
carrying out the modernization of Taiwan. A liberal spectrum leads from
his moderation to the spirit of radical moral denunciation with which Chu
Kao-cheng or the popular writer Ho Huai-shuo confronts the KMT. Ho
blames it above all for lack of "sincerity" and held even in 1988 that there is
no significant difference at all between KMT rule and Communist rule on
the mainland.[46] His views epitomize the liberal belief that there is no middle
ground between "dictatorship" (*chuan-chih*) and "democracy" (*min-chu*), a
view which reduces any intellectual defense of gradual democratization to
an apology for vested interests.

---

[45]See Chu Kao-cheng, "Wo tui ling-tsu hsin-tang-te ch'en-ssu" (My thoughts about
organizing another political party), *Shih-chieh jih-pao*, April 29, 1990, p. 4.
[46]*Tang-tai*, vol. 29 (Sept. 1, 1988):147–48.

This belief has animated the liberals since at least the late 1970s. It lay behind the Chung-li riot during the late 1977 elections; it was expressed in Wang T'o's 1978 book of interviews *The Voices of Those Outside the Party (Tang-wai-te sheng-yin);* it drove forward the *Mei-li-tao* movement during the Kao-hsiung Incident of December 10, 1979; and it served as the basic rationale for the formation of the DPP in 1986.[47]

The TIM "Saga"

Our fifth and last type of political thinking in the ROC is here called "radical" and refers especially to the so-called Taiwan Independence Movement (TIM). The intellectual origins of this amorphous separatist trend can be at least partly sought in the memoirs of one of its earliest leaders, the political science professor P'eng Ming-min, born around 1923. His father was a prominent physician, and P'eng was part of the Chinese elite in Taiwan under Japanese colonialism. From kindergarten through all but the last year of college, he received a Japanese education, cultivating warm relations with young Japanese intellectuals, who often shared his objections to Japanese imperialism, his admiration of Western liberalism, and his contempt for Chinese backwardness. As the ROC forces took back Taiwan from the Japanese in October 1945, the local elite circles P'eng was part of had a view of the world vastly different from the KMT's. They expected to be treated with respect by a Chinese government which they saw as inferior to the Japanese even as they hoped it would simultaneously heal the ravages of war, bring efficient administration, and deal delicately with numerous sensitive questions, such as the disposal of enormous amounts of Japanese property.[48] The many kinds of tensions between the KMT and the Taiwanese were aggravated by gross KMT misrule. Protest actions in the form of mass violence occurred from February 27 through about March 8, 1947. Called the February 28th Incident, this uprising was followed by a reign of terror, during which ROC forces killed some 8–10,000 persons whom they linked to the dissidents.

---

[47]Lin Cheng-chieh and Chang Fu-chung, *Hsuan-chü wan-sui* (Elections forever!) (Taipei: Kuei-kuan t'u-shu kung-ssu, 1978); Wang T'o, *Tang-wai-te sheng-yin* (The voices of those outside the party) (Taipei: Ch'ang-ch'iao ch'u-pan-she, 1978). The vast literature on the Kao-hsiung incident includes *Kao-hsiung shih-chien chuan-chi* (Documents concerning the Kao-hsiung incident) (New York: Hsingtu Publishing Co., n.d.), and Liu Cheng-kuo and K'ou Wei-yung, *Mei-li-tao yü yin-mou chi-t'uan* (The magazine *Mei-li-tao* and conspiratorial groups) (Taipei: Huang-ho tsa-chih-she, 1980).

[48]P'eng Ming-min, *Tzu-yu-te tzu-wei* (The taste of freedom), trans. from English by Lin Mei-hui (Irvine, Calif.: Taiwan Publishing Co., 1986).

This episode stimulated the formation of what can be called a new political "saga" or "community of memory." According to this TIM saga, the Chinese immigrating to Taiwan since the seventeenth century had started a "struggle" to escape the miseries and hegemony of the mainland, had gradually found that Western and Japanese influences benefited them more than Chinese, and were destined to found an island nation related to Chinese culture much as the United States was related to British culture, one developing at the intersection of the great maritime powers of the Pacific and the great land powers of east Asia. Built on liberal ideals that young Taiwanese like P'eng Ming-min had imbibed already under Japanese rule, the TIM was filled with anger directed at the miseries on the mainland that Chinese had fled to brave the dangers on a disease-infested, uncivilized island; at the ways in which the Ch'ing Dynasty had misgoverned Taiwan, provoking twenty uprisings; at the abandonment of Taiwan by the Ch'ing in 1895; at the KMT misrule beginning in 1945 and culminating in the terror of 1947; and at the continuing refusal of the KMT to allow total and immediate democratization.[49]

This "saga" of course collided with the KMT saga. After the 1947 Uprising, Taiwanese with such views could not freely express them in Taiwan but did form a vigorous international network, especially in the United States. Today they are influential in the DPP, but, especially since a Taiwanese became president of the ROC in 1988, separatist thinking has partly become more moderate and subtle.[50]

The Eightfold Teleological Vision Basic to Modern China's Political Discourse

If, then, political discourse in contemporary Taiwan has consisted mainly of variously nuanced views forming five main clusters—the official doctrine, the "petty bourgeois" outlook, modern Confucian humanism, Chinese liberalism, and the TIM "saga"—we can also see that an eightfold teleological vision was interwoven with much of this ideological spectrum as well as with Chinese Marxism. (The extent to which it was part of the TIM saga need not be debated here. The extent to which it was part of the "petty bourgeois" outlook is discussed below.)

1. The first of the eight premises is an emphasis on Chinese patriotism

---

[49]See M#1 and Lai Tse-han, Ramon H. Myers, and Wei Wou, *A Tragic Beginning: The February 28, 1947, Uprising* (in press at Stanford University Press).
[50]See, *e.g.*, Chang Fu-mei, ed., *T'ai-wan wen-t'i lun-wen-chi* (Essays on the Taiwan issue) (Irvine, Calif.: Taiwan Publishing Co., 1987).

and global centrality. Without trying to analyze Chinese nationalism, which often enough, as Sun Yat-sen deplored, has failed to overcome feelings of indifference to the fate of one's countrymen, we should note an idea usually basic to contemporary Chinese political thought, Sun's demand that China be "second to no other nation" (*pu hsun yü jen*), including any of "the great powers." Chu Yuan-hung's study, for instance, shows that in *Min-pao,* the magazine published by Sun's organization from 1905 to 1910, a central concern was to "catch up with Europe and the U.S. . . . if not surpass them."[51]

This reflects the traditional idea of being "the central kingdom." After the eighth century A.D., the power of the steppes steadily increased at the expense of China, and in the twentieth century a superpower was established in this vast region to the north. In the nineteenth century, China along its maritime border started to face foreign nations more powerful than itself. Yet no major Chinese thinker to my knowledge has ever accepted this shift in China's global position as just a normal change in the course of history. Instead, China's increasing lack of centrality in world affairs has been regarded as a shockingly aberrant condition. That is a major reason that the writings of Hu Ch'iu-yuan, who focuses on these geopolitical issues, have attracted so much admiration.

2. A second premise is a form of what can be called "epistemological optimism," the assumption that human beings can conveniently obtain knowledge about all the major moral and factual aspects of human life. Usually "reason" (*li-hsing*) is used in the traditional sense as a human capacity to grasp not only logic but also universal, objective moral norms valid whatever the "differences between the present and the past or between east and west or north and south," as T'ang Chün-i put it.[52] No modern Chinese that I know of has ever questioned the possibility that reason can turn all culturally disparate viewpoints that have any "true value" (*chia-chih*) into a single, logically unified, universally valid understanding of life (*hui-t'ung*).

---

[51]See, *e.g.,* Chu Hung-yuan, p. 228.
[52]Thomas A. Metzger, "Some Ancient Roots of Modern Chinese Thought: This-worldliness, Epistemological Optimism, Doctrinality, and the Emergence of Reflexivity," *Early China,* vols. 11–12 (1985–1987):70. See also Thomas A. Metzger, "T'ang Chün-i and the Conditions of Transformative Thinking in Contemporary China," *The American Asian Review,* vol. 3, no. 1 (Spring 1985):1–47. For a discussion of the May Fourth generation's "historical consciousness" that at least partly coincides with my account here of an eightfold teleological vision, see Leo Ou-fan Lee, "In Search of Modernity: Some Reflections on a New Mode of Consciousness in Twentieth-Century Chinese History and Literature," in Cohen and Goldman, eds., *Ideas Across Cultures,* pp. 109–35.

Only a very few Chinese intellectuals much exposed to contemporary Western skepticism, like Chang Hao and Tu Wei-ming, are wary of using "reason" (*li-hsing*) in this broad, transcultural sense. Even Ch'eng Chung-ying, with a Harvard Ph.D. in philosophy, has spoken of "joining together reason in its traditional sense with reason in its modern sense" as "the basis of the Three Principles of the People in Chinese and Western philosophy."[53] Chinese less exposed to Western skepticism have still more easily agreed with the famous nationalistic conservative Hu Ch'iu-yuan that "Because human nature is the same, there are no basic differences between the cultures of mankind east and west. At the center of the creative power of any culture are human values, reason, morality, and the cognitive capacity."[54]

In other words, while Alasdair MacIntyre has equated modernity with the doubt that reason can establish objective moral principles, this doubt has been, at best, peripheral to the modern Chinese intellectual world, not to mention popular Chinese culture.

The few Chinese scholars aware of it have hardly been alarmed by it. A good example is Li Ch'ang-ching's 1989 article on John Dewey's theory of valuation. Li is quite aware that in rejecting the idea of "transcendent" moral absolutes, many thinkers have fallen into ethical relativism, subjectivism, and emotivism. Yet Li sees no crisis here leading to moral degeneration or cultural disorientation, certainly none comparable to the one that Chinese usually blame on their failure to grasp the relation between Chinese culture and modernity. For Li, the threat created by the ethical relativism that alarms MacIntyre is minor, because John Dewey's refutation of emotivism, relativism, and subjectivism was partly successful, because Dewey "must have realized" that cultures the world over honor the same moral principles anyway, and because people in fact can recognize the difference between a "prejudiced" and an "unprejudiced" way of discussing moral choices. Therefore, for Li, Dewey's failure to make clear how objectively to distinguish between a moral and an immoral goal is merely a theoretical shortcoming, not part of a cultural failure to establish moral standards clearly.[55]

Indeed, for virtually all Chinese, it is beyond doubt that moral principle

---

[53]Ch'eng Chung-ying, "Lun hsien-tai yü ch'uan-t'ung-te li-hsing-te chieh-ho: San-min chu-i-te che-hsueh chi-ch'u" (On the joining together of reason in its traditional sense with reason in its modern sense: The basis of the Three Principles of the People in Chinese and Western philosophy), Monograph Series of the Institute of the Three Principles of the People, no. 15 (Academia Sinica, 1984), pp. 18 and 23.

[54]Hu Ch'iu-yuan, p. 217. This is the fourth edition of this famous book.

[55]Li Ch'ang-ching, "Tu-wei-te p'ing-chia li-lun" (Dewey's theory of valuation), monograph no. 23 in *San-min chu-i yen-chiu-so ts'ung-k'an* (Academia Sinica, April, 1989), pp. 31, 47, 50, 53–56.

coincides with the ascetic goal of unselfish devotion to the public good (*ta-kung wu-ssu*). Traditional ascetic concepts of virtue have scarcely been criticized in modern China, except by a few Taiwan psychologists influenced by the abundant Western literature denouncing "repression" and "guilt feelings."

Even when seemingly rejecting the Confucian concept of virtue, early modernizers have actually used the Confucian ideal of unselfishness to denounce the traditional way of life. While unwary observers assumed they were rejecting Chinese in favor of Western values, they actually were making an assumption unquestioned in China but strange to Western ears: a philosophy is adequate only if the people following it actually are motivated by it fully to realize its ideals, creating a society free of human weakness. In other words, the Neo-Confucian ideal of *chih-hsing ho-i* (the unity of knowledge and action) was treated by them not just as a goal but as a goal necessarily realized by the propagation of a correct philosophy. Making this assumption, the famous Chang Ping-lin, known as a fearlessly incisive thinker, denounced Confucianism on the eve of the 1911 Revolution for having failed to abolish selfishness in China and called for a new way of thought that would abolish it:

> The vilest thing about Confucian teachings is that they made men unable to free themselves from preoccupation with wealth, high position, profits, and official salary. . . . We now want to realize the Revolution and introduce rule based on the sovereign authority of the people. If we permit this desire for wealth, high position, profits, and official salary however slightly to adulterate our efforts, it will be like a tiny worm or a spot of mildew that can eventually destroy all of whatever it enters. Thus we absolutely cannot employ Confucian teachings.[56]

We should also remember that while early modernizers like Liang Ch'i-ch'ao criticized Confucian culture as insufficiently nourishing a spirit of risk-taking activism, they of course viewed this heroic spirit as ascetic.

Moreover, as illustrated equally by Lao Ssu-kuang's, T'ang Chün-i's, Mou Tsung-san's, Yang Kuo-shu's, and Hu Ch'iu-yuan's philosophies of history as well as the Three Principles of the People, Chinese Marxism, and many other examples, Chinese intellectuals typically believe that moral and factual knowledge can be used to establish a single, overarching, correct doctrine or standpoint clarifying all basic ontological, cosmological, histor-

---

[56]Cited in Chu Hung-yuan, p. 249. At the heart of Sun Yat-sen's revolutionary ideology as expressed in *Min-pao* on the eve of the 1911 revolution was a concept of "loving others and discarding all selfishness," which was intertwined with an emphasis on "equality." See ibid., p. 237.

ical, moral, and political questions (a *t'i-hsi*; or *hsi-t'ung*). True, Chinese Marxism and Sunism posit that one or more "great" men have already found this doctrine, while Chinese liberalism and modern Confucian humanism instead view this quest for a doctrine uniting all the truths of mankind (*hui-t'ung*) as still drastically unfinished. The importance and feasibility of this quest, however, is seldom if ever doubted, even today.[57]

Often linked to this quest for the correct doctrine is that for a brief verbal formula which can serve as the lodestar of change. Again, the formulae differ but not the belief in the importance of finding the right formula. The first famous formula, Chang Chih-tung's in 1898, "Chinese learning for the basis, Western learning for instrumental purposes," has remained enormously important, whether for those who lean to it or those who reject it. Lao Ssu-kuang's formula, discussed above, can be seen as another recent attempt to refute Chang Chih-tung: "Treat the Confucian tradition as a fact, not a norm" (*Kuei-fan-hsing-chih chieh-ch'u yü shih-t'i-hsing-chih she-li*), that is, retain Confucian norms to the extent that they are factually integral to the cultural identity of the Chinese, not because they necessarily are universally valid as norms. We have also noted Hu Ch'iu-yuan's formula: "Progress by transcending all Chinese and foreign ideas not in accord with the autonomous, rational will of the Chinese people" (*Ch'ao-yueh ch'ien-chin-lun*). In an 1988 meeting in Beijing organized by the PRC's Academy for the Study of Chinese Culture, Wei Cheng-t'ung, a prominent liberal and humanist from Taipei, introduced the thought of Lin Yü-sheng, an historian and liberal spokesman well known in the ROC too, by praising Lin's formula, "creative transformation" (*ch'uang-tsao-hsing-te chuan-hua*) and explaining how the latter had replaced the earlier "wholesale Westernization" and "modernization" in Taiwan.[58]

3. Third, epistemological optimism having rationally defined transcultural moral standards, the leading Chinese ideologies never use the word "culture" in the descriptive way developed by Western anthropologists. Even when citing the definitions of culture devised by anthropologists like Clyde Kluckhohn, Chinese scholars from Yin Hai-kuang to Yü Ying-shih have used "Chinese culture" in a strongly normative way, holding up standards like democracy, modernization, human dignity, rationality, and respect for

---

[57]Thomas A. Metzger, "A Confucian Kind of Modern Thought: Secularization and the Concept of the *T'i-hsi*" in *Proceedings of the Conference on Chinese Modernization,* Institute of Modern History, Academia Sinica, summer 1990 (in press).

[58]"Liang-an hsueh-che t'an Chung-kuo wen-hua" (Scholars from both sides of the straits discuss Chinese culture). A photographic copy was kindly given to me by Dr. Richard Wang. Originally published in *Chung-kuo lun-t'an,* around late November 1988.

law, and then asking whether or not Chinese culture accords with these values. When Tu Wei-ming writes about "Chinese culture" for Chinese audiences in Chinese, he divides it into "poisons inherited from the feudal era" (*feng-chien i-tu*) and "the finest aspects of Chinese culture" (*Chung-kuo wen-hua-te ching-hua*).

While culture in Chinese eyes is thus primarily an object to be evaluated by referring to universal or current standards or goals, it is also often seen as a determinate, systemic, "integrated whole" based on a "central" feature, whether a source of backwardness, such as the agricultural ecotype (Yang Kuo-shu's view of Chinese culture); an unfolding ideal meshing with modern values, such as the "inner transcendence" emphasized by Yü Ying-shih; the goal of "grasping the ultimate while finding the perfect balance in daily affairs" (*chi kao-ming erh tao chung-yung*), emphasized by Fung Yu-lan; or the traditional ideal of *nei-sheng wai-wang* (within a sage, without a true king), emphasized by Mou Tsung-san.

4. Fourth, history is similarly seen as a determinate series of "stages," and it is currently in the process of moving into the next, virtually perfect stage. This shift is seen as a global "tide" (*ch'ao-liu*) of events, and moral action is defined as action in accord with this historical "tide."

5. The idea of this shift is integral to that of the ideal society, and the criteria of successful modernization derived from this ideal are often used to judge political life in the present. "Democracy" is part of this ideal and, as already noted, refers not only to rule based on majority vote but also to "rule by the enlightened" (*hsien-jen cheng-fu*). This enlightened group is conceptualized as either an actual political party (such as the CCP, the KMT, or the new party envisioned in 1990 by Chu Kao-cheng), or as those true to "the Chinese intellectuals' corporate, morally critical, self-aware consciousness," to use Tu Wei-ming's concept. This enlightened group understands the historical shift currently occurring, realizes that virtue of unselfishness implied by reason, and so is able to transcend partisan interests.

As already noted, this assumption that there are people who can wield power in a completely unselfish way has been common to Chinese Marxism, Sunism, and Hu Chiu-yuan's philosophy. It has been common also to humanistic and liberal thought. In other words, it is part of what David Laitin has called culturally defined common sense.

For instance, for the brilliant Hsu Fu-kuan, writing in 1953, the central political problem was to *ko-chün-hsin-chih fei* (understand and remove any bias or other mistaken idea in the ruler's mind). The Confucian approach to this problem relied unsuccessfully on persuasion, but "democracy" succeeded by relying on "legal institutions": "In a democracy, the likes and dislikes of political leaders are separated from the 'source of sovereign authority' [that is, 'the hands of the people']. Thus, there naturally are objective limits on the implementation of [the leaders'] like and dislikes, which they do not dare act on to the point of disrupting affairs. Thus anything wrong in their minds is rectified without even trying. . . . They cannot but follow the results of the elections, and they cannot but take into account the arguments made in the representative assembly. Anything that objectively has to be done is something that subjectively is the easiest thing possible to do . . . even if a political leader is not a sage, he cannot but act as a sage would."[59]

Yin Hai-kuang, a famous liberal critic in Taiwan then, praised this essay of Hsu's without raising any questions about its highly optimistic view of democracy.[60] In 1935, Hu Shih had similarly assumed that leadership free of partisan interest was possible. He argued then that the national crisis demanded an all-powerful leader, but this leader could not express the interests of one party or faction: "Certainly he himself can continue being part of a party and being its leader, just as he can continue being part of the military and being its leader. But his perspective must far transcend the interests of his party. He has to pursue the interests of the nation as a whole. If he is unable to do this, he definitely is not qualified to lead the nation."[61]

"Democracy" also connotes realization under this elite of a morally, intellectually, politically, and socially unified society. T'an Ssu-t'ung's and K'ang Yu-wei's vision of a society without "barriers" or "fissures" alienating people from each other has remained basic. The oneness of the ruling group with "the people" is basic to the Sunist concept of "government by all the people" (ch'üan-min cheng-chih), not to mention Maoism. Even Yang Kuo-shu, a representative liberal thinker today much influenced by American scholarship, takes for granted that in China's coming "open, pluralistic" society, "people will be of one mind, their thinking based on the same principles" (jen t'ung tz'u hsin, hsin t'ung tz'u li).

In 1986, he even dealt with the problem of Taiwanese separatism, still urgent in 1990, by holding that turning Taiwan into a "truly open, pluralistic

---

[59]Hsu Fu-kuan, *Hsueh-shu yü cheng-chih-chih chien* (Between the realms of scholarship and politics) (T'ai-wan hsueh-sheng shu-chü, 1980), pp. 124–26. In this book's next essay, Yin Hai-kuang praises this article by Hsu, obviously agreeing with its conceptualization of democracy. In other words, this conceptualization was a cliché, a widespread idea. (Yin was then an iconoclastic liberal, a follower of Bertrand Russell, while Hsu was a profound Confucian scholar.)
[60]Ibid.
[61]Cited in Chang Chung-tung, "Tsai tung-luan-chung chien-ch'ih min-chu-te Hu Shih" (Hu Shih's resolute commitment to democracy in a time of upheaval), *Chin-tai-shih yen-chiu-so chi-k'an*, vol. 15, no. 2 (Dec. 1986):133.

society is the most effective way to eliminate the psychological and social boundaries separating those with different provincial origins."[62]

Democracy, moreover, is typically identified with an era of global oneness. K'ang Yu-wei saw this coming stage as one of a "great moral oneness of mankind" (*ta-t'ung*), while T'ang Chün-i preferred the idea of a "great harmony" (*t'ai-ho*). This teleological viewpoint is so basic to modern Chinese thought that it has been retained even by Chinese scholars greatly exposed to contrary Western ideas. Both the Princeton professor Yü Ying-shih and the Hong Kong philosopher Lao Ssu-kuang hold open the hope that "perhaps all of mankind will really create a shared value system merging together all cultures," as Yü put it.[63] The Harvard-trained philosopher Ch'eng Chung-ying sees "the greatest test through which Chinese culture must pass" as taking Confucian thought and "making it one with Western scholarship and thought." In this way, he hopes, the Chinese can extend to the "rest of the world" a "way of thinking emphasizing peace and moral rule," putting "an end to the international power struggles in all the Western countries."[64]

When intellectuals of the ROC lean toward such a vision, it usually affects their criteria of successful modernization and hence the way that they evaluate the political performance of their government. Instead of evaluating it by using statistical indices or other empirically based standards to compare its record with the records of other developing and modern nations, they often derive sublime, if not utopian, criteria from this vision of what is bound to be. An *a posteriori* understanding of what is politically practicable is thus superseded by an *a priori* faith in what Chinese with moral intentions can in fact do.

It is not enough, then, for citizens to be law-abiding and industrious. As demonstrated by the famous debate in April 1987 between Ting Pang-hsin and Ho Huai-shuo, it is taken for granted that citizens should be thoroughly virtuous. Ting demanded they get rid of "selfishness," while Ho went on at length about the lack of "sincerity" throughout society.[65] High social mobility rates are not enough, because in a democracy, Yang Kuo-shu has said, status simply accords with what every individual deserves.[66] An interesting, vital, free marketplace of ideas is not enough,

---

[62]Yang Kuo-shu, *Shui-pien*, p. 228.
[63]Yü Ying-shih, *Ts'ung chia-chih*, p. 116.
[64]Ch'eng Chung-ying, pp. 18 and 23.
[65]*Lien-ho-pao*, April 9 and 10, 1987, and *Chung-kuo shih-pao*, April 20 and 21, 1987.
[66]Cited in Metzger #6, p. 83. See Yang Kuo-shu, *K'ai-fang*, p. 3.

because a moral-intellectual consensus is the indispensable basis of social harmony. Democratization must be quick and lead to a polity free of selfish interests. Economically, "growth with equity" is not enough, because the ROC should be technologically independent, free of dependence on foreign trade, and as affluent as Japan or the United States. Finally, China's normal international position is one matching that of any other nation, including the superpowers. All these criteria of success are commonly found in Taiwan political writings, although there is also a definite tendency to use more modest criteria, as illustrated by Ku Ying's views, those of some social scientists, like Wei Yung and Chin Yao-chi, or indeed Lao Ssu-kuang's own emphasis on practicality.

6. Sixth, given the belief that current history is a teleological "tide" bringing one culture after another into an era of democracy, prosperity, and moral harmony, as well as the belief that reason can fully grasp the nature of this historical movement and its relation to older values, cultural change is a matter of applying reason. In other words, cultural change is something to be properly directed by the elite able to use reason, rather than a hetero-geneous, indeterminate process shaped by disparate impulses coming from all social sectors. Lao Ssu-kuang's views above are typical. Cultural change is thus seen not as crescive, but as enacted; not as accommodative, but as transformative; not as unplanned and uncontrolled, but as planned and controlled. To use Tolstoy's distinction, Chinese ideologues confront history and the process of cultural change with the spirit of Napoleon, not Kutuzov. The enlightened are to control cultural change, not only the democratic political process.

7. The seventh part of this teleological vision is the view that modern Chinese history has consistently failed to meet this standard of normative cultural change, and that China today is still in a deep predicament, a crisis in no way mitigated by any successful economic or political development that has occurred in Taiwan (see "The Prevalence of the Sense of Predica-ment," below). Apart from some Maoist views in the past, China's current historical reality is invariably seen as contradicting the "tide" of history.

8. Eighth, given this failure of Chinese in modern times to grasp and carry out the principles of normative cultural change, a vehicle of rectification is needed, a "sense of moral mission" (*shih-ming-kan*) embodied by either the Party or "the intellectuals," depending on the ideological standpoint. Thus a major difference between Maoism and the Three Principles of the People was that official propagation of the latter, even though exalting the role of the Party, coexisted with contrary claims giving this mission of rectification *entirely* to "intellectuals," the position taken in both Chinese liberalism and modern Confucian humanism.

History itself having determined that goal of global centrality and moral harmony which Chinese culture should realize, and reason having grasped that goal, an ascetic commitment to "struggle" for the realization of this goal by transforming Chinese culture was the only conceivable path to be taken by any Chinese person true to his or her conscience. The eight premises outlined here thus formed a logically and affectively unified vision revolving around an ascetic morality implied by reason and demanded by the movement of history. Conversely, these premises defined much of the current society as perversely resisting this historical "tide." In other words, Chinese to a very large extent have defined their national situation not as just a mix of desirable and undesirable tendencies to be dealt with in a practical way but as an inexcusable predicament caused by perverse refusal to respect history's immanent moral logic. The difficulties of modernization and state building were thus defined as inherently abnormal phenomena due to normally avoidable human weaknesses. Citizens with this commonplace view thus reacted to these difficulties not by calmly considering practicable alternatives but by angrily denouncing leaders or lapsing into feelings of alienation or passivity.

This worldview is very different from a Western intellectual mainstream today that Alasdair MacIntyre and others have described. This mainstream has been heavily influenced by nominalism, empiricism, historicism, cultural relativism, ethical skepticism, and legal positivism. Much influenced by David Hume, these trends deny that "reason" can establish objective, impersonal moral norms transcending culturally distinctive norms. Studying the cultures of the world, these Humeans emphasize value-free description and, despite Lawrence Kohlberg's complaints, believe that there are no metacultural standards by which one cultural pattern can be judged as superior or inferior to another. Conversely, Western intellectuals tend to see "the crisis of culture" as based on this lack of access to universal moral standards, while Chinese intellectuals more typically define such a "crisis" as due to misunderstanding about the relation between modernity and their traditional culture. While Chinese intellectuals take for granted that morality is ascetic, Western intellectuals often deny that ascetic values objectively supersede other "life-style preferences."

There is also much more skepticism in the West than in the Chinese cultural arena about the possibility of constructing any macroscopic philosophy of history. When John A. Hall recently tried to outline such a philosophy in even a modest way, he noted he was going against the trends of the day. To be sure, many Western scholars today still see in Western history an admirable economic and political transformation reminiscent of the teleological historical vision of Marx or J. S. Mill. Yet they usually deny that this transformation followed any historically necessary laws of development. They thus view history as hovering between random events and only partly coherent tendencies, rather than following a determinate, coherent, teleo-logical path of progress publicly promulgating objective moral norms all individuals should respect. Filled with Tolstoyan doubts about the human ability to control the course of history, they agree with Tolstoy that Kutuzov showed more wisdom than Napoleon: history consists of events largely outside the control of any elite, political or intellectual.

In the Western, Millsian tradition, moreover, democracy is more a procedural, constitutional form maximizing equality and freedom rather than a system necessarily putting a morally and intellectually enlightened elite in control of the government. In other words, the Oxford philosopher J. R. Lucas was expressing a widespread Western view when he distinguished between "agreement about the rights and wrongs" of a particular "dispute," and "agreement about a method, a procedure, or a form, for settling dis-putes," such as an adjudicative procedure. For him, because the former kind of agreement is often impossible, a community must be based on the latter kind.[67] Liberal and other Chinese thought, however, typically assumes the former is both feasible and indispensable (*jen t'ung tz'u-hsin, hsin t'ung tz'u-li*).

We Westerners who are wed to the above views often use them to rank cultures epistemically, claiming that "we know how to know" and looking down on outlooks like the Chinese one above as naive and unsophisticated. Yet in fact, how to rank cultures epistemically is a vast problem only ob-scured by such presumption.[68] My point here is just to emphasize the dis-parity between two intellectual worlds, not to rank these worlds.

Given this disparity, scholars who hold that the West has come to exercise cultural hegemony over the East have to argue that this disparity is unimportant.

To be sure, the disparity between Eastern and Western thought is less if we compare the former to Western thought one or two hundred years ago. An important example is John Stuart Mill's (1806–1873) long essay "On

---

[67]See J. R. Lucas, "On Processes for Resolving Disputes," in Robert S. Summers, *Essays in Legal Philosophy* (Berkeley, Calif.: University of California Press, 1972), pp. 179–80; John A. Hall, *Powers and Liberties: The Causes and Consequences of the Rise of the West* (Oxford: Basil Blackwell Ltd., 1985); Alasdair MacIntyre, *After Virtue* (Notre Dame, Ind.: University of Notre Dame Press, 1981); and Lawrence Kohlberg, *The Philosophy of Moral Development* (San Francisco, Calif.: Harper & Row, 1981). With regard to studying Kohlberg's thought, I owe a great debt to Profs. Uwe P. Gielen and Richard Wilson and to Mr. Lei Ting.

[68]See Thomas A. Metzger, "The Normative Way to Make Normative Statements: Some Reactions to Recent Kohlbergian Work on Chinese Moral Thinking," *The American Asian Review*, vol. 8, no. 1 (Spring 1990):1–62, and Metzger, #4.

Liberty." Although Mill emphasized the fallibility of the human mind, he combined this emphasis, whether logically or not, with great epistemological optimism. Thus he viewed "reason" as able to discover moral as well as factual truths, referring to the "'eternal or immutable dictates of reason.'" He viewed the history of the West as an accumulation of "uncontested" "truths" that had been revealed especially by the Greek philosophers, Christianity, the Reformation, science, and German humanism. Morality for him was ascetic, consisting of the Aristotelian and Biblical virtues. Thus becoming increasingly civilized, the West, according to Mill, existed in a state of objective contrast with "those backward states of society in which the race itself may be considered in its nonage." In dealing with such "barbarians," "despotism is a legitimate mode of government . . . provided the end be their improvement," while liberty is suitable for civilized societies.[69] Moreover, the Chinese concept of democracy as uniting universal moral principle and "the will of the people" had even more in common with the Rousseau-Hegel-Marx vision of the polity than with the Millsian tradition.

Certainly, both of these European traditions had a major impact on Chinese political thought after the turn of the century. Marx and especially Rousseau, for instance, had a profound influence on the thinking of Sun and his followers in the years just before the 1911 Revolution,[70] while J. S. Mill's influence on Yen Fu in the 1890s is well known.

Given this similarity between much Western thought in the nineteenth century and the still-current Chinese teleological vision, there is room for argument about whether this Chinese vision was originally imported from the West at the turn of the century or was also rooted in what I have tried to describe as the "optimistic this-worldliness" of the Confucian tradition.[71] In other words, there is still much controversy about the extent of the discontinuity with the Confucian tradition which occurred at the turn of the century as the generation of K'ang Yu-wei, Liang Ch'i-ch'ao, T'an Ssu-t'ung, Chang T'ai-yen, and Sun Yat-sen turned Chinese thought in the direction of modernization.

---

[69]Edwin A. Burtt, ed., *The English Philosophers from Bacon to Mill* (New York: The Modern Library, 1939), pp. 956, 964, 982, 993, 1000–1. See also David Held, p. 94.

[70]Chu Hung-yuan, p. 205 and elsewhere.

[71]See Metzger, #4.

The Teleological Vision and
the ROC's Intellectual Marketplace

No matter how this Chinese teleological vision originated, it carried with it an agenda of unresolved questions.[72]

Has a "great" man or two already discovered that correct doctrine needed to "save China"? To what extent is the quest for this doctrine an ongoing project requiring free and open intellectual discussion, rather than a largely finished project identifying the false doctrines which should be prevented from entering China?

Given the Chinese perception of the world's current intellectual resources as including available ideas which can be the foundation of a total, correct doctrine needed to restore China's globally central position, what are these ideas? Should Marxism be used? Some mix of Kant and Neo-Confucianism? Bertrand Russell's philosophy? Western social science or psychology? Hermeneutics? Some mix of Habermas and Wittfogel? How should various historical events, especially revolutions, be interpreted? This open-ended argument about how to think was intertwined with that about how to design the "Revolution," about which forces to extirpate, which to cultivate.[73]

In dealing with ideas perceived as wrong and behavior perceived as selfish, should Chinese seek reform in a tolerant, peaceful, gradualistic, accommodative way, or in a transformative, radical way aiming for the intellectual-moral purification of society? This problem was central because of the nature of capitalism, of the contemporary flow of ideas and information, and of political pluralism.

On the one hand, as already noted, modernization seems to require a basically capitalistic economy; a rather free and therefore confusing marketplace of ideas open to the global flow of information; and tolerance for legal political competitors seen as selfishly motivated. On the other hand, the teleological, eightfold vision described above focused on an ideal society free

---

[72]See Metzger, #2.

[73]This conflation of practical and highly philosophical questions has been basic all along, as illustrated by Chu Hung-yuan's study and even by Dr. Chu's own perspective. He criticizes the T'ung-meng-hui's "revolutionary theory" as incomplete or impractical but does not ask whether the T'ung-meng-hui's quest for such a total theory is a valid approach to the practicalities of political-economic development. See, *e.g.*, Chu Hung-yuan, p. 5. In other words, like the other Chinese writers cited here, he assumes that this quest is valid. Again, this is not necessarily a criticism. Whether his view is valid or not is a question we do not treat here, except to warn Westerners against presuming they are necessarily smarter than Dr. Sun.

of any economic inequalities that were morally unjustified, free of confusing intellectual competition blocking grasp of right doctrine, free of any power structure out of accord with the true will of the people (*min-i*), and free of any competition between selfishly inclined interest groups. Should Chinese then deal with these morally unacceptable conditions in a gradualistic, accommodative way, or try to extirpate them, violently if necessary, in order to transform China and turn it into a morally purified society?

This question was connected to that of the relation between state and society. If evil or "selfishness" was identified with "feudalism" and "capitalism" in the Marxist way, it logically followed that the free-market economy, traditional familism, the traditional Buddhist-Taoist religion, and the traditional civilizational heritage, including Confucian learning, should be largely extirpated, while Chinese contacts with the Western world of capitalism and democracy should be minimized. Moreover, there would be no practical way to do this except the expansion of state power to control most aspects of Chinese life. Thus Mao's definition of evil directly justified the huge centralized structure he erected to control Chinese life.

On the other hand, the KMT identified evil much more with the CCP than with "feudalism" or capitalism. Because Sun Yat-sen from the start rejected any wholesale denunciation of traditional behavior, saying that it was a mix of good and bad,[74] extirpation of the traditional familistic, economic, religious, and intellectual patterns could not be rationalized in KMT terms. On the contrary, the KMT honored many of these patterns and sought to build on them. Thus, even to the extent that the KMT had a transformative approach, its definition of evil did not imply a moral mandate vastly to expand the state in order to replace traditional patterns of life with new, state-centralized activities.

Another question pertained to the eighth premise. Given China's predicament, who or what was the agent of rectification? Both the Communists and the KMT identified this agent as a political party, but the humanists and the liberals saw this agent as "the conscience of the individual" or the "intellectuals"—what Tu Wei-ming called "the corporate, self-aware, morally critical, traditionally inherited consciousness of Chinese intellectuals."

Chinese Marxism and the other ideological trends of modern China can thus be seen as constituting a great variety of answers to the questions on a shared agenda implied by a shared, teleological vision of modern China's

---

[74]Lü Fang-shang, *Ko-ming-chih tsai-ch'i—Chung-kuo Kuo-min-tang kai-tsu ch'ien tui hsin ssu-ch'ao-te hui-ying, 1914–1924* (The revival of the revolution: The Kuomintang's response on the eve of its reorganization to the May Fourth Movement) (Taipei: Chin-tai-shih yen-chiu-so, Chung-yang yen-chiu-yuan, 1989), p. 228.

situation. The nature of this variety, however, requires further discussion. Certainly there was an obvious contrast between Chinese Marxism, on the one hand, and Sunism, Chinese liberalism, and modern Confucian humanism, on the other.[75] There was, however, also a major difference between all the intellectually most respected trends and Taiwan's actual ideological mix, which virtually all Chinese intellectuals have regarded as morally and intellectually shallow.

This dichotomy is well illustrated by the thought of Tu Wei-ming. In his many discussions with mainland intellectuals from 1978 through 1987, he repeatedly referred to Taiwan's ideological scene as "politicized" and "vulgarized" and sought a "profound" intellectual vision transcending that scene. Then in 1989 he spoke with unqualified enthusiasm of the student democracy movement on the mainland, seeing it as "joining together . . . Marxist humanism . . . an absolutely correct understanding of the spirit represented by Western democracy and freedom . . . and the Confucian tradition's best, most outstanding moral values, its spirit of protest against immoral rule."[76] In other words, in this intellectual synthesis which Prof. Tu hailed, three of the four leading modern Chinese ideologies had a place, but Sunism was excluded, not to mention the formless eclecticism of Taiwan's actual intellectual marketplace.

Similarly, when Lao Ssu-kuang and many other Chinese intellectuals describe modern China's intellectual development, they do not even mention the Three Principles of the People. Thus for such intellectuals, China's whole future—economic and political as well as cultural—depends on a fully coherent, "profound" intellectual vision, and a formlessly open marketplace of ideas allowing every individual to pursue truth in his or her own way cannot itself be equated with that "corporate" state of intellectual-moral well-being which they regard as the indispensable basis of successful Chinese modernization.

To be sure, we can question their view. Is their ambitious goal of intellectual success the indispensable basis of practical progress? Or is it a chimerical goal which conflates practical with philosophical questions, and the pursuit of which impedes practical progress?

Surely intellectuals like Tu Wei-ming and Lao Ssu-kuang have been right in rejecting many views in Taiwan as philosophically shallow, vulgar, and

---

[75]Metzger, #2, pp. 48–74.

[76]Tu Wei-ming, "Pei-ching hsueh-yun-te nei-tsai wen-hua tung-li (The inner, cultural force motivating the student movement in Beijing)," *Tang-tai*, vol. 39 (July 1, 1989):72–74. His repeated references to Taiwan's Confucian trends as "politicized" and "vulgarized" are made in his *Ju-chia ti-san-ch'i fa-chan-te ch'ien-ching wen-t'i.*

politicized. But were they right in expecting a concrete society to be free of "vulgar," "politicized" views? In holding that profundity and moral purity are the keys to practical economic and political progress? In looking for a single correct doctrine or intellectual response to the problem of cultural change and competing values in modern times? And in failing to point out that an open, vigorous marketplace of ideas is itself a major good, if not the best human beings can expect?

Yet who is right or wrong is not the key issue here. My goal here is just to identify Taiwan's eclectic marketplace of ideas as an empirical fact and to grasp the relation between the discourse of this marketplace as a whole and political life in Taiwan.

First of all, this marketplace did allow increasingly open access to the historical and global flow of ideas and information, thus meeting that requisite of modern life discussed by Karl W. Deutsch. Moreover, it entailed a stabilizing consensus. Thus in Taiwan the consensus legitimizing the actual order of things was a product of what many in the society believed, not just a set of forcibly imposed, propagandistic ideas.

What were these ideas shared by Sunism, Chinese liberalism, and modern Chinese humanism? All these trends rejected Marxism-Leninism and emphasized modernization, Chinese patriotism, and a partly Millsian concept of democracy; they also accepted capitalism, albeit with reservations. (Interestingly, this endorsement of capitalism harked back to the viewpoint propagated on the eve of the 1911 Revolution by Liang Ch'i-ch'ao.) They also in effect endorsed eclecticism, both because their coexistence with each other inherently constituted a form of eclecticism, and because Sunism, as its critics have never tired of pointing out, itself draws broadly and loosely on many major Chinese and Western schools in an eclectic way. Thus it inherently demonstrates the diversity of sources of knowledge.

Also important was the shared emphasis on Confucian ideals pertaining to personal and social life. While Sunism and modern Confucian humanism explicitly endorsed these Confucian principles, Chinese liberals from Hu Shih to Yin Hai-kuang have criticized the Confucian emphasis on hierarchy but taken for granted the Confucian concept of the "man of integrity" who autonomously stands by his conscience no matter what the social pressures (chün-tzu) may be. Iconoclastic liberals like to say that these Confucian ideals are just commonsense principles dictated by universal "morality" and have nothing to do with Confucian culture in particular,[77] just as they assume

---

[77]This point is made, for instance, in Lin Yü-sheng, *The Crisis of Chinese Consciousness: Radical Antitraditionalism in the May Fourth Era* (Madison: The University of Wisconsin Press, 1979).

that creating a polity without selfishness is a universal practical goal, not just a Chinese one.

Including this Confucian perspective, the ideological consensus in Taiwan put value on the morally and materially self-reliant, ascetic individual and on the intellectual community as morally bound to stand apart from and criticize the government. The government itself accepted this traditional relationship when in 1958 it made the famous liberal Hu Shih president of the most prestigious academic organization in Taiwan, the Academia Sinica.

True, some scholars today deny that Confucianism historically called for such autonomy. Yet the Confucian differentiation of sovereign power from individual conscience has been made clear by many Chinese scholars, from Hsu Fu-kuan and T'ang Chün-i to Chang Hao, Yü Ying-shih, and Tu Wei-ming. Many Western scholars have not understood this point and so concluded erroneously that the Communists' attempt to minimize individual autonomy was largely continuous with Confucian culture. In the Confucian view, individual conscience and the sovereign state merge only when the latter has fully met absolute moral standards, an ideal Confucians have invariably perceived as unrealized in the present.[78]

The ideological consensus in Taiwan, moreover, largely included the eight premises above. Thus this mix did to some extent reconcile the prevalent vision of sacred-moral values with the economic, intellectual, and political pluralism seemingly needed for modernization.

That is, thinking in terms of this mix, an individual participating in Taiwan's pluralistic life could link it to the sublime moral goals history had given Chinese by viewing the current situation as either a time of moral failure to which one should resign oneself, or a transitional stage during which some vehicle—whether the KMT, its opponents, or even some ambiguous mix of the two—would gradually effect realization of these goals. Consequently, this way of reconciling sacred-moral values with the mundane requisites of modernization was necessarily an outlook pregnant with intellectual uncertainty, political ambivalence, and moral despair. According to the eightfold teleological vision, after all, a morally, intellectually, economically, and politically diverse, heterologous society could not but be perceived as out of accord with the uniform, homologous, moral logic of history. This logic, in other words, was hard to reconcile with the increasingly apparent fact that modernization to a large extent requires institutionalization of society as an economic, intellectual, and political marketplace.

---

[78]See Metzger, article cited in note 34 above.

The Prevalence of the
Sense of Predicament

If, however, we can abstractly show that Taiwan's ideological mix thus combined a morally compelling, widespread teleological vision with some acceptance of the pluralistic requisites of modernization, can we also show that this sort of ideological reconciliation was important as part of the way leaders and other citizens in Taiwan actually thought about their moral, social, intellectual, occupational, and political situations?

What we can show is that, to a very large extent, people in Taiwan have viewed the contemporary condition of their society as far worse than it should be, despite all the pronouncements to the contrary by economists, political scientists, and government spokesmen. Thus, how one views the role in their lives of the eight-part teleological vision described above depends on how one interprets this distinctive way of feeling that there is something drastically wrong with Taiwan's current condition and course of development.

On the one hand, the Chinese citizens—intellectuals and others—who have this view see it as simply an objective reflection of reality. On the other hand, I argue that this view illustrates the seventh premise set out above. Thus I hold that this "sense of predicament" is less a reflection of objective reality than a way of evaluating the current situation by defining it as perversely contradicting the hopeful "tide" of history. In other words, this hopeful vision is an integral, if implicit, part of the way in which so many in Taiwan express deep dissatisfaction with their society's overall record of development. Whether the evidence supports this interpretation each reader has to judge for himself or herself.

This diffuse sense of failure is illustrated, first of all, by the widespread, if not unchallenged, view that Chinese history during the last century has been a series of disasters unmitigated by whatever success Taiwan has had. Historical disaster is no longer seen as a process beginning centuries ago after a golden age, but as a recent series of terrible mistakes. Lao Ssu-kuang's view, cited above, is entirely typical. In his eyes, the Chinese elite, hampered by a peculiar incongruence between Chinese culture and the "intrinsic" nature of modernization, were unable to grasp the principles of normative cultural change and so could not take "control" of the forces buffeting their society about in the twentieth century. Similarly, Yü Ying-shih's book on Chinese modernization omits any reference at all to any kind of successful modernization in Taiwan, an omission not so much forgiven as unnoticed by Taiwan intellectuals, who mostly admired his indeed eloquent treatise, though not a few felt he should have attacked the KMT.

Taiwan's current culture is similarly discussed as drastically failing to be what a culture should be. This perception of course is based not only on the normative concept of culture noted above but also on those extremely ambitious criteria of historical success that were part of the eightfold vision. As already noted, no Chinese writer has expressed enthusiasm about the open, eclectic character of the intellectual scene in Taiwan. Lao Ssu-kuang dismisses Taiwan's culture as "capitalistic," while the reporter who interviewed him in 1988 described it as "colonial" and "unevenly exposed to the good and the bad in the West."[79] Yü Ying-shih sees "value orientations in a state of confusion" owing to the fact that most Chinese wrongly regard modern values as incompatible with China's traditional culture.[80] Yang Kuo-shu, on the contrary, sees a mistaken clinging to the obsolete values of the "traditional" period. Given his definite though qualified iconoclasm, Yang Kuo-shu regards the heavy emphasis in Taiwan on Confucian values as a refusal to affirm the values of the emerging "modern, industrial society." Hu Ch'iu-yuan sees the intellectuals in Taiwan as mired in the confusions of eclecticism (*che-chung-lun*) and as thoughtlessly adopting foreign ideas or copying traditional ones. Tu Wei-ming has still another way of depicting cultural failure in Taiwan, as already noted. As he explains in his *Reflections on the Dawning of the Third Era in the Evolution of the Confucian Tradition*, published in Taipei in 1989, there is much serious interest in Confucian learning in Taiwan, but the cultural atmosphere there remains dominated by "politicized" intellectuals who substitute "flowery talk" (*t'ien-hua luan-chui*) for that uncompromisingly moral spirit of criticism and self-awareness which "profound reflection carried out in a comprehensive way" (*shen-ju ch'üan-mien-te fan-ssu*) can realize, and through which Chinese intellectuals will form a kind of morally critical, unified, "corporate" group (*ch'ün-t'i-te p'i-p'an-te tzu-wo i-shih*).

Another typical way of evaluating Taiwan's culture is illustrated by this passage set down in about 1984 by the Harvard-trained philosopher Ch'eng Chung-ying:

> To distinguish between what is right and what is selfishly advantageous, between the public good and private interests, this has been the precious morality of Confucianism, but real life has seldom amounted to more than pursuing selfish ends dressed up as moral goals, settling personal grudges while pretending to be acting impartially, and other such ways of borrowing the language of morality to cultivate selfish interests. China's moral ideals are the highest, but China's ability to realize them in institutional and social

---

[79]See note 42 above.
[80]Yü Ying-shih, *Ts'ung chia-chih hsi-t'ung*, p. 112.

terms has been insufficient. Moral ideals in the context of actual social life have degenerated, turning into dead dogmas. . . . From this we can see that a culture is an integrated whole, since in the actual course of history, its deficiencies as well as its points of excellence become manifest. Moreover, political actualities often cause originally noble moral ideals to become distorted and misunderstood, with the result that people lack any way to renew themselves morally in order to deal effectively with the needs of the present. . . . As for the effort [in Taiwan] to revive our traditional moral knowledge and capability, all kinds of teachings and public statements have pervaded the society, but this has just been lip service. In actuality, society as usual endorses a conservative and closed way of thinking, resisting any attitude or reform proposal suggested to deal with current shortcomings and corrupt ways. Thus efforts to revive the high ideals of the past are necessarily intertwined with the ignorance and widespread deficiencies of the inherited culture. With regard to grasping Western science, we are still behind Europe, America, and even Japan by several decades. We are not entirely without some successes, but these are limited and mostly just a matter of copying the fruits of Western creativity. What we have done is wholly surrender to the West's mechanistic civilization, wholly accepting the pathology of the Western mechanical civilization. Thus while the advantages of Western civilization have not yet been made manifest [in Taiwan], its bad tendencies have already entered our society.[81]

This evaluation also coincides with that of mainland intellectuals who recently visited Taiwan for the first time. One example is the mainland writer and Marxist Liu Pin-yen, who in the 1980s became famous as a critic of the PRC leadership and was expelled from the CCP. Taking part in a Taipei symposium in December 1989, he said without fear of contradiction:

The mainland can learn much from Taiwan's political and economic development these past few years, even though Taiwan is still in a transitional period. . . . but with regard to raising the quality of the human spirit, there is nothing good to report about Taiwan. In this respect, therefore, Taiwan's usefulness for the mainland is rather limited. . . . At present on the mainland, not a few people think that freedom and prosperity can solve the long-standing problems, overlooking that a great challenge faced by the mainland is how to turn broken human beings into whole, perfect ones.[82]

---

[81]Ch'eng Chung-ying, pp. 27–28.
[82]*Chung-kuo shih-pao*, Dec. 19, 1989. I am grateful to R. H. Myers for this reference and also for the reference to Wang Jo-wang's enthusiastic view of Taiwan cited in ibid., April 19, 1989. A PRC dissident, Wang on this occasion, which occurred during the period of hope before T'ien-an-men, was sending a letter to Teng Hsiao-p'ing urging him to imitate President Chiang Ching-kuo's democratizing reforms.

Naturally, much of the prevalent sense of predicament has been directed at the political structure, which many have long viewed as dominated by "unenlightened" people. The liberalization that began in 1986 has little changed this perception. In 1988, the well-known liberal Ho Huai-shuo said in an article that there was no real difference between Communist and KMT rule. In 1990, as discussed above, another famous liberal, Legislator Chu Kao-cheng, granted that the era of dictatorship (*chuan-chih*) was in the past, but said that the elected representatives in Taiwan failed to represent the will of the people. Not only were they all incompetent; they also were either opportunistic or overly idealistic. In his eyes, "society's elite" were "alienated" from politics. Until they held power, Taiwan would lack "healthy democratic politics" (*chien-ch'üan-te min-chu cheng-chih*).[83] As Ramon H. Myers and I predicted in 1989, "Even after full democratization, the dissident view of the power center as perverse will persist."[84]

Even more striking, this "sense of predicament" has not been much affected by economic progress. In 1955, Hsu Fu-kuan emphasized that according to classic Confucian ideals he embraced, among all the goals of government, filling "the material needs of the people must occupy first place." Yet in the two collections of his more political articles, he never once gave the KMT credit for meeting this supreme standard he so strongly emphasized.[85]

In 1960, as economic progress became apparent, Yin Hai-kuang said: "True enough, since the withdrawal of Japan, there have been some economic projects in Taiwan. But we must not forget: Taiwan is not an uninhabited, uncultivated island; it certainly is no such thing. Whenever there are people around to do something, one can more or less count on there being progress. As we know, since the Second World War, energetic economic revival has been a general tendency among the world's nations." Yin Hai-kuang went on to say that Taiwan's economic progress was just a façade, beneath which the economy was being "enervated by the government." No rise in mass living standards was possible given the government's current wastefulness, and "on the day that American aid stops, the true situation will come to light."[86] (American aid stopped in the mid-1960s.)

---

[83]See notes 45 and 46.

[84]See Metzger and Myers (M#1), p. 305, and Ch'en I-chung's article in *Tang-tai,* vol. 56 (Dec. 1, 1990):138–49.

[85]Hsu Fu-kuan, p. 299. The other collection of Hsu's political writings is *Ju-chia cheng-chih ssu-hsiang yü min-chu tzu-yu jen-ch'üan* (Democracy, freedom, human rights and Confucian political thought), ed. Hsiao Hsin-i (Taipei: Pa-shih-nien-tai ch'u-pan-she, 1979).

[86]Yin Hai-kuang, *Yin Hai-kuang hsuan-chi—ti-i-chüan—she-hui cheng-chih yen-lun* (The

Nineteen years later, in 1979, Chang Chung-tung sternly warned that "many feel we rely too much on foreign technology and capital, especially in the case of the U.S. and Japan. If we cannot quickly change this and energetically try to become wholly independent, we cannot be optimistic about our economic future."[87]

How Taiwan was to carry out export growth while becoming "wholly independent" of the United States and Japan was a problem Prof. Chang apparently regarded as solvable. Similarly, his goal of technological independence would be regarded by many as unrealistic for a small country traditionally outside the world centers of technological progress, but, believing in it, Prof. Chang expressed a view widespread in Chinese circles. Despite his worries, the ROC's U.S dollar reserves became the second or third largest in the world by 1989.

When in late 1982 I came to Taiwan to live for a while, I found such gloomy economic views prevalent. While many persons denied that the government deserved any credit for the ROC's economic progress, others— ranging from a cab driver to a famous scholar—insisted "there has been no economic progress." The most ingenious approach recognized the fact of progress but gave all the credit to "luck." A brilliant young editor at a leading newspaper made this point during a long conversation with me in 1983. Around the same time, a National Taiwan University professor with particularly strong scholarly credentials explained to me that Taiwan had been lucky to be able to take advantage of a boom in international trade, but "our luck has now run out."

Some two years later, after the running out of Taiwan's luck had still been delayed, another National Taiwan University professor published a well-received op-ed piece for the major newspaper *Chun-kuo shih-pao* which analyzed the ROC's economic failure in another way. He was alarmed by the fact that so much of the income of the rural population came from nonagricultural sources. In this phenomenon he saw not the inevitable result of industrialization, the enrichment of economic opportunities for the remaining rural population, and the demise of a backward economy based on agriculture. Instead, he deplored the erosion of the agricultural economy and of the Confucian ideal of a virtuous society based on agriculture. Thus while industrialization had always been regarded as the way out of economic backwardness, it also was often regarded as the key to moral disintegration

---

collected writings of Yin Hai-kuang—vol. 1—Social and political writings) (Kowloon, Hong Kong: Yu-lien ch'u-pan-she yu-hsien kung-ssu, 1971), pp. 600–1.
[87]Cited in T'ao Pai-ch'uan, p. 4.

and vulgarity. This was an ingenious way to define success as failure and so to preserve the sense of predicament in the face of success.

It is also unsurprising that recently in some academic circles on Taiwan, the Western neo-Marxist theories about "dependency," emphasizing how the "core" countries of the capitalist world system exploit the nations on the "periphery," like the ROC, have been warmly received. I saw this enthusiasm for the views of Immanuel Wallerstein in 1983 when participating in an oral examination of an M.A. candidate in sociology at National Taiwan University. Crosscutting Marxist and non-Marxist Chinese thought, the widespread Chinese emphasis on the nefarious effects of Western imperialism has been prominent in both ideological and scholarly writings and has been little affected either by the growing Western literature on the complexity of imperialism's economic impact or by the way the ROC used trade with the "capitalistic core" to achieve the material well-being of its people.[88]

Pessimism can also be nervously mixed with a proud emphasis on what the ROC has accomplished. Just after the elections of December 1986, as Taiwan's economy continued to boom, and when the establishment of an opposition party had earned the ROC widespread international praise, Chien Yu-hsin, a rising young KMT politician, said to a Japanese journalist:

> Actually in the city of Taipei the KMT has been subject to a lot of pressure. In the first place, because of our development up to now, there is a bottleneck in every area; the political, economic, and social structures have all arrived at the bottleneck stage. We now have to think of a way to break out of this bottleneck. The economic bottleneck is now very serious. The political bottleneck has a number of aspects. . . . The KMT in the past 30 years has not been bad. It was criticized, but generally speaking, Taiwan's still has been a stable society. In the past 30 years, the education of the citizens has been handled with extraordinary success. Whether in the case of primary, secondary, or higher education, one cannot say the educational level has fallen short. The success in education is a point of excellence in our record, but it puts pressure on the ruling party. As everyone's standards are raised, dissatisfaction increases.[89]

This sense of facing a bottleneck or predicament is thus expressed by people in virtually all walks of life in Taiwan. In 1984–1985, a radical and

---

[88]For the view that Taiwan's grave problems largely stem from its "dependent kind of modernization," see Hang Chih, *I-wei-chi* (Taipei: Yun-ch'en shih-yeh ku-fen yu-hsien kung-ssu, 1987), pp. 27–32.

[89]*Pai-hsing*, no. 138 (Feb. 16, 1987), pp. 34–35. I am grateful to Prof. William Tay for this reference.

very bright undergraduate student of mine was discussing politics with me in my apartment in Taipei. Having obtained an A from me despite our disagreements, he knew I differentiated scholarly ability from political views, and we had become good friends. Said he: "How can you say there has been progress here? This is not an ideal society. That shows there has been no progress." Similarly, a colleague of mine in Taipei who basically supports the KMT commented thus on a political scuffle between the KMT and some liberals: "Just dogs biting each other."

Free China Review (*FCR*), an officially sponsored magazine trying to give foreigners a realistic but still sympathetic picture of the ROC, is full of comments about this alleged collapse of morality and traditional values. "People must learn not to be so selfish," says Prof. H.C. Kao, interviewed by *FCR*.[90] "Radical shifts in income are bringing about a loss of traditional values which were based upon thousands of years of extended family life in rural settings," states an *FCR* editorial.[91] With "industrialization," says Prof. Shen Ch'ing-sung, chair of the Department of Philosophy at one of the ROC's leading universities (Cheng-ta), the old concern with "happiness for the whole" has turned to "an immediate concern with individual happiness."[92] An associate professor at another leading university (Shih-ta) agrees: "Today, the rules of life are different, and moral standards have collapsed."[93] A teacher is quoted: "The value judgments and morality we always esteemed as part of the virtue of man seem to have disappeared."[94] A high-school teacher who is a member of the KMT declared: "But ever since I have been eligible to vote, I have always cast a blank ballot. It seemed to me that there never was a candidate really willing to devote himself to serving the people. . . . There no longer seems to be a consensus among the people. Everybody just cares about himself."[95]

As already mentioned, when, in April 1987, Ting Pang-hsin and Ho Huai-shuo had their famous debate in Taiwan's two leading newspapers (*Lien-ho-pao* and *Chun-kuo shih-pao*) about whether the KMT was Taiwan's main problem or main benefactor, both took for granted that Taiwan was a moral wilderness, and they argued at length about whether the main moral problem was lack of "sincerity" or "selfishness."

Abundant evidence, therefore, demonstrates the prevalence in Taiwan

---

[90]*Free China Weekly*, vol. 39, no. 10:9.
[91]Ibid., vol. 39, no. 11:1.
[92]Ibid., vol. 39, no. 10:17.
[93]Ibid., vol. 39, no. 10:20.
[94]Ibid., vol. 39, no. 11:10
[95]Ibid., vol. 39, no. 12:13.

of a deep, diffuse sense that there is something drastically wrong about life there. This feeling has been shared especially by the more educated. Instead of pointing to Taiwan's economic and political successes and excusing its failures as due to inevitable human imperfections and the unavoidable difficulties of modernization, many in Taiwan have focused on its failures as revealing its true nature. In other words rather than viewing its failures as "blemishes on the face of success" (*mei-chung pu-tsu*), they have looked on its successes as "some bright spots amidst the darkness" (*o-chung-chih mei*, to try out a little American Chinese).

This leaning toward pessimism cannot be explained, I would argue, as just a reflection of objective reality. Instead, it is a culturally distinctive tendency that is completely consistent with the eightfold teleological vision described above. Taking for granted the sublime standard built into this vision of a political and civil life free of selfish interests—what we would call a saintly life—and assuming that a historical "tide" is moving mankind toward full realization of this ideal but for the perversity and incompetence of some powerful people, many in Taiwan angrily or disgustedly view what some would call usual human frailties as inexcusable moral degeneration. There is a *yu-an i-shih* (sense of darkness) about the current situation, but this kind of darkness is based on an enormously optimistic definition of normal life. As Prof. Chang suggests, a less optimistic standard of normal life would lead to a more tolerant view of current conditions.

An angry, intolerant view of them necessarily accompanies the feeling that Taiwan suffers not from normal problems, but from the inexcusable refusal of leaders and citizens to act in a normal way. Reacting to this perceived disaster, citizens identify a vehicle of rectification, whether the KMT or some intellectual or political movement or organization opposed to the KMT. Sunist doctrine has tended toward the former option, while Chinese liberalism and to some extent modern Confucian humanism have tended toward the latter, not to mention the Taiwan Independence Movement.

In point of fact, therefore, as China modernized, the eightfold vision could not be ignored. Indeed, since it consisted of a set of clichés identified with common sense, the Chinese did not even conceptualize it as we have here: an ideological option one could adopt or reject. Rather for them it has just been an unavoidable part of common sense. Yet at the same time, it clashed with the kind of economic, intellectual, and political pluralism integral to economic modernization and the institutionalization of Millsian democracy. How to deal with the powerful public feelings expressed by this eightfold vision thus turned out to be a central problem in the history of Chinese modernization.

Two main approaches to this problem were used: the transformative and the accommodative. Mao pursued this vision by claiming that China could promptly enter the great new stage of historical evolution by directly creating a moral and modern society free of the selfishness of capitalistic life, free of the confusing contradictions of an intellectual marketplace unguided by any one, true doctrine, free of any morally insufficient ruling group, and free of the threatening spectacle of interest groups legally competing to pursue selfish, immoral ends. Even after 1976, there was strong resistance, both inside and outside the CCP, to allowing such conditions to develop. In Taiwan, however, despite much fear of and opposition to these various kinds of pluralism, modernization was attempted by trying to tolerate them, and by debating diverse claims that in this diverse society there was a vehicle which could lead to an escape from this moral predicament. Diversity, in other words, was increasingly seen as both morally troubling and integral to modernization.

Conclusion: Political Attitudes and Social Strata

This is not to say, however, that political discourse in Taiwan has been shaped only by the eightfold vision described above. As just about all scholars today recognize, political discourse is always influenced by a complex variety of interacting patterns, situations, and personalities. To understand this whole process fully, one would have to discuss economic modernization in Taiwan and its psychological and social consequences, including the creation of an urbanized society with a large middle class. We would also have to analyze the "intellectual mobilization" that occurred from the 1970s on (to use Reinhard Bendix's term), international pressures, the KMT's own program of political liberalization, the leadership of Pres. Chiang Ching-kuo in particular, and the momentum inherent in the election system.[96]

Moreover, as already noted, political attitudes in Taiwan include a wide-spread "petty bourgeois" outlook. Many observers have seen "the middle

---

[96]I have tried to analyze these issues in another paper, "Political Change in Taiwan Since 1945 and Its Historical Background," presented at the Conference on Culture and Polity in the Developing World since World War Two, Hoover Institution, April 5–8, 1990. Tun-jen Cheng and others, as Andrew J. Nathan notes, have discussed how "conditioning factors making this democratic transition possible" were realized in Taiwan. See Andrew Nathan, "Chiang Ching-kuo's Decision for Political Reform," paper presented at the Conference on Chiang Ching-kuo's Leadership in the Development of the Republic of China on Taiwan, sponsored by Miller Center for Public Affairs, University of Virginia, March 16–18, 1990.

class" as having this "materialistic" outlook, being little interested in any of the ideological positions or even in political events, except as they affected the economic climate. Prudently avoiding any confrontation with the government and seeking stability more than reform, people with this "petty bourgeois" outlook have exhibited an authoritarian and passive attitude toward politics, though also evoking the Confucian option of "preserving one's moral purity by staying out of the worldly struggle" (*chüan*).

Yet this kind of passivity, typically combined with the sense of moral predicament noted above, also often involved ambivalent and complex feelings about those in society actively pursuing either a pro-KMT or anti-KMT position, or even about both groups. This element of complexity and ambivalence can be testified to by anyone familiar with life in Taiwan.

How then can this complex variety of ambivalent political feelings be socially located? Trying to identify the significant strata in Taiwan, the anthropologist Hill Gates and leading social scientists in Taiwan, such as Kao Ch'eng-shu and Ch'ü Hai-yuan, have discussed the rural-urban distinction; regional distinctions; ethnic ones (between mainlanders and the Chinese living in Taiwan before 1945, that is, "Taiwanese," between Hakka and other Taiwanese, and between Chinese and the aboriginal population); the gender distinction; distinctions based mainly on wealth, power, and prestige; and the problem of how to categorize "intellectuals," who play such a central role at least in the Chinese social consciousness.[97] With regard to stratification based mainly on wealth, power, and prestige, many agree with Gates' scheme: an upper class divided into political and business elites; a new middle class made up of employees on the higher rungs of governmental and private organizations; a traditional middle class made up of those owning and running small farms and small businesses; a working class (some hold that there are six million "laborers" in Taiwan);[98] and a stratum of unemployed or deviant persons, including the underworld.

How each of these strata views politics is a question we cannot yet answer precisely. Yet we can ask whether the demand for democratization confronted by the KMT from the late 1970s on represented the collective desire of a growing middle class produced by economic growth. Prof. Tien Hung-mao sees such a tendency: "It is the emergence of this second middle class that has changed the island's political landscape. With its rising political

---

[97]Hill Gates, "Ethnicity and Social Class," in Ahern and Gates, *The Anthropology of Taiwanese Society*, pp. 273–78. The rich issue of *Free China Review*, vol. 39, no. 11 (Nov. 1989) on the middle class should also be noted, especially the article by Kao Ch'eng-shu and the interview with Ch'ü Hai-yuan. Also see Tien Hung-mao, p. 31.
[98]*Free China Review*, vol. 39, no. 12 (Dec. 1989):56.

and social consciousness, the new middle class acts as a reformist force in electoral politics and social movements . . ." Yet Prof. Tien also sees much middle class support for the KMT.[99] Prof. Kao Ch'eng-shu, therefore, seems correct in viewing this middle class as having vacillating, ambivalent political attitudes.[100]

To be sure, determining the political attitudes of the "middle class" is hard because there is only the roughest agreement about who belongs to it, whether one looks for objective indicators or depends on how people subjectively define themselves. It is clear, however, that the KMT enjoys much support from middle-class voters (however defined), because the KMT's ability to attract a majority of the voters (usually around 60–70%) would be impossible without middle-class support; because the middle class has not flocked to join the main opposition party, the highly liberal Democratic Progressive Party (DPP), which, established in 1986, still had less than 10,000 members in 1988, as compared with 2.4 million KMT members;[101] and because there are findings that what Gates calls "the new middle class" tends to support the KMT. According to a study made in the early 1980s, KMT candidates "drew heavy support from the military, police, KMT functionaries, college professors, college students, civil servants, elected representatives, professionals (lawyers, physicians, engineers, and accountants), journalists, writers, those engaged in other media work, and mainlanders." The same study found that the KMT's liberal opponents received support from the "traditional" middle class, that is, from "youths other than college students, native Taiwanese, farmers, fisherman, workers, small entrepre-

---

[99]Tien Hung-mao, pp. 14 and 33. What "second" and "new" refer to is not clear, but the general thrust of Prof. Tien's view is. Putting together ibid., p. 33 and p. 191, we can infer that Tien sees the "traditional middle class" of small businessmen, etc. as the main class segment calling for more democratization, not the "new middle class" of people working on the higher rungs of the governmental, educational, industrial, and financial organizations. Yet whatever part of the "middle class" is seen by Tien as a "a reformist force," he himself suggests that the KMT "now has . . . perhaps even a dominant position among the middle class." See ibid., p. 194. Tien really ends up viewing the middle class as politically ambiguous, if not leaning toward support for the kind of gradual democratization the KMT came to stand for. In other words, since Tien certainly distinguishes between this KMT stance and the "reformist" demands in Taiwan, his picture of the middle class as both "a reformist force" and a class tending to support the KMT is indeed another way of picturing the middle class as politically ambiguous.
[100]*Free China Review*, vol. 39, no. 11: 4, 7, 9, 10.
[101]Tien Hung-mao, pp. 35–101.

neurs, business clerks and managers, and housewives."[102] In other words, one might say that most of the support for strongly liberal politicians comes from Taiwanese who are members of the lower or the middle class, but one cannot say most middle- or lower-class Taiwanese support these politicians.

In asking about the political orientation of the middle class or any other stratum in Taiwan, we must note that ambivalence was reinforced by the lack of any strong sense of class solidarity. This lack of class solidarity is doubtless rooted in the striking extent to which China's traditional society— far more than any other premodern civilization—divorced status from ascriptive qualities. Especially after about 700 A.D., the elite mostly did not institutionalize themselves as a hereditary aristocracy, and slavery—with the possible exception of the Period of Disunity (200–589 A.D.)—played a minor role in the economy and the society. Thus a disjunction between political views and social background arose. It was manifested in what should be called the Charles O. Hucker phenomenon: he showed, in the case of an early seventeenth-century protest movement (the Tung-lin movement), that there was little correlation between Tung-lin membership and class background, regional origin, governmental status, family standing, or any other social variable.[103] Undoubtedly a study of, say, DPP members would yield a similar result.

Most basically, social scientists have found that many families in Taiwan include members of different classes, that factions pervade most of Taiwan, crosscutting classes just as families do, and that voting behavior, especially outside Taipei, is often based on particularistic ties.[104]

An active focus on the ideological questions implied by the eightfold teleological vision, therefore, has not been typical of the majority of the ROC's citizens. Many are only remotely conscious of ideological issues and seldom even read the political sections of the newspapers. Just as many Americans care more about baseball than international relations, many in Taiwan yawn at the mention of the Three Principles of the People but are fascinated by a story that the magician David Copperfield (Ta-wei-wang) had to ask for White House permission to make the Statue of Liberty

---

[102]Ibid., p. 191.

[103]Charles O. Hucker, "The Tung-lin Movement of the Late Ming Period," in John K. Fairbank, ed., *Chinese Thought and Institutions* (Chicago, Ill.: University of Chicago Press, 1957), pp. 132–62, esp. pp. 157–61.

[104]Tien Hung-mao, pp. 164–71, 190. Also see Hsin-huang Michael Hsiao, "Development, Class Transformation, Social Movements, and the Changing State-Society Relations in Taiwan," a paper presented at the eighteenth Sino-American Conference on Mainland China, Hoover Institution, June 8–11, 1989.

disappear. As full democratization became ever more imminent in 1990, many in Taiwan—the vast majority, I would say—devoted barely a minute a day to commenting on or thinking about this momentous historical event. Mentioning it was just a boring conversational ploy for people thinking about travel, jobs, friendships, or real estate—the real meat of life for so many in Taiwan.

Politics and the design of institutions, however, cannot be carried on without public argument, and those in Taiwan who argue publicly about the political and institutional condition of their society have directly or connotatively evoked the teleological, utopian vision of historical evolution that arose in China around the turn of the century—a vision with a moral-sacred character. The ways in which they evoked it, however, constituted a relatively open, eclectic intellectual marketplace with a consensus favoring peaceful, accommodative change, a large degree of capitalism, intellectual pluralism, Millsian democracy, and anti-Communism. On the one hand, therefore, their relation to this moral-sacred vision entailed for them a deep sense of moral predicament and intellectual impotence, since they saw themselves as forced to live with actual historical tendencies contradicting the way in which history was inherently and morally bound to go. On the other hand, their sense of predicament not only expressed their high, inspiring ideals but also proved compatible with the economic, social, intellectual, and political pluralism objectively needed for modernization.

Thus the ideological mix or cognitive model in Taiwan has been an important part of a sovereign political center supporting the kinds of pluralism needed to promote instrumental rationality and so encouraging those revisions of the inherited culture needed to cultivate instrumental rationality.

It follows that we cannot understand the nature of political thinking in Taiwan by just using the rational-choice model or holding that progress simply depends on embracing universal ideals and struggling against vested interests. Like all societies, China entered the modern era evoking a culturally disparate heritage of sacred-moral values. Anyone trying to erect a sovereign state enjoying public support had to invoke these values and show that this government would be in accord with them. But a choice had to be made about how to invoke these values. This choice turned out to be crucial for the Chinese struggle to modernize.

Whether intentionally or not, the intellectual marketplace in Taiwan turned out to be compatible with modern pluralism, while the Communists' zealous, utopian way of evoking modern China's teleological vision turned out not to be. In the 1980s, many mainland intellectuals felt that Marxism was no longer viable, and that their society desperately needed the guidance which could be provided only by a new, intellectually correct formula or doctrine not yet conceptualized, or at least not yet sufficiently promulgated.

What few, if any, of them advocated was stopping the search for such a single correct way of thought and instead institutionalizing the kind of open, eclectic, diverse, and heterological intellectual scene that has in fact become so fundamental to the Taiwan way of life.

Yet in Taiwan, too, intellectuals have not yet explicitly endorsed this morally uncertain, heterological situation. In other words, as in many, if not all, societies developing in the twentieth century, finding a way to reconcile sacred-moral values with the idea of society as a marketplace remains an ongoing problem.

Change and Continuity in the CCP's Power Structure since Its Thirteenth National Congress

A "Line" Approach

Different Approaches to Understanding Political Change

Over the past decades, most Chinese scholars have cited changes in Beijing's leadership to explain political conditions in mainland China. For instance, the P'eng Te-huai affair and P'eng's subsequent downfall revealed that a subtle political change in leadership power had taken place. The purge of Liu Shao-ch'i during the Cultural Revolution indicated that a drastic change in the power structure and its policies had occurred. The disappearance of Teng Hsiao-p'ing from the political stage in January 1976 meant that Beijing's moderate policy was soon to be replaced by a radical one. The arrest of the Gang of Four and Hua Kuo-feng's rise to power in 1976 signified that the ultraleftist policies of the Cultural Revolution would soon be abandoned. The rehabilitation of Teng Hsiao-p'ing in 1977 indicated that Hua's political life would soon come to an end, and that Teng's reformist policies would guide socialist construction in mainland China. Similarly, the downfall of Hu Yao-pang in January 1987 and Chao Tzu-yang in 1989 implied that reformist policies had become stalled.

Speculations about, or interpretations of future policy orientations connected with the rise and fall of important Communist Chinese leaders are sometimes convincing and correct. Yet such an approach has shortcomings. First, such an approach is almost always used after the fact; it rarely predicts events correctly. Second, except during the Cultural Revolution, important personnel changes have not occurred with great frequency. In recent years, power struggles are not as frequent and bloody as during the Cultural Revolution; they are carried out behind the scenes, and with some moderation. Therefore, the approach of examining the changes in Beijing's power structure and its politics through the rise or fall of high-ranking Communist Chinese leaders has limitations, and it seems necessary to use another approach to interpret political changes when there are no obvious personnel readjustments. I will attempt below to analyze Communist Chinese politics from the perspective of Beijing's changes of "line."

Let us first clarify the difference between the party's line and its policies. The party's line consists of its basic guidelines for a relatively long period, while its policies govern its actions for a short period. A top-ranking Communist Chinese leader might readjust the party's policies in times of great difficulty without modifying its line. However, every change in the party's line is usually accompanied by a drastic change in its power structure. A review of the party's history shows that under the leadership of the same faction, its line has usually remained unchanged, but its policies have often been modified according to their success or failure.

Over the past four decades, Chinese Communist party leaders at all levels have used this method to observe and explain the political changes in the upper echelons of their own party. China watchers may have noticed that in important political speeches, Communist Chinese leaders have often referred to the party's line and the party's political, organizational, and ideological lines. In fact, at each of its national congresses, the Chinese Communist Party (CCP) has taken pains to redefine its line—that is, its basic guidelines and general policies concerning the understanding and reforming of the world in a certain historical period. Such action reconfirms the party's objectives and unifies the thinking of party members. Communist Chinese leaders have also re-emphasized at most important meetings the continuity of the party's line in its current stage.

CCP leaders and members are convinced that, while following concrete principles and implementing policies, they must firmly bear in mind the party's general line and policies so that they will not become confused about which direction to follow. The revolutionary line of this proletarian political party has always been formulated by applying Marxist-Leninist theories to interpret the concrete situation in China. The party line has to be tested in revolutionary practice, and the correctness of the line has a decisive influence on the success or failure of the revolutionary cause and socialist construction.[1]

---

[1]Hsia Cheng-nung, ed., *She-hui-chu-i tz'u-tien* (A glossary of socialism) (Kirin: People's Publishing House, 1985), p. 527.

The party line consists of three elements: the ideological line, the political line, and the organizational line. The ideological line is the theoretical basis for the formulation and implementation of the political line; the purpose of the organizational line is to guarantee the thorough implementation of the political line; and the political line is the general line for the party's action at its current stage.

According to General Secretary Chao Tzu-yang's report to the party's Thirteenth National Congress in October 1987, the general line of the party in the current stage focused on "one central task and two basic points." Chao explained that in order to build socialism with Chinese characteristics during the primary stage of socialism, the party's basic line is that it must lead the people of all nationalities within the country in a united, self-reliant, intense, and pioneering effort to turn China into a prosperous, strong, democratic, culturally advanced, and modern socialist country by making economic development the central task, while adhering to the Four Cardinal Principles and persevering in reform and the "opening-up" policy.

According to the same report, the party's ideological line is the seeking of truth from facts and the observing of actual conditions everywhere. Its organizational line is that the organization of the party is to be strengthened: any tendency to neglect or relax party organization must be prevented or overcome, and the tendency to simply concentrate on party organization without relating it to reform and "opening-up" policies must be eliminated. The party's political line calls for concentrating all energy on promoting modernization. Party members decided at the congress that the fundamental task of a socialist society is to increase productivity; that the expansion of the productive forces should be regarded as the party's central task; that helping to expand the productive forces should become the point of departure in considering all problems and the basic criterion for judging all work; that a comprehensive reform should be conducted; that the opening-up policy should be upheld; that a planned commodity economy with public ownership playing the dominant role should be established; that democracy should be developed on the basis of stability and unity; and that efforts should be made to build a society with an advanced culture and ideology under the guidance of Marxism.[2]

When observers understand the party's line in a specific historical period, they may then examine whether the Chinese Communists have been able to persevere in pursuing their line. If the line has not been thoroughly implemented, observers should find out whether the Central Committee has modified it because they have encountered serious obstacles in the course

---

[2]"Chao Tzu-yang's Report to the CCP's Thirteenth National Congress," *People's Daily*, Nov. 4, 1987.

of implementation, or whether serious conflicts within the Central Committee have obstructed implementing the line. Take the reform and opening-up policies advocated by Chao Tzu-yang in 1988 as an example. When Chao became general secretary at the Thirteenth National Congress and declared the expansion of the productive forces the central task in economic development, most China watchers speculated that Beijing's economic reforms and its opening-up policy would progress rapidly. Soon after, articles published in news media of mainland China revealed sharp disagreements within the party over which policies are best suited to develop the PRC's productive forces. Since the political line of the party at the current stage advocates expansion of those productive forces, and since some party leaders have openly expressed disagreement with this line in official speeches, it is reasonable to say that there are political conflicts within the party.

Using the "line" approach to analyze political changes in mainland China has both theoretical and practical significance. First of all, while being influenced by Marxist views and theories, most Communist Chinese leaders are subconsciously idealists. They have optimistic expectations about the future of Communism. They also believe it is a simple task to define right and wrong thinking and behavior. Such idealism in Beijing's politics affects its economic policies; even the conflicts over power are often referred to by the Chinese Communists as "the struggle between the two lines." During the Cultural Revolution, the struggle between the socialist line and the capitalist line became fierce. At present, disagreements center on how to build socialism with Chinese characteristics.

Communist leaders usually insist that there are no serious policy conflicts within the party. For instance, in September 1988 Teng Hsiao-p'ing told Susumu Nikaido, the ex-vice-president of Japan's Liberal-Democratic Party, the following:

> Based on their assessment of China's situation, some foreigners have asserted that there are disagreements within the highest echelon of our leadership. Their observation is wrong. It is normal for people to differ about means and measures during a discussion. Some people in Hong Kong have speculated that [mainland] China's leaders disagree with one another. They are spreading rumors. The people who desire to see China plunged into chaos will be disappointed.[3]

At a meeting with U.S. secretary of state George Shultz in May 1988, Chao Tzu-yang emphasized that, although Communist Chinese leaders have encountered many problems and have different views about the course of the

---

[3]*Wen wei po* (Hong Kong), Sept. 17, 1988.

reform, not one of them desires to return to the old track. He specified that China has to solve many problems and will have no choice but to push the reform and opening-up policies forward.[4] On March 15, 1989, Wu Hsing-t'ang, head of the party's International Liaison Department, asserted that high-ranking Communist Chinese leaders have no disagreement about the general guidelines and policies concerning the reforms and the opening-up of mainland China. He added, however, it was rather normal to hold different views on specific problems.

Judging by the "line" approach, these statements are not completely incorrect, because Communist Chinese leaders generally have a consensus on the general line of reform and opening up. Even Premier Li P'eng, a conservative, announced in his work report to the Second Session of the Seventh National People's Congress in March 1989 that mainland China will not return to the old policy of a planned economy. Yet leaders disagree over political and ideological lines.

Viewed from the standpoint of practice, the Chinese Communists have for a long time had great differences of opinion about how to realize their goal of socialism. Since establishing their regime in October 1949, conflict over these two lines has existed within the party. These lines often became entangled in power conflicts, causing severe policy and ideological struggles within the party. In the 1960s, a struggle erupted between the ultraleftists (headed by Mao Tse-tung and Chiang Ch'ing) and the capitalist-roaders (headed by Liu Shao-ch'i). In the late 1970s, a confrontation occurred between the pragmatists (headed by Teng Hsiao-p'ing) and the "whateverists" (headed by Hua Kuo-feng; for an explanation of this group's name, see chapter 6, note 46). In the 1980s, differences of opinion also existed between the reformists (represented by Hu Yao-pang and Chao Tzu-yang) and the conservatives (represented by Li P'eng and Yao I-lin). In short, factions within the CCP have been involved in power struggles because they have differed about policies, have interpreted Marxism differently, or were divided over how to build socialism. Without doubt, their differences are only relative, not absolute. Essentially, all factions share some basic principles. The conservatives, relatively inflexible about ideology and policies, advocate prudence when modifying the old; the more open-minded reformists are more eager to challenge the old systems and correct previous shortcomings.

[4]Ibid., May 17, 1988.

The Party's Current Power Structure— Gerontocracy

The "line" approach is a useful method of analyzing the CCP's power structure, but its limitation is that it only reflects objective problems. It does not allow for an understanding of the "human factor" in Chinese politics, a problem which, in contemporary politics, has become the "aged-revolutionary factor."

Gerontocracy is a longstanding problem in Chinese politics. Communist China is no exception. The aged are revered and endowed with great authority. In fact, old Communist veterans may still have great political influence even after they have retired. Since 1987, these leaders have played key roles in several important political events, including Hu Yao-pang's downfall. They were also involved in Beijing's economic policy failures in 1988. At a meeting with Museveni, president of Uganda, on March 23, 1989, Teng Hsiao-p'ing frankly admitted that old cadres had played a part in committing serious economic mistakes in the previous year.[5] Old party veterans not only intervene in economic and political policies from behind the scenes; they also meddle in decisions about who will replace the top leaders. The country is now under the rule of eight party elders.[6] Although

---

[5] *Ta kung pao* (Hong Kong), March 24, 1989.
[6] The ranking of the eight most important veterans according to political influence is as follows:

Classification	Name	Age	Posts
Most influential	Teng Hsiao-p'ing	85	Chairman of CCPCC Military Commission
	Ch'en Yun	84	Chairman of CCPCC Advisory Commission
Fairly influential	Yang Shang-k'un	83	State president, and permanent vice-chairman of CCPCC Military Commission
	Wang Chen	82	State vice-president
	Li Hsien-nien	80	Chairman of CCPCC
Influential	P'eng Chen	83	No post
	Po I-po	82	Vice-chairman of CCPCC Advisory Commission
	Sung Jen-ch'iung	80	Vice-chairman of CCPCC Advisory Commission

most of these party elders have given up their original leadership posts, they still intervene in the actual decisionmaking processes of the party's Central Committee, and they even play a key role in that decisionmaking. Teng Hsiao-p'ing, chairman of the party's Military Commission, is the most influential of the party elders, and his decisions are respected by the rest. These veterans have one attribute in common: they will not give up their power until they die.

These party elders use their power according to a single rule: if one among them has made a statement or issued a directive, the others will not contradict him. This tacit agreement has made relations among the party elders appear harmonious to all outsiders.[7]

Of course, such an operational rule does not mean there are no conflicts among the party elders. When faced with important political issues, they often engage in open debates to defend their own vital interests or goals. As a rule, such debates do not last long. If the most influential leader insists on his views, the debates will end immediately. However, normally even the most influential veterans show considerable respect for the views of other veterans because they wish to appear impartial and unselfish. This is why some senior veterans often confide in Teng Hsiao-p'ing their own views about the leaders of the younger generation. Hu Yao-pang's downfall was largely due to criticisms made to Teng Hsiao-p'ing by Wang Chen, Po I-po, and Li Hsien-nien.[8] The party elders in the Advisory Commission also played an important role in the "dump-Chao" movement of early 1989.[9]

Gerontocracy is now an indispensable element of the leadership structure. Old age formally affirms the ruling power of these party veterans. In fact, party veterans have a voice in everything, from national affairs to local administration.

Beijing's politics are normally characterized by factional activities. In their involvement in politics, these party veterans avoid taking sides and opposing each other. However, there is factionalism among the second and third generations of leaders of the CCP. Let us consider the above-mentioned eight party elders. They are old friends who have been through thick and thin together. They have experienced persecution in previous political strug-

---

[7]*Chiu-shih nien-tai* (The nineties), 1989, no. 2: 17–19.

[8]Shih Hua, "Talks by a Guest from Peking on Behind-the-Scenes Politics," ibid., 1987, no. 3:9–12.

[9]*South China Morning Post* (Hong Kong), March 22, 1989. Several leading members of the CCPCC's Advisory Commission asked Teng Hsiao-p'ing to dismiss Chao Tzu-yang. However, Teng brushed off the suggestion, arguing (1) that one of his close deputies had already been deposed, and (2) that there was nobody to replace Chao. It was reported that the question of whether to replace Chao would be put off at least until that summer.

gles, especially during the Cultural Revolution. They joined forces in the struggle against the "whateverists" and succeeded in overthrowing Mao's ultraleftist line, which had been the main cause of their past suffering. They treat one another as brothers in a traditional Chinese family, with Teng Hsiao-p'ing and Ch'en Yun as the revered eldest.

In this leadership structure, the leaders of the second and third generations are playing the role of "housekeepers," just as Teng Hsiao-p'ing has often said. Teng has referred to Chao Tzu-yang as the chief housekeeper and has specified that Chao and Li P'eng are jointly in charge of the main leadership work. His goal, obviously, is to confirm their leadership in the future.

However, leaders of the second generation do not have the unique background of the veterans. Most of them were promoted to high ranks because by chance their achievements in a certain field won them the appreciation of high-ranking party veterans, or because they are part of the veterans' patron-client network. Chao Tzu-yang, for instance, caught Teng's attention by his "Szechwan experience." Teng, himself a native of Szechwan, later transferred Chao to Beijing.[10] Li P'eng is the son of Li Shuo-hsin and the nephew of Chao Shih-yen, both important leaders of the party in its early stage. He is also the adopted son of Chou En-lai and Teng Ying-ch'ao and has rather close personal relationships with most senior veterans. Yao I-lin is an old client of Ch'en Yun. Ch'iao Shih, having worked in security departments, has organizational relations with Ch'en Yun and P'eng Chen, who were once in charge of security work. Hu Ch'i-li obtained Teng's support after being recommended by Hu Yao-pang.

These cadres were promoted to their positions by different party veterans. The brotherly relations among veterans, therefore, do not exist among them. Moreover, they compete for power. To consolidate their leadership positions, they have formed factions, resulting in a leadership structure with factional confrontation as its main element. The party veterans, for their part, have a similar attitude toward the factions consisting of second-generation leaders. They do their utmost to support the cadres they have selected, because they believe they could not have misjudged their clients. One example of this behavior is Teng's consistent support of Chao Tzu-yang's policies. To avoid unnecessary disputes among themselves, the veterans naturally take care not to openly criticize the cadres selected by other veterans because they are not willing to sacrifice their brotherly relations for any leader of the second generation. However, should a second-generation

---

[10]Chao Wei, *Chao Tzu-yang chüan* (Biography of Chao Tzu-yang) (Hong Kong: Cultural and Educational Press, 1988).

leader commit serious mistakes, it is possible that veterans other than his own patron would jointly express their dissatisfaction. His patron might then have to sacrifice him. Examples of such sacrifices were Hu Yao-pang's downfall and Chao Tzu-yang's dismissal from the post of general secretary of the party.

The Power Factor in Disputes over Political and Ideological Lines

To convince Teng Hsiao-p'ing that the party's general secretary was not a suitable successor, the other party veterans had to prove he had committed serious mistakes. Criticizing the policy mistakes of Chao Tzu-yang became fashionable.

Following the Thirteenth National Congress in October 1987, policy debates between the two party factions became open and intense. A major reason for this was the two factions' competition for leadership power.

Chao Tzu-yang served as general secretary of the party, and Li P'eng as the acting premier. On the surface, the general secretary's responsibilities concerned party affairs, and the acting premier managed government administration. In actual fact, however, no clear demarcation of their proper responsibilities existed. Chao Tzu-yang continued to direct the government administration, as he had done when he was premier. Li P'eng had to play the role of onlooker. The party always had merged government administration and party affairs; the general secretary took charge of everything as the "chief housekeeper." This rarely caused serious problems, because the general secretary and the premier usually belonged to the same faction, and policy coordination was easily achieved. For example, Hu Yao-pang and Chao Tzu-yang were both reformists. Nevertheless, Beijing's leadership structure had begun to change. Chao Tzu-yang and Li P'eng belonged to different factions and held different policy viewpoints. Their respective spheres of authorities and responsibilities began to clash more frequently.

Competition for power between leaders from different factions is usually more intense than that between leaders of the same faction. Because the party's second- and third-generation members had not participated in the early revolutionary movement to seize power, they had no legitimate right to leadership power. For one of them to gain power and lead the party, the policies he advocates will have to succeed. If the functions of the government were truly separated from those of the party, the policymaking power would be in Li P'eng's hands, and Chao would not have directed government policies. Chao would sooner or later have lost economic decisionmaking power, because he no longer played a role in economic policymaking. Losing control over policymaking would have lessened his chances to seize the highest level of leadership. For these reasons, after the Thirteenth National Congress Chao insisted on participating in economic decisionmaking. His decision certainly aggravated the power conflict latent within the party.

Meanwhile, the policy conflict between the two factions became more obvious. Dispute focused on the speed of economic reforms: the issue was whether to seek progress without loss of economic stability or to seek economic stability in reform. The reformists argued that the smooth implementation of economic reforms depended on adopting radical reform measures, such as a sound market mechanism to replace the old central-planning system as quickly as possible. The conservatives believed that replacing the old economic system should be a slow process, and that the switchover should never lose sight of the socialist road or endanger economic stability. They insisted that central macroeconomic control should still continue.

Chao Tzu-yang's economic policies were based on his political line that expanding productive forces was a centrally important task; that argument was logically connected to the ideological line: "practice is the sole criterion of truth." The reformists advocated both these positions. The first policy debate that emerged after the Thirteenth National Congress concerned the feasibility of the economic-development strategy for the coastal areas because it involved the issue of the productive forces.

From late 1987 to early 1988, Chao Tzu-yang made three inspection tours of the coastal provinces, including Chekiang, Fukien, Kiangsu, and Kwangtung. During his tours, he proposed an export-oriented economic-development strategy for the coastal areas. After receiving Chao's report, Teng approved the strategy and on January 23, 1988, urged that bold action be taken to accelerate its implementation so that a good opportunity would not be lost.[11] On February 6, the Politburo decided at its Fourth Plenary Meeting that this strategy should be resolutely implemented so as not to miss a good chance.[12] The strategy, however, was opposed by the conservatives within the party. Chao made that opposition public at the plenary meeting in an article entitled "Further Emancipate the Mind and Further Liberate the Productive Forces," which was designed to refute the conservatives. The conservatives Li P'eng and Yao I-lin contended that economic stability should be the key objective of economic reforms. Chao replied in his article that in the last nine years, every reform policy had originated from the emancipation of thought. He asserted that further emancipation of thought

---

[11] *Ming pao* (Hong Kong), Feb. 9, 1988; *Ta kung pao,* March 1, 1988.
[12] *Ta kung pao,* Feb. 7, 1988.

could increase productivity. He also accused the conservatives of being overscrupulous, pointing out that they ignored the forces obstructing productivity because they did not clearly observe reality and dared not emancipate their thought. He insisted that the government must be empowered to push forward those measures conducive to developing the country's productivity and promoting the country's commodity economy. Later, when Li P'eng and Hu Ch'i-li visited Ch'en Yun at the time of the Spring Festival, Ch'en Yun also expressed support of the coastal economic-development strategy.[13] Political support had tilted in favor of the coastal provinces.

The conservatives remained cool in their support of the coastal economic-development strategy, however. In a speech at the 1988 Spring Festival, Li P'eng pointed out that this strategy was Chao Tzu-yang's.[14] He intended to stand aside and take no responsibility for it. Vice-Premier Yao I-lin, a conservative who has always supported Ch'en Yun's concept of a "birdcage economy," argued at the end of March 1988 that the coastal areas must not indiscriminately import raw and semifinished materials on a large scale regardless of local conditions. He asserted that this strategy should be promoted in a systematic way, with a view to enhancing the economic stability of the whole country.[15] Very shortly thereafter, heated debate erupted within the party. The *People's Daily* published in May and June 1988 articles by seven commentators. They emphasized the importance of thoroughly implementing the coastal economic-development strategy and lashed out at critics who doubted its prospects for success. These commentators criticized unnamed skeptics who feared that the strategy's opening-up policy meant adopting capitalist practices, and that the opening up of the country would restore colonialism and foreign economic aggression. The commentators criticized these skeptics for worrying too much, for being indecisive, for lacking courage, and for being unable to distinguish right from wrong. They went on to say that some skeptics made the relationships of production, the social system, and property ownership the criteria for distinguishing right from wrong. These skeptics maligned that theory of developing an export-oriented economy by using such concepts as small-scale production, small-scale peasant economy, planned economy, and production economy. Still other skeptics created difficulties for the export-oriented economy and the strategy of opening up the coastal areas by referring to them as a colonial economy, economic aggression, capitalism, dependence on the outside world, or dependence on foreign countries. The essays published in the *People's*

---

[13]*Ming pao,* Feb. 16, 1988.
[14]*Wen wei po,* Feb. 20, 1988.
[15]Ibid., March 27, 1988.

Daily also pointed out that the deep-rooted small-production mentality and small-scale–peasant-economy mentality had restricted the thinking and productivity of the people and might impair implementation of the opening-up policy.[16]

The next "line" debate concerned the price reform, which was at the heart of the socialist economic system. The conservatives support a planned commodity economy, while the reformists stressed the role of the market mechanism in a commodity economy. To improve the economic system by expanding the market mechanism, Chao Tzu-yang originally hoped to push the price reform further with Teng's support. He hoped that the prices of commodities could be decided by the needs of the market fairly soon. His main objective was to enable producers to obtain reasonable rewards for what they produced, thereby encouraging them to increase their productivity. In May 1988, price controls for four kinds of nonstaple foods—meat, sugar, eggs, and vegetables—were relaxed for the first time. This policy was formally affirmed at the Ninth Plenary Meeting of the Politburo in June 1988. However, these price readjustments immediately produced sharp price increases and serious inflation, causing widespread discontent and economic instability. Many people opposed further price reforms because they suffered a decline in their living standards. The conservatives now seized the opportunity to announce that the price reform advocated by Chao Tzu-yang and the reformists was an erroneous policy. At the Peitaiho Conference in late July 1988, Chao Tzu-yang came under serious criticism and was temporarily deprived of economic decisionmaking power, being replaced in that sphere by Premier Li P'eng and Vice-Premier Yao I-lin. These two officials immediately proposed new measures to stabilize the economy in the hope of

---

[16]The strength of the reformists' defense of the strategy was unprecedented; seven commentaries were published in the *People's Daily*. See "A Major Event of Historical Significance: On the Economic Development Strategy for the Coastal Areas," *People's Daily*, May 19, 1988; "Emancipate the Mind, Work Boldly: Second Commentary on the Coastal Economic Development Strategy," ibid., May 21, 1988; "Study the State of the Nation and also Understand the World: Third Commentary on the Coastal Economic Development Strategy," ibid., May 23, 1988; "Develop the Coastal Areas, Promote National Development: Fourth Commentary on the Coastal Economic Development Strategy," ibid., May 25, 1988; "Don't Bungle the Chance to Develop Labor-intensive Industries in the Coastal Areas: Fifth Commentary on the Coastal Economic Development Strategy," ibid., May 27, 1988; "Import and Export in a Big Way and Ensure Exports with Imports: Sixth Commentary on the Coastal Economic Development Strategy," ibid., June 3, 1988; "Advance Steadily by Discovering the Facts, Avoid Stirring Things Up: Seventh Commentary on the Coastal Economic Development Strategy," ibid., June 25, 1988.

ending the economic chaos. Their policy was to slow the pace of economic reform and to achieve economic stability. The Third Plenary Session of the Thirteenth Central Committee in September 1988 endorsed that new policy.[17] The economic reform now entered a new phase. Meanwhile, Chao Tzu-yang's political status slipped because he was perceived as pushing price reform with undue haste.

According to the September issue of the Hong Kong magazine *Chengming* (Contending), strong pressure from the conservatives had forced Teng Hsiao-p'ing, the backstage supporter of the reformists, to say that he would not guarantee the leadership position of any person, and that any one not doing his job well should step down.

---

[17]The Chinese Communists held the following meetings in 1988 to deal with the inflation crisis caused by the price reform:

Date	Meeting	Important points
July 15	Second Plenary Session of the State Council	Decided to reduce the scope of capital construction to ensure economic stability
July 20–30	Peitaiho Conference	Discuss price and wage reform policies
Aug. 15–17	Tenth Plenary Meeting of the CCPCC's Politburo	Adopted price and wage reform policies
Aug. 30	Tenth Executive Meeting of the State Council	Extended timetable for completion of the price and wage reform
Sept. 15–21	CCPCC Work Conference	Agreed that economic development should focus on stabilizing the economy and restoring economic order
Sept. 26–30	Third Plenary Session of the CCP's Thirteenth Central Committee	Decided that economic stability should be the main objective of economic-development policies for the next two years

Evaluating the Political Succession of
Chao Tzu-yang and Hu Yao-pang

After Hu Yao-pang was removed from the post of the party's general secretary, Chao Tzu-yang became Teng Hsiao-p'ing's successor. Like Hu, Chao was at the peak of his career when he formally became the party's general secretary at the Thirteenth National Congress. To carry out his succession plan, Teng Hsiao-p'ing removed many old cadres from the Central Committee. That rejuvenation of the central leadership provided Chao with a new opportunity to exercise his power. Moreover, Teng Hsiao-p'ing had learned something from the downfall of his first successor-designate, Hu Yao-pang. No successor can now hold real leadership power in Beijing politics if he does not have the backing of the military. Therefore, Teng deliberately promoted Chao to first vice-chairman of the Military Commission, the number-two leader of the People's Liberation Army, second only to Teng. Hu had never held these important military posts when he was in power.

After Chao became general secretary of the party, he took the advice of members making up his "think tank" and proposed a new theory called the "initial stage of socialism." He made expansion of the forces of production the criterion of all party work and the basic concept for justifying the reformers' policies for socialist construction.[18] He hoped that mainland China's protracted economic difficulties could be quickly solved by launching the export-oriented economic-development strategy for the coastal areas while initiating price-reform measures. These economic-reform measures, on which the consolidation of his leadership power depended, failed. The conservatives had every reason to attack Chao's policies and to oust him from the post of general secretary. Let us consider these developments in the context of three "lines."

---

[18]Members of Chao's "think tank," social scientists from the Institute of Economic Structural Reform, believed in the market mechanism, and it was they who helped Chao to formulate his reform policies. Since the failure of these policies, some of these researchers have gone to study abroad or have gone into business; others have been transferred to research offices under the party's Central Committee.

The Ideological Line

The immediate cause for Hu's downfall had been the democratic movement initiated by students in 1986–1987. The conservatives within the party argued that the lenient attitude toward spreading "bourgeois liberalization" had arisen under Hu's leadership. The failure to maintain ideological orthodoxy had caused the large-scale student movement. Hu, as the general secretary, must be held responsible for that undesirable result. Before the student movement, there had been the campaign in late 1983 to eliminate ideological pollution. Then in 1986, the liberalization trend in academic circles produced the Ma Ting affair and the Liu Tsai-fu affair, which intensified debate and confusion over economic theories and theories of art, respectively. These ideological conflicts in the party gradually led to an ideological struggle over whether Marxism could serve as the only guiding ideology for Chinese socialism. This struggle was an important reason for Hu's downfall.

The anti–bourgeois-liberalization movement which followed Hu's dismissal suddenly restored the influence of conservative ideology. Beijing's economic reforms were soon seriously affected. With Teng Hsiao-p'ing's support, however, Chao Tzu-yang made strenuous efforts to counter the influence of this backlash of conservatism. Chao managed to close *Red Flag*, the CCP's theoretical magazine for more than 30 years, because he regarded it as the mouthpiece of the antireform forces within the party. This act caused much bitterness among the conservatives. From February to May 1988, a heated debate flared up in the party concerning the emancipation of thought and its linkage with productivity. Chao was personally involved in that discussion. Although Chao won this ideological dispute, his theory proved wrong in practice. Later, the Peitaiho Conference and the Third Plenary Session of the Thirteenth Central Committee concluded that the criterion of expanding productivity is not absolutely correct. Apart from this affair, Wang Chen, a senior veteran, expressed his dissatisfaction with more demands for the emancipation of thought, as reflected in the television documentary "River Elegy."[19] Ch'en Yun was also unhappy about these new trends in the ideological sphere. In November 1988, he told Chao Tzu'yang that according to an investigation he himself had conducted, students in party schools did not understand socialism. He remarked that "socialism is planned and orderly economic development. Now, how many socialist ingredients does our country still have?" He then said, "Now almost

---

[19]Lu Ching-shih, "The Leftists' Counteroffensive Before the National Congress of Writers and Artists," *Chiu-shih nien-tai*, 1988, no. 11:62–63.

all proletarian ideological bridgeheads have been occupied by bourgeois ideologies. It is time that we must counterattack."[20] In April and May 1989, the vigorous campaign for human rights and democracy and against bureaucracy launched by intellectuals finally led to the downfall of Chao Tzu-yang.[21]

The Political Line

Before Hu Yao-pang stepped down, many criticized him for rashly advocating high consumption and setting excessively high economic goals regardless of the country's real conditions.[22] When the Central Committee called for unifying the thinking of the whole party, Hu said that all party members should correct their attitude toward economic issues; that the purpose of the party-consolidation movement was mainly to promote economic development; and that economic performance should be the criterion for judging the party's consolidation work. However, when Hu was the general secretary, economic work was mainly under the supervision of Chao Tzu-yang. Therefore, Chao was spared making mistakes involving the political line.

Before Chao Tzu-yang was deprived of his power as secretary general, he made expanding productivity the criterion for judging whether one supported economic reforms.[23] Ignoring the opposition of the conservatives, he implemented policies of large-scale economic restructuring and of price reform. Without effective macroeconomic control, however, these policies only spawned spiraling price rises, demoralization in the bureaucracy, and widespread discontent. Li P'eng commented that these policy mistakes were based on the belief that one could obtain quick returns in economic and social development; such a view failed to take into consideration the country's vast population, the shortage of natural resources, and the prevalent pattern of unbalanced economic development; the lack by many of full understanding of the complexity of these reforms, the lack of good sup-

---

[20]Ho Yan-cheng, "Ch'en Yun on Counterattacks in the Ideological Sphere," *Ching-pao* (The mirror), 1989, no. 1:29.

[21]Ch'i Hsin, "An Unprecedented Move by China's Intellectuals," *Chiu-shih nien-tai*, 1989, no. 3:20–21. In response to calls from intellectuals for the release of Wei Ching-sheng and for democracy and human rights, the Chinese Communists announced that they had no intention of granting an amnesty.

[22]*Pai-hsing* (The people) (Hong Kong), no. 138 (Feb. 16, 1987):4. Hu believed that high consumption would promote production.

[23]"Li P'eng's Government Work Report at the Second Session of the Seventh National People's Congress," *Ta kung pao*, March 21, 1989; *Wen wei po*, July 2, 1988.

porting measures, and the failure to pay enough attention to whether price reforms were acceptable to business enterprises and the people.[24]

The Organizational Line

Hu Yao-pang always had attached great importance to the cadre problem within the party. He made strenuous efforts to train cadres for the third echelon. Believing that cadres' ranks should be rejuvenated and professionalized, he did not want party elders to interfere in political affairs. This view enraged the veterans and was another important reason for his downfall.[25]

Chao Tzu-yang, more experienced in economic work, did not have much experience in party affairs and never devoted much attention to the party's organizational work or to cadre problems. In fact, Ch'iao Shih was in charge of the party's organizational work. This spared Chao from committing mistakes in that area.

Still, Chao Tzu-yang's downfall reflects the party's "line" conflict and the power struggle within the party for leadership. Mounting criticism from the conservatives and their anger forced Teng Hsiao-p'ing to withdraw his support from Chao. The main reasons for Teng's decision are the following.

First, there were political repercussions caused by the failure of Chao's economic-reform policies. The power base of leaders of the second generation, including Chao, differs from that of leaders of the first generation. The first-generation leaders were revolutionaries whose personal prestige rested on their contributions to the revolutionary cause. They did not need policy achievements to legitimize their leadership power. Even when they committed serious policy mistakes, they were not held accountable. The failure of Mao's "Three Red Banners" policy was an example of this. However, leaders of the second generation must prove their leadership ability by means of policy achievements. This is the only way they can win the confidence of the first-generation leaders. Moreover, in Beijing's politics, which lacks an institutionalized political system, the transfer of power is not carried out in an orderly and rational manner. Therefore, power struggles

---

[24]"Li P'eng's Government Work Report at the Second Session of the Seventh National People's Congress," *Ta kung pao,* March 21, 1989.

[25]A commentary in *Liao-wang* (Outlook), a weekly published by the party's Secretariat, demanded that first-generation leaders should live quiet lives without interfering in political affairs, that second-generation leaders should support younger cadres, and that third-generation leaders should devote themselves to their work. See *Liao-wang,* 1985, no. 8:4.

between different factions often occur, and policy mistakes by a leader soon bring political pressure and and criticism from the second-generation leaders.

Second, there are special practices governing political power struggles. Another reason for Chao's fall may be that other leaders held grudges against him because of the longstanding practice of struggling for power. As soon as Chao was appointed Teng Hsiao-p'ing's successor-designate, he became the center of Beijing's power struggle, regardless of whether or not he had committed any policy errors. In the party's history, all previous successors-designate eventually have been forced to step down, starting with Liu Shao-ch'i, Lin Piao, the "Gang of Four," Hua Kuo-feng, and Hu Yao-pang. It has now become a political practice that the heir-apparent becomes the obvious target of political struggle. Different viewpoints and interests exist, yet various factions within the party often quietly join forces against the successor-designate for different reasons, either because of political ambition, jealousy, or dissatisfaction with the successor-designate's qualifications or political record.

Conclusion

Following the party's Thirteenth National Congress, the power structure of the reformist faction quickly changed after the downfall of Chao Tzu-yang. The new power structure is basically characterized by the collective leadership of party elders headed by Teng Hsiao-p'ing. The leaders of the younger generation are only the policy executors. In every case of intervention by the party elders to designate a successor to the first-generation leaders, such as Hu Yao-pang, Chao Tzu-yang, and even the newly elected general secretary Jiang Jue-ming, those successors found it very difficult to implement policies to achieve their goals. Moreover, the old veterans bear latent hostility toward their successors, which is another obstacle preventing a smooth political succession by second-generation leaders. Those successors can be blamed for anything. Among the leaders of the second and third generations, factionalism has become a pervasive, informal pattern of political life.

The Labor-Reform Camps in the PRC

The prison system of the People's Republic of China (PRC) is a great deal more than a means of punishing and reforming wrongdoers. It is a critical component of the PRC's autocratic political structure. The labor-reform camp (LRC), or *lao-gai-dui* as this prison system is generally known in the Chinese Communist Party's (CCP) technical terminology, is a necessary product of the totalitarian PRC state. The *lao-gai-dui* is one of the most extensive and brutal prison systems in human history. Three forms of treatment—"arrest and sentencing," "re-education through labor," and "forced job placement"—constitute the *lao-gai-dui*.

An Overview

The three policies governing the *lao-gai-dui* were promulgated during the 1950s. According to various sources, at least fifty million people have been assigned to *lao-gai-dui* over the past forty years, but no one really knows how many people have disappeared into them. There are about five thousand labor-reform camps in the PRC, and they hold approximately sixteen–twenty million people. This author has identified nearly one thousand such camps by maps.

The low-paid and submissive, but disciplined and hardworking labor force of the *lao-gai-dui* plays an important role in the "socialist construction" of the PRC.

In economic activity, each *lao-gai-dui* is called a "special state-operated enterprise." The "labor-reform enterprises" make up an enormous national economic system of agriculture, industry, communications, transportation, engineering, and construction. "Labor-reform production" (LRP—CCP's technical term) makes up a significant portion of the PRC's economic output. Politically, the *lao-gai-dui* is an enormous instrument for supporting the totalitarian rule of the Chinese Communist Party. Given a minimal supply of food and forced to labor in order to be "reformed into socialist new people," terrorized and hopeless prisoners are asked to "reform" their ideological attitudes, morality, religious and political convictions, and even their most basic human natures, to make them accord with the demands of the CCP. In scope, length of duration, method of implementation, and social influence, the *lao-gai-dui* exceeds all similar dictatorial instruments in human history—even the Nazi concentration camps and the Soviet Union's labor camps.

From Mao Ze-dong, Liu Shao-qi, and Hua Guo-feng to Deng Xiao-ping, political policies and slogans have changed. Some policies have even been publicly repudiated and altered. The three policies mentioned above, however, have never been repudiated. After Deng Xiao-ping came to power in 1978, new policies in government, economy, and culture, as well as the appeals for "reform" and "openness" have attracted the attention of the public around the world. But the Labor-Reform Policy, about which the world knows almost nothing, has only been expanded and strengthened.

In October 1949, the CCP established its political power. The regime relied on the Marxist-Leninist theory of class struggle as a guiding principle. The party made use of various methods, including the LRC system, to eliminate "class enemies," "counterrevolutionaries," and those who were "counterparty" and "countersocialist."

In 1957, Mao Ze-dong, who led the PRC during its first 26 years, set forth six political criteria for the Chinese people to live by:

1. Words and actions should help to unite, and should not divide, the people of our various nationalities.
2. They should be beneficial and not harmful, to socialist transformation and socialist construction.
3. They should help to consolidate, and not undermine or weaken, the people's democratic dictatorship.
4. They should help to consolidate, and not undermine or weaken, democratic centralism.
5. They should help to strengthen, and not discard or weaken, the leadership of the Communist Party.

6. They should be beneficial, and not harmful to international socialist unity and the unity of the peace-loving people of the world.[1]

Whoever opposes these six political criteria is an "enemy of the people." Mao said: "towards the enemy, the CCP uses the method of dictatorship, that is, for as long a period of time as is necessary it does not permit them to take part in political activity and compels them to obey the law of the People's Government, to engage in labor and, through such labor, be reformed into new persons."[2]

In 1978, Deng Xiao-ping, the leader of the PRC for the past ten years, said: "In our society [there is] still a special form of class struggle . . . it is still necessary to exercise dictatorship over these countersocialist elements . . ." In 1979 Deng set out "Four Cardinal Principles:"

1. We must uphold the socialist road.
2. We must uphold the dictatorship of proletariat.
3. We must uphold the leadership of the Communist Party.
4. We must uphold the Marxism-Leninism and Mao Tse-tung Thought.[3]

In the past ten years, whoever has opposed those Four Cardinal Principles has been regarded as an enemy of the state and sent to the *lao-gai-dui*.

In recent years, especially since 1983, the labor-reform system has undergone some changes. The backlog of problems from the past 40 years required solution if change was to occur. Further, large changes in society in general sparked change.

Introduction to the Labor-Reform Camp

The LRC system consists of six parts: (1) detention centers; (2) prisons; (3) labor-reform discipline-production camps; (4) juvenile offenders' camps; (5) re-education-through-labor camps; and (6) forced-job-placement camps.

Each LRC (*lao-gai-dui*) in the PRC has two names. One is for the internal use of the Public Security Department and the Judiciary Department; examples of such names are: "Beijing No. 1 Prison," "Shanxi Province No. 4 Labor-Reform Detachment," "Hunan Province No. 2 Prison," and "Beijing Tuanhe Re-education-Through-Labor Camp." The other name is for public

---

[1]Quotations from Chairman Mao (Beijing: Foreign Languages Press, 1968), p. 48.
[2]Ibid., p. 42.
[3]Deng Xiao-ping, *Selected Works of Deng Xiao-ping* (Beijing), March 30, 1979.

use: such names are, for example, "Beijing Knitting Mill," "Shanxi Province Wangchuang Coal Mine," "Hunan Province Heavy Truck Plant," and "Yingte Tea Farm." The LRC organization follows that of the military. In the LRC the "squad" (10–15 inmates), "company" (80–150 inmates), "battalion" (800–2,000 inmates), and "detachment" (from 2,000 upward, with some having more than 10,000 inmates) correspond to the squad, company, battalion, and regiment of the army. There is a political instructor who is responsible for the inmates' "thought reform" at every organizational level of the camp.

Within the public-security and judiciary system, an internal, technical distinction is made among three types of personnel. The first type of personnel consists of people who have been arrested and sentenced to prison, labor-reform discipline-production camps, or juvenile-offender camps. The second type of personnel are those sentenced to re-education-through-labor camps. The third type of personnel are those in forced-job-placement camps. *Lao-gai, lao-jiao,* and *jiu-ye* are the terms applied, respectively, to these three types of personnel. The CCP clearly defines these three types of personnel as "targets" for elimination.

The category of *lao-gai* embraces at least 25 million people who have been arrested and sentenced in the past 40 years. This estimate does not include those arrested secretly or without legal process through various unofficial means—a number undoubtedly very large—such as those arrested during the Cultural Revolution (1966–1976). There are three–five million people who have been arrested and sentenced, and are now locked up as *lao-gai*. Only 13 percent of them are in prison, as they require strict incarceration. The remaining 87 percent are being held in the labor-reform discipline-production camps.

Lao-jiao covers those who are subjected to re-education through labor, a penal program launched in 1957. At least twenty million people have been sent to the LRCs as *lao-jiao*. There are now about three–five million people in those camps. Before 1980, most of the *lao-jiao* prisoners were organized in companies or battalions together with the *lao-gai* prisoners in the same LRC.

The CCP declared that the *lao-jiao* policy "is an administrative measure, a method for dealing with the contradictions among the people."[4] As an administrative measure, it is different from criminal-law processes because there are no steps for investigation, arrest, trial, prosecution, and sentencing.

---

[4]*Laodong jiaoyang shixing banfa* (Experimental methods for re-education through labor), article 1: Jan. 21, 1982 (Internal document of the Chinese Communist Party).

The program gives the CCP a simple, effective means—unnoticed by world opinion—of stripping people of their freedom and rights.

Jiu-ye was a policy carried out in 1954. Before 1980, 95 percent of *lao-gai* prisoners and 90 percent of *lao-jiao* prisoners were forced to resettle and accept jobs in the *lao-gai-dui* after they had completed their terms of imprisonment. There are about ten million *jiu-ye* personnel in the *lao-gai-dui*. *Jiu-ye* does not refer to an ordinary person who has lost his job and is placed in a new one. *Jiu-ye* personnel are in the labor-reform enterprises controlled by the Public Security Department. These individuals do not have the right to choose their own work or life styles. Their political and social positions are completely different from those of an ordinary citizen. Keeping people in this category is justified by the "thorough implementation of the policy of labor reform and the consolidation of social security."[5] Prisoners are completely deprived of their freedom, and they must work at primitive handicraft jobs overseen by the party's labor-reform production organ. The demands of "administrative and technological improvements of modern enterprises" require that a labor supply be dependable and have limited freedom. The *jiu-ye* category of penal labor satisfies the regime's political and economic requirements.

Labor-Reform Production

The CCP's policy has clearly stipulated that labor-reform production (LRP) be included in the statistics of national production. LRP falls under the jurisdiction of financial commissions of the People's Government of various levels. Labor-reform administrative commissions made up of the financial units from the central, provincial, and municipal departments formulate and implement the LRP plan.

Lao-gai prisoners are not paid; *lao-jiao* prisoners receive about 20–30 percent of the ordinary citizen's salary; and the *jiu-ye* are paid about 50–60 percent of the ordinary citizen's salary. Thus this penal system controls a cheap and submissive labor force.

All PRC prisoners are forced to work. Even if a prisoner is in a detention center awaiting trial, he is also forced to labor. Some special, important prisoners not permitted contact with other prisoners are organized into special labor teams that bind books, seal envelopes, and perform other such work.

During the 1950s, the LRP managed the physically strenuous labor

---

[5] *Fa xue yan jiu* (Beijing), April 1983, p. 44.

projects, such as cutting roads through mountains, building mines, water-power projects, large-scale reclamation projects, and farm construction. The LRP force has participated in most of the PRC's socialist construction projects. The LRCs also participated in many large projects of the national five-year plans. While these projects were being planned, arrangements were concurrently made to fund and equip the LRCs for different work systems. LRCs of different provinces and cities are placed under the direction of the Public Security Department. For example:

- The enormous Hui River water-power project employed a combined total of up to one million prisoners from Shanghai, Anhui, Chiangsu, Zhechiang, Hunan, and Shandong provinces and took ten years to complete.
- In the northern part of Changes province, 2,500,000 *mu* (1 *mu* = 0.1647 acres) of saline soil was opened up for more than ten state-operated farms. This project involved 200,000 prisoners from Shanghai and Changes province.
- In the Peitahuang region of Heilongjiang province, more than 500,000 prisoners from Beijing and the Northeast reclaimed wasteland of about 300,000 *mu* in area.
- The world-famous An-Shan Cooperative Steel & Iron Project and the Bao-Tou Cooperative Steel & Iron Project involved, from start to finish, tens of thousands of prisoners.
- No one can estimate how many *lao-gai dui* and their inmates were employed in the Xingjiang Autonomous Region and Qinghai province. These two areas are China's Siberia.

None of the prisons and buildings of the public-security system built since 1949 have been state-financed, but rather have been constructed by the prisoners themselves. The salaries, bonuses, welfare benefits, health insurance, uniforms, and other necessities of the LRC police are supplied entirely by the labor-reform production system.

During the 1960s, a large group of technologically advanced, modernized labor-reform enterprises appeared: the Linfen Automobile Factory in Shanxi province; the Liang-xiang Elevator Factory in Beijing: the Guangzhou Electric Fan Factory in Guangzhou; the Hunan Heavy Truck Plant in Hunan province; the Huadong Electric Welder Factory in Shanghai; the Bengpu Rubber Plant in Anhui province; the Yinyin Coal Mine in Shanxi province; the A-er-tai Gold Mine in the Xinjiang Autonomous Region; the Chaoyang Lead Plant in Guizhou province; the Chendu Machine-Tool Factory in Szuchuan province; the Xianyang Machine-Tool Factory in Hubei province; the Yingte Tea Farm in Guangdong province; the Qinghe Farm in Beijing, etc. The products from these labor-reform enterprises are sold domestically and abroad.

These labor-reform enterprises are active in their respective areas, as the following passage from a report from the Labor-Reform Bureau of Hupei province published in 1989 shows:

> A high-quality shaping machine (model B6050B) produced by Xiang-yang Machine Tool Factory was sold to more than 40 different countries and regions through different dealers in Hong Kong. The dealers' names are Tai-dong Co. (Hong Kong) and Singapore Machine Co., Ltd. This factory is a labor-reform camp which is controlled by the Judiciary Bureau of Hupei province and has 700 prisoners in custody. Before 1984, the annual profit of this LRE was 400,000 yuan; in 1984–1988, the annual profit rose three times.[6]

Political Prisoners in the LRCs

The CCP has always insisted that political prisoners do not exist in the PRC. The political prisoners in the PRC naturally have special names, such as "active counterrevolutionary," "ideological reactionary," etc. During the past 40 years, the CCP has engaged in class struggle. Criminals convicted of the same crime but having different class statuses and political backgrounds have been treated very differently. Many dissidents have been persecuted as criminals.

There are five major types of political criminals in the PRC:

Type one: "Counterrevolutionary landlord element." In the "land reform movement" from 1949–1951, approximately five million members of the landlord class were executed, and many were sent to LRCs.

Type two: "Historical counterrevolutionary." These people were somehow connected with the political or military network of the preceding regime. About ten million such people were politically persecuted. Most of them were sent to LRCs.

Type three: "Active counterrevolutionary." The scope of this category is very large; by rough estimate, in the past 40 years, twenty to thirty million people have been persecuted, and of those twenty million have been sent to the LRCs. Examples include the Catholic bishop

---

[6]*Fazhi jianshe* (Law and order) (Beijing: Ministry of Justice, 1989), vol. 2, p. 32. (Cited hereafter as *Law and Order.*)

Kung Pin-mei (arrested in 1955), and fighter for democracy Wei Jing-shen (arrested in 1979) and a student studying in the United States, Yang Wei.

Type four: "Counterrevolutionary rightist." In 1957–1958, some 550,000 intellectuals were labeled "counterrevolutionary rightist"; later, a portion of them were sent to the LRCs.

Type five: "Ideological reactionary" or "antisocialist element." Since 1956, many people have been seized because they expressed discontent in daily conversation, in articles, or even in their own letters or diaries. Even people who listen to radio broadcasts from Western countries have been considered criminals. Between 1958–1962, approximately ten million people were persecuted, mostly by means of re-education through labor (*lao-jiao*).

In the 1950s, people convicted as members of the "landlord element" or as "historical" or "active" counterrevolutionaries made up about 80–90 percent of all those in *lao-gai-dui*. In the 1960s and 1970s, political prisoners accounted for 50–60 percent of their inmates; in the past ten years, for about 10–20 percent.

Most political prisoners in *lao-gai-dui* are mixed up in the camps. Political prisoners are in an especially difficult position, even though they usually obey the rules better than other criminals and are less likely to attempt escape or to get into fights. The reasons for this are: (1) in the CCP's eyes, those prisoners are the most dangerous of enemies, who cannot be trusted; (2) these prisoners are educated, and their ways of thinking are complicated, so they are difficult to reform; (3) as these prisoners are not accustomed to physical labor, it is often difficult for them to meet the labor-production quotas, and that makes the public-security cadres very unhappy; (4) most of these people have a strong sense of morality and do not comply with the "law of the jungle" that dominates life in LRCs; and (5) most of these people have backgrounds that are economically and culturally superior to those of the public-security cadres, which provokes the latter to resentment and jealousy. Consequently, the instances of torture, term extensions, and forced resettlement in *lao-gai-dui* are more numerous among political prisoners than among ordinary prisoners.

Torture in the LRCs

By law, torture is totally forbidden in the LRCs. In fact, the torture of body and spirit is everywhere. Torture is common in ordinary prisons, as one would expect, but in the PRC it has some distinctive features.

In the LRCs, the first step for a prisoner is to confess, then to promise to accept the designated punishment, and finally to become a model "socialist new person." In the LRCs, humanity and dignity absolutely do not exist. There are many different means used to "reform" a person: "study classes"; "criticism meetings"; "disciplinary teams"; "attack-antireformists meetings"; "launching of movements to confess and denounce"; "confinement cells"; "reduction of the food allotment"; "thought summaries"; and various kinds of punishment. Spiritual torment, too, never ceases.

Torture, beatings, the controlling of prisoners, and managing them according to set procedures are routine features of the *lao-gai-dui* system so that the CCP has each camp running smoothly without disturbances and difficulties.

The Current Status of the LRCs

Since 1978, three crises of belief—disbelief in the ideal of communism, skepticism about the "socialist road," and mistrust of the leadership of the CCP—have come to be shared by more and more Chinese, even within the Communist Party. A sense of moral emptiness and a weakness of ideology has encouraged that new trend. These and other difficulties forced the ruling elite of the party to face up to a serious challenge: Deng Xiao-ping's "Four Cardinal Principles" were being openly challenged.

To maintain political control, the party now must yield some ground and allow for reform. This new leniency is being reflected in law, in the public-security system, and in labor-reform policy. In order to increase the efficiency of forced labor and to carry out new economic reforms, some thinking was required. In 1978, Deng Xiao-ping said the following about the role of class struggle and its connection with government organs and law:

> . . . we must recognize that in our socialist society there are still counter-revolutionaries, enemy agents, criminals and other bad elements of all kinds who undermine socialist public order, as well as new exploiters who engage in corruption, embezzlement, speculation, and profiteering. And we must also recognize that such phenomena cannot be all eliminated for a long time to come. The struggle against these individuals is different from the struggle of one class against another, which occurred in the past (these individuals cannot form a cohesive and overt class). However, it is still a special form of class struggle or a special form of the leftover, under socialist conditions, of the class struggle of past history. It is still necessary to exercise dictatorship over all these antisocialist elements, and socialist democracy is impos-

sible without it. This dictatorship is an internal struggle and in some cases an international struggle as well; in fact, the two aspects are inseparable.[7]

He then said:

Under the present circumstances, therefore, it is in complete conformity with the desire of the people and the needs of socialist modernization to use the repressive power of the state apparatus to attack the counterrevolutionary saboteurs, antiparty and antisocialist elements and criminals guilty of serious offences and to split their ranks in the interests of social stability.[8]

Deng Xiao-ping's speeches, like those of Mao before him, are accepted as infallible and used to establish new laws and policies. The above ideas became the basis for today's labor-reform policy.

The labor-reform policies responded in two ways to the great number of penal criminals in the last ten years and to the fact that many criminals were CCP members. In Shandong province, in 1986, 95 percent of prisoners were penal criminals; 60 percent were under 25 years of age; and 80 percent came from the revolutionary class." The party recognizes that the penal criminals are harmful to national interests and to the interests of the current government, and that they must be punished. Yet the party must also consider the social background of these criminals and treat them differently.

Since 1978, more orders and policies on *lao-gai, lao-jiao,* and *jiu-ye* have followed.

In 1987, 30 years after enactment of the re-education-through-labor policy—*lao-jiao*—this policy was applied to the People's Liberation Army (PLA). Conditions in the army had worsened, and the party had to act.

In 1983, the judicial system took over the LRCs from the public-security system. The organs of labor reform and re-education through labor are still component parts of the public-security organ; the nature of the latter's work and its responsibilities have not changed. The public-security system, the courts, the procuratorate, and the judicial system (with its categories of *lao-gai, lao-jiao,* and *jiu-ye*) are all organs of the dictatorship of the proletariat.

The numbers of the police are larger than ever in the past. The LRC police numbered more than 300,000 in 1986. In 1985, for the first time a "Labor-Reform College" was established for special training of police who will serve in the *lao-gai-dui.*

A policy of "three extensions" (*san yen-shen*) was approved by the Central Committee of the CCP in 1987 in the "Summary of the Panel on the

---

[7] *Selected Works of Deng Xiao-ping,* p. 92.
[8] Ibid., p. 156.

Political and Legal Work of the Nation." The "three extensions" are "forward," "outward," and "backward" extensions.

"Forward extension" means that in the process of preliminary investigation, prosecution, and sentencing, organs such as the public-security police and the courts will intensify their efforts to "educate" the criminal so that he admits his crime and accepts punishment. "Outward extension" refers to the goal of involving relatives and society at large in "reform" work. "Backward extension" means that upon fulfillment of sentence or release from *laogai-dui*, prisoners will continue to have jobs arranged for them by the Ministry of Public Security in order to impart to them complete labor reform.

In 1980, the party began changing the forced-job-placement policy. First, there was a new forced-job-placement policy; second, the old forced-job-placement personnel were terminated; third, a new policy handled these personnel when they returned to society. Those who returned to society "are only a portion of the total and not all. The function of the forced-job-placement policy as an extension of the labor-reform policy is still emphasized and made use of." A new condition of "good performance" has been imposed for those who are allowed to be "returned." The criteria for this condition are determined by the party.

The important role played by labor-reform production in the national economy of the PRC has still not disappeared. On the contrary, newly formulated policies encourage labor-reform production, as confirmed in the party's new guiding principle: "Reform comes first, production second."

The "Decision on Reforms in the Economic System" passed by the third session of the Twelfth Central Committee of the CCP stated: "We must incorporate and model ourselves after the advanced management and administrative methods for all production patterns that reflect modernization in all modern countries of the world, including developed capitalist countries." The labor-reform enterprise (*laogai qiyi*) is a component part of the state-operated enterprises and therefore must face similar reform. Of course, the labor-reform enterprises is a special type of state-operated enterprise and cannot completely adopt the reform.

In 1980, the LRCs, from top to bottom, began to undergo reform. They began to experiment with "A System of Contractual Responsibilities in Discipline and in Production." The National Meeting on the Work of *Lao-gai* and *Lao-jiao*, held in July 1984, required that "the economy be made more efficient, deficits made up, and surpluses increased." The national system of LRCs was to implement the policy: "Contractual Responsibilities in Discipline and Production." What did "contractual responsibility" mean?

The disciplinary and production criteria for each *lao-gai-dui* are based upon the two responsibilities that LRCs have always had: the responsibility of creating wealth for socialist construction and to maintain prisoner discipline. The disciplinary criteria are: the rate of escape and capture; the rate of cases solved; the rate of abnormal deaths; the rate of rule violation and repeat offenses in the *lao-gai-dui*; and the rate of entrance into educational programs for cultural and technical fields. The production criteria are economic, technical criteria, such as production value, quantity, cost, consumption, and profit. The manner of operation of the labor-reform enterprises is similar to the implementation of the nationwide responsibility system which requires that the "factory leader take responsibility"; like other state-operated enterprises, the labor-reform enterprise has done away with the "big iron rice bowl" and uses profits to improve labor-reform productivity.

These economic and political criteria are now emphasized in each detachment, battalion, company, and squadron, and even for the individual. All public-security cadres and all prisoners are given specific tasks according to these two sets of criteria.

A certain portion of the profit from LRCs is used for taxes and expenses. Surplus profit is used in the LRC budget. Usually, 30 percent of the surplus is used to expand production (as capital for the purchase of technologies and equipment); 30 percent is used to improve living conditions in the enterprises (new houses for public-security cadres; establishment of schools and nurseries; repairs, etc.); and 40 percent is allocated for incentives (only a very small portion of this gives the public-security cadres material incentives to make greater efforts.

After introducing the policy of contractual responsibility, some LRCs made economic gains. Consider the following example:

> The unpopulated wasteland of alkaline soil originally called the "Great Northern Wilderness," in the northern part of Shandong province along the Bohai sea, is now occupied by the "Weipei Labor-Reform Detachment," containing more than 30,000 prisoners. In addition to agricultural products (grains and fruits) and livestock (chickens, ducks, fish, pigs, cows, and sheep), they now produce soap, paper, a kind of general universal reinforcing welding machine, as well as textiles, and bedding for export. In 1986, the products made by this *lao-gai-dui* were worth 11.76 million yuan [*renminpi*], or approx. US$3,000,000.[9]
>
> Before 1985, administration of Ku-Che Labor-Reform Detachment (Xingjiang Autonomous Region) was poor, and it lost from 100–200 thousand yuan per year. After it began to implement "contractual responsibility," police in areas that had problems were required to carry out inspections, that may result in disciplinary, economic sanctions (suspension of rewards, etc.). In 1985, according to the regulations, the political com-

---

[9]*Law and Order*, Dec. 1987, p. 35.

missioner of the detachment, Shi Wei-Min, was fined 80 yuan, the vice-commissioner, Li Kuan-lue, was fined 60 yuan. Some police officers also received financial sanctions. In 1986 the situation changed. The rate of prisoner escapes decreased by 75 percent. Revenue and expenditure were basically balanced.[10]

The labor-reform enterprise is naturally a production unit. It has the same problem as other enterprises operated by the socialist state: production efficiency is low; production expenses are high; personnel avoid responsibility; there is little creative energy; economic efficiency is low; and most police lack knowledge of production, and so on. The purpose of contractual responsibility is to ensure that, while the suppressive aspect of the LRCs continues to operate normally, two groups are inspired to activity: public-security police and prisoners. Responsibility, power, and benefit are to become linked together. Material benefits—incentives—are to promote labor, and the coercive, political techniques of the past are to be abandoned. Labor and production in LRCs are to be promoted and encouraged by means of individual benefits. This further brings the function of production by slave labor into play in the socialist national economy. In the last ten years, the party has emphasized export of the products of LRCs:

1. The Ying-Te brand of black tea, famous in the tea markets of the Far East and with a long history, is supplied by a LRC enterprise named the Ying-Te Labor-Reform Detachment in Guangdong province.[11]
2. According to a report from Fuchien province, several LRCs joined together to create a new company for export business—Ming-Xing Supply & Marketing Co. (New Fu-Chien Supply & Marketing Co.). This LRC export company also joined with another twelve labor-reform enterprises from other provinces to organize a big new export company, named Xing-Lian Trading Co. (New Union Trading Co.) for exporting their products.[12]

How effective has the contractual-responsibility system been? LRCs have "independently" formulated various kinds of measures and regulations intended to develop the production of individual labor-reform enterprises in order to increase material benefits. Here are several examples that achieved those results:

---

[10]Renmin ribao (Beijing), March 14, 1987, p. 4.
[11]*Zhongguo fazhi bao* (Beijing), June 2, 1986, p. 2.
[12]*Law and Order,* March 1988, p. 32.

1. According to a report from the judiciary of Zhejiang province after labor-reform enterprises of the entire province had implemented the "System of Contractual Responsibility," public-security police and prisoners (including those in the categories re-education through labor and forced job placement) were inspired to activity. It is efficient in that, first, the rate of attempted escapes and repeat offenders in labor-reform camps has declined; second, in the first half of 1985, the total production value of labor-reform enterprises has increased by 57 percent from the same period in 1984, while profit increased by 35.8 percent; third, the number of labor-reform agricultural units that have been operating at a deficit for a long time greatly decreased.[13]

2. A report from Fuchien province stated: "The total production value of labor-reform enterprises (of Fuchien province) in 1982 amounted to 13.61 million [yuan]; in 1987, it has increased by 42.5 million [yuan], an increase of 312.3 percent. In 1982, there was a deficit of 1.64 million [yuan], but in 1987, there was a surplus of 40.5 million [yuan]."[14]

3. According to a report from the Labor-Reform Bureau of Bai-hu County, Anhui province, the total production value of LRP has increased by 15.2 percent from 1984; the total production value of 1984 was 34.91 million [yuan].[15]

4. The total production value of LRCs in Chiangsu province amounted to 247 million [yuan] in 1986, an increase of 15 percent from 1985.[16]

5. The profit target of Hua-Tong Welding Machine Factory in 1984 was 7.9 million [yuan]. This factory has about 1,000 forced-job-placement personnel [jiu-ye]. In 1984, from January to November, the production value amounted to 32.24 million [yuan], and the profit was 14.56 million [yuan].[17]

6. The vice-minister of the Judiciary, Jin Jian, said on Dec. 7, 1988, that in the past five years, more than 700 medium or small LRP projects had been rebuilt, extended, or built, and that 50 percent of them had gone into production. In 1987, the LRCs' fixed assets had increased 1.5 times from 1983, and the production value had increased 56 percent. Eight labor-reform enterprises became second-level national enterprises, and 350 became enterprises of the provincial and ministry level.

---

[13]Ibid., Nov. 1988, p. 20.
[14]Ibid., March 1988, p. 30.
[15]*Zhongguo fazhi bao,* March 4, 1986, p. 1.
[16]*Renmin ribao,* March 24, 1986, p. 4.
[17]*Zhongguo fazhi bao,* April 12, 1986, p. 3.

More than 30 LRC products won the national high-quality medal.[18] (The eight LRCs referred to are: the Xing-sheng Chemical Plant, Cheng-yang City, Liaoning province; Wa-fang-dian Machine Tool Plant, Liaoning province; Sheng-jian Graphite Mine, Bei-shu, Shandong province; Sheng-jian 83 Factory, Shangdong province; Lao-tong Steel Tube Plant, Shanghai City; Xu-zhou Forging Press Machine Factory, Jiangsu province; the 5–1 Machine Plant, Zhejiang province; and the Wu-ling Machine Factory, Hangzhou City, Zhejiang province.)

The party now believes that its reforms have improved the work of labor-reform camps.

Lingering Difficulties

Revision of the labor-reform policy in recent years has eliminated the extraneous and retained the essential: the early policy of Mao Ze-dong and the party was adjusted. Yet the fundamental intent of the labor-reform policy has not changed. The target has not diminished, but expanded. Organizational procedures have changed. Measures and policies have been perfected. The scope of the LRCs has not decreased. Their two aspects of dictatorship and production by slave labor are still being expanded and maintained.

For many reasons the regime could not force all released prisoners to resettle in the LRCs; thus most of them were released. The return to society of the two types of ex-prisoners: *lao-jiao* and *lao-gai*, for job placement causes the authorities great trouble. There are few jobs; the authorities must supply new residential permits to the ex-prisoners; and some returnees might return to crime. Because the policy of forced job placement (*jiu-ye*) was used in the past, these problems did not exist. By releasing more ex-prisoners, the party lost some control over them. While some were freed between 1980 and 1983, the release of prisoners then suddenly halted, and new regulations were implemented. Appraisal of these policies cannot be made at this time.

The current crime rate remains high and does not decrease. There also has been a rapid increase in party cadres' corruption and economic crimes. Can the labor-reform policy put a stop to these activities with the same degree of efficiency with which it has liquidated class enemies and counter-revolutionaries? What theory and what policy are needed to more effectively carry out the new "special form of class struggle" and preserve the ruling order?

---

[18] *Renmin ribao,* Dec. 11, 1988, p. 4.

The policy of re-education through labor (*lao-jiao*), a law labeled "the highest administrative sanction," which strips citizens of their freedom and fundamental rights, is increasingly being questioned and recognized for what it is by the people. How much longer can it be maintained?

The social atmosphere of corruption and power-brokering is vividly reflected in the labor-reform camps. All prisoners (including *lao-jiao* and *jiu-ye*) are vitally concerned with sentence reduction; being placed in labor-reform camps close to one's home region; avoiding being sent to distant provinces to serve their terms; being released for vacation; being able to leave the LRC for medical treatment; being allowed to visit relatives; avoiding any cancellation of a city residence permit and relatives' visiting hours; receiving gifts from home; and permission for sick leave. These conditions are all decided upon by public-security cadres. The ability of some persons to bribe these cadres to gain the favorable circumstances described above has produced a wave of corruption in the camps. Here are some examples:

1. A report stated: "Some relatives of prisoners serving sentences, in order to obtain a reduction in sentence, or the opportunity of outside medical treatment for their children, engaged in bribery, giving gifts to cadres of the labor-reform camps. Over the past year throughout the province [Hubei], 848 cadres of the LRCs rejected gifts and bribes worth 50,000 yuan. At Sha-Yang Farm alone, 435 cadres [party members] rejected gifts and cash worth 14,000 yuan."[19]

2. Chiang-Chen Prison [on the Yangtze River, in Wu-Hu City of Anhui province] holds repeat offenders. In recent years it has been successful in "reform" but not in production. It is responsible for more than one million yuan. In 1984, the newly appointed prison commissioner [named Fu] implemented "contractual responsibility," calling a meeting of the entire prison, including members of the police and prisoners, and encouraged them to improve production according to a rationalization proposal. All were included—members of the police could receive awards, and prisoners could have their sentences reduced.

In the cotton-goods workshop of the prison, a long-term prisoner named Shi Cheng sentenced to twelve years, suggested that they use the influence that he had [before he was arrested] to obtain steel materials and several thousand yuan in capital to set up production equipment to produce nails. Because of the lack of goods in the market, it is claimed that this prison makes 100,000 yuan a year. Effective use

---

[19]*Law and Order*, April 1988, p. 28.

was made of Shi Cheng's suggestion. Fu took Shi out of the prison to Ma-an-shan City [Anhui province] to make connections for the steel materials. Commissioner Fu, with the approval of the party commission for the prison, established the "Yangtze River Trade Co." He made himself manager and Shi assistant manager and purchasing agent. Fu called this "using laborers for cadres." [This expression is Fu's invention; the party has the policy, "using workers for cadres," which is to say, using people with worker status to do the work of national cadres.] Further, the company seal and work ID were handed over to Shi by Fu. Shi, who operated as someone with cadre status, controlled 220,000 yuan in funds.

On Nov. 22, 1984, Manager Fu and Asst. Manager Shi went to Ma-an-shan City and signed a contract worth 1,240,000 yuan with a businessman named Li, to whom Shi offered a bribe. Then, using introductions given by Li, Fu and Shi went to Shanghai, where they were given foreign currency [U.S. dollars] by a Hong Kong businessman. They agreed to exchange at a rate of 1:4.60 for US$2 million. This included a 0.1 yuan processing fee for every dollar. They also gave the Hong Kong businessman 6,000 yuan and HK$3,000 for him to go to Tientsin City to take care of business matters. At the same time, Fu sent Shi to Guangzhou City to determine the black-market quotation for the U.S. dollar. Shi claimed that it was 5.40 yuan for one U.S. dollar. They then purchased as much as 1,400,000 yuan. Fu supplied Shi with money for his expenses and for staying at a luxury hotel. Fu also promised that, if the business went smoothly, Shi could receive a reward of five thousand yuan and a six-year reduction in sentence. At that time Fu planned, by these means, to make the Chang-Chen Prison the nation's most progressive model of a *lao-gai-qiyi*. While in Guangzhou City, Shi drew on what was then 50,000 yuan to eat, drink, and enjoy himself with women. Later, the prison dispatched a policeman named Hu to Guangzhou City to check up on Shi. Shi gave Hu 1,645 yuan and HK$400 for traveling expenses. Shi suggested to Hu that, as he, Shi, was going to Tientsin City to deal with some two million U.S. dollars and would thus be carrying a huge amount of cash, as well as a train or boat tickets, Hu lend him his police uniform and pistol in order to make it easier for him to stay in a hotel. Hu agreed. [Shi took a picture of himself in the police uniform in Guangzhou City.] And so the prisoner became a policeman, wearing a police uniform and carrying a pistol, and went to Tientsin City and Beijing. At that time, a party decision made it illegal to purchase foreign currency, which ruined Shi's plan. Shi was brought back to the prison by police dispatched by the prison. The entire process had taken four months, during which time 30,000 yuan were spent. Twelve years were added to Shi's sentence, and policeman Hu was disciplined. Commissioner Fu wrote a will and then committed suicide, shooting himself in the head.[20]

From the above, we observe that in its core function, the contractual-responsibility system tried to achieve two goals: maximum reform through labor and maximum production. The system operates in different ways.

The amount of profit earned by an LRC determines the wages and welfare benefits received by its prisoners, as well as rewards such as good treatment when they serve in *lao-gai* and *lao-jiao*. The LRCs make use of both positive and negative means to increase the intensity and duration of prisoners' labor. They give financial rewards, reduce sentences, and provide other incentives. The LRC can also increase sentences, use torture, and deny prisoners certain rights. All of this creates greater tension in the labor–reform camps.

How should we judge reform of prisoners and production in the *lao-gai-dui*? *Reform* is an ambiguous term that is difficult to evaluate. As long as prisoners do not escape, cause trouble, or riot, it is very difficult to evaluate a given labor-reform camp's ability to reform its prisoners. But production output, value, quality, waste, and so forth are all "hard" criteria. Not only do these measures demonstrate the achievements of the group, team, battalion, and detachment, they also affect the purse of every public-security cadre. The party is aware of the danger that cadres can become corrupt as LRCs earn more money.

As in other enterprises, labor-reform camps face the "open door" problems of finding raw materials, obtaining markets for consumer goods, and deciding what type of products to produce. This is particularly evident in some labor-reform agricultural units that are becoming more complex in their management in order to earn income from sources other than agriculture. Public-security cadres are not skilled in management; nor are they skilled in the techniques of production. Moreover, the central producers of labor-reform enterprises are the targets of the system: they are the people who have been stripped of their freedom. The Public Security Ministry of the Judiciary stipulates that "outside prisoners" (labor-reform and re-education-through-labor prisoners, who, because of particular production needs, live outside the camps) should make up 5 percent of all prisoners. But in some camps, particularly agricultural ones, this number reaches 10 percent, and even 20 percent. Having so many prisoners of these types increases the

---

[20]*Democracy and the Legal System* (Beijing), Sept. 1987, p. 24.

costs of monitoring them and separating their activities from those of the other prisoners.

Labor-reform camps often append other regulations to those handed down by the Public Security Ministry in their attempts at reforming prisoners. For example, if there are escapes or serious offenses committed in a particular group, rewards will be taken away from the entire group or they will not be allowed to see relatives for half a year, or the group will be given a demerit. If a particular group has no problem with reform and meets its production responsibilities, then the group leader may be given a merit (a reduction of sentence), or the whole group may be given rewards. This kind of "linked production," or "linked implication," raises serious ethical questions, and the number of people murdered in labor-reform camps has greatly increased. Duty prisoners (like capos in the Nazi camps) who perform monitoring in the camps help group leaders and public-security cadres. Yet they cheat their superiors and deceive their inferiors, confuse right and wrong, encourage unfair activities, and use influence and force to serve their own interests. Their role has become even more important under the new contractual responsibility system.

Over the past several years, the Ministry of Public Security and the Judiciary have increased their demands for a complete set of labor-reform regulations. These entities have even suggested that the system of labor-reform camps be separate from the Public Security Ministry and the Judiciary and be placed under the jurisdiction of the independent national labor-reform ministry directly supervised by the National People's Congress. The national labor-reform ministry has even proposed that it be given the power to decide on reduced sentences and vacations for prisoners (they are currently decided by the local people's courts), as well as the power to re-examine prisoners' cases on appeal (currently decided by the legal courts). Indeed, the system of labor-reform camps is likely to undergo even further change.

Part Two
Developmental Aspects of the ROC

A Historical Perspective on
Economic Modernization
in the ROC

In the second half of the twentieth century, a major, epoch-making event took place. More and more societies demanded a modern way of life, particularly among the less-developed countries (LDCs), which contained the overwhelming majority of the world's population. This demand for modernization has economic as well as political dimensions. In the case of the LDCs, both dimensions can be traced to their desire to change from "traditionalism," characterized by a largely rural society and culture, to a more commercial and industrially advanced society, as in the advanced countries (DCs). This desire for change is referred to as the demand for modernization. If we consider only the Western countries as modernized, what is distinctive about their modern way of life is the persistent search for new science and technology and their application to production and distribution. Their successful adoption of knowledge to organize economic activity is typical of what Simon Kuznets described as a new epoch of modern growth (EMG), which began in the late eighteenth century because of new advances in science and technology.[1]

Demand for modernization in China can be traced directly to Western influences after the Opium War in the mid-nineteenth century. Their technological superiority enabled various Western countries to expand trade and investment in China and to insist on treaties giving them special privileges in that huge empire. China's leaders responded to these threats by launching a "technological" self-strengthening movement in the second half of the nineteenth century. That movement later evolved into a demand for a "total Westernization" of the country after the May Fourth Movement in 1919. Despite these new demands, the Chinese mainland experienced only a partial modernization in some of its coastal provinces. Meanwhile, some Chinese territories became colonized by foreign powers, such as Taiwan by Japan.

The post–World War II years were a period of transitional growth for LDCs toward achieving "modernization." In the case of the ROC after 1949, Chinese political culture assumed new forms as economic modernization rapidly took place. By 1990, Taiwan's people have almost fulfilled their long-cherished demand for modernization in the political and economic senses, and that small state is ready to join the camp of industrially advanced states by the end of this century.

The ROC's transitional growth differs from that of the PRC. The ROC opted for a pragmatic, evolutionary approach rather than for the politicized, revolutionary one chosen by the PRC, and retained many traditional cultural values instead of destroying them as did the PRC. The ROC became a "laboratory" in which the compatibility of traditional values with the requirements of modernization were tested. The findings of this experiment have been quite conclusive: traditional Chinese cultural values made a positive contribution to modernization, rather than obstructing that process. How did that happen?

The Origin of the Modern Way of Life

Modernization, as initiated by the Industrial Revolution in England, brought about a sustained increase in consumption levels; the production structure changed; and humans lived longer. Even more important was the continuous exploration of the unlimited potential of science and technology, which have

---

[1]Simon Kuznets, *Modern Economic Growth: Rate, Structure, and Spread* (New Haven, Conn.: Yale University Press, 1966).

provided an opportunity for a vast majority of mankind to control their own destiny in a rapidly changing world.

Western societies and those in East Asia strongly influenced by Confucianism have highly valued the exploration of the human potential and therefore find the modern way of life irresistible. For this reason, once started in England, modernization in economic growth rapidly spread to the rest of the world by means of trade, investments, and other forms of human exchange. The characteristics of that process were well documented by Kuznets.

By 1950, approximately one-quarter of mankind had entered modern economic growth. In this historical process, the postwar transitional growth of the LDCs reflects the spread of modern economic growth. The ROC was most successful in this transitional-growth process, especially after it had entered the "technological," intensive phase of development in 1980.

Industrial capitalism was the new social, political, and economic system that spread through Western Europe when the modern epoch began. Industrial capitalism possessed "peculiar" organizational features necessary to facilitate modern economic growth. Industrial capitalism explored the frontiers of science and technology; evolved a high capability to save, which nurtured the accumulation of new industrial capital; met the demand for new management from firms acquiring technological complexity and large scale of production; and satisfied the demand for risk-taking and entrepreneurship that would develop new technology to meet society's demands.

The Politicized "Mixed Economy" of Taiwan in 1950

Just as England experienced a gradual process in which state controls over markets were dismantled, so too did some LDCs, like Taiwan after World War II, experience a similar trend of liberalization in their economies. The vast majority of the contemporary LDCs, including Taiwan, at first opted for a mixed economy. While accepting the principles of "private property and markets," the LDCs still tolerated pervasive market interference. Although lacking a cultural tradition of constitutional democracy, these countries preferred political regulation of the economic system because of their acute sense of backwardness and their colonial heritage. Even though colonialism, in which "primary products" were exchanged for "factory-produced products" by colonies with their rulers, represented the spread of modern economic growth, the LDCs feared what free trade might do to their economies in the years of postwar reconstruction.

In 1950 Taiwan was a Confucian society. The political culture of Confucianism can be called cultural nationalism. It has an "internal" dimension related to government and social relations and an "external" dimension related to "international relations." The traditional Chinese "polity" was considered an extension of the "natural" kinship relationship. Strictly speaking, the Western definition of a "society" (understood to be made up of "strangers") is very different from a society in which the relationship between the government and the people it governs is one of political paternalism. The "political fathers" in the government had the moral obligation to take care of their "citizen sons"; these "sons" have no "human right" to make demands on the "father."

The daily contacts between human beings in this political family are conducted in hierarchies and ceremonies codified as *li*, according to Confucian tradition. Such political paternalism assumes that government power is "uninhibited" but responsible for the "moral discipline" of all the people. Such political paternalism also empowers the political system to behave as a moralizing polity. Indeed, the Chinese government behaved like the Western organized church in enforcing the observation of moral principles in the regulation of human behavior.

It was the widely shared political culture and social-behavior code of the Chinese that made them so different from the non-Chinese. For the Chinese, "all men are brothers" and belong to the same "universal empire" when and only when they adhere to Chinese kinship–oriented behavior codes.

One can reasonably argue that the Chinese political culture has been a major stumbling block for the modernization of political and economic institutions. Without the principles of "human rights" and recognition of a constitution (*i.e.*, contractual consent), there cannot be checks on state power and support for constitutional democracy. Prof. Yu Ying-shih also expressed the view that Chinese kinship–related values could not serve as the basis for modernizing the political system of China along the lines of constitutional democracy.[2]

Political paternalism contributes to political patronage. Such patronage influences economic policies to promote the profits of all firms and the welfare of all families. This form of political behavior involves the government in the marketplace and prevents the modernization of the economic system. In the case of Taiwan, its economic system in the postwar period only modernized as the process of depoliticization of the economic system took place.

---

[2]Yu Ying-shih, "The Modern Significance of Chinese Culture from the Viewpoint of Value System," *Time Press* (Taipei), March 1984, p. 96.

Yet depoliticizing the economic system proved difficult, because after World War II economic doctrine and theory strongly argued in favor of state intervention in the economic system. A major reason for this new belief was the awareness of leaders in many countries of their "colonial backwardness."

Therefore, the LDCs' officials and economists argued for using political force to promote growth. Even in the ROC, there was support for "economic construction" through government control of public enterprises and for equalization of private land ownership based on a widely shared nationalistic sentiment against colonialism. This sentiment was at the heart of the "Three Principles of the People" that provided the ideological guidance for the ruling Kuomintang party. Minister K. T. Li, a major policymaker, recently alluded to the shift in government policy away from large-scale intervention to selective policies to make the market work better as a reason for Taiwan's successful transitional growth:

> The thirty years 1950–1980 were a process of transition growth, the termination of colonialism and the initiation of the epoch of modern economic growth . . . By nearly all accounts, the development experience of Taiwan has been highly successful . . . The art of economic policy making [in this period] involves the use of a variety of market-related policy instruments [for example, foreign-exchange rate, interest rate, monetary expansion rate]. The exercise of these concrete policy instruments is predicated on the assumption [of the acceptance] . . . of the market mechanism.[3]

The Operation of the Mixed Economy (1950–1962)

In the 1950s, Taiwan's economy, like that of so many LDCs, still exported primary products and imported manufactured goods. Anticolonialist sentiments encouraged Taiwan and other LDCs to adopt a strategy of import substitution (I-S) that required state efforts to develop the domestic I-S industries.

Yet Taiwan did not behave like the vast majority of other contemporary LDCs. Its I-S strategy lasted for only a short period of some twelve years and then was abandoned in 1962 in favor of a strategy to promote trade-oriented growth. This new phase lasted for some eighteen years, until it was replaced by a strategy emphasizing technology transfer and diffusion as the

---

[3]K. T. Li, *The Evolution of Policy Behind Taiwan's Development Success* (New Haven, Conn.: Yale University Press, 1988), p. 101.

main source of growth. The cardinal, guiding principle for this evolutionary process was liberalization, or a process of depoliticizing the economic system.

The I–S strategy worked as follows. The government used many macropolicies and foreign exchange–rate control.[4] These macropolicies did not focus on managing aggregate demand to stabilize economic growth. Instead, the "management of expenditures" by the government was oriented toward supply of production. The "uninhibited" power of the government in Taiwan in this early phase involved the central bank's regulation of a multiple–exchange-rate system and allocation of investment funds to commercial banks and other agents.

In the advanced countries, aggregate-demand management in the Keynesian manner was based on the belief that the monetary authority can "manufacture profits" for private industries by lowering their investment costs if more money can be created. This monetary philosophy of Anglo-Saxon monetary managers was adopted by the less-experienced LDCs. Indeed, a cardinal principle that underlay the growth strategy of the LDCs was using political power to help make money. This philosophy amounts to a strategy of "covert income transfer" from politically weak groups, like farmers and urban consumers, to benefit urban entrepreneurial groups whose support is crucial for the government. This "covert" income transfer takes place because of the "ignorance" of so many, as well as the technical complexity of the state's carrying out of such transfers. At the same time, a political culture of paternalism, sloganized as "United we stand" or "Out of many arises one," contributed to widespread ignorance of what was taking place.

This covert income-transfer strategy was implemented by all of the policies being used. A high protective tariff wall or a "tax holiday" benefits certain "favored industries" at the expense of consumers and/or "nonfavored industries." Yet this transfer mechanism is far from easy to detect, even for professional economists, for all growth-promoting policies involve the use of money. An overvalued exchange rate (a common import-substitution strategy) allowed for export of primary products while making it possible for urban entrepreneurs to import machinery and raw materials for their "infant" industries. Average citizens, especially the "exporting farmers," never understood how severely they suffered price discrimination and exploitation.

Quantitatively speaking, the most important mechanism for income transfers in the LDCs related to the operation of monetary and interest policies. The government was all-powerful, because there were no checks

---

[4]Ibid., p. 153.

on central-bank policies. Few sovereign governments can resist the temptation to indulge in the benefits of "taxation without consent" by printing money. Thus, money is printed to allow the entrepreneurs to acquire goods and services from the market at artificially low interest cost, with their repayment burden further lightened by price inflation. Pre–World War II loanable-funds theorists derogatorily referred to this mechanism as an "act of burglary" or as "legal counterfeiting." The average citizen of an LDC hardly knew what was happening. Such prewar wisdom was rendered obsolete by the Keynesian revolution, so that an expansionary monetary policy enjoyed an unprecedented popularity even among professional economists in the advanced countries.

Commenting on the transferability of the policy experience of the ROC to the other countries, Minister K. T. Li offered this advice:

> What can contemporary LDCs learn from Taiwan's unquestioned economic success? More specifically, given this book's emphasis, what can other countries learn from Taiwan's policy experience? There are obviously some experiences that are transferable and some that are not. What is transferable is the determination to *control inflation by adopting high interest rates to absorb savings and the policy of growth with stability*, maintaining realistic exchange rates; establishment of export processing zones, promoting automation and technology as the labor surplus disappears . . . [5] (emphasis added)

Taiwan eventually renounced use of the covert income-transfer mechanism of money printing, and that major lesson has great value for contemporary LDCs.

The covert income-transfer mechanism suggests that the import-substitution strategy is inappropriate for a modern economy. Such a strategy was insensitive to distributional justice and violated a key moral principle of the modern market economy: namely, distributional fairness must be accompanied by equalization of opportunity for all. Taiwan's leaders adhered to this moral principle as a key guideline for depoliticizing the economic system.

The import-substitution strategy was also consistent with a political culture of internally oriented nationalism; such a strategy called for excluding foreign products, investment, and nationals from the domestic market. The government used political force to achieve economic as well as political independence after decolonization.

From the economic standpoint, market closure really means avoiding international competition. What lies behind the "pride" in a national flag (or

---

[5]Ibid., p. 148.

the chimney of a national enterprise) is that the "weak" fear the "strong." This mixture of "insecurity" and "inferiority" directly violates the principles of independence, free choice, and self-reliance so essential for a healthy market economy.

Opening the domestic market of Taiwan to international competition was a major evolutionary change after 1980. Yet nearly two decades of "external orientation" had to pass before producers on Taiwan gained enough confidence to compete in foreign markets. Such confidence required jettisoning a fear of international competition before the domestic market could be opened to foreigners.

Modernizing the ROC's Economic System (1962–Present)

As the transitional growth process unfolded, facilitated by a politicized economic strategy, Taiwan's political-economic system became more open in the 1960s. The state's arbitrary use of political force declined as the market system became more internationalized and influenced by technological change. Some called these developments the "liberalization movement," a clear indication that economic and social changes had brought about a "new" culture of political economy.

Taiwan had inherited a colonial economic structure based on exporting primary products and importing manufactured consumer goods. That economy's factor endowment had been characterized by a comparative advantage of natural resources and deficiency of capital, technology, and entrepreneurship, and a skilled, educated, disciplined, labor force suited to a modern "factory" way of life.

The import-substitution strategy used by the ROC government was supposed to divert foreign-exchange earnings from primary-product exports to use for importing producer goods (machinery and raw materials) to build industries like textiles that would supply a domestic market from which these same foreign goods were excluded. Because the earners of foreign exchange produced primary products, this strategy worked well as long as there was an abundant supply of natural resources to sustain expansion of the production of primary products. An abundance of natural resources was an incentive for a poor country not to develop its human resources.

Taiwan did not have such abundant natural resources, and yet it was still a labor-surplus economy. Taiwan was compelled to find employment for this labor and to find something to substitute for its scarce resource, land. A solution was found in the export of labor-intensive manufactured products (*e.g.*, textiles) to the markets of the industrially advanced countries. Expanding foreign trade put more people to work and generated more foreign exchange. As more production became trade-oriented, businessmen and workers improved their skills and productivity and lowered costs. Rising employment was associated with more capital accumulation, and the capital-labor ratio rose. Individuals acquired more assets, and income distribution became more equal until the 1980s, when it began to become unequal again.

Partial Liberalization in the Externally Oriented Phase (1962–1980)

The atrophy of Taiwan's political forces in the economy came about in stages. First, there was partial liberalization, with some protectionist policies being maintained in the domestic market; meanwhile, Taiwan's producers were free to enter the world market. This partial liberalization was popularly described as "fostering external sale by internal selling."

One step to liberalization of the external market was to create export-processing zones and introduce a tariff-rebate system. The latter was designed to return import duties on imported producer goods to exporters using those products to produce export goods. In addition, the overvalued foreign-exchange rate was abandoned. Many Chinese producers had been deprived of political patronage and were forced to become self-reliant in order to compete in the international market. The spectacular growth of the economy in the 1960s can be traced almost entirely to these reforms intended to depoliticize the economy.

In sharp contrast with this "external liberalization," the domestic market was still highly protected by high tariff walls and restrictions on foreign investment. These governmental regulations were justified by the slogan "fostering exports by internal sale," yet these politically favored industries, such as those producing passenger cars and tape recorders, received windfall profits. Meanwhile, consumers were victimized. Consumers were unaware of being exploited. The various enterprises protected by governmental patronage owed much to the culture of political paternalism. For example, the import duties on imported passenger cars are still no less than 40 percent of their sale price even today.

By the 1980s, pressures had built up in Taiwan for the acceleration of "liberalization" and "internationalization." Many groups wanted more competitiveness in the domestic market, such as the privatization of commercial banks in order to break the governmental monopoly of loanable funds. Competitiveness in the domestic market can be further strengthened by opening it to international competition. It is expected that this opening will be achieved by lowering the protective tariff wall and by eliminating the barrier to international investment.

The integration of Taiwan's economy with that of the rest of the world is expected to be reinforced by ongoing innovations in international monetary management. The new freedom to import gold and to hold foreign currencies will most likely become more and more privatized. The ROC's central bank is also beginning to learn to manage the foreign-exchange rate like other mature members of the international community. That action means that political force should not be used by the central bank to benefit exporters by means of an artificially undervalued Taiwanese currency and to accumulate excess foreign-exchange reserves.

Demands for "liberalization" and "internationalization" originated from the very successful trade-oriented development of the economy in the 1960s and 1970s. As a consequence, the export surplus increased, as did the stockpile of foreign-exchange reserves. These new trends gradually moved Taiwan's major trading partners, such as the United States, to demand that Taiwan reduce its export surplus. Just as certain businessmen resisted liberalization in the late 1950s, so too do other businessmen now resist further liberalization that would lower trade barriers and allow more foreign investment in service industries. Such resistance will gradually crumble as banks become privatized, barriers to trade and investment collapse, and the foreign-exchange rate is allowed to float according to market forces.

Modernization of the ROC's Political System

A notable political accomplishment of the ROC occurred in the 1970s and mid-1980s with political reforms, such as the ending of martial law, the granting of new freedom to the press, the permitting of street demonstrations, the legalizing of opposition parties, etc. These reforms occurred only between 1986 and 1988, and they have drastically changed the political life of the small republic.

The rapidity of political change should not blind the observer to the fact that much time had to pass before sociocultural change was able to promote greater acceptance of democratic values and ideals. Western democracy had been glorified in China, by such events as the publication of Dr. Sun Yat-sen's *Principle of People's Rights* and the May Fourth Movement in 1919. However, such "empty" "glorification" could not bring about political democracy until state and society had fostered the economic prosperity that paved the way for acceptance of democratic ideals.

Marketization and Democratization of the ROC

Constitutional democracy implies a particular government-society relationship in which the power of the government is "inhibited." Under democracy, governmental public services such as defense, maintenance of law and order, enforcement of contracts, and promotion of growth should be merely responsive to the demands of society conveyed to the government by such means as competing political parties, free elections, and open debate. These arrangements make government accountable. In a pluralistic society, there will be concern about income distribution, justice, mediation of group interests, and achieving compromise before measures of economic policy can be enacted.

The import-substitution strategy of the early postwar years (1950–1962) was obviously the product of an undemocratic, paternalistic political culture. Few in the ROC's society were aware of the consequences of these state policies for various social groups. The very notion of covert income transfers by such economic growth-promoting policies implied that their distributional impact on various social groups did not need to be clarified or compromised. The very definition of "paternalism" also implied a "common family budget," and that meant the "credit" and "liability" of individuals did not ever need to be meticulously accounted for in the first place.

A tax reform or government-guaranteed loans to a financially troubled Chrysler in the United States must be justified by explicit and meticulous accounting of the cost and the benefits to various social groups. The covert income transfers represented "executive privilege" under a paternalistic culture. From the economic standpoint, when the political culture is still paternalistic, the social relations between families are not yet commercialized or characterized by a meticulous accounting of "indebtedness" of individual families in monetary terms. The atrophy of such paternalism, however, is unavoidable if more and more groups enjoy new economic opportunities and out-compete those special interest groups favored by government policies.

The mushrooming of new interest groups like labor, which demanded a New Year's bonus; environmental protectionists, who demanded compensation; and veterans, who demanded subsidies for their visit to the mainland, brought these groups into the streets seeking government help. These actions show the bankruptcy of political paternalism. These demands for redistributing income can only be blocked if the government decides that a fair distribution of income can be achieved by promoting competition to bring about greater opportunity for all groups. The political culture of the ROC is slowly moving in this "competitive direction." If that trend continues, the strategy of covert income transfer might be entirely abandoned.

In the past 40 years, political modernization and economic modernization have been complementary. While these two modernizations definitely have a Western origin, they also have been nurtured by the Confucianism of traditional China.

I have argued that traditional Chinese values such as Confucianism played an important role in facilitating Taiwan's modern economic growth.

> The economists have identified two causal factors behind this economic miracle, namely the openness in orientation and the depoliticization of their economic system . . . I would like to argue that their roots reside deep in traditional Chinese cultural values . . . While the arguments of Professor Kuznets were based on historical evidences from the West, I will argue that the "internally oriented" traditional values have always satisfied the criteria of nationalism, secularism and egalitarianism. . . . [6]

That the East and the West share some basic cultural values is hardly a surprise. The discovery and the exploration of the "inner human potential" was important for the secularization of Western culture after 1350. Yet, in fact, the exploration of the unlimited human potential through self-cultivation involving interactions among learning, practice, and introspective self-examination is also one of the basic cultural values of Confucianism.

It is well known that freedom and independence may be interpreted as the key values consistent with the exploration of creative human potential in the West. When traditional Chinese cultural values were threatened and then suppressed by the brutality of political forces in the socialist PRC (1949–1978), some argued that "spiritual independence and freedom of thought" were identified as the highest cultural values of traditional Chinese. These gave spiritual strength and moral support to the silent protests of the Chinese intellectuals on the mainland when they wrote and spoke in their sarcastic, humorous, and poetic ways.[7] Moreover, scholars like Yu Ying-shih believe

---

[6]John C.H. Fei, "Economic Development and Traditional Chinese Cultural Values," *Journal of Chinese Studies,* vol. 3, no. 1(April 1986):111.
[7]Yu Ying-shih, "The Modern Significance of Chinese Culture from the Viewpoint of Value System," *Time Press* (Taipei), March 1984.

"traditional Chinese cultural values are suitable for modern life with only slight modifications."[8]

Chinese political culture has always been described as incompatible with democracy for two reasons. First, political paternalism seemed utterly incompatible with human rights when "despotic governments of the Orient" exercised "uninhibited" power. Second, an element of that culture was a feudal inequality of social status implied by the Confucian emphasis on relationships such as father-son, emperor-subordinate, husband-wife, and older-younger, in which the former member dominated the latter. There was no principle of equality as in the West. Yet such interpretations are unwarranted.

A modern version of the *li* means that values are internalized which effectively regulate the behavior of human interaction to ensure social order, and that these values, together with music, bring about social harmony. Non-Chinese may be surprised to learn that laws and music are naturally combined in the Confucian tradition to describe an idealized country. That tradition's inequality of status is only a moral discipline that carries an orientation of obligation to other human beings. This obligation is quite compatible with the spirit of democracy that also presumes a moral discipline of an "obligation orientation," such as tolerance of debate, amenability to persuasion, or propensity to compromise. In view of the overwhelming importance attached to the "cultivation of oneself," as noted above, the orientation of obligation to others may be viewed merely as a by-product of "self-cultivation."

Denying citizens the right to make demands on the government can be interpreted as upholding the principle of self-reliance. This is just as important for Hong Kong as it is for the United States, which faces an unbalanced budget due to its huge welfare expenditures. Similarly, the "political patronage of welfare statism" that plagued the PRC as well as the Western democracies in the early postwar years (1950–1978) should be rejected. In the case of traditional China, an economic policy consistent with the high principle of self-reliance was the fostering of the political culture of laissez-faire in the Confucian tradition.[9]

It is relatively easy for a democratic polity to operate smoothly or reach compromise between conflicting interests if the citizens do not make excessive demands on their government. Traditional Chinese political culture prepared the Chinese for modern democracy, if we understand Chinese paternalism to mean a moralizing policy (but only a moralizing one) in

---

[8]Ibid.
[9]Chou Ching-hseng, *Chinese Economic History* (1959), vol. 2, p. 192.

which the "citizen-sons," instead of being spoiled, were always taught to be independent and to take care of themselves when raised to adulthood by the "political father." Taiwan's modernization experience shows that democracy and markets are perfectly compatible for the Chinese who have a personality governed by traditional, that is, Confucian cultural values.

References Not Cited in the Text

John C.H. Fei, "Sino-American Economic Relations from an Evolutionary Perspective of Taiwan's Economic Institutions," *U.S. Congressional Club Reprint Series No. 1*, vol. 133, no. 137(Sept. 11, 1987) (Washington, D.C.)

John Fei and G. Ranis, *Development of the Labor Surplus Economy* (Homewood, Ill.: Irwin Press, 1964).

Political Modernization in the ROC

The Kuomintang and the Inhibited Political Center

Contrary to long-standing claims, the Kuomintang has never been a Leninist-type party. Although similar in party design to its archrival, the Chinese Communist Party, the Kuomintang never has functioned as a Leninist-type party. The Kuomintang has never espoused a party "line" or practiced "democratic centralism." It has never held a monopoly of power that enabled it to dominate society and eliminate all groups critical of its authority. The major differences between the two parties since 1949 have to do with their ideology, control over party membership, party recruitment, and party functions.

Kuomintang Ideology

In terms of ideology, a typical Leninist party usually takes its ideology much more seriously than does the Kuomintang. The purity of Marxism-Leninism is usually jealously maintained, particularly in the early phase of Leninist state rule. The top leadership alone determines how ideology will be interpreted and imposed on both party and society. The party will purge its ranks in the name of ideological orthodoxy. The Kuomintang, however, has always adhered to the Sunist ideology of the Three Principles of the People. The Sunist ideology is flexible, tolerant, and pragmatic: party leaders have never demanded an orthodoxy. The ideas of Dr. Sun Yat-sen were eclectic and served as guiding principles for a modernizing nation. There was no ideological basis for establishing a closed system of beliefs and values. To the party's credit, it never made the mistake of making Sunist ideas into a secular religion and thus avoided the mistakes of slavishly following outdated ideas. Even today, the Kuomintang can embrace all kinds of people, such as industrialists and workers, farmers and businessmen, idealists with high principles, and different politicians who might only pursue power and profit, simply because it eschews a rigid ideological straitjacket.

The Kuomintang Party Membership

A Leninist party attaches great importance to party discipline. To maintain discipline, it usually carries out periodic purges to eliminate those members who fail to live up to the standards set by the leadership, who disobey the orders of their superiors, or who deviate from the party "line." The Kuomintang, however, has never required its members to observe any rigid disciplinary code. It has never purged any members for disciplinary reasons. The Kuomintang rarely expels a member for criticizing the party or refusing to support a party candidate in elections.

Nor has the party leadership practiced "democratic centralism," in which the top, core leaders freely discuss policy and after agreement is reached, impose those decisions on the members who must all obey.

A Leninist party claims to represent a particular class or group of classes and takes a strong stand against the enemy of that class or group of classes. Fearful of class opposition, a Leninist party suspects that any group or association will mount opposition to its rule and foment class struggle against it. The Kuomintang has always claimed that it represents all Chinese people. It has always wanted to recruit people of diverse backgrounds as members. Its very catholicity has made it tolerant of different viewpoints.

The Role of the Kuomintang

The self-set purpose of a Leninist party is to achieve a proletarian revolution. Even though such a purpose need not account for all of the party's real activities, adhering to the pursuit of that purpose is bound to influence party behavior. For example, to achieve a successful proletarian revolution, the party must impose its dictatorship on society in order to suppress all class enemies. In the Leninist state, ideology justifies the party's having a monopoly of power. The Leninist party only resorts to the tactics of bourgeois democracy to preserve its monopoly of power. The Kuomintang leaders shared the ideals of Dr. Sun Yat-sen, which included a sincere commitment to establish a democratic form of government. The Kuomintang leaders believed that a strong party-state relationship was merely temporary and justified for reasons of national security because the nation-state was threatened by the communist regime on the mainland. The Kuomintang intended to be the only party to rule, but that state of affairs was to be only temporary and to be ended when conditions so dictated; then the party-state relationship would change. Unlike a Leninist party, which is bent on preserving its monopoly of power, the Kuomintang stands ready to share power with other parties.

The Nature of the Inhibited Center

During the 1950s, the Kuomintang leaders and members used party organizations to work through patron-client networks in society in order to penetrate the entire social fabric to obtain compliance with party-state policies. The docile and politically apathetic Taiwanese, still reeling from the shock of the suppression of the 1947 Uprising and the reforms that followed, remained unorganized and very susceptible to these party-state policies. The party leaders and top-echelon cadres carefully inspected their rank and file in 1950–1951 and relegated the officials identified as inept and corrupt to lower-level tasks or made them leave the party. By 1953, the party membership, much reduced in number, had become more dedicated and eager to serve. The top officials and military officials had sworn loyalty to Chiang Kai-shek. Moreover, they made up an experienced, efficient group of officials with considerable experience on the mainland. They were eager that the party should not fail a second time.

The party exerted control over society by two separate, interdependent systems: a territorial party organization existed to parallel the state administration; the other was an organization of various functional groups for educated youth, public-media workers, the civil service, transport personnel, merchant seamen, the military, etc. Finally, the party also established auxiliary organizations, such as the youth corps for high-school and college students, a women's association, the farmers' association, unions for workers, and a commissar system in the military. Through these networks and organs the party managed to have a presence in every community, whether urban or rural.

In the 1950s and 1960s, Taiwanese politicians still played virtually no role in the political process. The few Taiwanese who reached high positions had either served on the mainland in the party for many years before returning to Taiwan after the war with Japan had ended, or they were respected community leaders without political ambitions, merely willing to accept ceremonial posts.[1]

However, ever since 1949, regular elections of local officials have been held. In the 1950s and 1960s, Taiwanese politicians won minor posts through this channel, but unless they were co-opted by the national leadership, they never became high-ranking officials at the national or provincial levels. This sharp separation between the holding of local and national offices facilitated the maintenance of a homogeneous official, political culture until the early 1970s. Both party and government leaders were outwardly committed to the goal of making Taiwan a model province that would serve as the base for "the recovery of the mainland." These leaders constantly adhered to the Three Principles of the People as the guidelines for national construction. These principles endorsed economic reform that would pave the way for a more equitable distribution of income, while allowing the establishment of a flourishing free-market economy.

In these same decades the party selected and screened its cadres to fill the important posts in national government and local administration, schools, civic associations, etc. The party coordinated the implementing of state policies and the resolving of disputes between various branches of the government, such as those at the county level, and between the Provincial Assembly and the county executive offices, and settled disputes that arose during election campaigns. Supervising election campaigns has usually required little time and energy of party functionaries, and national party leaders and cadres were spared these monitoring activities.

In this way, the Kuomintang built a powerful, robust political center with firm but elastic connections to Taiwan society. In Taiwanese civil society the autonomous, self-propelled adult and his or her family have remained free to pursue their interests. Individuals could freely join together in groups or associations to achieve their goals, but they could not use these organizations to severely attack or threaten the Kuomintang, the state, and the political center itself. Yet this political center remained sensitive to the political sensibilities in civil society and always was inhibited to some extent in the use of its full power.

---

[1]Prior to 1972, only three Taiwanese had served as cabinet members. For an account of the discontent and frustration of the Taiwanese elite, see Li Hsiao-feng, *T'ai-wan chan-hou ch'u-ch'i ti min-i tai-piao* (The representatives of the people of Taiwan during the early years following World War II) (Taipei, 1968).

The Transformation of the Kuomintang

In the 1970s and 1980s, the party was still dominant in the ROC, but its position and role began to change. First, the Kuomintang was challenged by a small, yet vigorous, expanding opposition group that eventually formed the Democratic Progressive Party (DPP). Further, it increasingly had to deal with a variety of civil associations not under its control and which eventually resolutely refused to accept any orders from the party. In addition, the party began to be made up in large part of younger members, so that the Kuomintang became more diverse in ideas as well.

In the early 1970s, a group of politicians began to refer to themselves as "outside the Kuomintang" (*tang-wai*) and became the first effective opposition movement in the political history of the ROC. In numerous national and local elections, the *tang-wai* politicians began to win consistently more than 20 percent of the election votes. This performance showed that the *tang-wai* were not just a transitory phenomenon, and that these politicians could become a serious opposition force if allowed to form a party. Even though these politicians established a genuine political party in 1986 and became a legal party in 1989, these politicians were still regarded as a de facto party by the voters in the early 1970s. Despite the fact that in the Legislative Yuan the *tang-wai* had only about 4 percent of the seats, they posed a serious, vigorous challenge to the government by conducting interpellations of officials and examining the state budget.

In addition, since the mid-1970s, various social protest movements have erupted, and many "autonomous" associations have emerged. These movements staged street demonstrations and public rallies and gathered enormous numbers of names on petitions to pressure the government agencies on various issues such as environmental pollution and advancing the material interests of workers, farmers, veterans, students, women, aborigines, etc. The activities of these groups have not only severely tested the mediation skills of the Social Affairs Department of the party's Secretariat, but also weakened the unity of the party-controlled civic associations.

In the past two decades, the Kuomintang has been undergoing significant internal change. Two developments account for this. First, conducting elections campaigns in an evolving pluralistic society has made election monitoring the principal occupation of the party. This new trend has also obligated the party to seek favors from local factions in the counties and cities. Unlike the veteran leaders of the Kuomintang, the politicians affiliated with local factions are not concerned with ideals or ideas; they see politics as a means to promote their careers and the economic interests of their kin or factions.[2]

In the 1950s and 1960s, national politics was insulated from local politics. Decisionmaking by the national government concerning major issues rarely involved corruption and scandal. A high moral stance could be maintained by officials in their pursuit of national goals. In the 1970s and 1980s, though, the politicians affiliated with local factions became more influential at the national level, largely because of the more important role the Legislative Yuan came to play when in 1968 and thereafter more seats in it could be won through election. This new development changed the nature of politics in the ROC as well as in the Kuomintang. While ROC politics became less ideological and moralistic and more concerned with people's bread-and-butter issues, the Kuomintang had to take on the new role of power broker.

Another development was the entry of a new generation of young, educated members into the party. Veteran party leaders were gradually being replaced by this new generation. This came about in two ways. First, Chiang Ching-kuo pushed the policy of Taiwanization of the party after becoming premier in 1972. As a result of his new policy, more well-educated Taiwanese began to serve in the government in the early 1970s. Some of these people later became a new core in the top leadership of the post-Chiang era.[3] Second, new people joined the leadership through the election process. This process of succession is a gradual and protracted one. By the mid-1980s, however, with the formation of the party's Central Committee and its Standing Committee for the Thirteenth Party Congress, the leadership succession was almost complete.

Prior to this congress, policy disagreements and disputes between more conservative veteran leaders and the newly recruited leaders had occasionally occurred. But when Chiang Ching-kuo (and before him, in 1975, Chiang Kai-shek) was in charge, these disagreements and disputes rarely were visible outside the party. These two powerful leaders and their supporters maintained a high degree of party unity and cohesiveness, at least at the highest level.

Then Chiang Ching-kuo died on January 13, 1988, and Li Teng-hui succeeded him as president of the ROC in accordance with the Constitution.

---

[2]On the local factions, see Chao Yung-mao, *Ti-fang p'ai-hsi yu ti-fang chien-she ti kuan-hsi* (Local factions and their building) (Kaohsiung, 1980).

[3]On Chiang's policy of recruiting younger Taiwanese into the bureaucracy and its implications, see Peng Huai-en, *Chung-hua min-kuo cheng-chi t'i-hsi ti fen-hsi* (An analysis of the ROC's political system) (Taipei, 1983), pp. 335–61.

But there was considerable controversy about Li's becoming the acting chairman of the party. Some party leaders enlisted the support of Mme. Chiang Kai-shek to block Li's elevation to the top party post. That move failed. Then, at the Thirteenth KMT Congress in July 1988, Li's position became stronger after he was elected chairman because he was able to appoint some of his staunch supporters to the party's Standing Committee. But Li certainly is not as powerful as either of the Chiangs. Until the present, serious disputes in the top leadership still seem to be rare, but the party must make major changes because of the demands of younger members.

These new demands have been expressed by party members in the legislatures and through the public media. They usually focus on two issues. The first concerns the procedure of the election and nomination of party officers and candidates. The second concerns the labeling of the party as "revolutionary-democratic party" or a "democratic party." On the eve of the last party congress, these two issues were heatedly debated between the younger party elite and the conservative party leaders and National Assemblymen. The younger party members demanded not only that delegates to the congress should be elected by the ordinary members, but also that the entire Central Committee should be elected by delegates to the congress, and the Standing Committee should be freely elected by the Central Committee. The conservatives opposed this radical departure from the past practice because it would weaken their authority in the party. A compromise was eventually reached: delegates to the congress were elected by the rank-and-file members in the various party branches. With regard to the selection of the 180-member Central Committee, the party chairman reserved the power to nominate 180 candidates, but an equal number of candidates might enter the contest on their own. (Previously, the chairman had nominated all candidates.) But the chairman would still choose the Standing Committee.

The nomination of candidates for public offices is an even more controversial issue. Many younger party members have repeatedly expressed their dissatisfaction with the traditional rules for nominating candidates. They believe the traditional nominating procedure gives too much power to professional party functionaries and favors the local factions at the expense of the ordinary rank-and-file members. They demanded more "democratic" procedures for the selection of candidates. Recently, the party's Organizational Department made a bold proposal to the top leadership that the United States' primary system should be adopted for nominating candidates for the forthcoming election. Despite the reservations of several prominent party leaders, the Standing Committee approved this proposal with some minor modifications. Observers generally agree that this was a decisive step in the party's rapid democratization.

To outsiders, the controversy concerning the party's description seems purely academic. It is not. This description defines the party's real role, its relationship with society and the government, and its future evolution as a force in the political center. The Kuomintang has been described as a "Leninist" party by Western scholars. During its brief period of collaboration with the Communist Party and Soviet advisers, the party adopted certain features of Bolshevik organization and tactics in its efforts to control society. As demonstrated at the outset of this chapter, the Kuomintang has never behaved as a typical Leninist party.

By adopting the description of "revolutionary-democratic," the Kuomintang alluded to its revolutionary heritage, the selfless devotion the party expected from its members, and the party's great struggle to destroy communism in China. In recent years, many younger members demanded that the first of these adjectives be dropped. They wanted the party to be described as "democratic" because "revolutionary" implied an unwillingness to compete with opposition parties on an equal basis and to promote democracy within the Kuomintang. Before the last party congress, several younger Kuomintang leaders openly declared that the old description should be eliminated from the party's charter. The younger members welcomed that suggestion with enthusiasm, but the conservative old guard insisted on keeping the old description. During the Thirteenth Party Congress, the party leadership clung to the old description but tried to mollify the younger members by arguing that the word *revolutionary* should be understood within a particular historical context: the Kuomintang still was a "revolutionary" party because of its struggle against the Communist Party and had no relationship with other parties and social forces in the ROC. Moreover, they continued, the label had nothing to do with internal party affairs.

The Changing Relationship between Political Center and Society

Taiwanese society in the early 1950s allowed a tight, single party-state relationship and the establishment of an inhibited political center. The Taiwanese had never gained experience in self-rule. Taiwanese society had once consisted of a small stratum of rural-urban gentry and a broad mass of people of different occupations. Among the elite were a few professionals, mainly medical doctors, who enjoyed high social prestige but lacked political sophistication. These people usually participated in local elections. The successful land reform carried out in the early 1950s broadened property rights and expanded opportunity for more people. Most important, that reform made the Kuomintang highly popular in rural areas. Owing to the rapid economic development in the 1950s and 1960s, a new middle class composed of professionals, businessmen, and white-collar employees of industrial and commercial firms made its appearance in Taiwan by the late 1960s. These urban dwellers were young, moderately well-educated and more Westernized in their outlook than the gentry or the mass of the people. They facilitated the diffusion in Taiwan of Western ideas and values to make the island's society pluralistic and one in which the same mixture of tradition and cosmopolitan views was commonly shared.

The Kuomintang remains the dominant political force in this pluralistic society. It continues to maintain its presence in nearly all administrative, socioeconomic, and educational organizations. Most important positions in the ROC government, including those of university presidents, ranking military commanders, and leaders of representative institutions, are still held by Kuomintang members.[4] Yet there are two new developments that have been influencing the old party-state relationship. First, there are the changes in the Legislative Yuan. Before the 1970s, the Legislative Yuan did not play a significant role in the ROC's political system. It merely served as a symbol for national unity. After 1969, however, more legislators were elected to the Legislative Yuan. Their number gradually changed that body's relationship to the Kuomintang, the Executive Yuan, and the society at large, as well as the role the Legislative Yuan played in politics. Unlike the senior legislators, the new legislators must be re-elected periodically in their districts. Therefore, they must respond to the interests and views of their voters, which, in practical terms, often means the interests and views of their local supporters from varying groups in society. The Kuomintang legislators are now subjected to two conflicting pressures: their party and their constituencies, and at times to the pressure exerted by a particular issue of burning importance. Whenever an issue arises that involves a conflict of interests between the Kuomintang and Taiwanese society, such as whether all senior National Assemblymen should be retired immediately or allowed to freely retire, the Taiwan-elected Kuomintang legislators then defy their party. By such defiance these politicians often win the praise of the general public and the

---

[4]The percentages of members of important governmental bodies who also belong to the KMT (as of 1972) are:

National Assembly. 86.54%	Taiwan Provincial Assembly	
Legislative Yuan 93.18%	Taipei City Council 77.47%	
Control Yuan 81.08%	Kaohsiung City Council 76.19%	
County magistrates	Cabinet 100.00%	
(city mayors) 78.94%		

Source: Peng, p. 205.

media. Aware of the unpopularity of its position, the Kuomintang refrains from disciplining these party members.

Until the 1970s, the Legislative Yuan only approved bills submitted by the executive branch without insisting on any major change. In recent years, the Taiwan-elected members of the Legislative Yuan are unwilling to accept this former passive role. All major bills submitted by the Executive Yuan are now closely examined, heatedly debated, and often rejected, or passed only after major amendment. Take the example of the budget. In the 1950s and 1960s, the budget submitted by the executive branch was almost always passed without discussion. The budget session was very brief, and the general public was not aware of what occurred in the budget process. Since the early 1970s, the budget session has become the most exciting legislative session. ROC society now eagerly waits to see how the budget submitted by the executive branch is handled by the legislators. To improve their public image and their chance for re-election, the new legislators usually scrutinize the budget very closely. In a typical budget session, the opposition legislators will harshly criticize the budget. The Taiwan-elected KMT legislators usually defend certain items of the budget while criticizing other appropriations. Only the senior legislators wholeheartedly support the executive branch. In recent years, legislators usually criticize the government budget on two major grounds: first, the government subsidies given to various KMT-owned enterprises, such as the China Broadcasting Corporation, the Central News Agency, etc.; second, the funds for national defense. Some legislators now feel that defense expenditures are too large and must be cut so that more money can be allocated for education, social welfare, and environmental protection. Although these criticisms of the budget have not produced major reallocations of government funds, the debates have attracted societywide attention. For example, in 1988 the defense budget was cut for only the second time since 1949 by the amount of NT$30 million (the first cut came in 1969, but only by a few NT$) from a defense budget of over NT$300 billion. In 1989, a compromise was reached between the Kuomintang and opposition legislators that cut about NT$1 billion from the defense budget.

Kuomintang legislators often ignore their party's instructions or even vote against the party for political reasons. In the legislative elections, the Kuomintang party can give a candidate very little genuine help either financially or by mobilizing voters to elect that candidate. The candidate must rely on the local factions for support and to elicit the support of voters, as well. The party label is useful for a beginner in politics, but for the veteran politicians its usefulness is usually not very great. In the multimember constituency system the ROC adopted from Japan, the personal image of the candidate and his personal connections are of major importance to win an election. Moreover, in a system in which a single party is dominant, voters usually cast their votes according to their evaluation of candidates instead of by party ideology and program. In the past, the Kuomintang headquarters could mobilize several voter groups such as veterans, military dependents, etc., to elect candidates loyal to it. But in recent years these former "iron votes" have not been so reliable, and their number is declining.

Another development influencing the political center's relationship with society is that "autonomous" civic associations are more active and protest movements more frequent. Until the mid-1980s, mass protest movements were rare. Except for the rebellion of February 28, 1947, the Chung-li riot, and the Kaohsiung Incident, no mass movement took place. In 1983, a few street rallies and demonstrations occurred, and a number of times angry citizens surrounded a few polluting factories. That year marked the beginning of mass protest movements in the ROC, for thereafter, protest movements of various kinds increasingly erupted. Political dissidents, students, women, workers, farmers, shareholders, veterans, aborigines, etc. took to the streets to protest against any real or imagined grievances and to demand that the government solve their problems.[5] Along with mass protest movements, various "autonomous" civic associations such as labor unions, farmers' rights associations, and teachers' rights associations have been founded. Some of these associations have ties with the DPP, while others are not affiliated with any political party. All of these groups are competing for members and for social backing from the Kuomintang-sponsored civic associations.

The sporadic outbreaks of hundreds of protest movements have caused serious concern. The conservatives have wanted the government to take stern measures to stop this "anomalous state of affairs," but most of the educated public, while worried, has recognized that these actions are typical of a transition era when a close, single party-state relationship changed to a pluralistic polity. During such a transition, the old rules and norms lose their validity, but new ones have yet to become firmly rooted. More people become aware of their rights, but a civic culture has yet to be solidly nurtured. Most observers believe this transitional phase will pass, and that a new political era of stability will follow.

---

[5]In 1988, over 1,500 street demonstrations of various sizes occurred in the ROC. See the *Tu-li wan-pao* (Independent evening post), March 25, 1989.

Toward a New Political Center:
The "Subordinate" Political Center

In order to speculate about the new political center that will take form in the ROC, we must understand why the Kuomintang opted for an "inhibited" rather than the "uninhibited" political center the Communist Party established on the mainland. I have already mentioned the special features of the Kuomintang, especially its Sunist ideology, which committed the leaders and members to a democratic polity and the eventual rollback of Kuomintang political power in the political center and society. The party's modernization policies, as described in the next chapter on economic development, improved incentives and lowered the transaction costs for businessmen, to give the ROC high, stable economic-growth rates fueled by rising productivity. Rapid economic growth brought enormous urbanization of the island and the rise of a differentiated urban work force with middle-class aspirations.

By the 1970s, Taiwan was already a prosperous, partially industrialized and highly urbanized society. The middle class had gradually become a potent political force, not only in terms of size but in political sophistication and assertiveness. Apart from the middle class, the literate working class also made its presence felt. These groups provided the political opposition with leadership, financial and electoral support, and mass membership. In the early 1980s, many not only enjoyed the fruits of rapid economic development but were observing new ecological crises, severe pollution of air and water, and a widening gap between earnings from wages and assets. All these new issues proved hard to resolve. Many citizens became impatient with the slow pace of the bureaucracy and the lack of adequate response from a hard-pressed political leadership. They decided to exert stronger pressure on the government, and mass demonstrations suddenly became the fad in the 1980s.

Just as its society changed, Taiwan's close connections with the West, particularly the United States, greatly changed the nature of knowledge and information there. Two consequences followed, one cultural, and one political. The schools and colleges taught new, Western ideas and the ideals of liberal democracy, such as human rights, the doctrine of separation of governmental powers and intragovernmental checks and balances, and limited government. Increasing numbers of faculty members of social science departments of universities were educated in the West, particularly the United States. Many new leaders in the formation of opinion are also products of Western institutions. The cumulative influence of these people has been considerable. This cultural influence from the West has had its critics, however. Some of them argue that traditional Chinese culture has been undermined by the powerful cultural influence from the West; others express worry about the United States' imperialist influence and argue for the validity of "dependency theory" to make their point. But these critics are decidedly in the minority. Most educated people believe the influence from the West is, on balance, beneficial to the ROC.

Direct political influence from the United States also has contributed to the recent political democratization of the ROC. That political influence has taken such forms as the report of the U.S. State Department on the ROC's human-rights record; the personal concern expressed by powerful U.S. Congressmen for ROC political issues such as the fate of certain political prisoners; the views expressed by certain U.S. media; and open hearings held in the U.S. Congress in connection with the sale of arms to the ROC. All these influences resonate in the ROC and are intensely discussed in the public media.

Finally, unique political leadership paved the way for major reforms in the political center. There are several views on the role played by Chiang Ching-kuo in facilitating the reforms. One position argues that Chiang Ching-kuo's actions, his foresight, astuteness, and moral courage played a decisive role in making those reforms possible. This view tends to ignore other factors and exaggerates the role of a single individual in shaping historical events. Another view belittles Chiang's role, arguing that he was forced by domestic and external pressures to undertake political reform. Moreover, some of those reforms were merely cosmetic, because the basic structure of the Kuomintang party-state still remains intact.

I regard both of these views as unacceptable. The political changes in the ROC flow from a variety of factors. They certainly are not the achievements of a single individual. Yet Chiang's role in accelerating these changes cannot be ignored. Without Chiang's personal attention, these changes still might have occurred, but they would have occurred much later. The ROC polity might have become more unstable if that had been the case. Chiang's personal authority eased the anxiety of leading party conservatives and gave the military confidence in the party's reforms.

As for future political developments in the ROC, what kind of a political center will evolve and how will that center relate to civil society? Three trends must be reviewed before those questions can be answered: the first is Taiwan's modernization, then "factionalization" and decentralization, and, finally, the rise of a "pragmatic" elite.

The process of Taiwan's modernization has been twofold. First, over 75 percent of the 2.5 million members of the Kuomintang are native Taiwanese. In the formation of Kuomintang leadership, Taiwanization has been a recent development. After the death of Chiang Ching-kuo, a Taiwanese, Lee Teng-hui, became chairman. As for the Central Committee elected at the Thirteenth Kuomintang Party Congress, Taiwanese representation in that body came to 34.4 percent of the total, a higher figure than for the previous Central Committee (19.3 percent). A more significant fact is that in the current Standing Committee, Taiwanese form the majority. The other aspect of Taiwanization concerns the shift of the general orientation of the party. After the central government moved to Taiwan in 1949, the ruling party's main concern was "to recover the mainland." Taiwan was to be the "base." For the Kuomintang at that time, it was important to develop Taiwan, but that was not the party's ultimate goal. Now this party goal is no longer shared by all party members. The Kuomintang still pays lip service to the "recovery of the mainland" or the "unification of China under the Three Principles of the People," but its main preoccupation is to develop Taiwan and advance the ROC into the ranks of developed nations.

At the national level, the Kuomintang was free from factionalism from 1949 until recent times. At the local level, the party is closely tied to local factions; at that level factionalism has become the essence of party life. National politics and local politics were separate until the last decade or so. Local politics now greatly affects politics in the government. In the Legislative Yuan, for example, factions have appeared. Like-minded members form "clubs." The Kuomintang Committee in the Legislative Yuan often has difficulty in mediating the differences between these clubs. So far, factionalism of the type observed in the Liberal Democratic Party (LDP) of Japan has not developed in the Kuomintang. In Japan, cabinet members are selected from the Diet according to party affiliation. Factionalism in the Diet as well as the cabinet are two sides of the same coin. As cabinet members are all affiliated with factions, the top leaders of the LDP are divided according to party factions. In the ROC, in contrast, cabinet members have not been members of the Legislative Yuan, and the members of the Legislative Yuan are usually not top Kuomintang leaders. Factionalism in the Legislative Yuan has not yet influenced the top party leadership.

Before Chiang Ching-kuo died, the Kuomintang was still a highly centralized organization. The chairman made practically all important decisions. Even at the session of the Central Standing Committee, members did not speak much unless asked. In fact, Chiang once instructed the Central Standing Committee members to speak out. After Chiang's death, Central Standing Committee meetings became a genuine exchange of views. An even more significant sign of the widening of decisionmaking power in the party is the leadership's relationship with Kuomintang members in the Legislative Yuan. The party leadership previously had instructed these Kuomintang members of the Legislative Yuan to support government bills or budget proposals, and those party members did so without question. In recent years, extensive exchange of views between the executive branch and the legislators must be conducted, and revisions of legislation then follows. If legislators do not agree, bargaining must take place. Even after the party leaders make their position known, they still cannot be sure the Kuomintang legislators will support a particular bill or proposal. Mobilizing enough support from party members in the Legislative Yuan requires much patient work and persuasion by party leaders. As senior members retire in the near future, the Kuomintang faction in the Legislative Yuan will have to work even harder to mobilize support for the party's legislative program. Recent demands by its rank-and-file members forced the Kuomintang to use the primary system to choose its candidates for public offices. This decision will certainly decentralize its political power even more so.

In the early 1950s, the party had stood for staunch, uncompromising anticommunism. The party insisted on recovery of the mainland by force, and its policies tried to achieve that goal. The Kuomintang boasted of being a revolutionary party with a noble mission. It never worried about mundane politics, to which an ordinary democratic party must pay much attention. As time passed, the ideal of recovering the mainland slowly faded to become an impossibility. Economic development in Taiwan became the primary goal for both party and state. Economic planners replaced party ideologues and organizers as wielders of influence in the ruling circles of the party. Pragmatism reigned supreme. Many still gave lip service to the goal of recovering the mainland, but few took that goal seriously. Monitoring elections in an evolving pluralistic society on a day-to-day basis compelled party cadres to devote their time and energies to nurturing ties with local factions. The revolutionary party became a political party concerned with its survival. As the pragmatic ethic was shared by more party leaders, the Kuomintang acquired the features of an ordinary political party in a democratic society.

The Kuomintang will undoubtedly become more "Taiwanized." It will have to deal more and more with factionalism. Its decisionmaking power will become more diffused and decentralized, and it will become more pragmatic in order to survive in Taiwan's evolving pluralistic society. But with the enormous resources it commands, its political experience and leadership, and the broad popularity it still enjoys in influential segments of the people, and its success in adapting to new circumstances, the Kuomintang will continue to play an important role in the ROC's political center.

Meanwhile, that political center will take on a new form. Opposition parties will demand that the Kuomintang's power be further reduced, particularly in military affairs, government administration, and in educational institutions. If successful in rolling back Kuomintang influence in these sectors, new opposition parties will eventually play an important role in the new political center. How the KMT will respond to these demands is difficult to say. The KMT's role in the military will certainly be a troublesome problem.[6]

Although state and society relations can assume different forms,[7] the framework organizing the discussion presented in this chapter has adopted the concept of a political center and whether or not that center has successfully avoided political decay or experienced a process of crystallization. In essence, the ROC's political center evolved over 40 years by gradual crystallization. Strong individual leadership influenced the activities of the Kuomintang. Yet party and state policies initiated rapid socioeconomic modernization. Such modernization in turn brought about dramatic political changes within the Kuomintang and the manner in which the Kuomintang exercised its power. While eliciting broad popular and intellectual approval for its policies, the Kuomintang changed the very rules by which the party governed its members and tried to influence the state's and the center's activities in Taiwanese society. By the mid-1980s these developments had culminated in the making of new laws: the Assembly and Demonstration Law, a National Security Law, a Civic Association Law, etc.

Opposition parties were now registered with the government. The public media could print news as it saw fit. The political center became more complex in its political dynamics. Debates became more complex and sophisticated. Political maneuvering became more complicated and time-consuming. Monitoring elections and preparing for them required greater energy and resources. Politics became a full-time business for more and more people.

The political center was becoming more subordinated to the demands of interest groups in society. The once-dominant ruling party in the political center was experiencing new changes leading to new views and groups in the Kuomintang that decided policies.

A new era had begun.

---

[6]Because the army was founded by the Kuomintang as a revolutionary component of itself, that party still exercises some control over the ROC's armed services. The main opposition party is perceived as supportive of Taiwanese independence, so that separating the military and the Kuomintang is very difficult.

[7]Cf. John Keane, "Despotism and Democracy," in John Keane, ed., *Civil Society and the State* (London and New York: Verso, 1988), pp. 35–72.

The Changing State-Society Relation in the ROC

Economic Change, the Transformation of the Class Structure, and the Rise of Social Movements

There are many ways to examine the complex changes and development of Taiwan's society in the past 40 years. One approach is to consider distinctive changes or patterns in family structure and functions, urbanization and industrialization, demographic transformation, social institutions, and class relations from either the micro or the macro perspective in order to show these changes or patterns in quantitative terms. Cross-sectional or time-series data can be used. This chapter summarizes the quantitative and descriptive work found in many recent studies and tries to relate these insights to the relationship of state and society of the past 40 years.

First, what major social changes flow from the various state policies pursued in the past decades, and how have such societal changes influenced relations between state and society? The interaction of state and civil society cannot be ignored in Taiwan's developmental experience. The East Asian state has a tradition that cannot be defined as "soft," "passive," or "minimal." Instead, most experts regard it as "active" or "strong" in trying to influence civil society.[1] Even so, civil society is not simply putty to be molded by the

---

[1]H.H. Michael Hsiao, "Development Strategies and Class Transformation in Taiwan and South Korea: Origins and Consequences," *Bulletin of Ethnology* (Academia Sinica), 61(1987):183–217.

state; it flexibly adapts to changes and assumes new forms because of complex changes produced by social units.

Macro-Societal Change

The year 1945 marked the end of World War II and 50 years of Japanese colonial rule of Taiwan. The Chinese central government took over Taiwan in October 1945, but could allocate few resources to its new provincial administration on Taiwan and help the island in its postwar rehabilitation. Between 1945 and 1949, the society of Taiwan experienced major social and economic chaos. Inflation was rampant; unemployment was high; urbanization did increase, but largely because of the influx of mainland refugees.

Taiwan's socioeconomic structure was still primarily rural, with tenant and landless families outnumbering those owning their own farms. The landlord and gentry strata still provided traditional local leadership in the countryside and maintained limited commercial interests in the townships and cities. The tenant farmers and landless possessed no political and economic power. The large size of the floating population without employment made for an unstable society in these years, especially in the cities.

Poor economic policies by the new provincial administration along with other complex factors created tensions and grievances, which boiled over into a massive riot on February 28, 1947. Some nine cities were taken over by rebels, and some rebel leaders even demanded major political reforms of the provincial administration as well as of its relationship to the Nanking government. The central government, viewing the uprising as a rebellion in its rear, sent poorly trained, undisciplined troops to Taiwan, and these soldiers harshly suppressed the rebellion. This complex and tragic event was responsible for much of the bitter Taiwanese-mainlander relations in subsequent decades.

This tragic event certainly weakened the role of the Taiwanese elite, dividing it and demoralizing some of its members. Still others fled abroad, many going to Japan, to form the backbone of a new political movement bent on toppling the Nationalist government on Taiwan. The majority of the Taiwanese elite preferred to "lie low," but many gradually joined the government as civil servants or turned their efforts to business and farming.

The political and social turmoil of postcolonial Taiwan diminished by 1949, when Nationalist officials moved their government from the mainland to Taiwan because of the defeat of the KMT forces by the Communists. A new political era commenced. A successful socioeconomic "land reform" quickly came in 1949 and ended in 1952. Political and social reasons, rather than economic reasons, dictated the reform. Yet it was a great success.[2] The new regime was not persuaded by appeals from the landlord class to preserve its property rights. The reform did compensate the landlords, though.

The most favorable, immediate consequence of this reform was the creation of small landowners and the elimination of the old landlords' rural property base. The predominance of small farmers after the land reform later entirely changed the political character of Taiwan's countryside. More conservative in outlook, these farmers posed no threat to the new Nationalist state. Nor was there a large, differentiated urban society to challenge the government. The party-state political center enjoyed dominant power over civil society in the post–land-reform era.

After land reform, the Nationalist government launched the first four-year economic plan, carried out in 1953–1956, and pushed an import-substitution program to build a small industrial base. This new strategy, lasting through the second four-year plan, until 1960, protected new industries, whose products would be sold domestically to replace imported consumer goods. The state also set up extensive protectionist machinery, which helped a small group of businessmen in this period. Nearly a decade had to pass before the government vigorously promoted opportunities for businessmen to expand their activities and for a real private sector to emerge. Part of the reason for this time lag was the Sunist doctrine shared by officials who took Sun at his word that "regulating capital" (*chieh-chih tzu-pen*) meant protecting a group of businessmen at the expense of other businessmen. Perhaps, too, some officials still clung to socialist ideas and did not trust local businessmen. The small, feeble private sector in these years did not give officials very much confidence that they could launch economic modernization. For them, "large" was beautiful and the vehicle for economic development. Therefore the state-owned enterprises and the mainlander-owned private industries became the leading beneficiaries of the import-substitution program. Yet a new generation of Taiwanese industrialists began to emerge, many being former landlords. Among their ranks were bold entrepreneurs, who quickly responded to the governmental policies of the late 1950s.

One significant result of the import-substitution strategy was the creation of a small urban industrial working class in the new state and private

---

[2]H.H. Michael Hsiao, *Government Agricultural Strategies in Taiwan and South Korea: A Macrosociological Assessment* (Institute of Ethnology, Academia Sinica, 1981); H.H. Michael Hsiao, "Land Reform in East Asia Revisited: An Ingredient of East Asian Development Model?" in John Tessitore and Susan Woolfson, eds., *Asian Development Model and the Caribbean Basin Initiative* (New York: CRIA, 1985), pp. 149–50.

industries. Meanwhile, many farmers shifted to service industries, as did some self-employed and unpaid family workers. More white-collar workers entered the private sector, finding employment in both the government bureaucracy and state enterprises. In short, the new mix of private industries and state enterprises, along with the state administrative bureaucracy, provided opportunities for many to find work and change their residence from the countryside to the cities. In these occupations, however, mainlander bureaucrats and professionals still occupied the upper-level positions of supervisors, department heads, and so forth.

As the economy took off in the 1960s, government policies had become more liberal and trade-oriented. Having no overall plan except to provide new monetary incentives for businessmen anxious to export, the government rigorously promoted exports to the world market, particularly the United States. During the period of the third four-year plan (1961–1964) and through the time of the fifth plan (1969–1972), the private sector became an engine of growth manned by tens of thousands of small businessmen, the majority being Taiwanese who operated small and medium-sized enterprises along with some large-scale firms still controlled by both mainlanders and Taiwanese who had gained their start a decade before. Society, too, was changing. The urban industrial working class grew by leaps and bounds, employed entirely in the private sector. More and more urban families began to perceive themselves as belonging to the middle class, and in their ranks were managers and professionals of the new industrial and commercial sectors. Meanwhile, the state bureaucracy at both central and local levels grew and employed more white-collar workers.

The development strategies of the ROC's government had established the foundation for a market system supplied by private entrepreneurs, economic sectoral change, and the rise of the services and industrial sectors. Land reform boosted agricultural production for export, which earned much-needed foreign exchange and expanded demand in the domestic market. These favorable developments launched Taiwan's modern economic growth. Meanwhile, powerful new market forces propelled as well as attracted more rural people into the cities. The population was now concentrated in the already large urban centers in Taiwan, which had become distinctive by the end of World War II. These large urban centers became the environment in which new social forms and activities emerged. Then new changes became more clear by the mid-1960s, and marked a new era of social change.

As economic activity, oriented to world markets as well as the new urban centers, accelerated, and when urban manufacturing industries were at their production peaks (1973, 1979, and 1980), the outflow from the rural labor force was probably greatest. In other years, such as 1975 and 1981, this outflow nearly stopped, with reversals even recorded in some areas.[3] Meanwhile, agriculture's share of the GNP steadily declined, and the share of the GNP from manufacturing and services climbed. The share of the labor force in the primary sector fell from more than half in 1953 to less than one-fifth in the mid-1980s. During this same period, the share of the labor force in both the secondary and tertiary sectors had increased by half. For the secondary sector, the absolute number of people employed rose almost sixfold, while the number of those employed in the tertiary sector quadrupled.

A simple way to see this pattern of urbanization is to consider the proportion of population that resides in cities of 20,000 or more. By 1952, the proportion of the population in Taiwan residing in cities of 20,000 or more had increased substantially, from around 16 percent in 1935 to nearly 48 percent. This shift originated in part from the influx of mainland Chinese. In 1940, mainlanders in Taiwan numbered 31,721, but in 1950 they were more than 500,000, and by 1957 exceeded one million. As most of these mainlanders were government bureaucrats and their families and members of the military services, they mainly lived in large cities and the military bases. By 1955, this population was distributed thus: 56.2 percent in provincial cities; 12.4 percent in larger county cities; and only 20.9 percent in towns and the rural areas.[4]

In 1962, the proportion of the population in cities of 20,000 or more had increased to 52 percent, almost a 5 percent increase in ten years. In 1972 the figure had jumped by almost 10 percent to 61.1 percent. Similarly, in 1976 the figure was 66.3 percent, and by 1980 it had reached 70.3 percent, an increase of roughly 1 percent per year.

Looked at from another angle, the number of cities with a population of 20,000 or more had already increased to 67, and by 1980 it exceeded 90. Within that same decade, the increase of the urban population was more than 3.3 million, from 7.6 million to 11 million, or an increase of 43 percent. Most of this growth occurred in cities of more than a half-million, and their share of the increase amounted to 1.7 million out of the total 3.3 million. The growth rate was most substantial in smaller cities of 50,000 to 100,000 inhabitants, which increased in population by 85 percent. The northern part of the island absorbed the largest number of people—1.8 million, or a 45

---

[3]Cheng-hung Liao, "Changes in Agricultural Human Resources," in Hai-yuan Chiu and Ying-hwa Chang, eds., *Social and Cultural Changes in Taiwan* (Institute of Ethnology, Academia Sinica, 1986), pp. 184–85.

[4]Ying-hwa Chang, "Changes in Urban Taiwan Since the End of the Ch'ing Dynasty," in Hai-yuan Chiu and Ying-hwa Chang, eds., *Social and Cultural Changes in Taiwan* (Institute of Ethnology, Academia Sinica, 1986), pp. 233–76.

percent increase; the central region took 0.47 million, or a 62 percent increase; finally, the southern and eastern regions, with the smallest growth, absorbed 0.70 million and 0.48 million people, respectively.[5]

As urbanization changed, so did the spatial distribution of production. One study showed that between 1966 and 1977 there was nearly a one-to-one correspondence between the growth rate of urban population and the spatial distribution of production.[6] Industrialization and urbanization had become closely linked.

After World War II, Taiwan had rapidly moved from a colonial, agrarian society to a modern, urban society.

Social Strata Change and the Political Center

Two important social changes had meanwhile occurred. First, people lived better, saved more, and consumed more goods and services. Second, social differentiation took place.

Social differentiation and economic affluence usually occur together. The 1961 GNP per capita was a mere US$100; by 1970 it had increased to US$400, and by 1981 to US$2100. Such a measure describes tangible improvement of living standards but also reveals the slow advance over a long period of several decades as rapid population growth also takes place. Yet consumption did change. The need for the basic necessities of food and shelter were quickly satisfied, and households increased their spending for health care and social and recreational activities. The proportion of income saved also greatly increased, marking a new pattern in Taiwan as compared to other Third World nations.

Income distribution in the first three decades had avoided the "Kuznets trap" by becoming more equal. In 1964, the income share of the top 20 percent was 5.33 times higher than that of the bottom 20 percent. The same figure fell to 4.49 in 1972 and to 4.29 in 1984. Using the Gini index to

---

[5]Ching-lung Tsai, "Growth and Distribution of Urban Population in Taiwan," in Chau-nan Chen, Yu-lung Kiang, and Kuanjeng Chen, eds., *Essays on the Integration of Social Sciences* (Sun Yat-sen Institute for Social Sciences and Philosophy, Academia Sinica, 1982), pp. 221–22 and 225–26.

[6]Fu-chang Tang, "The Diffused Development of Taiwan's Industries," *Proceedings on Industrial Development in Taiwan* (Institute of Economics, Academia Sinica, 1983), pp. 276–77.

measure income distribution, that index was 0.6206 in 1953; by 1972 it had fallen to 0.2955, and even lower to 0.2806 by 1979.

Even so, some sectoral disparities in income distribution did occur; they were within rural areas and between the countryside and the cities. Income distribution after 1980 also became more unequal as Taiwan entered a new era of complex economic restructuring.

With economic affluence, new social strata emerged in the late 1960s. One stratum consisted of households in which one or more members worked as factory workers; another was made up of households in which one or more members worked in services or in skilled occupations.

From the social-class point of view, these changes in employment status could be far more influential than mere occupational structural change.[7] Between 1951 and 1981, the proportion of "working for someone else" or "non-self-employed" had increased annually, from 22 percent to 52 percent. This rapid change began in 1966, and by 1978 the figure had surpassed the 50-percent mark. At the same time, the proportion of employers had also increased by 1970. The 1981 figure of 4.5 percent was more than double the 2-percent figure of 1960. These figures were offset by the rapid decline of the proportion of the "self-employed" and the "non-gainfully-employed household workers." The figures for those working in the government remained unchanged. These numbers show the rapid growth and importance of the private-manufacturing and services sectors. Their growth in absolute numbers was even more pronounced.

It seems a small-landowner stratum dissolved to become a new laboring stratum, with many other strata perceiving themselves as belonging to the middle class. By 1980, only 18 percent of the island's employed worked in farming. Of these farming households, over 90 percent were only part-time farmers. The new stratum of workers had increased from less than 15 percent to more than 35 percent in 1980, while the broad middle class rose from 20 percent to around 30 percent.

Within this middle class, there were shifts and changes. Sen used various census data to delineate Taiwan's new social structure.[8] Table 6.1 presents his findings. Note the upward trend of the working class and new middle

---

[7]R. V. Robinson and J. Kelley, "Class as Conceived by Marx and Dahrendorf. Effect on Income Inequality and Politics in the United States and Great Britain," *American Sociological Review*, 44(1979):38–58; and E. O. Wright and L. Perrone, "Marxist Class Categories and Income Inequality," *American Sociological Review*, 42(1977):32–55.

[8]Yow-suen Sen, "A Preliminary Analysis of the Transformation of Class Structure in Taiwan" (unpublished manuscript, Department of Sociology, University of Hawaii, 1986).

Table 6.1
Class Transformation in Taiwan, 1956–1980

Class Category	1956	1966	1970	1975	1980	Ratio of Increase (1975/1956)
Upper class	1.8	1.5	1.2	2.3	1.5	1.27
New middle class	10.1	14.2	13.5	14.9	19.3	1.47
Old middle class	11.9	7.7	9.8	9.7	12.2	0.81
Working class	14.4	22.2	25.9	32.5	35.4	2.26
Marginal class	17.8	21.8	16.5	13.4	13.2	0.75
Farmers	43.9	32.6	33.1	27.2	18.4	0.62
TOTAL	100	100	100	100	100	
	(2900)	(4289)	(4525)	(5589)	(6417)	— (Unit: 1000)

SOURCE: Based on Yow-suen Sen, "A Preliminary Analysis of the Transformation of Class Structure in Taiwan" (unpublished manuscript, Department of Sociology, University of Hawaii, 1986), p. 44.

class and the downward trend of the small farmers, marginal class, and petty bourgeoisie (at least until 1975) between 1956 and 1980.

These changes in social structure also reflect the changing nature of society. State policies had speeded up a rural transformation and the growth of cities with many new social strata. Within the upper classes, businessmen predominate. It is inappropriate to speak of this group as a capitalist class only in quantitative terms. So-called capitalists exerted their power in a very disproportionate way in 1980, when their group only accounted for slightly more than 1 percent. The other extreme is a working class having a very large membership, but still not organized in the marketplace.

What is unique about this class structure is that the household and its kinship ties still play an important role in shaping individuals' views of their status and rank in society. In fact, most individuals who might be assigned to a certain class still live in families whose members work in different occupations, such as in the service industry. Kinship ties also influence attitudes individuals hold toward other groups. The phenomenon of people under the same roof or in kinship relations working in different occupations exists throughout Taiwan's society. Therefore Taiwan can at best be called a complex, differentiated society composed of many strata and certainly not a "class society." "Class" has not been a determining force in shaping social and political actions.

In the immediate post–land-reform period, small farmers had little political power to influence state policies. As a conservative group, small farmers could not organize to demand new policies from the political center. Marginal groups also were weak during this same period. They became totally dependent on new opportunities generated from urban development and had little direct access to the political center to impose their demands.

The working class had also been excluded from political and economic organizations that could demand new policies from the political center. Their unions have been restrained by the state, and the dynamic market system also discouraged people from organizing union demands for new price and wage policies. International competition served to dampen increase of wages, and labor markets functioned well to allocate labor to new occupations. The government carefully watched unionization of the working class to ensure urban stability. Finally, the conservative, rural background of the "first generation" of the Taiwanese working class and the short careers of young, unmarried female workers also accounted for a passive labor force.

After the late 1970s, a "second generation" of the working class emerged, one that had a longer urban industrial life experience, was younger, and had more education. This group is more oriented to "activism" but is not necessarily "radical." These members now make for a new labor movement. Consequently, in the 1980s labor disputes broke out for the first time since 1950.

The new liberalization of the late 1980s forced new restructuring, which took place when the social changes described above were also occurring. The political center is now being confronted with new demands from organized groups in society that represent all strata, ranging from the homeless to small businessmen and professionals.

The broad middle class benefited from the economic modernization but remained politically conservative. Its members eschewed radical change. Like the working class, the middle class has not developed any class consciousness. Its members advocate no clear and strong ideological opposition to the government and ruling party. They have served as a crucial stabilizing force in society.

By the late 1980s, many in the middle class had begun demanding "reforms" from the political center. They organized on such issues as those of the environment, consumerism, human rights, women's rights, and so on. Still not politically motivated, these groups are now pressuring the political center for new laws, new policies, and more spending by the government to deal with their special interests.

New Social Movements and
a Changing Civil Society

As the 1980s unfolded against the background of three decades of economic expansion and rapid change, civil society had become more prosperous, more differentiated, and more fluid. The circulation of new information had become immense. New expectations and new perceptions of problems became the major topics of the day. Society and state, too, had begun to change in their relationship to each other.[9] Some of these new hopes and demands have roots in events of the distant past, such as the rebellion of February 1947. Various groups also had tried to form, like the Free China Group, the aborted Chinese Democratic Party in the 1950s, followed by the Intellectuals, who called for political reform, and a new opposition force in the 1970s, and finally the first opposition party, the Democratic Progressive Party in 1986.[10]

These examples of group efforts to influence the political center only reflected elite attempts to organize new political forms. They had no real social base. Therefore when various social movements formed in the late 1980s, a dramatic new set of conditions began to take shape.

A total of seventeen social movements making claims on the political center can be identified in civil society. They are: (1) consumer movement (1980–); (2) antipollution protests (1980–); (3) a natural-conservation movement (1982–); (4) a women's movement (1982–); (5) aboriginal human-rights movement (1983–); (6) a student movement (1986–); (7) New Testament Church protests (1986–); (8) labor movement (1987–); (9) farmers' movement (1987–); (10) a movement for teachers' rights (1987–); (11) protestors for the welfare of the handicapped and disadvantaged (1987–); (12) protesters for military, veterans' welfare (1987–); (13) a political victims' human-rights movement (1987–); (14) a mainlanders' visiting-rights movement (1987–); (15) a Taiwanese visiting-rights movement (1988–); (16) an

---

[9]Yang-san Chou, *Social Movements and the Party-State in Taiwan* (Ph.D. dissertation, Columbia University, 1988); H.H. Michael Hsiao, "Emerging Social Movements and the Rise of a Demanding Civil Society in Taiwan" (paper presented at the Conference on Democratization in the ROC, IIR, Taipei, Jan. 9–11, 1989); and H.H. Michael Hsiao, "Changing Theoretical Explanations of Taiwan's Development Experience: An Examination," *International Journal of Comparative Sociology*, forthcoming.

[10]Hsiao-fung Lee, *Taiwan's Democratic Movement in the Past Forty Years* (Taipei: Independent Morning Post, 1987).

anti–nuclear-power movement (1988–); (17) a Hakka-rights movement (1988–); and (18) nonhomeowners' "snail" movement (1989–).[11]

These eighteen social movements have different, specific objectives; yet they make demands on the political center, calling for new policies, laws, and support. Their appeals were presented to government officials, to the ruling party, to state organs, to the press, and even to the public to gain their support. The composition of these new social groups demanding change transcend social class. These groups embrace all sorts of people of different age, sex, occupation, ethnicity, religion, education, and so forth.

Key participants in different social movements come from a wide range of social backgrounds: they are small farmers, workers, intellectuals, women, students, veterans, members of welfare groups, pollution victims, political prisoners, and church members. These groups do not articulate clear-cut class interests, although unions, farmers' associations, and antipollution protesters express some basic sentiments. The main sentiment expressed by these social movements is a sense of "being ignored and excluded." Their collective actions are justified as a rational demand on the political center to provide justice, compensation, or some privilege to protect their group interests.

A typology of these seventeen social movements is presented in table 6.2. The political center has been most challenged by the antipollution protests, labor unions, farmers' associations, the veterans' movement, the mainlanders' home-visiting movement, the Taiwanese home-visiting movement, and the political victims' human-rights movement. These groups do not necessarily possess a great capability to mobilize resources on their behalf. These seventeen social movements, however, challenge the center to debate and consider new environmental policy and to reconsider its policy toward mainland China. In the public sector, social groups such as farmers, laborers, and veterans now demand more compensation from the government. Yet their ability to mobilize resources is also not great.

The government, the ruling party, and other elements in the political center have responded to these new demands in a cyclical fashion. Figure 6.1 illustrates this response. The government permitted mainlanders to visit their homeland and allowed the New Testament Church to settle on a remote mountain. Thereafter, these two movements began to fragment and dissolve. Consumers, workers, farmers, students, and the Taiwanese home-visiting movement have made demands that the political center slowly

[11]H.H. Michael Hsiao, "Emerging Social Movements and the Rise of a Demanding Civil Society in Taiwan."

Table 6.2
A Typology of Social Movements in Taiwan (December 1990)

Challenge to the Political Center	Capability to Mobilize Internal Resources	
	Low	High
Low	1. Aborigines' human-rights (1983–) 2. Handicapped or welfare-group protests (1987–) 3. Women's movement (1982–) (I)	1. Consumers' movement (1980–) 2. Conservation movement (1980–) 3. Teachers'–rights movement (1987–) 4. Student movement (1986–) 5. Anti–nuclear power movement (1988–) 6. New Testament Church protest (1986–1989) 7. Hakka-rights movement (1988–) 8. Nonhomeowners' "snail" movement (1989–) (II)
High	1. Antipollution local protest movement (1980–) 2. Labor movement (1987–) 3. Farmers' movement (1987–) 4. Veterans' welfare protests (1987–) 5. Mainlanders' home-visiting movement (1987–1988) 6. Taiwanese home-visiting movement (1988–) 7. Political victims' human-rights movement (1987–) (III)	(IV)

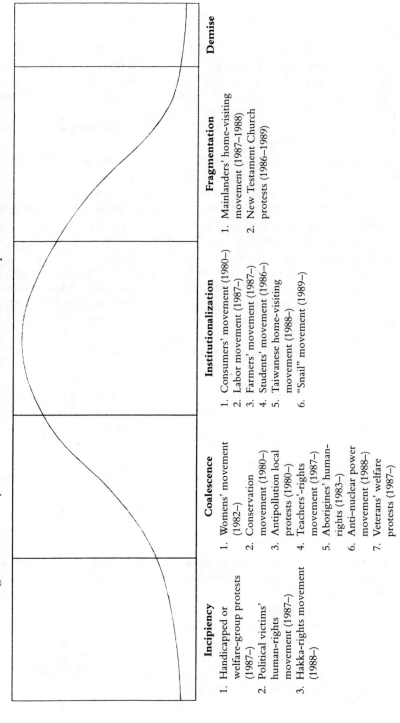

Figure 6.1: Life Cycle of Social Movements and State's Response as of December 1990

Incipiency

1. Handicapped or welfare-group protests (1987–)
2. Political victims' human-rights movement (1987–)
3. Hakka-rights movement (1988–)

Coalescence

1. Womens' movement (1982–)
2. Conservation movement (1980–)
3. Antipollution local protests (1980–)
4. Teachers'-rights movement (1987–)
5. Aborigines' human-rights (1983–)
6. Anti-nuclear power movement (1988–)
7. Veterans' welfare protests (1987–)

Institutionalization

1. Consumers' movement (1980–)
2. Labor movement (1987–)
3. Farmers' movement (1987–)
4. Students' movement (1986–)
5. Taiwanese home-visiting movement (1988–)
6. "Snail" movement (1989–)

Fragmentation

1. Mainlanders' home-visiting movement (1987–1988)
2. New Testament Church protests (1986–1989)

Demise

granted through policy change, legal reforms, or administrative reorganization. The Consumers Protection Act, the new University Law, and regulations governing Taiwanese on the mainland who want to visit Taiwan or take up residence there are now before the Legislative Yuan; a housing program is being proposed; a Labor Commission has been established at the cabinet level; and the formation of a Ministry of Agriculture is also being considered.

The other ten social movements are either still incipient or are striving to coalesce at a new stage of vigor. Again, the center will most likely respond to their demands as it has met others.

In the 1980s Taiwan's civil society was no longer passive. Individuals and their social groups mobilized to demand action from the political center. These same groups now form networks for their causes and seek support from the grass-roots of society.

Some groups seek new coalitions and alliances with other groups. As they identify some common goals, that task becomes easier, but so far these groups have not become politicized and aligned with any particular political party. The political center has become more sensitive to such interest-group pressures and demands. The ruling party and government now try to anticipate these demands and satisfy them before they become politicized.[12]

---

[12]Ibid.

References Not Cited in the Text:

Tun-jen Cheng, "Democratizing the KMT Regime in Taiwan" (paper presented at the Conference on Democratization in the ROC, IIR, Taipei, Jan. 9–11, 1989).

Reginald Harrison, *Pluralism and Corporatism* (London: George Allen & Unwin, 1980).

Guillermo O'Donnell and Philippe Schmitter, *Transitions from Authoritarian Rule: Tentative Conclusions About Uncertain Democracies* (Baltimore, Md.: Johns Hopkins University Press, 1986).

Philippe Schmitter, "Still the Century of Corporatism?" *Review of Politics,* vol. 36, no. 1(1974):85–131.

Philippe Schmitter, "Models of Interest Intermediation and Models of Societal Change in West Europe," *Comparative Political Studies,* vol. 10, no. 1(1977):7–38.

Edwin Wincker, "Taiwan Politics in the 1990s: From Hard to Soft Authoritarianism" (paper presented at the Conference on Democratization in the ROC, II4, Taipei, Jan. 9–11, 1989).

Impressions of Mainland China Carried Back by Taiwan Visitors

On November 2, 1987, the Republic of China on Taiwan lifted its 38-year ban preventing its residents from visiting the Chinese mainland. Since then, around 230,000 residents of Taiwan have been registered as traveling to the mainland, while unknown numbers have gone there unofficially. Remaining restrictions very likely will be relaxed in the future, and the number of these residents visiting the mainland will increase. The new views of returning visitors might influence relations between the two governments that face each across the Taiwan Straits.

The ROC's Visitation Policy

As early as 1979, many residents of Taiwan secretly traveled to the mainland via third countries as tourists. Beijing willingly allowed residents of Taiwan to come and go, and for humanitarian reasons the Taipei government did not prosecute these people. In the years 1979–1987, over 10,000 residents of Taiwan probably visited the mainland.[1] In the 1980s, pressures mounted to lift the ban on traveling to the mainland. In 1984, Yu Chen Yueh-ying, an

---

[1] *Tzu-li wan-pao* (Independence evening news) (Taipei), March 3, 1988, p. 2.

independent legislator, asked the government to allow military veterans to make contact with their families on the mainland.[2] In 1986, legislators Hsieh Hsueh-hsien and Chiang Peng-chien requested that the government allow postal exchanges and visits. You Ching, a member of the Control Yuan, even suggested that contacts be allowed between parliamentarians of the two governments. These politicians were mainly non-Kuomintang and native Taiwanese eager to win the votes of mainlanders.

In early 1987, Pres. Chiang Ching-kuo, the ruling party's chairman, instructed Mah Soo-lay, the party's general secretary, to review the ban on mainland visits. That review did not begin until July, by which time Lee Huan had replaced Mah as general secretary.[3] Meanwhile, the Executive Yuan replied to the legislators' demands by cautioning that Beijing wanted its people to contact their relatives in Taiwan by mail and invite them to visit the mainland to see their families or conduct business. This stratagem conveyed the false impression of voluntary contacts between the two sides.[4] Even so, secret visits to the mainland had become so popular that pressures to lift the ban on travel continued to mount.

Then, on August 15, the *China Times* and the *United Daily News* deliberately leaked information that the government was considering lifting the ban on mainland visits and revising its mainland policy. On August 28, the *United Daily News* declared that in September the Executive Yuan would announce new terms for visits to the mainland by residents of Taiwan.

At the meeting of the ruling party's Central Standing Committee on September 16, Chiang Ching-kuo appointed a committee comprising Lee Teng-hui, Yu Kuo-hwa, Nieh Wen-ya, Wu Poh-hsiung, and Ho Yi-wu to report on the travel-ban rules. The committee finally submitted its report at the October 14 meeting of the Central Standing Committee.[5] The Executive Yuan then drew up new regulations, and on October 15 Interior Minister Wu Poh-hsiung announced the lifting of the ban. On November 2, the Red Cross formally began accepting applications from Taiwan.

The Central Standing Committee justified its new policy with humanitarian reasons and as compliance with traditional Chinese ethics. The government's anti-Communist stance and its resolve to reunify China had not changed. National security would be safeguarded to prevent Communist infiltration. All residents of Taiwan except government employees and servicemen on active duty might apply to visit their parents, siblings, uncles,

---

[2]*Li-fa yuan kung-pao* (Bulletin of the Legislative Yuan), vol. 73, no. 98(Dec. 6, 1984).
[3]*Hsin hsin-wen* (New news) (Taipei), no. 25(Aug. 31–Sept. 6, 1987), pp. 9–11.
[4]*Li-fan yuan kung-pao*, vol. 76, no. 52(July 1, 1987).
[5]*Hsin hsin-wen*, no. 32(Oct. 9–25, 1987), pp. 20–25.

aunts, and in-laws. Chiang Ching-kuo also reaffirmed the government's basic anti-Communist policy, its goal of reunifying China, and the need to safeguard national security.[6] Thereafter, family visits became a new element in the government's "mainland policy."

Taipei still maintains its policy of "no contact, no negotiation, and no compromise." The government insists that residents of Taiwan visiting the mainland refrain from any actions harmful to national interests, and that they do not carry out propaganda for the Communists upon returning to Taiwan. Individuals were limited to one family visit a year, of no more than three-months' duration. People making illegal trips to the mainland could not leave Taiwan for two years after returning. The new mainland-visitation rules would be reviewed after six months.

In May 1988, the Interior Ministry's Bureau of Entry and Exit held two meetings with the Central Personnel Administration, the Ministry of Justice, and intelligence and public-security units to review the new policy. On May 23, the ministry published its review and announced that restrictions would be relaxed to permit visits of first cousins.[7] The ministry also suggested that some public servants as well as nonmanagerial personnel of state-owned businesses be allowed to visit the mainland. The Executive Yuan rejected this proposal. On April 18, the Red Cross opened indirect mail service between the two sides of the straits.

On July 12, 1988, the KMT's Thirteenth National Congress pledged that family visits would continue and restrictions further relaxed. The resolution also allowed mainland residents to visit their ailing spouses or other close relatives in Taiwan or to attend family funerals there. The mail service would be conducted through civic bodies.[8] On August 1, the government formally extended the scope of visits to include first cousins. On November 9, the authorities started accepting applications from mainland residents to visit Taiwan.

In early December 1988, Taipei agreed in principle to allow Taiwanese veterans of the Nationalist army who had been stranded on the mainland since 1949 to come to Taiwan with their spouses and children. On March

---

[6]Chung-kuo ming-jen chuan-chi chung-hsin (Center for biographies of eminent Chinese), ed., *Ta-lu t'an-ch'in hsü-chih* (Information concerning family visits to the mainland) (Taipei: Chung-kuo ming-jen chuan-chi chung-hsin, 1987), pp. 1–15.

[7]*Lien-ho pao* (United daily news) (Taipei), May 24, 1988, p. 1.

[8]Hsiao Ch'ang-lo, "A Note on the Formulation of 'Current Policy Toward the Chinese Mainland,'" in *Chung-kuo kuo-min-tang hsien-chieh-tuan ta-lu cheng-ts-e* (Current KMT policy toward the mainland) (Taipei: KMT Central Committee Department of Cultural Affairs, 1988), pp. 9–15.

14, 1989, the Ministry of the Interior announced that it would begin to accept their applications on March 31. In summer of 1989, public-school faculty members were permitted to visit mainland China.

Surveys of Taiwan Residents
Returning from the Mainland

On February 17, 1989, Ma Ying-jeou, executive secretary of the Executive Yuan's task force for affairs concerning mainland China, announced that in 1988 over 316,000 applications had been received for family visits to mainland China. Of the 237,000 applicants who had made the trip, about 220,000 had already returned. Most of the visitors were over 50 years of age; 70 percent were male and 30 percent female; and 80 percent had no education above junior high school.

Ma also said that since November 9, 1988, when applications were first accepted, 1,694 mainlanders had applied to come to Taiwan; of those, 1,376 were approved, 545 had arrived, and 72 had returned to the mainland. There had been no reports of mainlanders overstaying their time limit in Taiwan.[9] According to the latest statistics issued by the Bureau of Entry and Exit, up to March 30, 1989, 2,351 applications had been received from mainlanders, of which 103 had been rejected and 820 accepted. Of these, 250 applicants had left within their allotted time, and over half of the 181 who had overstayed their time had applied for an extension.[10]

At the end of last year, the private Chang Jung-fa Foundation sponsored a survey of 1,495 residents of Taiwan of whom 1,028 had never visited the mainland and 467 had returned from mainland visits (hereafter referred to as "returnees"). Among the latter, 71.7 percent were male and 28.3 percent female; 2.6 percent were in their twenties, 5.8 percent in their thirties, 6.9 percent in their forties, 20.3 percent in their fifties, 47.1 percent in their sixties, 15 percent in their seventies, and 0.9 percent in their eighties or older. People with only elementary-school education or below accounted for 33.2 percent of the returnees; 20.8 percent had middle-school education; 18.4 percent had high-school education; 12.8 percent had attended junior vocational schools; 11.1 percent were college graduates; and 0.4 percent had been educated above college level. As for their occupations, 22.5 percent were retired servicemen; 0.7 percent were public employees; 0.6 percent teachers;

---

[9]*Chung-hua shih-pao* (China times) (Taipei), Feb. 18, 1989, p. 2.
[10]*Chung-kuo shih-pao* (China daily) (Taipei), April 1, 1989, p. 2.

11.1 percent businessmen; 20.1 percent housewives; and less than 0.5 percent had other occupations.[11]

Ma Ying-jeou also pointed out that most residents traveling to the mainland had no complaints about the application formalities, although some suggested that transportation might be more convenient. Visitors have generally recognized the superiority of Taiwan's system over that of the mainland, and their travels served to inform the mainland people of Taiwan's achievements. Family-reunion fever, however, has overtaken the people of Taiwan, distracting them from other important issues and making them less vigilant against Communist propaganda.[12]

In this opinion survey, returnees gave detailed accounts of their impressions of the mainland and their evaluation of the ROC government's policy.

Over half of the returnees claimed they had encountered no problems during their trips to the mainland, which seems to contradict most media reports.[13] Among them, 21.4 percent considered the degree of mutual trust among the mainland people to be "high," while 37.3 percent found it "low" or "very low"; 11.1 percent said it varied according to different situations, and 29.3 percent had no opinion or did not know.[14]

Over 60 percent of the returnees felt that mainland people are not conscientious in their work. This finding suggests that laxness has set in over the past 40 years of Communist rule, which is behavior unlike traditional Chinese industriousness and reflects a basic difference between the Communist and non-Communist economic systems.[15]

The impression created by Chinese Communist officials was generally favorable: 69.4 percent of returnees regarded them as either "very friendly" or "friendly." Such conduct, however, may be due to Beijing's united-front policy and its officials' policy of ingratiating themselves with foreign visitors and compatriots from Taiwan.[16]

As for their feelings toward their relatives, 70 percent felt "very close" to "close" to their families on the mainland. Forty years of separation evidently had not affected family ties. Nevertheless, this high rating might

---

[11]Ch'ü Hai-yuan et al., *Ta-lu t'an-ch'in chi fang-wen te she-hui ying-hsiang* (The impact of family visits to the mainland on society) (Taipei: Chang Jung-fa Foundation, Dec. 1988), Appendix 3, pp. 14–15.
[12]See note 9.
[13]Ch'ü et al., *Ta-lu t'an-ch'in*, p. 19.
[14]Ibid., p. 20.
[15]Ibid., p. 22.
[16]Ibid.

reflect the fact that most of these elderly people were born on the mainland. Their Taiwanese native spouses and their children might feel differently.[17]

The returnees' assessment of mainland China's economic condition was not optimistic: nearly 70 percent believed that it would take more than 60 years for the mainland to catch up with Taiwan. But the rest believed that after that time span the mainland could compete with Taiwan or even leave it behind.[18]

Nearly 70 percent said that they definitely planned to go back to the mainland again; 84 percent of that group wanted to see their relatives, and 25.1 percent wanted to go as tourists. Those not planning to go back cited as reasons financial difficulties, adjustment problems, physical weakness, or few relatives on the mainland.[19] Responding to the question whether the Chinese Communists would welcome them if they decided to live on the mainland, 56.2 percent gave no opinion or said they did not know, but 59.5 percent stated that their relatives would certainly welcome their living there.[20] Over 80 percent of returnees said that they approved of relaxing the ban on family visits,[21] while 30 percent wanted all government employees to be allowed to visit; 20 percent would allow lower-ranking public servants to go; 10 percent suggested that each application should be decided on its merits; and a mere 10 percent objected to the new policy.[22] Around 80 percent welcomed mainlanders visiting Taiwan, while less than 10 percent objected.[23] The percentages were similar for those endorsing or opposing competition in Taiwan of mainland sports teams.[24] Yet 30 percent objected to opening direct trade across the Taiwan Straits, and less than 40 percent gave their support to that step. The conspicuous lack among the returnees of enthusiasm for direct trade may be due to ignorance, as over 50 percent of the nonreturnees questioned in the survey favored such trade.[25]

Almost 80 percent of the returnees approved the suggestion that residents of Taiwan be allowed to travel directly to the mainland rather than via a third country.[26]

---

[17]Ibid.
[18]Ibid., p. 23.
[19]Ibid., p. 24.
[20]Ibid., p. 26.
[21]Ibid., p. 27.
[22]Ibid., p. 28.
[23]Ibid., p. 29.
[24]Ibid., p. 30.
[25]Ibid., pp. 31–33.
[26]Ibid., p. 34.

Finally, nearly 60 percent of the returnees either "distrusted" or "strongly distrusted" the Beijing regime, while 40 percent held the opposite view.[27] Less than 20 percent of them believed that the two sides would hold talks within the next 30 years.[28] Over 40 percent believed that relations would remain unchanged for the next 10 years; 20 percent said 30 years; and less than 10 percent said 50 years.[29]

In response to the assertion that the future of Taiwan should be decided by the residents of Taiwan themselves, 50 percent of them said they believed that the act of self-determination would provoke an attack from Beijing, and 30 percent said they did not know what would happen.[30] Only 10 percent believed that the Taipei government would succeed in reunifying China, while less than 10 percent believed Beijing would.[31]

The Research, Development and Evaluation Commission of the Executive Yuan published a similar survey in February 1989.[32] Of the returnees it had questioned, 44 percent had been received by officials while on the mainland, and 30 percent of these evaluated their treatment as good.

As for cultural interchange between the two sides, 61.3 percent of the returnees supported a partial opening in this regard, and 21.3 percent a full opening, while 50 percent favored only sports interchange, and 32 percent wanted to see complete exchange. Over 60 percent of the returnees favored limited academic exchange, while 19.2 percent supported complete exchange. As for direct trade, 38.4 percent approved; 20.2 percent disapproved; and the remaining 41.4 percent held no opinion.

Of these returnees, 57.8 percent welcomed the decision to allow mainlanders to visit Taiwan, while 63.3 percent of those who had never been to the mainland also approved. The percentages of those satisfied with the governmental policy on family visits were 85.5 percent for returnees and 81.21 percent for others. The former group had a higher opinion of Taiwan's

[27]Ibid.
[28]Ibid., p. 35.
[29]Ibid., p. 37.
[30]Ibid., p. 36.
[31]Ibid., p. 38.
[32]At a work conference on united-front work in Fukien, held on Jan. 20, 1987, Yen Ming-fu, director of the CCP Central Committee United-Front Work Department, pointed out that there are two strategies for getting Taiwan to talk to Beijing: the first through attraction, and the second involves creating a force within Taiwan that will impel the KMT to talk to Beijing. For this speech, see CCP Fukien Provincial Committee United-Front Work Department, *T'ung-chan kung-tso t'ung-hsün* (United-front work newsletter), no. 44(March 28, 1987):1–19; and *Chung-hua jih-pao*, Feb. 28, 1989, p. 2.

current situation than the latter, but they expressed more caution about interaction between the two sides of the Taiwan Straits. Yet more than 50 percent of both groups were optimistic that China would be reunified within 30 years.

Personal Interviews

I was born in mainland China and came to Taiwan with my family in 1948. As a state-university faculty member, I am not permitted to visit the mainland. However, I have taken every opportunity to talk with people who have been there. Without research funds to conduct a formal survey, I could only interview a random sample of informants, most of whom were in their fifties. They included taxi drivers, veterans, government employees, housewives, a small number of professors, and some businessmen who had illegally traveled to the mainland. Conversations were held in markets, barbershops, parks, and elsewhere. Many of these people were unknown to me; many of those known to me did not wish to be quoted by name. In addition to these conversations, I also referred to unpublished material provided by government agencies. The information I gleaned from these interviews presents only a sketch of how these travelers observed the various mainland provinces.

Kiangsu Province (including Shanghai and Nanking)

The buildings in Shanghai are those of 40 years ago. The streets swarm with pedestrians, bicycles, and crowded buses. Few taxis and trolley buses operate. Still very backward, Shanghai people must mend their broken teapots and use the same basin for personal washing. They bathe once every three to five days in a public bathhouse. Electricity exists in the urban area, but only at given hours in the countryside. One telephone exists for every 1,200 households. Local cadres strictly supervise telephone use. Few public toilets exist, and people queue up to use them.

A Shanghai person with a college education earns 86 yuan per month, and one having vocational training, 63 yuan. Each individual receives a monthly subsidy of 8 yuan to offset inflation, plus food coupons for 18 to 30 *chin* of grain (1 *chin* = 0.6 kg), half a *chin* of grain oil, 1 *chin* of sugar, and 3 *chin* of meat. The one-child policy is more strictly enforced in the cities, and most one-child families receive a nutrition subsidy of an extra 5 yuan. Families with two children, however, must pay 500 yuan.

Shanghai, like other mainland cities, has been swept by "Taiwan fever" and the craze for going abroad. Every day, people queue up at the public security bureau to apply for passports. Shanghai has reception centers, along with special hotels and restaurants, for visitors from Taiwan; because of lingering ultraleftist sentiment and prejudice and the lack of manpower, visitors from Taiwan have not received a warm reception. They are invited to few banquets but spared official interrogations.

A lack of sincerity is also evident in Nanking. Nanking agencies overcharge visitors from Taiwan for food, board, and transportation.

In Soochow, bribery of cadres is widespread. There is a saying that "those who eat crabs do not need to spend money, and those who spend money cannot eat"; in other words, nothing can be done without money changing hands.

Chekiang Province

On the mainland, most enterprises are state-run and close at 5:00 p.m. Restaurants close at 7:00, and tourists who miss their evening meal must wait until the following day. Local train stations are crowded with people.

The monks of the famous Ning-yin Monastery in Hangchow either busily collect admission tickets or stand sentry; they have no time to read their sutras. Some say that monks may get married, and that to be a monk is an occupation like any other, with regular working hours and an entrance examination.

In this province's rural areas, one radio station broadcasts nothing but basic farming information all day. Ten years ago, the province suffered a famine, and even three years ago there was much hardship. Chekiang people in general welcome their relatives from Taiwan who come to live in the province, but they must first obtain permission from the local cadres and have US$10,000 to cover living expenses. The local authorities have built some attractive four- or five-story apartment blocks for ex-residents of Taiwan, but these lack basic facilities, such as bathrooms.

While touring the West Lake area near Hangchow, one elderly veteran from Taiwan had several thousand dollars extorted from him by his taxi driver and a policeman.

This province set up offices in each area to provide services for visitors from Taiwan. These offices entertain the visitors in order to gather information about Taiwan.

Fukien Province

The authorities keep a close watch on visitors from Taiwan. As soon as an application is received in Hong Kong, it goes to the united-front work department in the locality the applicant intends to visit. The department then assembles the visitor's relatives and other people from the same village for questioning. The united-front work department entertains the visitors from Taiwan, as does the local overseas Chinese association. Sometimes the visitors are invited to listen to a report at the county government offices.

Formerly, visitors from Taiwan could simply arrive at the coastal areas of the mainland with only their personal identification and their relatives' names and addresses. That has changed. Controls are now tightened, and visitors must first apply to the local public-security bureaus for a permit.

A visitor to Changpu County said that visitors from Taiwan are warmly received by the Taiwan-affairs office of the local united-front work department, but the office also takes their photographs and keeps them on file.

Changpu County is still very poor. Few jobs exist apart from farm work; thus many men in their forties still cannot marry. There is a shortage of electricity; the transportation system is inadequate, and many roads are not paved. Almost everybody smokes. Corruption and privilege-seeking among cadres seems serious.

In Amoy, public buses and bicycles are the main means of transportation. Buses are overcrowded, and the bicycles create traffic problems. Because most households use coal-fired stoves, air pollution is quite serious. There are few goods in the large state-run stores, but the small, private shops have plenty to offer.

Individual household businesses have the largest incomes in Amoy, some earning over 1,000 yuan per month. As confidence in the yuan is low, the black market flourishes: HK$100 can be exchanged for 75 to 80 yuan, instead of 48 yuan at the official exchange rate. It once was said in Amoy that "no matter whether you work or not, you can obtain 36 yuan a month." Now everyone is trying to leave for Hong Kong or abroad.

One veteran who returned to Amoy in April 1988 said that his wife, who had already married another man, at first greeted him warmly, but when she learned that he had not brought a television set and a refrigerator, and that he had had to borrow money to cover his traveling expenses, her smiles turned into a stream of curses. She would have hit him, had the neighbors not intervened.

Hunan Province

The one-child policy is implemented in Hunan's urban areas. Families living in the countryside are permitted to have two children, but they are not allowed to move their household registration to the city. Outside the cities, electricity is scarce. In Anjen County there is only one television set per 500 households, and a single movie theater. This county has twelve deputy magistrates. The united-front department pays close attention to the opinions of visitors from Taiwan on "reunification" and "Taiwanese independence."

According to one returnee, each township in Chen County has one mayor and at least three deputy mayors. Each village has a brigade with three or four cadres, some of whom are illiterate. These cadres always spouted the "one country, two systems" slogan to visitors from Taiwan. United-front department cadres had to invite the visitors for meals and were punished if their guests failed to attend.

Another returnee from Huang County said that on his arrival at the train station, the county magistrate, a deputy magistrate, and the director of the united-front work department met him. The magistrate and the department director said that people from Taiwan were welcome to visit or to return to live in the county. The authorities would help them to settle or build factories there. They talked about the benefits of "one country, two systems" and "peaceful reunification" and asked for the visitor's opinions. Finally, they asked for criticisms and suggestions. According to the visitor's relatives, they had been told by the local united-front work department to clean and whitewash their houses, including their ancestral tablet. The man's schoolmates from elementary school held a banquet at the county seat. The visitor said that many beggars followed visitors from Taiwan around, and that employees at tourist spots asked them for foreign exchange or even extorted it from them.

Honan Province

Honan's farmland is divided equally among the villagers, except for government employees. The additional children (that is, those in excess of the limit) do not qualify for a land allotment. Each individual receives about 0.5 to 2 *mu* of farmland (1 *mu* = 0.0667 hectares). At first, this allocation was to be changed once every ten years to allow for population change, but this is now done once every five years. Farms have their own equipment and seeds and must transfer 80 *chin* of grain to the state each year; they may keep any surplus. Many farms use surplus grain to feed chickens, ducks, and pigs. Although few households make over 10,000 yuan, living conditions have improved.

Honan's rural areas do not have running water or enough electricity. Most people use candles and do not watch television. Electricity is limited to schools and public offices. Each township has a public-health center, which forces people to practice birth control. Families having more than one child are fined up to 600 yuan. Honan people have a low opinion of Mao Tse-tung and speak favorably of Teng Hsiao-p'ing.

In Chengchow, the local united-front work department admitted to the

Taiwan visitors that Taiwan was superior to the mainland in every way; yet they declared that they could never give up the Four Cardinal Principles. People have little confidence in the yuan. Grass-roots cadres joke that Teng Hsiao-p'ing advocates *shang-min chu-i* (that is, capitalism), which sounds similar to Dr. Sun Yat-sen's *San-min chu-i* (the Three Principles of the People). Visitors complained much about the fact that stores close at 5:00 p.m., and that service is poor.

Shensi Province (including Sian)

A returnee from Chien County said he had been received by the secretary of the county party committee and cadres of the united-front work department and the department of public security. Visitors from Taiwan had to fill out forms giving their name, age, family origin, and dates of entry and exit.

Shensi people can bribe their way into universities and schools or use their privileged position to gain entry. Profiteering is rife, and farmers have to pay much more than the market price for chemical fertilizers. Many long-haired, jobless youths loiter about, and some rob people.

Returnees from Sian said that, in public, the local party secretary and the director of the united-front work department put on airs and lauded the mainland's progress. But they privately admitted that the country was backward and reunification would be difficult. Every month, the united-front work department holds a seminar about compatriots in Taiwan and asks people to help reunification by writing to their relatives in Taiwan. The department has a list of people they try to contact, and the cadres question visitors from Taiwan. They ask visitors to bring telephone books from Taiwan with them on their next visit.

In Sian, the intellectuals complain about low pay, and that peddlers earn much more than they do. They boldly criticize the Chinese Communist leaders in public, no longer calling Mao Tse-tung "chairman." They offer favorable comments about Teng Hsiao-p'ing and sympathize with Hu Yao-pang.

Kiangsi Province

One returnee to Kiangsi reported that at first he was always being invited by the local united-front work department, the propaganda department, the military subdistrict, the Chinese People's Political Consultative Conference (CPPCC), the association of overseas Chinese, and the association of Taiwan compatriots. As a result, he could not visit his mother until five days after his arrival.

This man was asked for his opinions on "one country, two systems." When he inquired about old people's returning to the mainland to live, the cadres did not offer him much encouragement. They said that any individual who returned would receive assistance to obtain land and build a house, as well as receive a subsidy of 30 yuan each month. Nevertheless, they said that anyone wishing to return to live should think carefully before making a decision. It would be inconvenient for both the cadres and the individual concerned if he or she failed to adapt to life and then wanted to leave. The cadres would most likely be blamed.

According to this visitor, workers who receive wages and buy their food have no need to fear natural disasters or grain shortages. But farmers live off the land and do not receive a wage. As the rural areas are poor, young people eagerly seek work elsewhere.

Because most administrative organizations lack a formal system for recruiting personnel, an official may transfer his post to this son on retirement.

Kiangsi people complain that government policy changes with the waxing and waning of the moon. They do not like cadres and complain that while ordinary people work, cadres enjoy themselves.

Szechwan Province

In this province it is difficult to find transportation or a telephone. Even if you can find a telephone, it is difficult to put through a call. One returnee had a good impression of commercial services, but he also said that in both government and private offices too many people performed little work.

A visitor to Chengtu and Chungking received a very bad impression of some young people on the mainland who did not even know their table manners or how to talk to their elders. He also strongly disapproved of his relatives' avarice, which came close to blackmail. He pointed out that, although people in Taiwan are often criticized for lacking public spirit, the mainland people were worse. Traditional Chinese virtues had all but disappeared.

Kwangtung Province

In Swatow, meetings are held almost every day for relatives of old soldiers from Gen. Hu Lien's army who live in Taiwan. Cadres all over the province are busy investigating each family to see if it has any relatives in Taiwan.

In Wan County, both ordinary people and cadres admire Taiwan. In their eyes, visitors from Taiwan are wealthy and educated; they believe

Taiwan can replace Hong Kong as a source of financial assistance to the mainland.

Anhwei Province

Many jobless young men loiter on the streets all day in Anhwei. Finding a job depends on family background and influence. The people are well-fed and -clothed, but the environment is very dirty. Transportation is satisfactory, but it is hard to obtain air or train tickets. People strongly dislike the untidy policemen who smoke on duty.

The man who reported on Anhwei Province was a graduate of Whampoa Military Academy, and wherever he went, cadres from the united-front work department and the local CPPCC greeted him. His impression was that officials below the county level received him more warmly. The reception given by big-city officials, who tend to be jealous and prejudiced, is superficial; they do not provide any concrete help with accommodations or transportation. He also warned that the Chinese Communists still keep a wary eye on visitors from Taiwan, and they should not forget that public-security agents are always watching them.

Beijing

One visitor complained of the traffic chaos on the mainland. Beijing Airport was at least 30 years behind Taipei's Sungshan Airport. Conditions are even worse at Hangchow Airport. Most of the planes are Boeing 737s with 140 seats.

There are express and regular trains, but the expresses are slower than regular trains in Taiwan. It takes four hours to travel by rail from Hangchow to Shanghai. In the southern provinces, there are only single-track railways, so trains have to stop to let others pass. Many farmers lease out their land and start up other businesses. Because people travel mostly by train, the stations and trains are overcrowded, and tickets are difficult to obtain. Even if you have a ticket, it is difficult to get on the train. The roads are therefore full of all kinds of ancient, rickety vehicles—tourist buses, vans, and sedans—which often break down. Cars on official business pay a lower price for gasoline than private vehicles.

Conclusion

All returnees claimed that visits to their families on the mainland had relieved their longstanding homesickness. Having seen the backwardness and poverty on the mainland, they have become more attached to Taiwan. Some plan to return to see their relatives or to travel, but few declared that they wanted to spend the rest of their lives there.

Taiwan residents finally have seen how people live on the mainland and how different the two societies have become. Returnees are less optimistic about the prospects for reunification than those who have never been to the mainland. Beijing's united-front effort has failed. Even so, the family visits have greatly decreased the enmity between the two sides.

Although people would like the policy on family reunions and interactions between the two sides to be relaxed even further, most doubt Beijing's sincerity. They are not optimistic about China's reunification, but neither do they think Taiwan should or could be independent.

The more educated the returnees, the less they seem satisfied with Taipei's mainland policy of banning visits by government employees, public-school and college teachers, and journalists, and of not having cultural and sports interchanges and direct trade and communications between the two sides. Nevertheless, most of them are cautious, believing that Taipei's mainland policy should take into account national security and national interests.

Finally, visits of residents of Taiwan to the mainland might diminish the demand for Taiwan's independence. This was the original aim of Chiang Ching-kuo and the KMT, and Beijing seems to want that as well. In the past, insistence on "one China" produced civil war. Today, family reunions are facilitating people-to-people contact.

Part Three
Developmental Aspects
of the PRC

The Business Climate in the PRC

A legal private business sector is one of the newborn things of socialism with Chinese characteristics. Virtually nonexistent at the time of the Third Plenum of the Eleventh Central Committee of the Chinese Communist Party (CCP) in December 1978, one decade later over 26 million Chinese officially worked in more than 14 million registered private enterprises, some of which had hundreds of employees. In a dramatic case of historical irony, the CCP, after decades of concerted effort to stamp out "tails of capitalism," has legitimated private business as a way of solving some of China's deep economic and social problems. The state has undertaken numerous reforms, which include creating a business climate suitable for private entrepreneurs. However, for a number of reasons, neither the business climate nor the behavior of entrepreneurs has turned out as intended.

This chapter argues that although the party and state have made several reforms on paper to create a climate conducive to private business, in practice, private entrepreneurs face a range of formal and informal constraints. The paper first examines reasons for the party's decision to encourage private business and steps it took to create a suitable investment climate. Many of the consequences were not well thought through, and the private sector expanded and evolved more rapidly than the leadership expected or intended. I then look at constraints on private business. The events of spring 1989 gave opponents of the program a pretext to crack down on private business.

Under the guise of more strictly enforcing regulations, they will try to restrict it even more.

Why Encourage Private Business?

After declaring victory in its campaign to socialize private business in 1956, the CCP mounted constant attacks against any re-emergence of what it termed "tails of capitalism." Under the leadership of Liu Shaoqi, Deng Xiaoping, and others, it loosened up a bit after the disastrous Mao-inspired Great Leap Forward (1958–1960) in order to revive the economy, but then went on the offensive again. The Cultural Revolution (1966–1976) marked an extreme point in the suppression of private business. China appears to have gone beyond the East European socialist countries in its efforts to stamp out the second, or nonstate, economy.

As an integral part of the shift in focus from class struggle to the Four Modernizations after the Third Plenum in 1978, the CCP has criticized its earlier policies as extreme and unrealistic and has taken the unprecedented step of encouraging private business and creating conditions conducive to it. What did the party hope to achieve by reviving private business?[1]

First, it wanted to use private business to fill a number of gaps caused by shortcomings of the state and collective sectors. China's unique Maoist experiments had done serious damage above and beyond the problems seemingly inherent in all actually existing socialist economies. In urban areas, these were especially evident in the areas of services and commerce. Freeing up the rural sector could increase production of food as well as the production of other agriculture-based sideline industries. "Individual households" (*getihu*) could be flexible and respond quickly to fill perceived needs. Relying on their own capital, they would not drain already tight state funds, which then could be applied in critical areas.

Second, taxation of private business could enhance state revenues, providing funds for the numerous projects then on the drawing board.

Third, permitting private operations to compete directly with state and collective enterprises in some sectors (the latter would be made responsible for their own profits and losses) could bring about an improvement in the

---

[1]Some of these points are covered in the chapter *"Woguo xianjieduan weishemma yao baoliu geti jingji?"* (Why should our country preserve the individual economy at the present stage?), in Guojia gongshang xingzheng guanliju geti jingjisi and *Beijing ribao* lilunbu, eds., *Geti laodongzhe shouce* (Handbook for individual laborers) (Beijing: Beijing ribao chubanshe; Gongshang chubanshe, 1984), pp. 73–76.

strength, efficiency, and productivity of the socialist sectors. This would also free the state from the responsibility of shoring up money-losing ventures as well as raising the overall level of production.

A fourth attraction of private business was that it would absorb many of the tens of millions of surplus rural workers.[2] The CCP had eliminated the urban labor market, but with economic stagnation, China did not have enough available slots in state and collective enterprises for the millions of new job seekers annually. In addition to school graduates, there were "socially idle personnel" who needed jobs. This category includes former inmates of reform-through-labor camps and education-through-labor camps; workers fired from other jobs; and ex-Red Guards who had returned to the cities from the countryside, where they had supposedly settled during the Cultural Revolution. There were also handicapped citizens and the elderly on fixed pensions or, if they had never worked, with no pensions at all and needing incomes.

In spite of the fact that, in theory, the private sector could solve these pressing problems, why would the CCP take that option—a tremendous political volte-face—instead of trying to muddle through? For starters, Deng had the precedent of the post–Great Leap years when, under his leadership, partially decollectivized farming had rapidly revived production in a situation more desperate than that of the late 1970s. By 1978, China's state and collective sectors were more dominant and secure than in 1960, so that the Dengists felt confident that, even if they permitted private business in the rural and urban areas, it could never replace the socialist sectors. Whereas most rural folk would participate in the private economy as the communes were disbanded, the targeted urbanites were almost entirely marginals. This could ensure that private business would not have too much attraction for urban Chinese and would retain a cachet of being somewhat disreputable. Through close regulation and supervision, private entrepreneurs would be prevented from expanding to such an extent that they would actually threaten the socialist economy.

In addition to these factors, at that time the CCP began to change its approach to reunification with Hong Kong and Taiwan, stressing the "one country, two systems" idea, whereby the latter could retain their capitalist systems long after returning to the embrace of the motherland. Demonstrat-

---

[2] In 1981, 26 million urbanites were unemployed (Wojtek Zafanolli, "A Brief Outline of China's Second Economy," *Asian Survey,* vol. 25, no. 7(July 1985):715–36; 726, n. 35). In 1988, a survey of eleven provinces revealed that 8–15 percent of the labor force in state enterprises was surplus; see *Beijing Review,* North American edition (hereafter, *BR*), 1988, no. 51(Dec. 19–25):22.

ing that the CCP could tolerate private business, and even provide an environment in which it could thrive and expand, could pay handsome dividends in the Communists' attempt to assuage the fears of the citizens of Hong Kong and Taiwan.

All told, then, the reformers believed that the potential economic benefits of private business within the larger reform program outweighed the downside risk. If properly regulated, private business would have limited social consequences. It would demonstrate the sincerity of the CCP's condemnation of Maoist excesses and of its desire to win popular support through improving the masses's quality of life.

Creating an Investment Climate

In the decade since the Third Plenum, the CCP has undertaken profound reforms in order to stimulate the economy, preserve its power, and eliminate discontent. A comprehensive review of the reforms is beyond the scope of this chapter.[3] In this section I will consider aspects of the reforms that affect the climate for private business.

We should not dismiss out of hand the potential role of a communist state in creating and maintaining an investment climate for private business. The successful economic development of Japan and the Four Little Dragons of East Asia has drawn attention to the potential positive role of the state in creating and manipulating the business climate,[4] including creating the conditions and institutions for a market economy. The East Asian capitalist economies have proven that a large state role in the economy is not necessarily antithetical to the growth of a market economy. Not all elements of the business climate are manipulable, nor are outcomes predictable, but the state can use instruments such as fiscal and monetary policies, state enterprises and banks, allocation of scarce (often imported) resources, direct assistance, provision of infrastructure, labor control, access to information, protectionism, and so on to try to influence the investment decisions of business enterprises in desired directions. The stability of the state itself, its respect for its own laws, and its ability to guarantee social peace also influence investment decisions and business practices.

---

[3]For an overview of the reforms, see Harry Harding, *China's Second Revolution* (Washington, D.C.: Brookings Institution, 1987).

[4]Chalmers Johnson, *MITI and the Japanese Miracle* (Stanford: Stanford University Press, 1982); Thomas B. Gold, *State and Society in the Taiwan Miracle* (Armonk, N.Y.: M. E. Sharpe, 1986).

The socialist state has even more instruments at its disposal to influence the business climate. By definition, the state and collective sectors, operating under a plan, dominate in a self-styled socialist economy. In practice, some degree of market activity and a second economy exist, and enterprises enjoy a certain amount of autonomy. These offer variables for manipulation, a phenomenon described by Chinese economic *genro* Chen Yun as "a bird in a cage."[5]

Institutional Reforms

The guiding principle for economic reform has been to be "open to the outside and [to] enliven the domestic economy" (*duiwai kaifang; duinei gaohuo jingji*). China's opening to the outside has provided models for private investors, Special Economic Zones, and open cities with an especially free-wheeling environment and opportunities for linkages with foreign firms. It is, however, the latter part of that equation which has more direct bearing on the fate of the private sector.

Enlivening the domestic economy includes the following steps which affect private business:[6]

1. Introducing markets for many commodities, in particular agricultural goods, but also many raw materials and manufactured goods above those covered in plans. The state has attempted to reduce the scope of the plan, while expanding that of the market, claiming that it was establishing a socialist commodity economy and regulating the market and the "market guide enterprises." More and more goods are being exchanged, with their prices free to fluctuate. Many goods are

---

[5]Jan S. Prybyla, *Market and Plan Under Socialism* (Stanford: Hoover Institution Press, 1987). I use "second economy" to refer to the nonsocialized or nonplanned economy and "informal economy" to refer to that part of the second economy which goes unregistered and skirts the bounds of illegality. For more discussion on this, see my "Urban Private Business in China," *Studies in Comparative Communism,* vol. 23, no. 2/3(Spring/Summer 1989).

[6]For an excellent discussion of the role of the state in creating a market economy in the rural sector, see Victor Nee, "Peasant Entrepreneurship and the Politics of Regulation in China," in Victor Nee and David Stark, eds., *Remaking the Economic Institutions of Socialism* (Stanford, Calif.: Stanford University Press, 1989), pp. 169–207.

to be made equally accessible to private businesses at the same price as that charged state and collective enterprises.[7]

2. Establishing thousands of free markets, initially for agricultural goods, then expanding to markets and commercial zones for a broad range of consumer manufactures.

3. Introducing responsibility systems. For agriculture,[8] this step involved dismantling the collective commune system and the mandatory purchase of grain, and introducing a system of contracts between the *xiang* government and households, groups, or individuals to sell grain or other crops at a fixed price. Everything produced above the contracted amount may be sold to the state at a higher price or sold on free markets. Households and individuals are encouraged to become specialized (*zhuanyehu*), and permitted to leave agriculture in part or completely and undertake ventures in services such as transportation, as well as household sidelines, and industry. The State Council pledged assistance in the form of loans, prices, tax breaks, and technical aid for needy rural ventures in handicrafts, repairs, services, and catering.[9] Although farm families cannot own the land, they can contract plots for fifteen or more years, giving them a sense of ownership, which then encourages them to invest in improving the land, in equipment, and in their own techniques.

With regard to urban industry and commerce, the state began a reform push after the Third Plenum of the Twelfth Central Committee in October 1984, which encourages entrepreneurship even among managers of state and collective enterprises. This involves decentralizing control from Beijing to provinces and local authorities, and then introducing enterprise autonomy. Under this system, former bureaus become companies which change the way of dealing with enterprises from commandist administration to contracts. The enterprise is re-

---

[7]The eighth policy regulation in "Some Policy Regulations of the State Council Concerning Urban and Township Non-Agricultural Individual Economy" (July 7, 1981) states: "For the supply of that part of materials and supplies needed by individually managed enterprises that belong to the plan, local commercial, supply, and other relevant departments should aggressively bring them into the orbit of the plan, rationally allocate them and aggressively arrange them according to the principles of unified planning with due consideration for all concerned and treating equally without discrimination." (In *Handbook for Individual Laborers*, p. 7).

[8]For a review of agricultural reforms, see "Food and Agriculture in China During the Post-Mao Era," a special symposium in *China Quarterly*, no. 116(Dec. 1988).

[9]"Some State Council Regulations Concerning Village Individual Industry and Commerce" (Feb. 27, 1984), in *Handbook for Individual Laborers*, p. 15.

sponsible for its own profits and losses, and pays taxes instead of receiving and remitting allotments from the state. It applies for loans from state banks. This substitutes hard for soft budget constraints. Chronic money-losers may go bankrupt. The enterprise director has decisionmaking power, while the party committee and its secretary remove themselves from day-to-day administration to concentrate on matters of general policy. Efficiency is to replace a focus on quantity and speed; intensive growth will replace extensive growth.

This has evolved into some other forms of managerial responsibility, including subcontracting or leasing of some state and collective enterprises by individuals or groups (not always originally belonging to those units) who pay taxes to the state and retain the profits, disposing of them as they please.[10] An element of high-stakes competition among all parties has changed the face of Chinese business.

4. Wage reforms that dismantle the "iron rice bowl" system, which guaranteed a job, wages, and benefits, no matter how hard people worked. The reforms also attack the principle of "eating from one big pot," or egalitarianism, where everyone received the same wage or bonus. Bonuses are now to be based on results, with penalties for shirkers, including the risk of being fired.

5. Replacement of the job-assignment system with a labor market. Urbanites who finish school will no longer be subject to (or entitled to) automatic assignment to jobs by the state. Instead, they will search for jobs and sign term contracts, renewable if they perform well. Enterprise directors have the right to hire and fire workers. Employees have more opportunities to switch jobs.[11]

6. Introduction of mixed ownership. The state sector will be held relatively constant, while expansion will occur in the collective and private sectors. As some state and collective enterprises are subcontracted to private persons, this gives a sense of ownership of the means of production. Some state enterprises will sell shares of stock to individuals and other enterprises. The permitted scope for the private sector has expanded beyond merely supplementing state and collective enterprises to actually competing head-on with them in many cases, in particular in retail selling and services.

To sum up, the institutional reforms grant, and compel individuals

---

[10]See Xie Youqiao, ed., *Chengbao jingying zerenzhi zhinan* (Guide to the subcontracting management-responsibility system) (Beijing: Jingji guanli chubanshe, 1988).
[11]Liu Jialin and Mao Fenghua, eds., *Zhongguo laodong zhidu gaige* (Reform of China's labor system) (Beijing: Jingji kexue chubanshe, 1988).

to take personal responsibility for their economic well-being. Through decentralization to the localities and enterprises, restriction of the plan, expansion of the market, price reform, and elimination of many guarantees, the leadership encourages everyone to be more entrepreneurial in the hope that this will stimulate economic activity across the board.

Legal Reforms

China had virtually no body of law prior to the Third Plenum of 1978. To end residual disorder from the Cultural Revolution and to prevent further abuses of power, the state first promulgated a body of criminal and administrative laws, including an attempt to limit the terms of officials. It supplemented this with a media campaign stressing the role of law and the equality of all citizens before law. As economic development proceeded, and in order to promote it, the state promulgated a wide range of laws relating to the management of enterprises, and introduced a system of contracts enforceable by law.[12] Many of the laws relate to foreign investment and trade, and the authorities have shown great responsiveness to the criticisms and suggestions of foreign businessmen and lawyers active in China. The training of lawyers specializing in economic law has expanded rapidly.

Of particular importance to domestic private business is Article 11 of the state constitution promulgated in December 1982. It reads:

> The individual economy of urban and rural working people, operated within the limits of law, is a complement to the socialist public economy. The state protects the lawful rights and interests of the individual economy. The state guides, helps and supervises the individual economy by exercising administrative control.

In the 1978 constitution, a similar provision had the rider that the state guides the individual economy toward collectivization. The 1982 document also protects the right to own and inherit property.

In the planners' original conception, the individual economy would really be individual—one person plying some trade, possibly helped by family members or hiring some outsiders. The key document on the private sector came out on July 7, 1981: "Some Policy Regulations by the State

---

[12]See David Zweig, Kathy Hartford, James Feinerman, and Deng Jianxu, "Law, Contracts and Economic Modernization: Lessons from the Recent Chinese Rural Reforms," *Stanford Journal of International Law*, vol. 23, no. 2(Summer 1987):319–64. It includes a discussion of individuals as parties to contracts.

Council on the Urban Non-Agricultural Individual Economy." The fifth regulation limits individual operations to two assistants (*bangshou*) and at most five apprentices. But some continued to grow, and in March 1988 the National People's Congress officially created a new category of "private business" (*siying qiye*), granting legal status to private enterprises with eight or more employees, with no upward limit. A set of "Interim Regulations on Private Enterprises of the People's Republic of China" went into effect on July 1, 1988. Under the heading "Rights and Duties of Private Enterprises," Article 20 states:[13]

> Investors in private enterprises have the proprietary rights of the property, which can be inherited according to law.

The "Interim Regulations" also differentiate three types of private enterprises: sole investment, partnership, and limited liability (Articles 6–10). Private enterprises may set up joint ventures and other sorts of relationships with foreign companies (Article 22).

The state has promulgated numerous tax codes for individual operators and private enterprises. It has also published several handbooks for rural and urban private business. These typically introduce theoretical underpinnings for private business in socialist China, relevant laws, tax codes, and hints on successful operation.[14]

The legal reforms, in sum, protect private property and codify a number of rights and obligations of private businessmen.

Social Reforms

The CCP has retrenched from its earlier efforts to "lead everything" and to unify all thought and action. It now acknowledges that China has a complex social structure, and that different social forces have different in-

---

[13]Published in *BR*, 1989, no. 10(March 6–12): ix–xiv.

[14]Some examples: Wu Handong, Chen Di, and Min Feng, eds., *Getihu zhuanyehu falu zhishi* (Legal knowledge for individual households and specialized households) (Changsha: Hunan renmin chubanshe, 1985); *Geti laodongzhe shouce* (Handbook for individual laborers) (Beijing: Beijing ribao chubanshe; Gongshang chubanshe, 1984); Huang Jian and Liu Zhao, eds., *Siying qiye zhinan* (Guide for private enterprises) (Beijing: Jingji kexue chubanshe, 1988); and Huang Zhengang and Xu Fuchang, eds., *Geti gongshangyehu nashui zhishi* (Tax payment knowledge for individual industrial and commercial households) (Shanghai: Fudan chubanshe, 1987).

terests.[15] It has granted people more scope to manage many of their own affairs, such as businesses, and also interferes less in personal beliefs (including religion), taste, consumption, artistic expression, interpersonal relations, love, and family life. This opens the way to more diversity in social life. Smashing the iron rice bowl and terminating the job-assignment system have compelled many people to take control of their own lives, like it or not.

One of Deng Xiaoping's tenets is that it is permissible that some people get rich as a way of stimulating effort by the rest and of increasing general social wealth.[16] This means that China's society not only includes more diversity of life-styles, but also inequality of income and all that goes with it.

As part of the shift from class struggle to modernization, the party removed labels from many former class enemies, such as landlords. It has accorded former capitalists a place of honor and encouraged them to revive contacts with former acquaintances, in the interests of soliciting business ties with China.

The new crop of individual entrepreneurs is called "individual laborers" (*geti laodongzhe*), not "capitalists" or even "petty bourgeoisie," thus granting them a legitimate status in a society nominally run by and for the proletariat. (The owners of "private enterprises" have an unclear status at present.) Many works of popular culture—fiction, reportage, songs—portray entrepreneurs in a sympathetic and favorable light. The CCP and Communist Youth League (CYL) have recruited many entrepreneurs, and many party and state leaders have received them and made positive pronouncements on their endeavors. In 1989, there were more than 200,000 entrepreneurs in the CCP (1 out of every 235 members), as well as 10,000 model laborers, 260,000 advanced laborers, 5,500 delegates to people's congresses at various levels, and 6,500 delegates to the Chinese People's Political Consultative Conferences at various levels among the corps of private businessmen.[17]

In the rural areas in particular, the dismantling of the commune-brigade-team structure has resulted in the re-emergence of the family as the main producing, investing, and consuming unit. Family-based strategies of investment, risk diversification, occupation, and so on have re-emerged in the countryside and among many urban business families as well.[18]

---

[15]Gu Jieshan and Zhang Xiang, "Shehuizhuyi chuji jieduan liyiqunti lun" (On interest groups in the primary stage of socialism), *Guangming ribao,* Feb. 29, 1988, p. 3.
[16]See discussion of this in Orville Schell, *To Get Rich Is Glorious,* rev. ed. (New York: New American Library, 1986).
[17]*Wenhui bao,* April 9, 1989.
[18]This latter phenomenon is discussed in Ole Bruun, *The Reappearance of the Family*

Ideological Reforms

Party theoreticians have been busy justifying the wide-ranging reforms and the changes they have brought about. The general rubric, proposed by Deng Xiaoping, is "building socialism with Chinese characteristics." This leaves both socialism and Chinese characteristics undefined,[19] granting great scope for experimentation in order to arrive at suitable definitions of both.

Since the 1978 Third Plenum, the CCP has undertaken a far-reaching review of the history of the party and of the PRC, criticizing many of its past actions. The 1981 "Resolution on Some Questions of Party History" opened the way to a reconceptualization of the role of the party and the nature of Chinese socialism. Economic theorists in particular began to criticize the socialist transformation of industry and commerce in the early 1950s and the collectivization of agriculture in the latter half of that decade as being premature, hasty, and overly simplistic.

Although theorists such as Su Shaozhi[20] had hinted at a major theoretical reconceptualization some years earlier, the major post hoc statement justifying the reforms was Zhao Ziyang's speech to the Thirteenth Party Congress in October 1987, when he discussed "the primary stage of socialism." In this formulation, China is already socialist, as the state sector dominates the collective and private ones, the plan dominates the market, and distribution is based on work. The proletariat's party runs the state. But China's level of productive forces is far below that envisioned by Marx when he discussed the transition from capitalism to socialism. A fundamental reason for China's recent tragic mistakes was the effort of Mao and other leaders to establish socialist relations of production when the material base was too immature. Therefore, the major task for the party in the present stage is to concentrate on raising the level of productive forces by whatever means possible (including private business, foreign capital, etc.) to bring China out

---

as an Economic Unit: A Sample Survey of Individual Households in Workshop Production and Crafts, Chengdu, Sichuan Province, China, Copenhagen Discussion Papers, no. 1 (Copenhagen: Center for East and Southeast Asian Studies, University of Copenhagen, Dec. 1988).

[19]"Socialism" is defined tautologically by reference to the "Four Cardinal Principles" of socialism, the first of which is that China is on the socialist road. (The others are: Marxism-Leninism-Mao Zedong Thought is the guiding ideology; the CCP must lead; and the form of the state is the people's democratic dictatorship.)

[20]See "A Symposium on Marxism in China Today: An Interview with Su Shaozhi, with Comments by American Scholars and a Response by Su Shaozhi," *Bulletin of Concerned Asian Scholars,* vol. 20, no. 1(1988):11–35.

of the preliminary stage of socialism to the point where it can implement full-scale socialism.[21]

This section has reviewed important formal aspects of the reforms as far as they affect private business. The party has provided belated ideological justification for the decision to permit private business and inequality; through the state, it has remade many of China's economic institutions to open numerous areas for private business activity, and promulgated laws to protect such undertakings. A business climate exists, on paper at least, that offers numerous legitimate opportunities for enterprising individuals. In the next section, I look at the growth of the private sector.

The Rebirth of Private Business

At the time of the Third Plenum, there were only 100,000 or so licensed individual enterprises (*getihu*) in China. The total number of licensed individual households in 1981 was 1.83 million, of which 868,000 were urban and 961,000 rural. At the end of 1987, the respective figures were 13,725 million, 3.38 million, and 10.34 million.[22] In 1988, the total passed 14 million.[23] The State Statistical Bureau estimated that in the middle of 1986 there were at least another 6 million unlicensed individual enterprises.[24] Officially, the number of people working in individual enterprises in 1981 was 2.27 million (1.06 million urban, 1.22 million rural). By 1987, these figures jumped to, respectively: 21.58 million, 4.92 million, and 16.66 million.[25] Personal observation convinces me that these figures are vastly understated, as family members and friends regularly help out in enterprises without ever entering the rolls as employees. The figures also do not include moonlighters, who include many intellectuals, professionals, and students, who do not need licenses. Nor do they include participants in the informal economy—prostitutes, moneychangers, smugglers, and so on.

---

[21]Theoreticians have elaborated on Zhao's points. See, inter alia, Yu Guangyuan, *Zhongguo shehuizhuyi chuji jieduan di jingji* (China's economy in the preliminary stage of socialism) (Beijing: Zhongguo caizheng jingji chubanshe, 1988).

[22]"The Individually Owned Economy," *BR*, 1989, no. 9(Feb. 27–March 5):27.

[23]*BR*, 1989, no. 3 (Jan. 16–22):43. According to *Shichang bao* (Market newsletter), there were 14.52 million enterprises and 23.04 million workers (March 30, 1989, p. 1).

[24]"Geti jingji di xianzhuang ji wenti" (The current situation and problems of the private economy), *Geti jingji diaocha yu yanjiu* (Investigation and research on the private economy) (Beijing: Jingji kexue chubanshe, 1986), pp. 3–12; p. 3.

[25]"The Individually Owned Economy," p. 27.

In addition, there are 225,000 "private enterprises" (*siying qiye*), those firms with eight or more employees. These are broken down into 115,000 privately owned enterprises with 1.847 million employees plus 50,000 collective and 60,000 cooperative units.[26] These figures are quite confusing, as the capital usually comes from several partners who sometimes register as "private enterprises," but at other times as collectives and cooperatives, mainly because the latter two sound more politically advanced and enjoy a better tax rate and higher social status. There are also subcontracted and leased state and collective enterprises. By the end of 1988, 81.9 percent of China's 87,000 small and medium-sized commercial enterprises had been subcontracted, nearly 35,000 to households.[27]

In the first years, socially marginal individuals accounted for most of the urban *getihu*, as they had no other choices of occupation. This is what the state intended. But as time went on, other people joined the private sector as a voluntary choice. Some did it for the money they could earn, others to be free of the bureaucratic control of state organizations, and others because they felt that in this way they could bring their talents into full play. The latter group includes university graduates who forgo state jobs for more lucrative and satisfying jobs in private business.[28] The most famous example of that is Wan Runnan, the computer whiz who left his job in a state research institute to establish the Stone Corporation, which grew into a hardware and software company with agents throughout China and abroad.

Workers in state enterprises also took advantage of opportunities to enhance their incomes. Some quit their jobs outright; others made arrangements for temporary leave. In many cases, one family member retains a state job for the iron-rice-bowl benefits it offers, while others embark on the private road.

In 1987, private-household retail trade accounted for 17.4 percent of the nation's total of 582 billion yuan, an increase from the 0.1 percent of 1978.[29] The growth rates have increased yearly. In 1985, individual enterprises paid 3.8 billion yuan in taxes.[30] In 1988, their taxes reached 9 billion, nearly 30 percent of the 30 billion they had paid since 1980.[31]

---

[26]*BR*, 1989, no. 3(Jan. 16–22):42–43.

[27]"Taking Stock of Commercial Reform," *BR*, 1988, no. 52(Dec. 25, 1988–Jan. 1, 1989):22.

[28]For more details on motivations, see my "Guerrilla Interviewing Among the *Getihu*," in Perry Link, Richard Madsen, and Paul Pickowicz, eds., *Unofficial China: Essays on Contemporary Popular Culture and Thought* (Boulder, Colo.: Westview Press, 1989), pp. 175–92.

[29]"Taking Stock of Commercial Reform," pp. 21–22.

[30]Hu Guohua, Liu Jinghuai, and Chen Ming, *Duosetiao di Zhongguo geti jingyingzhe*

In the late 1970s, markets were extremely hard to come by, but by 1988 there were approximately 70,000 of them in cities, towns, and villages.[32] At the end of 1985, private outlets numbered 8.73 million—11.6 percent of the nation's total number.[33] Many state and collective enterprises leased space to private enterprises, and in some places, such as Haikou, Hainan, private businessmen bought buildings and converted them into multistoried shopping centers, leasing space to individual investors. In Wenzhou, Zhejiang, marketization has proceeded so far that it is extremely difficult to distinguish private from socialist enterprises. I visited a three-storied private restaurant with theme rooms and a consumer electronics shop with very stylish staffers, which turned out to be state-owned. Wenzhou's atmosphere resembles that of cities of comparable size in Taiwan, down to the horseshoe-shaped graves on hillsides.

As supplies improved, the Chinese de-rationed most goods, freeing them from plans and subjecting them to market prices, although the prices of about one-fourth were still only allowed to fluctuate within limits.[34]

Private entrepreneurs were concentrated in commerce: in 1985, 53 percent of them were in this sector. Thirteen percent were in industry and handicrafts; 10 percent in catering; 7 percent in repairs; 4 percent in construction; 8 percent in transport and transportation; 6 percent in services, and the rest in miscellaneous activities.[35] Private entrepreneurs dominate in some sectors, in repairs in particular. Privately owned industries have expanded as well, mostly at the expense of the state sector. In 1979, state industrial production accounted for 81 percent of the total, with the rest coming from collectives. In 1989, the industrial production of the state sector had dropped to 59 percent of the total, while collective industrial production rose to 36 percent and private production to 5 percent.[36] (This figure includes wholly-owned subsidiaries of foreign companies as well as joint ventures of Chinese and foreign investors.)

These numbers demonstrate the tremendous growth and expansion of

---

(China's multicolored individual businessmen) (Beijing: Beijing jingji xueyuan chubanshe, 1988), p. 49.

[31] *Shichang bao,* March 30, 1989, p. 1.

[32] "Taking Stock of Commercial Reform," p. 22.

[33] Hu et al., p. 49.

[34] "Taking Stock of Commercial Reform," p. 21.

[35] Calculated from table in Hu et al., p. 29.

[36] Nicholas D. Kristof, "State's Share of Businesses Falls in China," *New York Times,* March 20, 1989, p. C10.

the private sector, but do not reveal the constraints it faces, as well as shortcomings in the actual implementation of policies and laws on the books.

Constraints on Private Business

Duly registered private businessmen encounter a number of constraints in the course of doing business. We can distinguish between formal and informal constraints that influence the business climate.

Formal Constraints

The most important formal constraints come from the plethora of agencies involved in regulating and administering the private sector. Foremost is the Industrial and Commercial Bureau at each level of administration. Below it are departments specifically charged with administering individual enterprises and markets. The Tax Bureau, Public Security Bureau, and Transportation Bureau also have a hand in this work. Other agencies check up on *getihu* within their purview. These include sanitation, environmental protection, urban construction, and city beautification. *Getihu* refer to them disparagingly as "mothers-in-law" (*popo*). The government has admitted that the division of labor among these agencies is unclear: the Industrial and Commercial Bureau does the lion's share of the work, while no one coordinates the work of the other agencies.[37] At the same time, relevant organs suffer from serious understaffing. For instance, in Chengdu each tax official is responsible for 718 enterprises.[38]

Officials make regular and unscheduled checkups on private enterprises. They certify that the *getihu* is not operating outside the scope of business as registered on the license, which is supposed to be prominently displayed (but rarely is). The cadres list the following as the main areas of illegal practices: speculation, cheating, smuggling, trying to monopolize markets, driving up prices, compelling purchases and sales, doing shoddy work and

---

[37]"Guanyu geti laodongzhe xiehui di jige wenti" (Some questions on the Self-Employed Laborers Association), in *Investigation and Research on the Private Economy*, pp. 281–88.

[38]"Buneng rang tamen kao touloushui facai" (Don't let them get rich by evading taxes), *Chengdu wanbao* (Chengdu evening news), March 22, 1989. Each state industrial and commercial cadre is responsible for 1,700 *getihu*, while local tax collectors average 3 to 400 (Wu Shuzhi, "Guanyu geti jingji di guanli" [On administering the individual economy], in *Investigation and Research on the Private Economy*), pp. 272–80, p. 278).

using inferior materials, not paying attention to quality, selling seconds as firsts, selling counterfeit goods, cheating on amounts, adulteration, purveying pornography, disregarding sanitation, and bartering licenses.[39] Many of these complaints are the same as the "Five Vices" attacked in the Five-Anti Campaign of 1952. In addition to these business-related practices there is a gamut of life-style activities that skirt illegality, such as fighting, prostitution, public drunkenness, and gambling, which the Public Security Bureaus deal with.

The media assist the work of these agencies through publicizing crackdowns on offenders and praising models, to educate *getihu* as to the limits of acceptable behavior.

Coming to the aid of professional cadres are many citizens who supervise *getihu* activities in markets and neighborhoods. Commonly retirees, some wear "on duty" red armbands; others just keep an eye out in the course of their daily life.

Getihu also face constraints because of their need to obtain supplies, most of which are monopolized by state enterprises operating under the plan. Despite the regulation cited earlier granting them equal access, the state and collective sectors grab the lion's share of goods, which means that *getihu* must go to state-run enterprises, wholesale markets, or free markets. The state also monopolizes land, buildings, market stalls, and means of production, which constrains *getihu* activity. Some establish linkages with state enterprises for protection and some legitimacy. One form is called *guahu* (hanger-on), where *getihu* do out-work or marketing for state or collective units.[40] There is also the *guakao* (leaning) system, where *getihu* register with a state unit and pay it money, but work on their own.

A final type of constraint is the Self-Employed Laborers' Association (SELA). Nominally, it is the *getihu*'s own professional organization, which, like a guild, supervises its members as well as representing their interests. In point of fact, however, these are set up by Industry and Commerce Bureaus, which appoint their own cadres onto the boards. For instance, in Haikou, Hainan, the chief of the Individual Economy Section under the Industry and Commerce Bureau established the local SELA in 1983 and served as the first head. It was reorganized in 1987. *Getihu* make up over half of the fourteen-member board, the others being cadres from various bureaus, the CYL, and the Women's Federation. The chairman is chief of the Industry and Commerce Bureau. The three vice-chairmen include one

---

[39]Ibid., pp. 276–77.
[40]Susan Young, "Policy, Practice and the Private Sector in China," *Australian Journal of Chinese Affairs,* no. 21(Jan. 1989):57–80, 64.

getihu, the municipal CYL secretary, and the deputy chief of the Industry and Commerce Bureau. In addition to soliciting the experiences and opinions of members (membership is virtually compulsory), the SELA teach business ethics, relevant laws, and how to keep books, transmit party policies, and organize healthy social activities. They help *getihu* carry out "self-education, self-regulation, and self-service."[41] *Getihu* do not have a work unit (*danwei*), and the *getihu* license gives them permission to travel widely throughout the nation. The SELA, then, is something of a surrogate *danwei,* a means of keeping track of them and tying them down.

Informal Constraints

The laws are on the books, but their enforcement is inconsistent. With the decentralization of economic control, local officials have increased discretion in their enforcement of regulations and implementation of policies. This provides authorities with leverage over entrepreneurs under their jurisdiction, and there is tremendous regional variation in the business climate.

Tax officials in particular have a great deal of discretion in estimating how much tax is owed, and the amount is usually settled orally, through "discussion." Most *getihu* either do not keep books, or they are unreliable. Everyone knows they underreport income and in other ways evade paying taxes—they even boast about it. The director of the State Taxation Bureau announced in August 1989 that *getihu* paid only one-third of the taxes they actually owed in 1988.[42] *Getihu* claim that the entire taxation system is corrupt, and that the amount set depends on whether or not the revenuers are satisfied with the bribes they receive.

This brings up another major constraint on *getihu,* namely, corruption. *Getihu* interviewed unanimously claim that the various "mothers-in-law"

---

[41]Yang Zengwen and Ye Cuihua, "Wuhan yikao geti xiehui jiaoyu getihu" (Wuhan relies on SELA to educate individual enterprises), *Liaowang* (Outlook weekly), no. 9(March 3, 1986):24. Also, see *Shanghaishi geti laodongzhe diyici daibiao dahui huikan* (Volume of the first congress of Shanghai municipality's individual laborers), April 1986; and Huang Jian, "Guanyu geti laodongzhe xiehui di jige wenti" (On some problems of SELA), in *Investigation and Research on the Private Economy,* pp. 281–88.

[42]Xiao Zhao, "State Sets Date for Tax Evasion Crackdown," *China Daily,* Aug. 2, 1989, p. 1. The director stated that the 9.2 billion RMB paid in taxes by *getihu* accounted for nearly 6 percent of the state's tax income, and estimated that in 1989 it would reach 8 percent. Considering that the 1988 budget deficit was 7.8 billion RMB (*BR,* 1989, no. 29[July 17–23]:9), collecting more taxes would go a long way to alleviating this problem.

supervising them demand meals, gifts, or outright cash bribes. Those in the restaurant business are particularly vulnerable and must wine and dine cadres or risk being cited for numerous infractions.[43] Sales agents in state and even foreign-invested enterprises also receive payoffs for making scarce goods available to private businessmen. As a *getihu* put it, you need someone "inside" in order to get things. Because state enterprises are now responsible for their own profits, they have incentives to increase incomes through selling goods at higher prices. In addition to marketing their own output, cadres in key positions can take advantage of the existence of the dual-price structure and partially implemented market system to resell goods they receive at the low official price for whatever the market will bear. This is the notorious practice of "official speculation" (*guandao*). Also, many bureaus involved in managing the economy have been converted into "companies" that must show a profit, and they have also engaged in these illicit practices. Rural cadres' control over the allocation of chemical fertilizer and motor fuel has provided opportunities to extort payoffs from peasants.[44]

Another source of control over *getihu* is popular resentment over their high incomes and ostentatious consumption. This is especially galling as so many *getihu* have very low levels of education and have spent time in reform schools or jail. Traditional ideas about modesty and egalitarianism, combined with socialist-Maoist teachings about equality, combine to fuel this popular attitude. The media provoke some of this with stories about outrageous activities of some *getihu,* such as burning cash or holding wedding parades with dozens of motorcycles, cars, bands in trucks, and so on—all for an impotent, handicapped groom.[45]

A number of *getihu* have gone out of business, crushed by the burden of payoffs to corrupt officials as well as the arbitrary levying of fees and general harassment. A survey in Yueyang, Hunan Province, found that 65 percent of those who quit business did so for these reasons, as well as the low social status of *getihu* and political discrimination against them.[46]

These informal constraints and popular jealousy (the "red-eye disease")

---

[43]"Free-Loaders Ruin Restaurant," *China Daily,* June 17, 1986, p. 3.

[44]Jean C. Oi, "Peasant Households Between Plan and Market," *Modern China,* vol. 12, no. 2(April 1986):230–51.

[45]Xie Dehui, *Qian, fengkuang di kunshou* (Money: The mad, cornered beast) (Changsha: Hunan wenyi chubanshe, 1988).

[46]Yueyang shiwei zhengci yanjiushi, "Yiwando geti gongshanghu weihe xieye?" (Why did more than 10,000 individual industrial and commercial enterprises stop business?) *Shehui* (Sociology journal), vol. 10(1988):13–14.

have taken their toll on *getihu*.[47] Some have developed a fear of getting too large, as a large scale of operation brings attention and trouble. Many consume madly as a way of gaining some status in the eyes of others, even though it backfires and adds to the resentment against them. *Getihu* believe that the higher authorities have given free rein to local officials in dealing with them. This arbitrariness plus a lack of confidence in the legal system and in the long-term existence of the private economy also constrain their interest in expanding.

We get a picture of a vicious cycle: *getihu* behavior is a rational response to the business climate as actually implemented. They take advantage of loopholes and shortcomings, but also must deal with arbitrary exactions by hostile and corrupt bureaucrats. This sets them up as lawbreakers and targets for campaigns.

Conclusion

We are left with a somewhat schizophrenic picture of the climate for private business in China. On a formal level, the state has introduced a number of reforms conducive to predictability, stability, protection, and encouragement of private business. It succeeded in sopping up surplus labor, enlivening the economy, making life easier, and generating tax revenues, as intended. The party's tolerance of private business's evolution and flexible management gave confidence to Chinese in Hong Kong and Taiwan. On the other hand, in practice, the authorities at all levels evince an ambivalence, if not outright hostility, toward the sector, especially in the urban areas.[48] This seriously constrains their activity and ability to expand operations.

The center has initiated attacks against "illegal" private businesses and practices several times since 1978. During the campaigns against spiritual pollution (1983–1984) and bourgeois liberalization (1986–1987), local cadres attacked *getihu* with a vengeance, arbitrarily charging them with committing whatever crimes the campaigns were targeting. But then the center made pronouncements "reassuring" the private sector that the policy of permitting private business was not a short-term tactic, but a long-term strategy nec-

---

[47]This paragraph draws from Xie, *Money: The Mad, Cornered Beast*, especially pp. 121–26.

[48]Linda Hershkovitz, "The Fruits of Ambivalence: China's Urban Individual Economy," *Pacific Affairs*, vol. 58, no. 3(Fall 1985):427–50.

essary to raise the level of productive forces.[49] Summing up the experience of the first 30 years of the PRC, the center says: We realize we socialized the economy too quickly and need private business for a long time to come. Other statements discuss raising the consciousness of cadres (*tigao renshi*) about the necessity of private business, assuring them that it does not signal a return to capitalism. This indicates that there is tremendous resistance to private business within official ranks.

The events of spring and summer of 1989 exposed the tremendous disagreement within the leadership over the speed, extent, and direction of reforms. Zhao Ziyang, the man most associated with liberalizing the economy, lost that battle. It is clear that in spite of protestations to the opposite, the policy on private business was conceived as an expedient measure, and that the rapidity of the growth and evolution of private business and its attraction to people outside the targeted groups caught the leadership by surprise. They have had trouble managing it, as well as managing their own cadres. To a certain extent, they want to keep private businessmen off balance to prevent their acquiring a sense of being a social class or controlling too many resources, which might have political consequences. As it is, many *getihu* were active in the Beijing Spring. They ran messages, provided supplies, and demonstrated support. Wan Runnan, manager of the large Stone Corporation, contributed funds and logistical support to the students in Tiananmen Square, confirming some of the regime's fears.

The 1989 crisis, fueled by public resentment over corruption, inflation, and inequality, provided a convenient scapegoat in the form of private entrepreneurs, as well as a timely pretext for establishing new guidelines for administration of the private sector. Reining in *getihu* and terminating some corrupt officials might, as in the Three and Five Anti Movements of 1951–1952, win enough popular support to buy time for the new leaders.

The successful evolution of private business depended on withdrawal of the party and state from some economic activities and their ability to constrain their own actions. There is no reason to believe that they ever intended to withdraw to the degree the Kuomintang state did in Taiwan, where there is now a very strong private capitalist class, market economy, and incorporation into the global division of labor. Nonetheless, on paper, the Communists created an environment that afforded enterprising individ-

---

[49]For instance, the chapter "Fazhan geti jingji shi changqizhen, haishi quanyi zhi ji?" (Is developing the individual economy a long-term direction or an expedient measure?), in *Handbook for Individual Laborers,* pp. 84–86. Also, Liu Zheng et al., *Siying jingji wenti jieda* (Answers to questions about the private economy) (Beijing: Dizhi chubanshe, 1988).

uals many avenues for making profits, and over the reform decade, the general trend was in the direction of predictability and institutionalization. The leadership is still constrained by its inability to discipline its own officials, its financial straits, its lack of credibility and prestige among the masses, the demands of foreign lenders and investors, and the nervous populations of Hong Kong, Macao, and Taiwan. While post-June policy statements promise a rule of law, strict enforcement of regulations, and punishment of corruption, the political lineup offers little hope that this will be achieved. For the time being, arbitrariness, corruption, and hostility will characterize the climate for private business in China.

Economic Developments
in the PRC

Introduction

From the perspective of the late 1980s, the first four decades of economic development in China under the leadership of the Communist Party exhibit what I regard as five salient characteristics. The first is high growth. While there are certain problems with Chinese data, there is widespread consensus among Western specialists that the long-term (1953–1987) rate of growth of national income at least approaches the officially reported 6.8 percent per annum in real terms, or 5 percent per annum in real terms on a per capita basis.[1] Suffice it to say that this is, by a significant margin, the best performance of any socialist economy and roughly twice the average rate for other low-income developing countries.[2]

Second, and here I am on weaker empirical ground, the economy has been characterized by relatively low efficiency in the utilization of its scarce resources. As measured by total factor productivity, which unfortunately does not differentiate between the diffusion of technology (the adoption by more firms of the technology of the best firms in an industry) and the improvement of the best technology, China's performance may actually be distinctly inferior even to other socialist economies, a group that in general

---

[1]Chinese Statistical Bureau, *Chinese Statistical Yearbook 1988* (Beijing: Statistical Publishing House, 1988), p. 29.
[2]For the growth rates of low-income developing countries, see the World Bank, *World Development Report*, various annual issues.

exhibits less productivity growth than more market-oriented economies. Whether China's poor performance is the result of systemic features of socialist economies that inhibit both the development of new technology and the diffusion of best practice, or is the result of misguided central-government policies, such as the Great Leap Forward and the Cultural Revolution, is less clear.

Third, China's development has been highly autarkic. China has pursued a highly protectionist trade policy. This is reflected in ratios of trade turnover (imports plus exports) relative to national income that have been unusually low even for a large continental economy. Moreover, even in periods such as the 1950s, when the volume of trade grew rapidly, the overall strategy has been one of extreme import substitution, that is, it has been driven by the desire to import the productive capability that would ultimately significantly reduce the need for imports. Whether or not this orientation is also characteristic of the past decade, one in which trade volume has again grown markedly relative to output, is a question to which I return below.

Fourth, China's economy has been less market-oriented than that of other socialist states. In my judgment, Western economists have tended to put too much emphasis in their analysis on the relatively high share of many goods, even certain types of investment goods, that are distributed outside the plan through market and various quasi-market mechanisms. That has led to the view that in some sense the Chinese economy is less planned and more market-oriented than other socialist economies. Yet, in its allocation of capital and particularly of labor, China appears, after a decade of reform, to be far less market-oriented than other socialist states. The implications of this are pursued below.

Fifth and last, China's attempts to decentralize its economy, at first in the period of 1957–1958 and more recently in the 1970s and 1980s, have been more complex than those of other socialist states. In short, the regional factor has loomed large in China. As a consequence, economic reform in China is a curious blend of increased market forces and enhanced powers of provincial and local governments. As will be discussed below, many of the problems of China's current reform may be the consequence of this ultimately incompatible mix.

Growth Performance

The growth performance of the Chinese economy is summarized in table 9.1. The long-term growth of national income in the years since recovery from wartime disruption was largely completed in 1952 is 6.8 percent. While, as stated in the introduction, this is impressive by the standards of perfor-

Table 9.1

Growth of Chinese National Income and Its Components

(compound average growth rates in percent per annum)

Period	National Income	Agriculture	Industry	Construction	Transport	Commerce
1953–57	8.9	3.7	19.6	19.4	12.0	7.9
1958–62	−3.1	−5.9	1.8	−7.8	−0.5	−4.3
1963–65	14.7	11.5	21.3	20.9	15.1	2.8
1966–70	8.3	3.0	12.3	8.0	5.6	9.3
1971–75	5.5	3.0	8.5	5.2	5.3	2.1
1976–80	6.1	0.7	9.2	6.9	5.6	7.6
1981–85	9.9	8.3	10.2	11.6	11.0	13.2
1953–87	6.8	3.0	11.2	8.4	7.5	5.7
1979–87	9.0	6.0	10.4	12.8	9.5	9.9

NOTE: Growth rates are calculated according to the underlying values of the variables measured in comparable prices. What is translated in Chinese practice as national income (*guomin shouru*) is actually net material product, which differs from the Western concept of national income chiefly by excluding certain portions of the service sector.

Manufacturing enterprises at the village level and below are included in the industry category.

SOURCE: State Statistical Bureau, *Chinese Statistical Yearbook 1988*, p. 53.

mance of other socialist economies and other low-income developing economies, several caveats must be noted. First, the newly industrialized economies of East Asia—Korea, Taiwan, Hong Kong, and Singapore—have experienced growth performance distinctly superior to that of China. Between 1965 and 1980, for example, their annual growth rates ranged from 2.1 to 4.0 percentage points above that of China's. Only in the decade of reform has China's growth surpassed that of the newly industrialized economies of East Asia.

Second, the growth rate has been highly variable over time. National income and its components contracted sharply in the early 1960s, in the aftermath of the catastrophic Great Leap Forward, and then recovered rapidly in 1963–1965, by the latter year roughly reaching their previous high levels. The pace of growth in the next five years was high but did not match that of the first five-year plan. In the next decade, performance was distinctly lower, followed by a sharp upturn once reform programs were initiated in the late 1970s.

Last, the sectoral pattern of growth has been relatively unbalanced. This is reflected largely in the slow pace of growth of agricultural output, which in per capita terms was stagnant between the end of the first plan in 1957 and the onset of rural reforms toward the end of the 1970s. By comparison, per capita output of manufactured goods more than quadrupled over the same period.[3] Moreover, the slow growth of services (transport and commerce) relative to the expansion of national income is another indicator of imbalance. Services provide neither the value added nor the employment that the same sector does in other Pacific Basin economies. Finally, the imbalance is reflected in the relatively slow growth of personal income and consumption between 1957 and 1978, compared with the growth of national income. For example, collective peasant income grew only 10–20 percent in total over this period, and per capita consumption of food for the entire population declined.[4]

Productivity Performance

In contrast to the absolute growth of output, the growth of output per unit of input utilized in the production process has been less impressive. Declining efficiency in the utilization of capital is made evident by comparison of the rising share of output devoted to investment, as opposed to consumption, with the falling rate of growth. As shown in table 9.2, the long-term trend in the rate of investment is upward while, as shown in table 9.1, the trend for growth (leaving aside the recent reform period) is downward. In short, a rate of investment of less than one-fourth of national income sufficed to generate a rate of growth of almost 9 percent per annum in the first plan. But by the decade of the 1970s, a distinctly higher rate of investment of about a third resulted in a distinctly lower rate of growth, under 6 percent. In short, growth was sustained by a pattern of extensive development demanding over time an increasing quantity of capital input per unit of output.

More significantly, total factor productivity, which measures the growth of output per composite unit of input, including both capital and labor, was zero or even slightly negative in the nineteen years prior to 1977.[5] This is distinctly inferior to the experience of developing countries since World War II. A survey of twenty developing countries for which calculations of total

---

[3]State Statistical Bureau, *Statistical Yearbook of China 1986* (in English), pp. 41 and 71.

[4]Nicholas R. Lardy, *Agriculture in China's Modern Economic Development* (Cambridge, Eng.: Cambridge University Press, 1983), pp. 146–63.

[5]Dwight Heald Perkins, "Reforming China's Economic System," *Journal of Economic Literature,* vol. 26, no 2(June 1988):627–28.

Table 9.2
Investment as a Percent of National Income

Period	Percent
1953–57	24.2
1957–58	30.8
1963–65	22.7
1966–70	26.3
1971–75	33.0
1976–80	33.2
1980–85	31.3
1986	34.8
1987	34.7

SOURCE: State Statistical Bureau, *Chinese Statistical Yearbook 1988* (Beijing: Statistical Publishing House, 1988), p. 60.

factor productivity have been made, generally for periods of 20 to 25 years, showed that growth of total factor productivity averaged 2 percent per year, accounting for over 30 percent of the growth of these economies.[6] Although China grew somewhat faster than this group of countries, it was distinctly different in that growth of productivity apparently either made no contribution to growth or actually reduced growth.

The stagnation, or even decline, in total factor productivity in China after 1957 appears to have been fairly widespread, but there are varying estimates for the trends in individual sectors. In agriculture, for example, the work of Prof. Anthony Tang shows that factor productivity fell 21 percent between 1957 and 1977.[7] This interpretation is borne out by later calculations of Prof. D. Gale Johnson and others.[8] He estimates that total factor productivity declined by 0.3 percent per annum between 1952 and 1978.

---

[6]Hollis B. Chenery et al., *Industrialization and Growth: A Comparative Study* (New York: Oxford University Press, 1986), pp. 21–22.

[7]Anthony M. Tang, "Food and Agriculture in China: Trends and Projections, 1952–77 and 2000," in Anthony M. Tang and Bruce Stone, *Food Production in the People's Republic of China,* International Food Policy Research Institute Research Report, no. 15 (Washington, D.C.: International Food Policy Research Institute, 1980), p. 28.

[8]D. Gale Johnson, "The Agriculture of the USSR in China: A Contrast in Reform" (unpublished manuscript, September 1985).

In manufacturing, analysis is complicated by inadequate data on the capital stock of the collective and private sectors. For state-owned industry the estimates vary. A World Bank study shows stagnation or declining total factor productivity from 1957 through the late 1970s.[9] More recent work by Prof. Thomas G. Rawski and his colleagues suggests that the long-term trend over the same period is more favorable, with average annual productivity improvements estimated to have been between 0.4 and 1.4 percent per annum, depending on specific assumptions made.[10] But these results depend on many adjustments to the input data, made in an effort to eliminate what the authors regard as the biasing effect of rising prices of investment goods. However, these adjustments are somewhat ad hoc, and many uncertainties remain.[11]

My own view is that, after exhibiting robust growth in the period of the first plan, productivity in state-run industry declined after 1957 at an annual average rate of 0.4 percent, and that this is likely to be an upward-biased estimate of the underlying productivity trend in state-run industry.[12] That is, the true underlying performance of the industrial sector between 1957 and 1978 is likely to have been substantially worse than that indicated by the figure of −0.4 percent per annum.

Three important factors, which have not been taken into account, almost certainly raised the measure of factor productivity reported above. These are the massive commissioning of new plants built with Soviet technical assistance; significant improvements in the quality of labor, that is, improvements in human capital; and the discovery and exploitation of new energy sources. These three factors are not taken into account in the multifactor-productivity estimates presented above. But in a proper accounting, which we cannot undertake for lack of adequate data, we would want to account for these influences separately, rather than attributing their effect to improved factor productivity.

Soviet-assisted investment projects absorbed fully one-half of all Chinese industrial investment during the implementation of the first five-year plan. Because the technology embodied in these plants was significantly more

---

[9]The World Bank, *China: Long-Term Issues and Options* (Baltimore, Md.: The Johns Hopkins University Press, 1985), p. 111.

[10]Chen Kuan, Wang Hongchang, Zheng Yuxin, Gary H. Jefferson, and Thomas G. Rawski, "Productivity Change in Chinese Industry, 1953–1985," *Journal of Comparative Economics,* vol. 12, no.4(Dec. 1988):585.

[11]Nicholas R. Lardy, "Technical Change and Economic Reform in China: A Tale of Two Sectors" (unpublished manuscript, 1987).

[12]Lardy, "Technical Change."

advanced that indigenous Chinese technology, their commissioning probably boosted multifactor productivity as it is conventionally measured. Yet this infusion of technology from an external source should not be included in a proper measure of underlying productivity growth. Since the vast majority of these plants was not completed until after 1957, when measured factor productivity began to decline, other factors apparently more than offset the enhancement of the transfer of Soviet technology.

Second, there has been a substantial long-term improvement in human capital that is not captured in the data on the increased numbers of workers and staff in state-owned industry that are used in conventional multifactor-productivity calculations.[13] On the eve of the Communist takeover, adult illiteracy in China is estimated to have been 70 to 80 percent. Resources allocated to education, particularly at the primary and secondary levels, rose markedly in the 1950s. Primary-school enrollment ratios are estimated to have increased from 25 to 90 percent between 1949 and 1983. Secondary schools expanded even more rapidly, so that the enrollment ratio rose from 2.5 to 40 percent over the same period. In short, by the late 1950s, and continuing into the 1960s and 1970s, the basic quality of the entrants into the industrial labor force was substantially higher than that of the initial labor force. A proper accounting for these improvements in the quality of the work force after the mid-1950s would result in an even more rapid estimated decline in total factor productivity in state-owned industry.

Third, the discovery in the late 1950s of immense, relatively easily exploited petroleum reserves in the Sungliao Basin, notably the Taching Field in Heilongjiang province, should have contributed positively to total growth of factor productivity in the 1960s and 1970s. The discovery of the Taching Field was followed by discoveries of major new fields in Shengli, Takang, Panshan, Itu, and Fuyu, which dramatically shifted the distribution of oil production from the remote west and northwest of China to the northeast and east, substantially closer to the country's major industrial centers. By the mid-1970s, China had become a major world producer of petroleum and had begun to export oil, instead of depending on petroleum imports as it had from the 1950s onward. This windfall, too, should have pushed productivity up.

In short, all three of these factors presumably pushed up the measure of factor productivity cited above. Apparently other negative factors, which more accurately reflect the true underlying trend of productivity growth, more than offset these effects.

---

[13]The data on education used are taken from the World Bank, *China: Issues and Prospects in Education*. Annex 1 to *China: Long-Term Issues and Options*.

Autarky

China's development strategy has been basically autarkic. By this I mean that its strategy seeks to minimize over-time trade and other forms of economic interaction with the world economy. By the most common measure of the degree of participation in the world economy, the ratio of exports to gross domestic product, China has been extraordinarily self-reliant.[14] Considering the period prior to 1978 as a whole, China's export ratio appears to have been only about one-fifth to one-tenth that of the average of more than one hundred countries. Obviously, China's export ratio is low in part because its resource endowment is relatively favorable, obviating the need for massive imports of raw materials, and because the large size of its economy allows the exploitation of economies of scale in production without the need to export. But even when compared only with very large countries, defined as those with a population of more than 50 million in 1985, China's export ratio is still unusually low—about one-fifth to one-third the average.

A strategy of autarky does not mean that trade is necessarily minimized at every point in time. For example, China's trade grew rapidly in the 1950s, when trade turnover expanded from less than two billion U.S. dollars on the eve of the first plan to more than four billion U.S. dollars in 1959.[15] However, imports in this period were overwhelmingly machinery, equipment, and other producer goods, and were concentrated in sectors in which China wished to become increasingly self-sufficient—machine tools, chemicals, steel, and so forth. The underlying objective—self-sufficiency in the production of investment goods—was reflected in periodic claims of an increasing share of investment goods produced within China. These claims have been borne out by Western estimates which show that the degree of self-sufficiency in producer durables rose from 58 percent in 1957 to 92 percent in 1973.[16]

The autarkic trend was even more evident in the 1960s. The Sino-Soviet split led to a collapse of China's most important bilateral trade relationship. And trade with the West was inhibited, since the restrictions on trade with China from the Korean War era were still in effect. The Cultural Revolution, with its strong nativistic bias, curtailed a modest trade recovery that was evident from 1963–1966. By the end of the 1960s, the absolute volume of

---

[14]Dwight Heald Perkins, "Reforming China's Economic System," p. 635.

[15]State Statistical Bureau, *Statistical Yearbook of China 1981* (in English), p. 357.

[16]Thomas G. Rawski, *China's Transition to Industrialism: Producer Goods and Economic Development in the 20th Century* (Ann Arbor: University of Michigan Press, 1980), p. 101.

trade was less in nominal terms than in 1959, despite the fact that real national income was up more than 15 percent.

Growth of trade resumed in the 1970s, but again was strongly import-substitution in character. There was a resurgence of purchases of complete plants in product areas in which the Chinese sought greater self-sufficiency, notably chemical fertilizers, petrochemicals, and synthetic fibers.

The autarkic nature of China's development strategy was also evident in its institutional structure. The central government, through its monopolistic import and export corporations under the Ministry of Foreign Trade, controlled decisions on China's trade. The flow of imports and exports was determined through the planning process, not the decisions of firms and consumers. Import needs were fixed first, largely with a view to overcoming the temporary shortages in needed materials and to increasing China's productive capability in the producer-goods sector. Exports were seen primarily as a means of financing imports. The majority of trade was carried out on a barter basis with the Soviet Union and other members of the Eastern bloc. Annual trade protocols specified the goods to be exchanged, facilitating the incorporation of the flow of goods, both imports and exports, into the annual production plan of each side. The exchange rate was made artificially high.

Relative Absence of Markets

China has in some ways been less market-oriented than other socialist countries. Analysis of this issue frequently focuses on product markets in countries than which China was probably more market-oriented, even prior to the onset of reform. As the work of Prof. Christine Wong has shown, in 1978, prior to the beginning of industrial reform, a relatively high proportion of key producer goods was distributed outside of the central materials-allocation system: cement, 64 percent; coal, 46 percent; steel, 20 percent; machine tools, 65 percent; trucks, 25 percent; and so on.[17] Soviet specialists are particularly struck by this indicator of the degree to which Chinese economy was unplanned even prior to the last decade of reform.[18]

---

[17]Christine Wong, "Material Allocation and Decentralization: Impact of the Local State Sector on Industrial Reform," in Elizabeth J. Perry and Christine Wong, eds., *The Political Economy of Reform in Post-Mao China* (Cambridge, Mass.: Council on East Asian Studies, 1985), p. 262.

[18]David Granick, *Chinese State Enterprises: A Regional Property Rights Analysis* (Chicago, Ill.: University of Chicago Press, 1990), chapter 3.

However, it has been less widely noted that in labor markets in the modern sector, China is actually less market-oriented than the Soviet Union. The two countries may not vary significantly in their procedures for assigning jobs to school graduates, particularly at the university, technical-school, and secondary-school levels, but thereafter their systems diverge significantly. China has a very widespread permanent employment system, which means that turnover in the predominant state sector is minimal, not only for unskilled workers, but for technical and engineering personnel as well. In short, interenterprise competition for labor scarcely exists. The typical Chinese state enterprise has virtually no quits, is sometimes even constrained to replace retiring workers with one of his or her children, and faces heavy constraints on its choice of new workers. Even among scientific and engineering staff, the turnover rate is surprisingly low, about 3 percent annually. By contrast, as Prof. David Granick has pointed out, in the Soviet Union the annual quit rate is 17 to 20 percent.

In part, this difference stems from different underlying conditions in each country. In the Soviet Union, where the industrial sector is relatively large, and the growth of the labor force much slower, there is a relative shortage of labor. A worker who quits need not have difficulty in locating a new employer. In contrast, China's modern-sector labor force is quite small relative to the potential available supply. Under conditions of excess supply, the cost to the individual worker of quitting may turn out to be unemployment. In part, however, the lower turnover arises from the multifaceted dependence of workers in their enterprises so effectively analyzed by Prof. Andrew Walder.[19]

The low turnover of workers in China, particularly among engineers and technical personnel, may be a significant source of inefficiency. In most market economies, labor mobility is one of the major means of diffusing new technology. Much technical knowledge is embodied in human capital; hence increased flexibility in hiring practices might improve the diffusion of technology.

It should be noted that China's system of permanent employment differs in two respects from that of Japan's, where it does not seem to have affected productivity adversely. First, in prereform China, permanent employment was far more pervasive in manufacturing than was the case in Japan. In China in 1978, the system covered more than half of industrial employment, whereas in Japan the proportion is under one-fourth.[20] Second, and perhaps

---

[19]Andrew G. Walder, *Communist Neo-Traditionalism: Work and Authority in Chinese Industry* (Berkeley: University of California Press, 1986).

[20]*Chinese Statistical Yearbook 1988*, pp. 154 and 163.

more important, in Japan the potential adverse effects of the system are largely offset by intraenterprise labor mobility. This is facilitated by the large size and multiproduct character of the Japanese manufacturing firms practicing permanent employment. In contrast, China has a large number of state-owned enterprises—more than 80,000 on the eve of the reform. Moreover, most of these enterprises are specialized in a single product.

The Regional Government Factor

China's post-1978 reforms are not simply expanding the market at the expense of planning. They are simultaneously bringing about a substantial change in the locus of bureaucratic authority, specifically an enhancement of provincial and local government authority and a diminution of bureaucratic authority at the center. This trend is particularly evident in the fiscal system, where the magnitude of extrabudgetary resources, mostly controlled by provincial and local governments, is now fully equal to budgetary resources. It is evident to a lesser extent in the foreign-trade system, where a growing share of export and import transactions is carried out by newly established provincial foreign-trade corporations, rather than by the former provincial branches of the national foreign-trade corporations.

The enhanced authority of provincial and local governments in China's reforms appears to come from two factors. First, the initial position of these governments was more important than in other socialist economies, even that of the Soviet Union. This is reflected, for example, in the large share of the state-owned manufacturing establishments that has fallen under the jurisdiction of provincial and local governments. In part, that may be a function of China's large geographic size and the underdeveloped character of its communications and transport systems. For example, in Hungary around 1980 there were only about 700 state-owned industrial enterprises in an area roughly the size of Fujian province. China, by contrast, had more than a hundred times more firms, diminishing the possibility for direct ministerial control of all enterprises from the capital.

Second, reformers at the center in Beijing have always apparently sought support from the provinces in their attempt to diminish the power of the central-planning and ministerial apparatus. This, however, is an unusual alliance, for, as will be discussed below, provincial and local authorities frequently do not fully share the interest of central reformers in enhancing the role of the market in resource allocation, but seek to arrogate to themselves a share of the central authority.

Prospects in Coming Decades

Economic reforms begun under the leadership of Deng Xiaoping in the late 1970s have brought far-reaching changes in the Chinese economy and in certain respects have modified the distinctive aspects of the economy sketched out above. Yet, as the analysis below seeks to show, in certain critical respects the salient characteristics of the economy have been largely untouched, suggesting the very partial character of the reforms to date.

Growth and Productivity Performance

Perhaps the most salient objective of the reforms is to change the character of the process of economic growth. The objective is to generate an expanding economy increasingly through the more efficient use of scarce resources rather than by simply, for example, building more and more factories that operate with the same degree of inefficiency as do existing plants. Thus the objective is not so much to increase the rate of growth, which, as we have seen, was already relatively high prior to the reform period, as it is to sustain the expansion of the economy by means of increased productivity rather than high rates of investment.

At the aggregate level there is some evidence that the productivity performance of the economy has been up during the first decade of reform. The growth of national income, according to the State Statistical Bureau Data shown in table 9.1, was 9 percent per annum in the years 1979–1987, a sharp increase from the long-term trend. On the other hand, the rate of investment from 1980–1985 (shown in table 9.2) was slightly below the rate of the previous decade, although it moved up above that level in 1986 and 1987. This combination suggests some improvement in productivity in the use of capital.

Dwight Perkins' calculations show that conventionally measured total factor productivity also improved sharply in the postreform years. By his calculation, almost 4 percentage points of the almost 9 percent average annual increase in the growth rate of net material product between 1976 and 1985 was accounted for by increases in productivity, rather than by increases in the capital stock or in the labor force.

Data for individual sectors of the economy show varying results. On the one hand, productivity in agriculture almost certainly rose after 1978. The rate of expansion of output more than doubled, whereas the quantities of incremental capital and labor showed much slower or even negative rates of growth. D. Gale Johnson's calculations suggest that through 1984 improvements in factor productivity account for fully half the growth of farm output after 1978.

In the manufacturing sector there is more uncertainty. Calculations by the World Bank for state-owned industries using official data on an unadjusted basis show total factor productivity declining at an accelerating rate through 1983. Extension of this analysis through 1985 confirms the general result of negative factor-productivity growth.[21] On the other hand, an analysis based on data for twenty state enterprises that were included in a World Bank survey shows that total factor productivity may have increased as rapidly as 4.7 percent per annum in the period of 1975–1982, a level of performance that is attributed to the economic reforms begun in the late 1970s.[22]

The study by Thomas G. Rawski and his colleagues, cited above, suggests that there was a sharp acceleration in productivity growth after 1978. Depending on which set of assumptions is preferred, total factor productivity grew at a rate between 4.8 and 5.9 percent per annum between 1978 and 1985.

What are the implications of these results for our understanding of China's growth prospects? Obviously, more research is needed to shed further light on the all important manufacturing sector, which is responsible for almost half of China's national income.

My own preliminary view is that the multifactor-productivity calculations that we concurrently calculate for China are so crude that they can be regarded as no more than a very tentative indicator of what we are really interested in: the capability of the economy to stimulate technological progress and innovation. I say this for several reasons. First, it is quite possible that the official data on the growth of manufacturing output is biased upward after 1978 for two closely related reasons. First, a growing share (which has now reached fully one-third) of industrial output is produced in collectively and privately owned establishments, where, we might surmise, that the reporting of output is subject to greater error than in larger, state-owned plants. Second, the development and expansion of multiple markets for the same product may have led to errors in factory reporting on the value of output. With varying portions of outputs sold at state-fixed and market-determined prices and an inflationary trend in the latter, it may well be that part of the output gain in recent years is spurious. As least one Chinese

---

[21]On the World Bank methodology, factor productivity in state-owned manufacturing firms declined at an average annual rate of 0.3 percent between 1978 and 1985 (see Lardy, "Technical Change").

[22]David Dollar, "Economic Reform and Allocative Efficiency in China's State-Owned Industry," UCLA Department of Economics Working paper, July 1988.

source reported that as much as 3 percentage points of reported industrial growth in recent years represented the effects of price inflation rather than real output growth. However, it is not clear whether this adjustment is adequate to cover all of the sources of distortion in the official data, including the accumulation of low-quality output that is added to already excessive inventories, rather than meeting final demands such as consumption or investment.

Second, even if the data were not flawed, or if we could adjust for these flaws, it is not clear how we should interpret the data on productivity. Would they support the view that the capability of the economy to generate innovation and technical progress has increased in recent years? Or would they indicate that the 1980s were a transition period, in which the gross inefficiencies of the Maoist years were undone, but in which the underlying pace of innovation and technical progress was unchanged?

The experience of the agricultural sector would appear to support the second interpretation. As already indicated, the growth of farm output and total factor productivity in the farm sector grew impressively between 1978 and 1984. But the performance of agriculture simply collapsed after 1984. The failure of grain output in the last four years to surpass the peak level of 1984, of course, has been widely noted. A common explanation of this, however, is that it reflects the reallocation of land to other crops that have become relatively more profitable than grains. In a household-based, as opposed to a collectively organized, farming system, exhortations by the state to increase grain acreage have little influence on the allocation of land to alternative crops. While this is in part true, it overlooks the fact that, once we take out the rapidly growing rural manufacturing sector, agricultural output growth in the period of 1984–1988 is no more rapid than the long-term performance of the period from 1957–1978.

In short, most of the gains in farm output in the early years of reform stemmed from the elimination of the most obvious sources of inefficiency in the collective system. Peasants' real income was more closely tied to their productivity under a system of land contracting by individual households than it had been under the awkward system of work points used in the collective era. The change clearly stimulated more efficient use of labor. Inefficiencies associated with the Maoist era's emphasis on self-sufficiency in food grains at the local or even community level were drastically reduced once constraints on rural markets were eased. Comparative-advantage cropping quickly re-emerged once potential producers of fiber, oil seed, and other crops could purchase the grain needed for their own consumption on the market.

But these relatively easy sources of gains were quickly exhausted. By the mid-1980s, the performance of the farm sector was constrained by

China's relatively unfavorable resource endowment, the effects of which were compounded by a shortage of farm investment, both governmental and private; by inadequate rural infrastructure, particularly in transport and electrification; by relative prices whose movement was unfavorable to the peasantry, and so on.

Although I have no evidence, it may well be that some of the increased growth of other components of the national income after 1978 has been due to a similar one-time catch-up. The rapid growth of services (transport and commerce) reflected in table 13.1 for the years after 1978 almost certainly in part represents the reversal of previous decades of neglect. For example, up through the late 1970s, the number of food and other service establishments declined not only relative to the population but even absolutely. In the 1980s, though, there has been a remarkable resurgence in these activities. Similarly, the boom in construction, which is due largely to the building of more housing, in part represents a catch-up after a period of more than two decades during which urban housing standards declined precipitously and rural housing standards improved little, if at all. The long-term expansion in this sector may be well below the nearly 13 percent annual pace experienced after 1978.

Over the longer run, China's growth will almost certainly be depressed by both the continuing failure to address structural issues, such as the shortage of infrastructure and energy, and the relative neglect of human capital investment in recent years. For more than a decade a significant share of China's industrial capability has not been effectively utilized, and production has been restrained by the backward state of China's transportation infrastructure. Although these problems have long been clearly identified, the Chinese government has failed to take appropriate steps and the problems appear to have worsened in recent years.

In education, China's once-model performance in the developing world has been almost entirely reversed over the past decade.[23] Primary-school enrollment rates appear to have peaked in 1978 or 1979 and fallen since then. This is presumably due to changes in both supply and demand. Since the mid-1950s, rural primary schools have been built, and their teachers largely paid, from rural-collective funds, rather than from central or local government budgets. But the rural townships that have replaced the communes apparently either lack the revenue base to sustain rural primary schools, or have made the maintenance of the rural primary-school system a low priority. Similarly, many primary-school teachers have left the field as the revival of the rural economy created more remunerative positions for persons with their skills. On the demand side, peasant households may prefer to have

---

[23] *China: Issues and Prospects in Education.*

their children work on the family land rather than attend school, now that the marginal returns to labor accrue entirely to the household.

The collapse of enrollment is even sharper at the secondary-school level, where the share of the cohort enrolled fell from a peak of 46 percent in 1977 to 20 percent by 1983. Whereas China's secondary-school enrollment rate was well above the average of developing countries during the 1970s, it fell to well below that average a few years after reform began.

Autarky Re-examined

On the surface, it would appear that China's reforms have decisively rejected the autarkic trade strategy of the past. Over the past decade China's trade has grown more rapidly than that of any other economy in the world. Total trade turnover in 1988 exceeded 100 billion U.S. dollars and was exceeded significantly by only about a dozen advanced industrial economies. Exports as a share of domestic products have risen sharply and on some calculations now exceed the average ratio for large economies.[24]

While China has moved from virtually complete autarky toward greater openness in the past decade, the current "open door" policy retains a strong bias toward import substitution. And, although exports have grown rapidly, it is not clear that increased trade has been a source of efficiency gains in the economy, either directly through the more rapid growth of low-cost comparative-advantage exports or indirectly through the stimulus that international competition could provide to Chinese domestic firms.[25]

In a market economy with an equilibrium exchange rate reflecting the underlying relative value of the domestic currency, a move from autarky to more open trade would generate significantly increased efficiency in the allocation of resources. This is referred to as the "gains from trade." In the Chinese case, although exports have grown, the persistence of severe distortions in the domestic economy gives rise to the possibility that trade is actually welfare-reducing rather than welfare-increasing.

The major problems stems from the—at best—semireformed character of the domestic price structure. The most profitable export goods may not

---

[24]Exports of 47.5 billion U.S. dollars in 1988 were equal to 15 percent of China's national income measured in yuan and converted to dollars at the official exchange rate. Since that rate significantly understates the purchasing power of the domestic currency, the export ratio is overstated, perhaps by as much as three to five times.
[25]The World Bank, *China: External Trade and Capital* (Washington, D.C.: The World Bank, 1988).

be comparative-advantage goods, but those for which state-fixed prices have been set artificially low. For example, the underpricing of nonferrous metals and nonferrous metal alloys on the domestic, relative to the world market led to a rapid growth of exports of these commodities in 1988. Because the domestic price was fixed, shortages soon emerged, and in 1989 the central government forbade any export of these commodities. Thus the inflexibility of the domestic price structure appears to have led to the export of a range of noncomparative-advantage products and, furthermore, to a bureaucratic intervention that reduced the degree of openness of the economy. Similarly, the foreign-trade regime still effectively insulates most domestic firms from international competition. A large share of China's imports, about 40 percent in the mid-1980s, fell under the command plan. These commodities are imported to fill shortfalls in domestic production and are priced at the same level as domestically produced goods, eliminating the prospect of international goods undercutting domestic prices. A large share of the remainder of imports is restricted by licensing, which sets quantitative limits on imports and thus results in highly variable levels of protection. In addition, tariffs that, including their so-called regulatory component, range as high as 200 percent provide substantial protection for many domestic industries.

Regionalism

Finally, the enhancement of regional power is an obstacle to achieving greater efficiency. Market reform raises efficiency by reallocating scarce resources from less to more productive uses. While these readjustments entail some costs, the long-term payoff is expected to more than offset those costs.

However, provincial and local governments in the past decade have used their increased authority to frustrate efficiency-increasing resource reallocation. Rather than allowing markets to work, they have all too commonly sought to enhance and exploit their own market power. The result has been increasingly segmented, rather than more integrated markets, a rising misallocation of resources as monopoly power is used to raise prices and local profits, and a rising level of inflation which undermines support for further reform. The result of this trend is a surprising low degree of local specialization in the production of manufactured goods. Although the number of state-owned firms has grown significantly since 1978, this apparently does not reflect an increasingly competitive market. Many of the new firms are small-scale, high-cost producers that survive only because local governments set up bureaucratic barriers that prevent products from other regions from entering the local market. One example discussed in some detail in a World Bank report was the proliferation of bicycle plants that occurred in the early

1980s in response to rapidly rising demand.[26] In 1982, only 11 of 140 factories produced at a volume sufficient to take advantage of economies of scale. However, the new entrants were able to sell their high-cost products because their local market was guaranteed by protectionist measures.

This problem is not confined to bicycles; rather it is pervasive. In 1987, in an attempt to enforce bureaucratically what should have been assured by competitive markets, the central government promulgated a series of norms setting forth the minimum production capability for new factories in light industry and in the textile, motor-vehicle, building-materials, petrochemical, chemical, nonferrous-metallurgy, iron and steel, and power industries.[27] These sectors account for almost half of all industrial output in China. The goal is to prevent the emergence of more small-scale, high-cost enterprises that frequently absorb raw materials which previously went to more efficient large-scale plants in other regions. In a competitive-market environment, such a directive would be unnecessary. No investment funds for such small-scale inefficient producers would be found.

Summary

Many articles and books have analyzed in great detail the specific economic-reform measures promulgated and implemented in China over the past decade. While in certain respects China's reforms are more far-reaching than those of other socialist economies, I have sought to show that some of the most salient characteristics of the economy persist. In short, China's reforms remain partial. However, this position most likely is not one of stable equilibrium, since it induces increasing inefficiency over time and has exacerbated inflation, unemployment, and other transitional costs of reform. If the distortions that cause these inefficiencies and transitional costs cannot be reduced through a further expansion of the role of the market, there almost certainly will be more bureaucratic interventions. These may seek to alleviate specific inefficiencies, but may ultimately abort the reforms.

---

[26]*China: Long-Term Issues and Options,* p. 81.
[27]"State Issues Production Capacity Norms," *China Daily,* Aug. 1, 1989.

Chinese Economic Reform

Intellectual Approaches and Political Conflict

Like the Chinese revolution itself, the Dengist reforms—which recently marked their tenth anniversary—have moved from the countryside to the cities and from relatively superficial change have become a more far-reaching and complex transformation of society. The early years of the reform were dramatic because they overturned, both in theory and in practice, central tenets that have governed Chinese economic and political life since the period of the Great Leap Forward. In recent years, however, particularly since 1984, when concerted efforts have been made to carry out "comprehensive urban reform," the reform process, while in some ways less dramatic, has nevertheless challenged the traditional economic structure of centralized administrative control in ways much more fundamental than the earlier rural reform did.

At no point in this process has reform been guided by a unified vision of reform. It was not until the Thirteenth Party Congress in November 1987 that any authoritative party document risked either limiting the extent of reform or provoking divisions within the party by elaborating in any detail on the meaning of "building socialism with Chinese characteristics," and there is evidence that that document has been, and remains, the subject of considerable controversy within the party.[1] A round of inflation and re-trenchment in 1984–1986 both revealed existing divisions among policy advisers and in the leadership and stimulated a new round of theoretical exploration and decisionmaking that exacerbated differences. The heightening of economic difficulties in recent years—the stagnation of grain production in the countryside, the failure of state-owned industries to match the performance of non-state-owned industries, continuing budget deficits, and particularly the emergence of serious inflation—have sharpened differences among policy advisers and the leadership alike.

Accordingly, consensus on economic decisionmaking has been increasingly difficult to achieve. In 1988 alone, four distinct economic policies were endorsed by the leadership. At the central economic conference in December 1987, Li Peng, who was then acting premier, endorsed a policy direction of "stabilizing the economy and deepening reform."[2] By the time the party's Second Plenum met in March, then–general secretary Zhao Ziyang reversed this policy direction, insisting that high growth could be combined with economic efficiency.[3] In May, Deng Xiaoping personally led the campaign to carry out a sweeping program of price reform, believing that "a short pain is better than a long pain."[4] And in September, a Central Work Conference and the party's Third Plenum decisively rejected Deng's course and endorsed a policy of full-scale retrenchment that put off further reform indefinitely.[5] That policy was reaffirmed at the session of the National People's Congress in March 1989.[6]

---

[1]One expression of the controversial status of this party document is that Deng Xiaoping, in his June 9 defense of the decision to crack down on prodemocracy demonstrations in Tiananmen Square, stated that "not one word" of it should be changed. Deng's statement seems intended to forestall a new round of party infighting over ideology. See *Renmin ribao*, June 28, 1989, p. 1.

[2]*Cai zheng*, no. 1(Jan. 8, 1988):1.

[3]*Renmin ribao*, March 21, 1988; translated in Foreign Broadcast Information Service, *Daily Report: China* (hereafter cited as *FBIS-CHI*), March 21, 1988, pp. 20–27.

[4]See Xinhua, May 19, 1988, trans. in *FBIS-CHI*, May 19, 1988; Xinhua, May 24, 1988, trans. in *FBIS-CHI*, May 26, 1988; Xinhua, June 3, 1988, trans. in *FBIS-CHI*, June 3, 1988; and *Renmin ribao*, July 16, 1988, trans. in *FBIS-CHI*, July 18, 1988.

[5]On the Central Work Conference, see Cheng Hsiang, "Central Work Conference Underway in Beijing," *Wen wei pao*, Sept. 19, 1988, trans. in *FBIS-CHI*, Sept. 19, 1988, p. 20. On the Third Plenum, see Xinhua, Sept. 30, 1988, trans. in *FBIS-CHI*, Sept. 30, 1988, pp. 18–19.

[6]Li Peng, "Resolutely Implement the Policy of Improvement and Rectification and

A look at authoritative policy statements in recent years reveals that, while there has been consensus on reform in general, there has been considerable disagreement over the type of economic system that reform should produce. In particular, Chinese leaders have disagreed over the extent to which market forces should be allowed to develop and the role of planning and "administrative measures" in guiding economic activity.

The first systematic attempt to lay out the principles and goals for reform was the "Decision on Reform of the Economic Structure," adopted by the Third Plenary Session of the Twelfth Central Committee in October 1984.[7] That decision defined the goal of Chinese economic reform as the creation of a "socialist planned commodity economy." The adoption of the term "commodity economy" was an important milestone in the development of Marxist thought in China. Traditionally, a socialist economy has been seen as the antithesis of a commodity economy . This understanding stems from Marx's belief that the advent of socialism will mean the end of a commodity economy. That understanding was taken over by the Soviet Union, particularly as it moved away from the bold experimentation of the New Economic Policies and adopted central planning. In 1953, reacting to accumulated difficulties in the Soviet economy, Stalin, in his book *The Economic Problems of Soviet Socialism,* modified that position to allow for the existence of a commodity economy outside the realm of the state economy. Although Stalin's restatement of the relationship between the commodity economy and the socialist economy provided greater room for the former, it nevertheless made clear, first, that the two economic forms were different and antagonistic, and, second, that the goal of socialism was to eliminate the commodity economy.

The declaration in the 1984 Third Plenum document that socialism and the commodity economy were not antagonistic, but were one and the same, was thus a major ideological breakthrough, one that permitted a much greater development of market forces in Chinese society. It was precisely on these grounds that a seminar on the late Sun Yefang's economic thought actually criticized Sun for being too conservative. Sun, who had been castigated in the antirightist campaign of 1957 and again in the Cultural Revolution for being too capitalistic, was now being criticized for giving insufficient importance to the commodity economy. Indeed, viewed from the vantage point of late 1984, Sun's thought was conservative; while always

---

Deepening Reform," *Renmin ribao,* April 6, 1989, trans. in *FBIS-CHI,* May 2, 1989, pp. 35–55.

[7]"Decision of the Central Committee of the Communist Party of China on Reform of the Economic Structure," *FBIS-CHI,* Oct. 22, 1984, pp. K1–K33.

arguing for the importance of economic rationality, Sun had maintained a sharp distinction between the socialist and the commodity economies.

Despite the importance of this ideological breakthrough for defining the direction of Chinese economic reform, the decision was a carefully crafted document that finessed a number of important issues. Most important, in defining the goal of economic reform as a "socialist planned commodity economy," the decision declined to define what was socialist about it, leaving open the question of the distinct characteristics of socialism and capitalism, as well as the relationship between planning and the commodity economy (market forces). While the decision not to define such issues no doubt avoided bruising ideological battles within the party and permitted reform to go forward on a pragmatic basis, it nevertheless meant that such issues would be revisited at a later time. Indeed, both of these questions have been taken up in ideological disputes since then.

Conflict over the meaning of the Third Plenum decision was admitted by the journal of the State Commission on Reform of the Economic Structure in May 1986, when it said that while everyone agreed that the goal of reform is to transform the "original, ossified model that does not suit the development of productive forces" into a "model of the planned commodity economy that is full of vitality and vigor" (the goal written into the 1984 decision), there was in fact little agreement as to what constituted a "model of the planned commodity economy that is full of vitality and vigor." On this critical issue, the journal said, "The understanding of various quarters is very disunited."[8] Similarly, Ding Ningning of the Central Party School stated that although the phrase "planned commodity economy" had already been written into the party's resolution, "academic circles up to the present time have not come close to forming a consensus on this concept."[9]

Despite evident controversy over both the means and ends of reform throughout 1986 and particularly during the campaign against "bourgeois liberalization" in early 1987, reformers were able to secure a strong endorsement of their position at the Thirteenth Party Congress.[10] The resolution of

---

[8]*Zhongguo jingji tizhi gaige*, May 1986, p. 1.

[9]Ding Ningning, *Jingji yanjiu*, April 1987, p. 37.

[10]Controversy over the direction of reform in 1986 was apparent both in discussions over political structural reform that unfolded that spring and summer and in discussions over ownership reform and the status of labor in a socialist society. See Joseph Fewsmith, "The PRC's Internal Political Dynamics," *Journal of Northeast Asian Studies*, vol. 6, no. 1(Spring 1987):3–25. During the campaign against "bourgeois liberalization," the charge was raised, allegedly by Deng Liqun, that it was necessary to attack not only those who advocate capitalism, but also those who engage in capitalism. On the Thirteenth Party Congress, see Joseph Fewsmith, "China's 13th

that congress in many ways went well beyond the 1984 "Decision" in endorsing a market orientation of the economy . Elaborating on the 1984 "Decision," the congress report defined the goal of economic reform as bringing about a situation in which "the state regulates the market and the market guides the enterprises," thus implying that economic management was to be indirect and that the plan would be more one of setting parameters for the economy than of determining specific targets for various industries.[11] Vice-Minister of the Commission on Reform of the Economic Structure Gao Shangquan underlined this formulation, stating that it "shed new light on the relationship between the state and the economy ."[12]

The party congress report further stated that the "fundamental task" (*genben renwu*) of socialism was to develop the "productive forces" and set their development as the criterion for judging work: "Whether or not something is advantageous to the development of the productive forces ought to become the point of departure for our consideration of all problems and the fundamental standard for judging all our work."[13]

Although the report did not explicitly say so, this statement of the criterion for judging work was in fact a reformulation of the classic Dengist slogan that "Practice is the sole criterion for judging truth"—the ideological battle cry that had ushered in the Dengist era. This implication became apparent in early 1988 when Zhao Ziyang wrote an article entitled "Emancipate Thinking and Liberate the Productive Forces." Sharply criticizing those who "worry about everything except the fettering of the forces of production," Zhao stated that the Thirteenth Party Congress had "made productive forces the highest criterion." The implication of Zhao's argument was that people were opposing the sorts of reforms that Zhao intended to implement (and thought he had laid the ideological basis for in the report of the Thirteenth Party Congress) on the grounds that they were not Marxist. Thus, as Zhao said, it was necessary to "put the stress on further emancipating our mind" in studying the party resolution.[14]

Party Congress: Explicating the Theoretical Bases of Reform," *Journal of Northeast Asian Studies*, vol. 7, no. 2(Summer 1988):41–64.

[11]"Advance Along the Road of Socialism with Chinese Characteristics," Beijing Domestic Service, Oct. 25, 1987, trans. in *FBIS-CHI*, Supplement (Oct. 25, 1987), pp. 10–34.

[12]Beijing Domestic Service, Oct. 26, 1987, trans. in *FBIS-CHI*, Oct. 26, 1987, p. 37.

[13]"Advance Along the Road of Socialism with Chinese Characteristics," *FBIS-CHI*, Oct. 25, 1987, p. 33.

[14]Zhao Ziyang, "Further Emancipate the Mind and Further Liberate the Productive Forces," *Renmin ribao*, Feb. 8, 1988, trans. in *FBIS-CHI*, pp. 12–14.

Zhao's argument was greatly elaborated upon later in the spring when reformers used the tenth anniversary of the start of the discussion on practice as the sole criterion of truth to push their thesis that further emancipation of the mind was needed to advance reform. A Commentator article in *Renmin ribao* declared that "for every forward step we have made in reform, we have met with ideological struggle in different guises." These ideological struggles, the paper said, could be boiled down to the question "Should we copy what the books and dogmas say intact, or should we seek truth from facts and start from the actual conditions of things?" Putting forth the "criterion of productive forces" marked a deeper understanding of the "criterion of practice."[15]

A long Commentator article in *Guangming ribao* on May 11, the anniversary of the special Commentator article "Practice is the Sole Criterion for Judging Truth," which had appeared in that paper and had launched the discussion on practice a decade earlier, went even further. Stating that it was necessary to re-understand the concepts of socialism and capitalism, the article said that always asking whether a given policy was "capitalistic" or "socialistic" was not scientific and invariably impeded the development of productive forces. The question of taking the socialist or the capitalist road, it said, had been resolved by history and need not be continuously raised.[16]

This progression of authoritative ideological statements over recent years suggests that reformers had—at least until the events of June—by and large been successful in gaining ideological endorsement for far-reaching reforms, including a far greater recognition of the importance of market forces, the diversity of the economy, and a reduced role for traditional planning. The degree to which this agenda faces deep-seated ideological objections has become abundantly clear in recent months. Some of the themes that have been criticized in the wake of Zhao's purge have been the "one-sided" emphasis on the criterion of productive forces, the campaign to "re-understand" socialism and capitalism, and efforts to promote "privatization" of the Chinese economy.

Such opposition to continued reform, even before the events of June, made itself felt in a variety of ways, including in the very long documents that had been used to push the reform agenda forward. The way in which the 1984 reform document finessed such issues—but without achieving

---

[15]Commentator, "A Great Turning Point, A Brilliant Prelude—Commemorating the 10th Anniversary of the Discussion on the Question of Truth Criterion," *Renmin ribao*, May 5, 1988, trans. in *FBIS-CHI*, May 5, 1988, pp. 17–19.

[16]Commentator, "On the Forces of Production Criterion," *Guangming ribao*, May 11, 1988, pp. 1 and 3.

consensus—has been mentioned. Similar problems were apparent in the report of the Thirteenth Party Congress. Two examples will suffice to illustrate this. First, there was disagreement over how precisely to state the goal of economic reform. The version of the congress report that was published in the PRC-owned Hong Kong papers *Ta kung pao* and *Wen wei pao* at the beginning of the congress, prior to the document's revision by the congress, stated that "the state *regulates and controls* [*tiao kong*] the economy, and the economy guides the enterprises." When Zhao presented the report, however, he modified this phrase to read, "the state *regulates* [*tiao jie*] the economy, and the economy guides the enterprises." This phraseology stayed in the amended version of the report that was subsequently published in *Renmin ribao*.[17] This goal apparently remains in dispute. The communiqué of the Tenth Politburo session in August 1988 restored the term "regulate and control," but, curiously, the conservative decision of the Third Plenum in September restored the term "regulate."

Secondly, the draft of the report submitted to the congress avoided explicit mention of administrative measures, stating that "the state *mainly* uses economic and legal means to regulate market supply and demand." This ambiguity was apparently not sufficient to satisfy critics who desired explicit mention of administrative controls. Thus, the final version of the report was amended to read: "The state uses economic and legal means and *necessary administrative measures* to regulate market supply and demand."

The use of administrative measures has, of course, become an important part of economic policy since the adoption of retrenchment in September 1988. In a speech to the National Planning Conference in December, Li Peng stated firmly that when purely economic means failed, "it is necessary to adopt some necessary administrative means, including some measures and methods that have been used before and which have proved to be effective."[18]

In early 1988, Li Peng further signaled his disagreement with the reform direction charted the previous year by twice using the formulation "new order of a socialist *planned* commodity economy"—in obvious contrast to Zhao's use of the term "new order of a socialist commodity economy."[19] Li

---

[17]The version of the report submitted to the congress appeared in *Wen wei pao* and *Ta kung pao* on Oct. 26, 1987. The approved version appeared in *Renmin ribao*, on Nov. 4, 1987. Emphases added.

[18]Li Peng, "Earnestly Put the Focus of Construction and Reform on the Improvement of the Economic Environment," *Qiushi*, no. 1(Jan. 1, 1989):4–9, trans. in *FBIS-CHI*, March 3, 1989, pp. 27–33. Li's speech was delivered on Dec. 5, 1988, to the National Planning Conference and the National Conference on Reform of the Economic Structure.

[19]Zhao first raised the concept of a new order of socialist commodity economy in

also took aim at the "productive forces criterion" in an article in the journal of the State Commission on Reform of the Economic Structure. "We also need to consider what is the criterion for assessing the results of reform," Li wrote. "Should we use the productive forces criterion or other target models as the criterion?" Li concluded that social stability was also an important criterion of success.[20]

This brief overview of efforts to advance, finesse, and retard the rapid implementation of market-oriented reform suggests that even before the prodemocracy demonstrations brought deep-seated political cleavages to the fore, there were significant differences of opinion at the highest level of the CPC. These differences were clearly exacerbated by mounting economic difficulties, including inflation, and by the apparent immanence of the succession.

Problems in Economic Reform

Disputes among policy advisers and the leadership alike have been fueled by the obvious difficulties that have appeared in reform over the past several years.[21] While there is considerable disagreement about the relative importance of various factors, it seems that a combination of the delegation of authority, a tax system that encourages local investment, a decentralized (and politicized) banking system, and negative interest rates have distorted economic growth, hindered economic competition, encouraged excessive investment in capital construction, and exacerbated inflation.

Efforts to "loosen the bonds" placed by the traditional economic order on enterprises have failed to produce the intended results for a number of

---

his speech to the ninth Politburo session in late May. See Xinhua, June 1, 1988, in *FBIS-CHI*, June 1, 1988, p. 22. For a more detailed version of Zhao's remarks, see *Ching pao*, no. 7(July 1988):25–26. For Li Peng's references to a new order of a socialist planned commodity economy, see *Renmin ribao*, Jan. 24, 1989, p. 1; and *Renmin ribao*, Feb. 2, 1989, p. 1.

[20]Li Peng, "Maintain Orientation, Firm Up Confidence, Advance with Steady Steps," *Zhongguo jingji tizhi gaige*, no. 2(Feb. 23, 1989):609, trans. in *FBIS-CHI*, p. 23. Although not identified as such, this appears to be the speech that Li gave to the group on Feb. 1. See *Renmin ribao*, Feb. 2, 1989, p. 1.

[21]Discussion of difficulties in rural reform and the ensuing policy debates as to how to address those issues goes beyond the purview of this paper. I have addressed those issues in "Agricultural Crisis in China," *Problems of Communism*, Nov./Dec. 1988, pp. 78–93.

reasons. First, because the price system is seriously distorted, with sections such as energy, raw materials, and transportation being seriously undervalued, while other sectors, such as processing industries, have high profits, investment funds have tended to flow to the industries that need them less. Thus, administrative decentralization, the distorted price system, and investment incentives have worked together to exacerbate irrationalities in China's industrial structure.

Second, the tax system of "eating in separate kitchens" (*fen zao chi fan*)—which was instituted in 1980 and made each administrative fiscal unit accountable for balancing its own revenues and expenses—has encouraged local areas to invest in industries that will provide them with tax revenues. This has, generally speaking, meant investing in various sorts of processing industries, which has led to great duplication of production facilities. At the same time, this tax system has encouraged local areas to engage in local protectionism in order to prevent erosion of their tax bases by outside competition. This tendency to local autarchy and protected markets is further exacerbated by the way taxes are levied. Since what is taxed is output value, rather than profits, industries of marginal profitability or that are even unprofitable still pay taxes to local government and are therefore protected by local governments.

China's decentralized banking system has been part and parcel of this structure. On the one hand, the fact that local bank offices must respond to the demands of local officials means that there is no effective restraint on the growth of investment funds. On the other hand, the fact that there is a negative interest rate in China means that local enterprises and governments are actually being encouraged to borrow money. As strange as it sounds, this negative–interest-rate structure has been used by the banks to make money, which then goes into state coffers, so there is reluctance to raise interest rates as inflation goes up.[22]

This decentralized system, however, has not necessarily meant greater autonomy for enterprises. Many of the powers that were originally intended to be delegated to the enterprise level have been retained at the municipal level. Thus, enterprises, even if they are less under the control of the central government, are not necessarily freer of government control in general.

This structure, it seems, has contributed to the emergence of serious inflation in China, though to what extent has been very much in dispute. For some economists, such as Wu Jinglian and Liu Guoguang (whose views are discussed in more detail below), inflation is caused primarily by over-

---

[22]Yang Peixin, "Use Stopgap and Radical Measures Simultaneously in Curbing Inflation," *Guangming ribao*, Dec. 10, 1988, trans. in *FBIS-CHI*, Dec. 28, 1988.

extended capital construction and excessive bank loans. These causes are in turn supported by the structure of interests just described.

Other economists, however, point to other factors, such as the changing structure of the Chinese economy, as the primary explanation of inflation. Perhaps the leading proponent of the theory that inflation is primarily the result of the "dualistic structure" of the Chinese economy is Wang Jian, deputy research fellow of the Institute of Planned Economy under the State Planning Commission. In Wang's view, for 30 years China's development strategy was based on extracting surplus value from the countryside in order to concentrate on heavy industry. At the same time, surplus labor was forced to stay in the countryside. As the reforms have been implemented over the past decade, this surplus agricultural labor moved quickly into nonagricultural occupations such as rural industry. The effect of this movement of labor, in Wang's opinion, is the reduction of agricultural input, which contributed to a decline in output, at the same time that it stimulated the development of the processing industry. The slowing of agricultural output at the same time as the growth of the processing industry increased has forced the prices of both agricultural commodities and basic industrial goods to increase, thus fueling inflation.[23] The result of this structure has been a rapid rise in extrabudgetary funds and greater decentralization, but without effective macroeconomic regulation. This has led to overextended construction and inflation.

Strategies for Dealing with China's Economic Problems

Both ideological concerns and real economic problems have produced a variety of evaluations about how serious the problems facing China are and what should be done about them. Most economists seem to agree that China's reforms have reached a crossroads and that a new policy direction has to be found. Unfortunately, there seems to be very little agreement about which direction to move in.

Here, I have attempted to differentiate five schools of thought that form relatively complete approaches to the domestic economic problems of China. These five approaches have been selected because they cover a wide range

---

[23]Wang's views, along with those of other economists who similarly see structural causes as the primary cause of inflation, are summarized in Cheng Wenquan, "Causes of Commodity Price Rises and Measures for Stabilizing Commodity Prices: Views of Economic Theorists in the Capital," *Renmin ribao*, April 8, 1988, p. 4.

of opinion, and because they appear to be highly influential, either directly or indirectly, among policymakers.[24]

These five schools of thought, it should be noted, do not represent the complete range of opinion in contemporary China. In particular, there are those who advocate privatization, and their views gained ground in 1988 before coming under vitriolic attack following the Tiananmen Square incident. Their views are not discussed, because they appear to have had limited influence on the leadership.[25] Also not considered are Wang Jian's views on the "great international cycle," which would require a discussion of foreign-trade policy. Nevertheless, it appears that the five approaches considered cover the most influential approaches to economic reform in China, including those adhering to a more "orthodox" interpretation of Marxism.

Wu Jinglian and "Coordinated Reform"

Perhaps the single most influential school of thought in recent years has been that championed by Wu Jinglian of the State Council's Economic, Social, and Technological Development Research Center. Wu's basic thesis is that reform can be carried out successfully only if it is implemented by means of a well-designed blueprint balancing reforms in different areas such as the price system, the tax structure, and the fiscal system. Because he believes that such reforms need to be carefully tailored so that the effects of one do not offset the achievements of another, he calls this approach "coordinated reform" (*peitao gaige*).[26]

---

[24]Four of the five approaches discussed here were included in a group of eight studies commissioned by the State Commission on Reform of the Economic Structure for consideration of the Chinese leadership at the Beidaihe conference in the summer of 1988. These studies were assembled in *Zhongguo gaige da silu* (Major ways of thinking about Chinese reform), published by Shenyang renmin chuban she in 1988. These essays were intended to form the basis of a comprehensive price and wage reform to be approved by the Third Plenum in September. Hua Sheng did not contribute to this effort, perhaps because he was studying at Oxford at that time. His influence has been apparent, however, in the adoption of the dual-track price system, of which he was a founder, and of other measures. Of the other studies included in that volume, one focuses on the rural reform, which is outside the scope of this paper, while the other three propose less comprehensive schemes.

[25]One indication of the rising influence of those favoring privatization was the publication of the article by Huang Youguang and Yang Xiaokai, "A Group Discussion on the Reform of the Ownership System—Why China Must Institute Privatization in One Resolute and Decisive Action," *Shijie jingji daobao*, Feb. 6, 1989, pp. 12–13.

[26]Wu presents his views in a number of places, but the most systematic presentation

In Wu's opinion, reform in China, like that in Eastern Europe, has been characterized by "delegating authority and granting benefits" (*fang guan rang li*). Believing that this approach has led Eastern European economies to "fall into dire straits," Wu asserts the necessity of "coordinated reform." Harshly criticizing the "prevailing opinion" of the past that it was "impossible and unnecessary" to formulate a general plan for reform, Wu says that this approach contributed to the lack of coordination among reform measures, so that "more and more frictions and loopholes unavoidably appeared and problems became more and more serious." In contrast, Wu holds that reform should be carried out in a coordinated manner, meaning "first, various reforms should be carried out in a reasonable and regular sequence; and second, reforms in all links which have close relations should be carried out synchronously."[27]

There are, perhaps, four theses that define Wu's approach to "coordinated reform." First, based on his belief that "delegating authority and granting benefits" has led to the "perverse" outcome that the least modern and most backward sectors of the Chinese economy—agriculture and rural industry—have become the most vital, while the most modern and best-equipped sectors of the economy remain sluggish and under the direct control of the stage, Wu believes that it is imperative to change the focus of reform to those large and medium-sized industries—the so-called "backbone" enterprises—that are the most technologically advanced industries in China. Without significantly increasing the efficiency of such industries, he believes, China will be able neither to absorb the increasing movement of labor out of agriculture nor to develop its most modernized sector.[28]

Second, because of the importance Wu attaches to this sector of the economy, he is highly critical of other approaches that encourage the growth

---

of how his views differ from others is in his article "Guanyu gaige zhanlue xuanze de ruogan sikao," *Jingji yanjiu*, Feb. 1987, pp. 3–14, trans. in *FBIS-CHI*, April 22, 1987, pp. K15–K33. See also Wu Jinglian, "Jingji gaige chuzhan jieduan de fazhen fangzhen he hongguan kongzhi wenti," *Renmin ribao*, Feb. 11, 1985, p. 5; "Zailun baochi jingji gaige de lianghao jingji huanjing," *Jingji yanjiu*, May 1985, pp. 3–12; Wu Jinglian, Zhou Xiaochuan, and Li Jiange, "Functions of Government and Management at Different Levels," trans. in *China Report: Economic Affairs*, JPRS-CEA 87–020 (March 17, 1987), pp. 12–20; and Wu Jinglian, Li Jiange, and Ding Ningning, "Ba guomin jingji de zengzhang sudu kongzhi zai shidu de fanwei nei," *Renmin ribao*, March 10, 1986, p. 5.
[27]Wu, "Guanyi gaige zhanlue," pp. 4–5.
[28]Wu et al., "Jingji tizhi zhongqi guihua gangyao," in *Zhongguo gaige da silu*, pp. 200–1.

of smaller industries, especially when such growth is accompanied by the formation of segregated markets based on local protectionism. Such an approach, Wu argues, will lead to the growth of a so-called "primitive commodity economy," thereby hindering the growth of a "unified commodity market." According to Wu, there are some people who believe that the essential problem is to break through the traditional vertical and horizontal (*tiao tiao kuai kuai*) controls of the command economy in order to "open up" (*fang kai*) and "enliven" (*gao huo*) the economy. The problem with this approach, in Wu's view, is that it can only lead to a "primitive, crude commodity economy" and "not the modern commodity economy that we need." The formation of such a primitive commodity economy, like that of the early capitalist economy to which Wu likens it, would be attended by the social ills of the Victorian age, polarization, and the development of small enterprises that, if not restricted within a certain scope, could "threaten the leading position of socialist large-scale enterprises."[29]

Apparently because of this strong conviction that it is necessary to focus reform efforts on the major state-owned enterprises, Wu argues strongly for concerted, central action to implement reform. Without invoking the now-chic term "new authoritarianism," Wu addresses the issue in terms consonant with this concept.[30] Noting that "we must not imagine that we can attain this [reform] through the spontaneous individual actions of the multitude of the masses without a situation of leadership and organization," Wu argues that the "prestige of the central government is especially critical," and that the government must "have a clear recognition and firm grasp of the trend of history and go and mobilize, encourage and guide the whole body of the people."[31]

Third, price reform is central to Wu's vision of reform. According to Wu, "the price mechanism is the pivot of the entire economic structure of the commodity economy." It follows, in Wu's opinion, that if the price structure is not first rationalized, reform may end in chaos. Clearly criticizing the approach of those who, like Li Yining (whose ideas are discussed below),

---

[29]Wu, "Guanyu gaige zhanlue," p. 7.

[30]The theory of "new authoritarianism" [*xin quanwei zhuyi*] was discussed extensively in the press from late 1988 until the suppression of the prodemocracy demonstrations. Though there are different versions of this theory, the basic approach is to emphasize that the creation of a modern, commodity (market) economy requires a strong, authoritarian hand at the top. The idea is that economic liberalization must precede political democratization. For an overview, see Liu Jun, "A Brief Introduction to the Debate on 'Neo-Authoritarianism,'" *Guangming ribao*, March 17, 1989, trans. in *FBIS-CHI*, April 6, 1989, pp. 30–32.

[31]Wu et al., "Jingji tizhi zhongqi guihua gangyao," p. 203.

put emphasis on enterprise reform, Wu writes: "If we force reform of the enterprise-management system before prices are basically rationalized, establish a short-term money market before a sound commodity market takes shape, and establish a capital market and a securities-circulation market in the form of securities exchanges before the short-term monetary market takes shape, we will certainly fail to achieve the expected results, and may even bring about a disorderly situation."[32] While placing greater emphasis on the need for enterprise reform and the implementation of the shareholding system in his plan prepared for the 1988 Beidaihe conference, Wu nevertheless maintained that price reform must precede enterprise reform.

Fourth, Wu believes that in order to carry out reform it is necessary to bring about a "relaxed economic environment," one in which supply slightly exceeds demand. Wu believes that such an environment is necessary because only in such an environment can the state concentrate sufficient fiscal resources to carry out technological transformation and protect society from the shocks created by reform, particularly by the price increases that would be bound to come through price reform. Without creating a "relaxed economic environment," Wu feels, reform will bring about a serious expansion of demand that the state would be unable to deal with. This would lead to budget imbalance, inflation, and perhaps to political instability.[33]

But unlike Liu Guoguang and others, Wu believes that it is possible to create such an environment in a relatively short period of time. In his plan for Beidaihe, Wu proposed that for one year capital construction and the money supply be strictly controlled (and also that a number of other steps to improve the market situation be carried out), and that then during three years a "fundamental transformation" in the price structure be effected.[34] For Wu, retrenchment is a means of accelerating, not delaying, the reform process.

Li Yining and Reform of the Ownership System

When Wu Jinglian criticizes the emergence of a "primitive commodity economy" and reform measures that threaten the state's control, one of his targets is Li Yining, professor of economics at Beijing University, who is probably the leading proponent of reform of the ownership system (*suo you zhi*). Viewing reform as first and foremost a microeconomic problem, Li's writings pose a frontal challenge to Wu's belief that macroeconomic reform,

---

[32]Wu, "Guanyu gaige zhanlue," p. 6.
[33]Ibid., pp. 11–12.
[34]Wu et al., "Jingji tizhi zhongqi guihua gangyao," pp. 208–16.

in the form of price reform, can solve the economic problems facing China. Li agrees that price reform is important, but does not believe that it alone will lead to success. As he puts it, "economic reform can fail through the failure of price reform, but the success of economic reform cannot be achieved through success in price reform; it can [only] be achieved through reform of the ownership system."[35]

Li bases his argument on the assumption that prices ultimately reflect ownership of the factors of production and thus, in the final analysis, "prices are the terms of exchange of ownership among people in the market."[36] Thus, unless the ownership system is first reformed, price reform will not, in and of itself, lead to a market equilibrium. Moreover, Li maintains that a rational price system is not something that can be dictated by the government, but rather something that must come about through the interaction of independent commodity producers. Thus, Li says, price reform "can only be based on enterprise reform and cannot be the breakthrough point for enterprise reform."[37]

Whereas Wu focuses on the creation of a good market environment to achieve economic rationality, Li looks to definition of the relations of production and power to bring about that result. As one writer characterized those who take this approach:

> They hold that the root cause for the inflated aggregate demand in the second half of 1984 lies in the fact that enterprises did not have a well-defined responsibility for the management of their funds. The enterprises used more state funds without correspondingly undertaking greater economic responsibilities. This has given rise to unfair distribution of funds among enterprises with different fund contributions and a strong impetus among local governments and enterprises to scramble for more funds and credit from higher authorities.[38]

The solution to this problem, in the approach championed by Li Yining, is to clearly define ownership relations and thereby give operational autonomy to enterprises.

Li hopes to unify production and power, as was done in the rural

---

[35]Li Yining, "Gaige de jiben silu," *Beijing ribao*, May 19, 1987, p. 3.
[36]Li Yining et al., "1988–1995 nian wo guo jingji tizhi gaige gangyan," in *Zhongguo gaige da silu*, p. 90.
[37]Ibid., p. 91.
[38]Xiao Jie, "Diversified Views on the Focus of Economic Reform in the Seventh Five-Year Plan Period," *Shijie jingji daobao*, Jan. 6, 1986, p. 3.

economic reforms, by having enterprises—including the critically important large and medium-sized corporations—implement a shareholding system. Li sees the ability of enterprises to buy and sell each other's shares as essential to the formation of "enterprise groups" (vertically or horizontally integrated conglomerates) and development of "horizontal economic ties" (*hengxiang jingji lianhe*). Without a clear definition of ownership relations, the free combination and recombination of economic interests would be difficult or would be controlled by traditional vertical administrative relations, and this would interfere with the rational circulation of factors of production.[39]

To free enterprises from ministerial and other governmental (either central or local) intervention, Li proposes establishing "stock asset management bureaus" (*guoyou gufen zichan quanli ju*) at various levels to manage government-owned shares. These assets-management bureaus would be responsible for handling the state's investments in enterprises, purchasing or selling stock as deemed appropriate, and appointing the requisite number of directors to the boards of enterprises. Bureaus would be established on all administrative levels (national, provincial, municipal, and county), but there would be no hierarchical administrative relationship between them. Local bureaus would manage local interests in enterprises, just as the national bureau would oversee the state's interests. Li is particularly emphatic that the state's shares would not be managed by the traditional ministries, departments, and bureaus. The responsibility of such administrative organs would be limited to deciding developmental plans and policies, harmonizing relations between enterprises, and overseeing the implementation of policies and laws. It would not involve the internal affairs of enterprises.[40]

In contrast to Wu Jinglian's belief in the necessity of a strong state that centralizes resources and guides investment, Li is highly skeptical of state planning, regarding it as often doing more harm than good. According to Li, "if planned management is subjective and unscientific, we would rather not have it; and if the government's regulative role is inefficient and confusing, we would rather not have it."[41] Similarly, in contrast to Wu's contemptuous dismissal of the "primitive commodity economy," Li states that "unscientific government regulation is certainly not needed, since it is not as good as market regulation."[42]

---

[39]Li Yining, "A Conception of Reform of the Ownership System in Our Country," *Renmin ribao*, Sept. 26, 1986, p. 5, trans. in *FBIS-CHI*, Oct. 22, 1986, pp. K5–K11.
[40]Li Yining, "Suoyouzhi gaige he gufen qiye di guanli," Part II, *Zhongguo jingji tizhi gaige*, Feb. 1987, p. 25.
[41]*Zhongguo xinwen she*, June 30, 1986, trans. in *FBIS-CHI*, July 7, 1986.
[42]Li Yining, "Jingji tizhi gaige di guanjian shi suoyouzhi," *Guangming ribao*, Aug. 4, 1986, p. 2.

Hua Sheng and Reform of the Enterprise Operating Mechanism

A group with a third approach to reform is made up of those who look first and foremost to the relationship between the enterprise and the individual, rather than to that between the enterprise and the state (as Li Yining does), or to the perfection of the market environment (as Wu Jinglian does). Most representative of this school of thought is Hua Sheng, a scholar of the Chinese Academy of Social Sciences (CASS), who has often collaborated with other young scholars, such as He Jiacheng, Yong Bianzhuang, Zhang Xuejun, and Luo Xiaopeng.

This school of thought criticizes the approach of Wu Jinglian for being unrealistic in its hope for a quick victory in reform and naive in its oversimplification of the complexity of reform. As these economists wrote in one article:

> For a period of time, people thought that for a period of a few years we could use a set of coordinated reform measures and achieve victory in one battle. However, both domestic and international experiences have caused us to realize that it is impossible to clearly see the developmental law and complete face of the socialist economic reform. Reform is a progressive self-perfection of socialist society and is a readjustment of interest relations among the people. Even if one could see things clearly, . . . it would still take time.[43]

In addition, this school of thought sees Wu Jinglian's desire to bring about a relaxed economic environment before implementing reform as unrealistic. They maintain that "economic stability can only be the result and not the condition of reform." To concentrate on creating a relaxed economic environment would, in their view, mean that it would be necessary to "slow down the reform inappropriately or even lose a chance."[44] The only choice, then, is to forge ahead despite the less-than-optimal economic environment.

Furthermore, they argue that Wu's call for coordinated price reform seriously underestimates the difficulties in creating a market. Accusing Wu of wanting to "regulate" the price system, Hua and his colleagues emphasize the need to change the price-formation system—a process which they see as emerging from the bottom up and taking an extended period of time.

---

[43]Hua Sheng, He Jiacheng, Zhang Xuejun, Luo Xiaopeng, Yong Bianzhuang, and Du Haiyan, "Lishixing di zhuanzhe yu xiwang," *Jingji yanjiu*, March 1983, p. 12.

[44]He Jiancheng, Bian Yongzhuang, and Du Haiyan, "Correctly Grasp the Relationship Between Reform and Economic Development: Reflections on Practice in Reform During the Past Eight Years," *Jingji ribao*, Feb. 14, 1987, trans. in *FBIS-CHI*, March 17, 1987, p. K26.

Like Li Yining, Hua is skeptical of the government's ability to guide economic change. As Hua and two colleagues have written in a recent article, "Those who advocate regulating the system [a reference to Wu and his school of thought] have shown great faith in the government's ability to control the process of price reform." In contrast, Hua believes that "it can be said with certainty that the central authorities' price readjustment will not be able to beat the local authorities' countermoves, and that the local authorities' measures will not be able to beat the countermoves adopted by enterprises."[45]

Hua Sheng, He Jiacheng, and others who accuse Wu Jinglian of being too simplistic in his hope to "achieve victory in a single battle" are similarly critical of Li Yining's one-sided concentration on reform of the ownership system:

> The risks of reform of the enterprise structure do not come only from one side. For a period in the past, a certain portion of comrades seriously underestimated the difficulty of the reform of the enterprise structure and did not pay enough attention to the reform of the management mechanism, hoping that they could resolve in one battle the question of ownership.[46]

They not only feel that Li Yining's approach is overly simplistic, they—like Wu Jinglian—dislike the apparently reckless way in which some reforms in the ownership system have been carried out, believing that such methods pose a threat to state-owned assets and to economic control. As they see it, "the great majority" of enterprises implementing the shareholding system are "directly or indirectly redistributing the state's assets." Without undertaking a clear determination of what assets belong to the state, these enterprises "arbitrarily restrict or abolish the state's authority to receive interest

---

[45]The differences between Hua's approach to price reform and that of Wu Jinglian are laid out in a strongly worded attack on Wu's school of thought in the first part of a three-part article by Hua, Zhang Xuejun, and Luo Xiaopeng, entitled "Ten Years of Reform: Review, Reflection, and Prospects," that appeared in *Jingji yanjiu*, no. 9(Sept.1988):13–37; no. 11(Nov. 1988):11–30; and no. 12(Dec. 1988):10–28 (trans. in *JPRS Report: China*, JPRS-CAR 89-004 [Jan. 11, 1989], pp. 16–45; JPRS-CAR 89-024 [March 23, 1989], pp. 16–37; and JPRS-CAR 89-036 [April 26, 1989], pp. 2–24). The sentence quoted appears on p. 19 of the first part as translated by JPRS (Joint Publications Research Service). A sharp rebuttal from the point of view of Wu Jinglian's school of thought was written by Shi Xiamin and Liu Jirui and appeared in *Jingji yanjiu*, no. 2(Feb. 1989):11–33, trans. in *JPRS Report: China*, JPRS-CAR 89-064 (June 22, 1989), pp. 5–29.

[46]Hua Sheng et al., "Lishixing di zhuanzhe he xiwang," p. 13.

or dividends on stock." One effect of this arbitrary action is to turn production funds into consumption funds, which, they maintain, "will inevitably
cause the cost of labor and the cost of goods to increase sharply." It will also
discredit the shareholding system, which they see as inappropriate for the
present time, but as having an important role to play in the future, if properly
organized and implemented.[47]

These authors are also critical of Li Yining's approach, because they see
the proposed reform of the ownership system as, in effect, becoming just
one more of the altogether-too-frequent changes in ownership relations that
have plagued the PRC since its founding. What is necessary at present, they
maintain, is not to change ownership relations and thereby introduce a new
element of instability into China's economic life, but to clarify and stabilize
property rights, infusing predictability into the economy.[48]

They maintain that the current stage of reform should concentrate on
reforming the "internal operating mechanism" of enterprises, something
that previous reforms have ignored. The key to this change is to enhance
the status of the manager, recognizing him as an entrepreneur, and bring
forth a contingent of "socialist entrepreneurs." In their view, it is necessary
to "separate the interests of entrepreneurs from the general interest of staff
members and workers" to form an "independent collective of interests."
Only by separating the interests of entrepreneurs from that of staff members
and workers, and linking the interests of entrepreneurs to the economic
performance of the enterprises, will it be possible to carry out wage reform
and otherwise rationalize the internal organization of enterprises.[49]

The way to link the interests of entrepreneurs to the economic performance of enterprises—as well as to clarify and stabilize property relations—
is to implement a contract-responsibility system that clearly defines the
relationship between government departments and the enterprise, that is
linked with the good or bad management of the enterprise, and which grants
large awards or levies heavy fines, depending on economic performance.

Liu Guoguang and "Advancing on a Basis of Stability"

The reform proposal drawn up for the leadership to consider at the 1988
Beidaihe meeting by the study group headed by senior economist Liu Guoguang, who is also vice-president of CASS and an alternate member of the

---

[47]Ibid., p. 14.
[48]Ibid.
[49]Ibid., p. 13.

CPC Central Committee based its approach on the belief that the economic policies followed over the past several years have contributed to inflation without resolving either the structural imbalances in the economy or fundamentally changing the economic mechanism that underlay the old economic order. Because they see the reform efforts of recent years as misguided in important respects, they reject as inadequate explanations that the current problems facing the economy are due to unavoidable factors in the course of reform. "We believe," they state, "that the cause of these problems is not entirely due to the effect of the old system or to the friction that is difficult to avoid in the course of reform, but has a close relationship to the concrete developmental strategy and the concrete measures of some policies."[50]

Chief among the problems that they see is that of inflation. Inflation in contemporary China, they believe, has been conditioned by three factors. First, the delegation of authority and the practice of "eating in separate kitchens" has greatly increased the amount of money retained and controlled at local levels and outside the state budget. This has formed a powerful inflationary force that is difficult to control by the traditional means of cutting construction and controlling the wage fund. Second, distortions in market prices lead localities and enterprises to invest in areas where profits are large, such as home appliances and textiles, and to ignore "bottleneck" sectors that need investment, such as energy and transportation, thus accentuating structural imbalances in the economy. The rapid expansion of investment funds accelerates this process; thus structural imbalances and inflation form a vicious cycle leading to greater economic irrationalities. Third, as the reduction in the scope of mandatory planning and the scope of state control over budgetary expenditures has been reduced, the ability of the central government to control the macroeconomy is correspondingly reduced. Moreover, because the state can most easily influence economic behavior in the sectors directly controlled by the state—which are generally the areas of the economy, such as energy and transportation, most in need of funds—retrenchment policies inevitably affect the areas that can least afford it. Although the state has little choice but to "cut with one knife," doing so inevitably leads to pressures to loosen controls.[51]

These factors, Liu argues, make inflation much more insidious now than under the old economic system and mean that anti-inflationary policies need to be implemented consistently and over a long period of time. The re-

---

[50]Liu Guoguang et al., "Zhongguo jingji tizhi zhongqi (1988–1995) gaige gangyao," in Zhongguo gaige da silu, p. 58.
[51]Ibid., pp. 60–61.

trenchment policies adopted in 1985 and 1986 were correct, they argue, but "it is too bad that they were not carried through."[52]

Liu's group further argues that economic stability is a prerequisite for the successful implementation of reform. Great fluctuations in the economy, which, they argue, remain a feature of contemporary China, are "not good for economic development, cause the structure to become worse, efficiency to decline, and make it impossible for a comparative comprehensive, complete reform to take shape, thus blocking the deepening of reform.[53] The decreased efficiency resulting from fluctuations in the Chinese economy, they assert, has resulted in growth rates of taxes and profits not matching the overall economic growth rate. This has led to a decline in the standard of living of some urban residents and created a "tense" atmosphere, which makes reform difficult. Thus, they argue, the "Central Committee's orientation toward stabilizing the economy and deepening reform is entirely correct."[54]

Based on this analysis of inflationary dangers and the need for economic stability, Liu's group argues that it is necessary to implement anti-inflationary policies for an extended period—at least three years—to break the back of inflation. Their goal is to bring inflation down to about 3 percent and control economic growth to 7.5 percent per year over the next five years. In particular, they argue that over the next three years it is necessary to implement a policy of "advancing on a basis of stability, with stability as primary."[55]

In contrast to Wu Jinglian's emphasis on price reform and Li Yining's emphasis on ownership reform, Liu's group believes that since both are necessary, neither should be emphasized at the expense of the other. They argue that the experience of Eastern Europe and China shows that "only by advancing these two aspects of reform in a coordinated and unified manner is it feasible to deepen reform." However, they also argue that, given the inflationary situation in which China finds itself, it is necessary to place the emphasis in the first three years on reform of the enterprise mechanism. After that, the emphasis can be shifted to price reform.[56]

Nevertheless, in discussing near-term reform, Liu's group places primary emphasis on stability, rather on a specific plan of reform. Thus, they warn that in the near term "those reforms that cost too much money and

---

[52]Ibid., p. 59.
[53]Ibid., p. 62.
[54]Ibid., p.. 59.
[55]Ibid., p. 65.
[56]Ibid., pp. 67–69.

that cannot be borne by [the state's] financial strength and those reforms that are not beneficial to controlling demand and are of no benefit to raising efficiency should not be promoted." They place into this category such reforms as major price reform measures, a rapid opening of monetary and stock markets, and "all methods of enterprise reform that might induce or strengthen short-term behavior and inflation of consumption."[57]

Wu Shuqing and the Limits of Reform

More than any other group advocating a reform program for the consideration of the leadership at the 1988 Beidaihe conference, that headed by Wu Shuqing, then vice-president of the Chinese People's University, was the most pessimistic about the conditions facing the country and the extent of progress that could be expected over the next eight years. Citing population pressure, employment pressure, unstable development of grain production, increasingly tense supplies of raw materials, and a severe shortage of capital facing China over the coming years, this group thought that hopes should not be set too high. In contrast to other groups, Wu's group maintained that it was necessary to set up an "appropriate goal" for reform over the next eight years, which they defined as meaning that "it is impossible to truly set up the framework of a new structure and [reform] can only create the fundamental conditions for a new structure."[58]

Wu and his group believe that the scope of the state-owned economy is still too large, and they recommend selling off smaller, less important industries. But unlike Wu Jinglian's approach, which seeks to create a unified, competitive market, and Li Yining's approach, which would radically transform the state-enterprise relationship, Wu Shiqing's group believes that it is necessary to concentrate state control in fewer, more important industries— what they call moving from a "quantitative pattern" [shu liang xing] of leadership to a "guidance pattern" [dao xiang xing].[59] One could say that they advocate a sort of "leaner and meaner" command economy.

While Wu favors continued experimentation with the shareholding system, he takes a much more cautious approach toward this issue than does any of the other approaches considered here. Wu advises that, while shares can be sold, stock prices should not be permitted to fluctuate.[60] Failure to

---

[57]Ibid., p. 72.
[58]Wu Shuqing et al., "1988–1995 nian Zhongguo jingji tizhi gaige guihua," in Zhongguo gaige da silu, p. 162.
[59]Ibid., p. 165.
[60]Ibid., p. 172.

allow a secondary market for stock, however, would mean that there would still be no way for the market to value assets and would make transfer of assets difficult. Shares would represent debt, not equity.

At the same time, Wu takes a very pessimistic view of the possibility of price reform, saying that there is little chance of effecting "fundamental change" of the price system, including the dual-track system, within the next five years. As a result, he writes, the relationship between the state and enterprises cannot become a "standardized-asset relationship," and "the degree to which enterprises can take responsibility for their own profits and losses will be limited."[61]

Because Wu sees little possibility of effecting fundamental changes in either the price system or the ownership system in the near future, he recommends concentrating on "perfecting" the contract-responsibility system. This system, which is based on signing separate contracts between the state and each enterprise that take into account the different conditions each enterprise faces, inevitably involves a process of negotiation between the state and the enterprise. Wu believes that problems of this sort can be minimized if various reforms, such as making contracts more competitive, are introduced.

It should be noted that, while all of these schools of thought seek to reform Chinese economy, the approaches of Liu Guogang and Wu Shuqing contain significant elements of orthodox Marxist economic thinking that have increased their influence in recent months, particularly since the crackdown on the prodemocracy demonstrators. Even before June 1989, Liu Guoguang had been tapped to head Li Peng's think tank; he was also one of the first academics to support the government's line of criticizing "bourgeois liberalization."[62] More recently, Wu Shuqing has authored a sharply worded attack on Zhao Ziyang and the trend of "privatization" among Chinese economists. Interestingly, in light of the debates on the criterion of productive forces and the "re-understanding" of socialism and capitalism mentioned above, Wu links these trends with privatization and, more generally, with bourgeois liberalization.[63] Wu subsequently has been named president of Beijing University.[64]

---

[61]Ibid., p. 167.

[62]*South China Morning Post*, March 4, 1989; also in *FBIS-CHI*, March 6, 1989, p. 28; and Beijing Domestic Service, July 1, 1989, trans. in *FBIS-CHI*, July 3, 1989, p. 40.

[63]Xinhua, Aug. 7, 1989, trans. in *FBIS-CHI*, Aug. 16, 1989, pp. 16–17.

[64]Xinhua, Aug. 23, 1989, in *FBIS-CHI*, Aug. 23, 1989, p. 47.

Economic Visions and
Political Constituencies

It is apparent that these various approaches differ in their assessments of the nature and seriousness of various obstacles facing reform, and that they disagree, sometimes to an extreme degree, with each other. The critical question is: do these different approaches propose different means to attain the same end, or are they in conflict over the more basic question of where Chinese reform should be headed? That is, are the differences about means or about goals?

This is a very difficult question to answer given the authors' reluctance to discuss explicitly their vision of a reformed Chinese economy. Wu Jinglian at one point states that disagreements are indeed over goals. According to Wu, "the basic reason why people have conflicting views over the primary content and method of implementing reform is that they, in fact, harbor different medium-range, and even long-term goals."[65] Unfortunately, Wu did not elaborate on this statement, leaving the task of speculating over such differences to outside observers.

It seems useful to try to assess the implication of these various approaches by comparing them along the following dimensions: planning vs. market, centralism vs. decentralism, high growth vs. low growth, interior vs. coastal provinces, and urban vs. rural.

Planning vs. Market

While most reformers envision China moving in the direction of a market-based economy, there are apparent differences in how quickly and how completely they would seek to abandon or alter the planning system. At the conservative end of the spectrum, Wu Shuqing wishes to restrict the scope of planning but nevertheless sees a continuing need for the planned allocation of goods and materials for the foreseeable future. In contrast, Liu Guoguang wants to change the nature of the relationship between enterprises and the state (what the Chinese call the "operating mechanism of the economy") and presumably the way planning is carried out, but his emphasis on bringing inflation under control and advancing reform on the basis of stability appears to accommodate a greater degree of compromise with the present order for a period of time (at least three years).

Wu Jinglian places great emphasis on managing the economy in accordance with market principles and accordingly places great emphasis on

---

[65]Wu, "Guanyu gaige zhanlue," p. 6.

changing the nature of the planning system. Nevertheless, Wu appears to give great weight to the role of central planning in the future economy, but wants it to operate more like Japan's MITI than like the current system of mandatory allocation of funds and materials. In contrast, Hua Sheng and Li Yining appear to give greater emphasis to the gradual formation of a market-based economy—what Wu derides as a "primitive commodity economy"—and less scope to state action. Their vision of the economic future appears more laissez-faire than Wu's more statist vision.

Centralism vs. Decentralism

These economists appear to differ on the degree to which they favor a more centralized or a more decentralized economy in a way closely corresponding to the difference of their views on the amount and type of planning. Wu Jinglian is perhaps most explicit on this point, stating baldly that the continued growth of smaller industries could threaten the "leading position" of the large, "backbone," state-owned industries. In contrast, Li Yining and Hua Sheng appear to favor the continued growth of smaller industries, particularly those outside the scope of the state plan. Like Wu Jinglian, Liu Guoguang views the growth of extrabudgetary funds and out-of-plan industries as a threat to the ability of the state to control the economy—and explicitly cites these developments as a reason why traditional methods of macroeconomic control are not as effective as before. Although he does not say so explicitly, Liu's emphasis on controlling inflation appears to entail some sort of reassertion of state control over these funds and industries, if only for the duration of retrenchment. Wu Shuqing's views on planning also seem to imply a higher degree of centralism.

High Growth vs. Low Growth

Economists' views on the appropriate macroeconomic policies to adopt, that is, whether to carry out a relatively permissive monetary policy or to strictly control the issuance of money, appears to correlate well with their views on planning and centralization. Those who favor a greater role for planning (of whatever type) and place greater emphasis on state control over the economy also favor a strict monetary policy and a lower rate of growth. Conversely, those who favor less planning and greater decentralization are highly skeptical of the efficacy of retrenchment policies and hence favor a higher rate of growth.

Thus, while both Wu Jinglian and Liu Guoguang have called for strictly controlling investment and the growth of the money supply, Li Yining and Hua Sheng have criticized their approaches. Li disagrees with Wu and Liu that China's inflation is demand-driven, arguing that it is basically pushed up by rising costs. Thus Li believes that "the macro policies demanded by the fundamental starting point of reform cannot be simply to contract demand but must adopt an orientation of simultaneously contracting demand and increasing supply."[66] Hua Sheng similarly believes that retrenchment measures have the effect of causing general supply to fall more quickly than general demand and thus concludes that "a 'relaxed environment' for reform cannot be created by the practice of bypassing the essential issue of economic mechanism and applying administrative measures at the expense of economic development."[67]

Interior vs. Coastal Provinces

Although none of the economists discussed above have directly addressed issues of regional economic development, it appears that, because of the regional distribution of various types of industries, an economic policy of decentralization, high growth, and minimal state planning will, in practice, favor the continued expansion of coastal provinces, particularly such areas as Guangdong, Zhejiang, and Jiangsu, which have large numbers of rural enterprises, long entrepreneurial traditions, and relatively well-developed regional infrastructures. Large coastal cities such as Shanghai, that have a high percentage of state-owned industries, might be an exception to this generalization.

Rural vs. Urban

Similarly, none of the authors discussed has explicitly discussed the relationship between the rural and the urban economy, but their prescriptions for the economy appear to have definite implications for the two sectors. Those who favor a wider scope for planning (of whatever sort) and a more statist approach to the economy seem also to give greater weight to the urban economy than to the rural. Wu Jinglian is quite explicit about this. In his view, the urban economy must lead the rural economy; the alternative is to slow down the overall pace of modernization. Similarly, those who favor strictly controlling inflation appear to be placing great emphasis on maintaining urban standards of living and keeping prices stable for workers. Conversely, those who favor a higher growth rate and greater decentrali-

---

[66]Li et al., "1988–1995 nian wo guo jingji tizhi gaige gangyao," p. 92.
[67]Hua Sheng et al., "Ten Years of Reform: Review, Reflection, and Prospects," p. 37.

zation appear to give greater weight to the rural economy, particularly in areas where rural industry plays an important role.

In short, debates over economic strategy in China appear not only to have a dimension of "conservative" versus "reformer" (that is, those favoring to a greater or lesser degree retention of an important element of state planning versus those who favor adoption of a market-based economy), but also to have different visions of the relationship between Beijing and the localities and between the urban and rural economies.

These different visions of the economic future can also be seen as appeals to differing political constituencies. Wu Shuqing's approach in particular, and Liu Guoguang's as well, would seem to appeal to those with the greatest stake in maintaining the status quo—central ministries, extractive industries that face large deficits, inefficient industries, the interior provinces, urban workers desirous of stable prices, as well as political "conservatives."

Wu Jinglian's approach could also appeal to some large industries, but would probably have its greatest appeal among those that are technologically advanced and think they could move ahead if freed from state constraints. This would seem to be more true of state-owned industries in places like Shanghai than of "third front" industries in the interior. Because any large-scale price reform would likely be accompanied by sizeable price increases (though Wu believes that adequate measures can be taken to prevent overly large increases), Wu's approach would be unlikely to appeal to urban workers, in the short run at least. Because of its emphasis on moving ahead quickly with reform, however, it would seem to appeal to central leaders who are anxious to maintain momentum in reform, concerned about the role of the state in relation to the localities, and wish to avoid the ideological obstacles associated with ownership reform.

Hua Sheng's willingness to find methods—such as the dual-track price system and the contract management responsibility system—that accept the status quo, but provide ways of pursuing reform within the present system, have apparently made some of his proposals acceptable to the leadership. But his calls for maintaining a higher rate of growth, nurturing the price-formation mechanism, and essentially ending planning are far more likely to appeal to localities than to the capital, to coastal provinces than to the interior, and to areas with a large amount of rural industry rather than to cities with heavy concentrations of large-sized, state-owned industry.

Finally, Li Yining's proposals, like Hua Sheng's, represent a frontal assault on not only the traditional planning system, but also on the ideological basis of Marxism. His approach is thus more likely to find favor with those favoring decentralization, coastal development, and rural industry.

Conclusion

Given the obviously different conclusions of Chinese economists and the existence of differences within the Chinese leadership about the direction in which reform should go, it is worth putting forth some tentative ideas on the relationship between the policy advisers, on the one hand, and the policymakers on the other.

Although individual economists may have a longstanding relationship with one or more policymakers, economists serve first and foremost as purveyors of ideas. On the one hand, these ideas may reflect the preferred policy of one or more policymakers, and in this sense economists can publicize and explain the rationale for adopting particular policies. They can also "float" ideas to see how they are received. Perhaps particularly important is their negative function: they can refute the ideas and approaches of other economists and (indirectly) leaders. On the other hand, economists appear to make genuine efforts to come to grips with the economic difficulties confronting China. When convinced of a diagnosis and prescription of a particular difficulty, they can try to "sell" the leadership on their ideas by circulating papers through the various think tanks that advise the leadership.

Viewed from the other end of that process, that of the policymaker, the ideas and studies that economics can marshal can be used both to address specific policy problems faced by the leadership and to provide a rationale for a broader policy position. Policymakers, however, are less bound to articulate a coherent vision of a problem, and thus their solutions are likely to pick and choose among the views of economists.

As generalists, policymakers exist in a wider political environment. It is their function to link individual decisions about economic reform with a broader policy position, and thus they are bound to filter their perception of economic policy through their broader political vision. Although an individual policymaker need not have a clearly articulated, logically consistent vision of the future, much less be consistent at all times, it does seem that the successful policymaker, particularly one who is striving for the top leadership position in the country, does need to have a general agenda and attempt to move the country consistently, if not always steadily, in the direction set by that agenda.

This broader political vision will include such noneconomic issues as ideology, political participation, public order, and a sense of nationalism. Although it is difficult to clearly define separate and distinct political visions, and there are a wide variety of emphases on different issues by different leaders, it seems useful to differentiate three broad currents of political opinion in contemporary China.

First, starting from the "conservative" end of the spectrum, one political tendency is to reassert traditional political and economic control in the face of an economic and social situation that appears to be getting out of control. The tendency of those who adhere to this school is to re-emphasize past political symbols, making greater appeals to the need for hard work and the spirit of sacrifice as well as to fall back, at least temporarily, on previous, administrative methods of economic control. Ideologically, this political tendency would be less willing to allow the expression of controversial ideas, though it would not necessarily be heavy-handed in suppressing views. In terms of its appeal to nationalistic values, this school finds itself in the "hinterland" tradition, emphasizing the unique characteristics of China and its differences form the rest of the world.[68] This school of thought is inherently less trustful of the outside world and less willing to see China integrated into the world economy.

Second, as recent discussions of the "new authoritarianism" have made clear, there is a school of thought that finds the notion of a strong state and liberal economy attractive. This vision addresses concerns that reform has brought about decentralization and an inability to exercise macroeconomic control by strongly reasserting the role of the state in exercising sufficient economic and political power to force its economic agenda through the opposition of reluctant bureaucracies and localities alike. Similarly, this vision can address concerns about social order and ideology by bringing the power of the state to bear. It addresses nationalistic concerns by asserting the power of the state and by mobilizing the nation in an effort to create a modern economy. This vision, which appears to have its roots in the historical tradition of the "foreign affairs clique" (*yangwu pai*) of the late nineteenth century, as well as in the developmental experience of nations such as Turkey, Chile, Taiwan, Singapore, and South Korea, but also Japan in the late nineteenth and early twentieth centuries, clearly relegates concerns about political reforms to a lesser position. Political democratization, the theory goes, will follow after economic reforms have been implemented.

Third, a more "liberal" political tendency looks precisely to economic decentralization and political liberalization (or perhaps just to continued

---

[68]Paul Cohen makes the distinction between "hinterland" and "littoral" traditions. In his words, the littoral culture was "more commercialized than agricultural in its economic foundations, more modern than traditional in its administrative and social arrangements, more Western (Christian) than Chinese (Confucian) in its intellectual outlook, and more outward- than inward-looking in its general global orientation and involvement." See Cohen's *Between Tradition and Modernity: Wang T'o and Reform in Late Ch'ing China*. I have used this distinction to delineate traditions of nationalism in my "Dengist Reforms in Historical Perspective."

depoliticization) as the solution to the various economic and political problems facing the nation. While recognizing the various social problems that have accompanied reform, this school of thought would argue that corruption, influence-peddling, and unfair distribution will be gradually resolved as the market economy becomes more complete and as competition becomes enshrined. This school of thought has, perhaps, more difficulty ideologically, if ideology is viewed in traditional terms, but it seeks to redefine ideology, sometimes radically, in "humanist" terms. It is this school of thought that has promoted efforts to "re-understand" socialism and capitalism, exploring the two social systems for areas of convergence. In addition, this school of thought sees political reform as a necessary part of economic modernization and can see no fundamental restructuring of the traditional economic system without greater freedom of expression and political participation. This school of thought appeals to a more "littoral" tradition of nationalism that is far more open to the West and far more willing that China be integrated into the world economy (and participate in world cultural and political trends) than the "hinterland" tradition.

Although these different visions represent very different political tendencies, it is possible for a leader to make simultaneous or alternating appeals to more than one. In fact, one of the strengths of Deng Xiaoping as a leader has been precisely his ability to appeal to these different visions in turn. Thus, he can be both the sponsor of a loosening of political controls and of greater intellectual freedom and yet endorse the criticism of the writer Bai Hua and the campaigns against "spiritual pollution" and "bourgeois liberalization." He is able to appeal to China's unique tradition ("building socialism with Chinese characteristics") and yet open the country boldly to the outside world. Nevertheless, Deng over the past decade has clearly had a political agenda and has been able to move the country along the line set by that agenda.

It might be suggested, however, that one of the crises which China has faced in recent years is that these currents have become more and more difficult to reconcile. As the economic reforms encountered difficulties, as problems of social order intensified, and as intellectuals—and students— raised unprecedented demands for greater freedom of speech and political participation, there was a tendency for the gap between the old values and the new demands to open more quickly, to be asserted more strongly and more contentiously. This polarization itself may account, in part, for the recent popularity of the "new authoritarianism," which in some ways moves in both directions at once. It also accounts in part for the tragic political confrontation that resulted in the violent suppression of the prodemocracy demonstrations.

In addition to the economic and social problems facing China, the imminent departure of Deng Xiaoping from the scene made potential contenders for power appeal more strongly to these different visions of the future. "Reformers" emphasized that only opening up and continued reform could make China truly "wealthy and strong," while "conservatives" argued that wholesale importation of foreign ideas amounts to "national nihilism." The controversy over the summer 1988 television series "He Shang" (River elegy), which strongly asserted the views of the "littoral" tradition and disparaged the value of China's traditions, was a clear expression of this conflict and prelude to the more serious conflict that explored in spring 1989.[69]

As political leaders sort through economic ideas, they will consider them in light of such political traditions and visions and in light of their effect on their own political positions. Economic debates in China are thus an integral part of the broader political debate over the direction China will follow and over the sort of leadership that is to emerge in the coming years. The divergence of ideas among economists and the apparent political implications of their ideas suggest, first, that China's developmental strategy remains the subject of intense debate, and second, that the outcome of these debates will have a very important role in shaping the sort of political-economic system China will have—and the sort of interaction China will have with the rest of the world—for some time to come. While recent events have seen those upholding the hinterland tradition and more orthodox economic views triumph over those subscribing to the littoral tradition and radical reform ideas, it seems certain that this conflict will be rejoined in the future.

---

[69]For a sharp critique of "He Shang" from a "conservative" point of view, see Yi Jiayan, "What Did 'River Elegy' Advertise?" *Renmin ribao*, July 19, 1989, trans. in *FBIS-CHI*, July 21, 1989, pp. 17–20. Yi Jiayan appears to be the pen name of Wang Zhen, who previously complained that Zhao Ziyang did not permit his criticism of "He Shang" to appear in *Renmin ribao*.

Change and Continuity in Chinese Communist Political Ideology

The development of the Chinese Communists' political ideology over the past four decades can be divided into three leadership phases: the period of dominance by Mao Tse-tung; that of Hua Kuo-feng; and finally that of Teng Hsiao-p'ing. From 1949 to 1976, Mao Tse-tung tried to establish Communism as quickly as possible by transforming the people's ideology and revising Marxism-Leninism with his own political theories. Under Hua Kuo-feng, from September 1976 to December 1978, the official political ideology remained unchanged. After Teng Hsiao-p'ing assumed power in 1978, he tried to revise Marxism-Leninism and Mao Tse-tung's thought to justify his reform measures.[1] These three stages of official political ideology show the following characteristics:

- The political center's official political ideology dominates and justifies restructuring society according to its ideological goals.
- All organizations and individuals have become subordinate to the

---

[1] For the concepts of transformation and accommodation, see Thomas A. Metzger, *Escape from Predicament: Neo-Confucianism and China's Evolving Political Culture* (New York: Columbia University Press, 1977), pp. 226–35. See also Ramon H. Myers, "Does the Chinese Communist Party Have a 'Line'?" *Issues & Studies*, vol. 23, no. 12(Dec. 1987):133–34.

party, the state, and the power-holders; people must live their lives in accordance with the demands of the political regime.

- The party's rule is monolithic; it spreads its ideology through political campaigns and serves as the major instrument for political mobilization.
- No other political ideologies or rival political groups are tolerated; Marx, Engels, Lenin, Stalin, Mao Tse-tung, and Teng Hsiao-p'ing are deified, and their writings revered as classics.
- Under a one-party dictatorship, the power-holder has absolute authority and power; he changes the lines of command and establishes hierarchies in the party, government, and army at will; he interprets ideology in any way beneficial to his own political interests and uses ideology to attack his political rivals.
- The use of violence is institutionalized through the police and other specialized instruments of coercion and intimidation.
- Under such a political ideology, simple political terms discriminate between friend and foe: these include "communists and capitalists," "proletariat and bourgeoisie," "orthodox and revisionist," and "internationalists and imperialists (or hegemonists)"; there can be no compromise between these opposites.[2]

Accepting the above premises, I offer three hypotheses to explain what has changed, and what elements have remained constant in Chinese Communist political ideology.

First, the Chinese Communists are genuine, serious Marxists whose final goal is to realize communism. They apply Marxist concepts of "class struggle" and "violent revolution" to mobilize support and weaken their enemies in order to seize political power. Since the Chinese Communist regime was established in 1949, that party adopted radical measures to speed up the transition to communism. Their Marxist theories have not worked in practice. To preserve their ideals, the Chinese Communists slowed the pace of transition to communism and reinterpreted Marxism-Leninism and Mao Tse-tung's thought to deal with current political and economic conditions through gradual reform instead of radical policies.

Second, political movements originally were launched to achieve the cherished goals of the official ideology. The incessant political movements

---

[2]For some of these characteristics, see Roy C. Macridis, *Contemporary Political 7Ideologies* (Cambridge, Mass.: Winthrop Publishers, 1980), p. 90; Reo M. Christenson et al., *Ideologies and Modern Politics* (New York: Dodd, Mead & Co., 1975), pp. 3–20.

of the past four decades produced political instability and economic stagnation. Although the Chinese Communists repeatedly proclaimed their intention to dispense with further political campaigns, they have not done so in recent years.

Third, the current Chinese Communist leadership has reinterpreted Marxism-Leninism and Mao Tse-tung's thought when it found them inadequate, but they have not abandoned those basic theories. They continue to use them to consolidate the Chinese Communist regime's power.

The Mao Tse-tung Era

Both Karl Marx and Frederick Engels advocated the speedy abolition of private ownership of the means of production. Marx said that the system of private ownership was the root cause of the alienation of labor, and that to eliminate the vestiges of alienation, the system of private ownership must be abolished.[3] Later, Marx and Engels categorically asserted that Communist theory was summed up in a single sentence: "Abolition of private property."[4] They claimed that "the Communist revolution is the most radical rupture with traditional property relations."[5] Lenin also devised a new theory of socialism: under a dictatorship of the proletariat and the leadership of the Communist Party, capitalist society, before becoming a communist society, must pass through a transitional phase governed by the principle of "from each according to his ability, to each according to his labor." Society would later advance to the higher phase of communism, in which individuals were rewarded according to their needs.[6]

To first overthrow the "bourgeois dictatorship" and eliminate private ownership of the means of production,[7] the Chinese Communists concentrated their efforts between 1921 and 1949 on seizing power from the Kuo-

---

[3]Marx and Engels, "Economic and Philosophic Manuscripts of 1844," in *Collected Works*, vol. 3 (Moscow: Progress Publishers, 1975), pp. 273–75.
[4]Marx and Engels, "Manifesto of the Communist Party," in *Selected Works of Marx and Engels*, vol. 1 (Moscow: Foreign Languages Publishing House, 1962), p. 47.
[5]Ibid., p. 53.
[6]Lenin, "The State and Revolution," in *Collected Works of Lenin*, vol. 25 (Moscow: Progress Publishers, 1964), pp. 464–67.
[7]Liao Kai-lung, "A New Road and the Second Long March," in CCPCC Party School, ed., *Tang-shih hui-i pao-kao chi* (Collection of reports of meetings on party-history), *Chung-kung tang-shih lun-ts'ung* (Collection of articles on the history of the Chinese Communist Party), vol. 2 (Beijing: Publishing House of the CCPCC Party School, March 1982), p. 179.

mintang and eliminating the system of private ownership of land in rural areas. As most of the areas occupied by the Chinese Communist at that time were poor and backward, they tolerated the existence of some capitalism; in 1945 Mao said: "It would be a sheer illusion to try to build a socialist society on the ruins of the colonial, semi-colonial and semi-feudal order without the development of the private capitalist and the cooperative sectors."[8] In March 1949 the Chinese Communists adopted a policy of using the private capitalist sector to develop a state capitalist economy (joint public and private management), while also restricting that sector.[9] Mainland China's economy then contained state-run enterprises, cooperatives, farmers and artisans, services, and jointly owned and managed state capitalist firms.[10] Later that year, the party launched a land-reform movement in the "newly liberated areas" (different from the nineteen rural bases established by the Communists before 1949), and completed that task by the end of 1952. Thereafter, the Chinese Communists succeeded in nationalizing all land and means of production through a step-by-step process of mutual-aid groups, elementary cooperatives, advanced cooperatives, and finally people's communes. By 1958 the system of private ownership of land practiced in China for over two thousand years had disappeared.

In late 1952, the Central Committee of the Chinese Communist Party (CCP) declared that a transitional period, begun in 1949, would continue until socialist transformation of agriculture, handicrafts, and capitalist industry and commerce had been completed. In June 1953, the CCP's Central Committee formulated the policy of "using, restricting, and at the same time transforming" capitalist industry and commerce, and "uniting with, educating, and transforming" capitalist entrepreneurs with the purpose of "eliminating the capitalist system of private ownership of the means of production."[11] By the end of 1956, the socialized sector constituted 85.6 percent of the total economy; the joint state-private sector accounted for 7.3 percent; and the individual economy, 7.1 percent.[12] Under the "Three Red Banners" policy emphasizing the socialist General Line, the Great Leap, and

---

[8]Mao Tse-tung, "On Coalition Government," in *Selected Works of Mao Tse-tung*, vol. 3 (Beijing: Foreign Languages Press, 1965), p. 283.

[9]*Kung-tang wen-t'i chuan-t'i yen-chiu* (Monographs on Communist affairs) (Taipei, 1983), no. 13, p. 103.

[10]Ibid., 1982, no. 10, p. 357.

[11]Hao Meng-hua and Tuan Hao-jan, eds., *Chung-kuo kung-ch'an-tang liu-shih nien* (Sixty years of the Chinese Communist Party) (Nanking: Liberation Army Publishing House, Dec. 1984), pp. 411 and 422.

[12]Ibid., p. 455.

the people's communes and the Cultural Revolution, the party eradicated capitalist farms and collectivized virtually all economic activity in the 21 years from 1957 to 1978. That development brought about serious economic stagnation in mainland China.[13]

To achieve the communist ideal, the Chinese Communists initiated many political movements at the same time to propagate communist ideology, elicit popular support, and overcome certain political obstacles. Mao Tse-tung described their purpose as follows:

> The history of all revolutions proves that the transformation of old production relations does not necessarily result from the sufficient development of new productive forces. Our revolution started with the propagation of Marxism, which created a new public opinion which propelled the revolution. In the course of the revolution, the destruction of old superstructures paved the way for the establishment of new relations of production and thus opened up the road for the development of new social productive forces. In the course of developing productive forces, we should simultaneously proceed with the transformation of relations of production and ideology.[14]

Mao has broken with orthodox Marxism. Marx predicted that socialist revolution could only break out in developed capitalist societies in which highly developed productive forces have outgrown their outmoded relations of production. Such a socialist revolution would end capitalism and establish socialism under a proletarian dictatorship.[15] Only highly industrialized countries like Britain could expect a socialist revolution. But this prediction was wrong; the first successful socialist revolutions occurred in agrarian Russia and China, where industry was underdeveloped. Since 1949, the Chinese Communist leaders have struggled to establish socialism in a poor and backward country. Mao optimistically asserted that the poorer a country, the easier it could achieve revolution and socialism.

> China has strong points. It is, first, poor and, second, blank [i.e., ignorant]. But there are two sides to the coin. The poor want revolution. Ignorance

---

[13]Yü Kuang-yuan, "The Economy in the Initial Stage of Socialism," *Chung-kuo she-hui k'e-hsüeh* (Social sciences in China) (Beijing), 1987, no. 3:82.

[14]Mao Tse-tung, "A Note on Reading the Textbook *Political Economy* (Socialism), 1960," in *Mao Tse-tung ssu-hsiang wan-sui* (Long live Mao Tse-tung thought), vol. 2 (s.l.: s.n., 1969; reprinted, Taipei: Institute of International Relations, 1974), p. 182.

[15]Marx, "Critique of the Gotha Programme," in *Selected Works of Marx and Engels*, vol. 2 (Moscow: Foreign Languages Publishing House, 1962), pp. 33–34.

is not good, but it is like a sheet of blank paper. If paper has been written on, you cannot write another article on it, whereas a blank sheet of paper is good for writing on.[16]

Mao also caustically critiqued Lenin's theory that the more backward the country, the harder it would be to achieve the transition to socialism.[17]

Mao maintained that changes in relations of production would bring about upgraded productive forces, denying the basic Marxist principle that productive forces determine relations of production and that mainland China could not leapfrog into socialism. Mao justified political movements as a means of altering the people's world outlook and removing political obstacles that obstructed the changing of relations of production. For example, land reform mobilized poor and lower-middle-level peasants to seize land from landlords and rich peasants and redistribute it equally among the tillers. Mutual-aid and producers'-cooperative movements then mobilized the peasants in a step-by-step advance toward socialism.

The party leadership, however, disagreed about these policies. Liu Shao-ch'i, Teng Hsiao-p'ing, Ch'en Yun, and others criticized Mao Tse-tung for being too hasty. In September 1956, the CCP's Eighth National Congress made two important resolutions directed at Mao: both followed Liu Shao-ch'i's "Political Report" and Teng Hsiao-p'ing's "Report on the Revision of the Party Constitution." The resolution on Liu's report stated that contradictions between the proletariat and the bourgeoisie in mainland China had been basically resolved, that exploitation of one class by another had in general ceased, and that the socialist social system had basically been established. The second resolution emphasized the importance of collective leadership and criticized Mao's personality cults.

Mao did not seem to agree with the policy line adopted at the Eighth Congress. In June 1956, he refused to read the draft of a *People's Daily* editorial written by a group headed by Chou En-lai which supported the Politburo's policy of guarding against impetuosity. Later, in November, Mao emphasized the importance of class struggle in mobilizing cadres and the masses to carry out the socialist transformation of agriculture.[18] In

---

[16]Mao Tse-tung, "Talks at the Central Meeting on the Problems of Intellectuals, Jan. 20, 1956," in *Mao Tse-tung ssu-hsiang wan-sui*, vol. 1, p. 34.

[17]Mao Tse-tung, "A Note on Reading the Textbook *Political Economy* (Socialism), 1960," in *Mao Tse-tung ssu-hsiang wan-sui*, vol. 2, pp. 181–82.

[18]Mao Tse-tung, "Talks at the Second Session of the Eighth Central Committee of the Communist Party of China" (Nov. 15, 1956), in *Selected Works of Mao Tse-tung*, vol. 5 (Beijing: Foreign Languages Publishing House, 1977), pp. 337–42.

December, Mao then complained that other leading cadres agreed with the decisions of the Eighth Congress but not with him.[19]

The antirightist movement launched in June 1957 also influenced Chinese Communist ideology. Prior to that movement, members of the minority "democratic" parties and prominent nonpartisans were urged to voice their opinions. They responded by demanding that the party share power with other parties, eliminate bureaucratism and factionalism, and abolish the socialist system. Their criticisms incurred merciless attacks from Mao. The attacks did not end until the first half of 1958, when a total of 552,877 people had been labeled as "rightists."[20] Mao said that the antirightist movement was a "class struggle" and a "war" between the bourgeoisie and the proletariat.[21] The antirightist campaign paved the way for Mao to wrest power from his rivals. Throughout China, people were put under strict ideological restrictions.

After the antirightist movement, Mao initiated the "Great Leap Forward" to enable mainland China to surpass Britain within fifteen years in the production of steel and other important industrial products.[22] To prepare for the "Great Leap," the Central Committee held a series of meetings in Hangchow, Nanning, Chengtu, Hankow, and elsewhere, followed by the second session of the CCP's Eighth National Congress. At these meetings, Mao severely criticized the policy of opposing "rash advances" adopted at the first session of the Eighth Congress, claiming that it violated Marxist principles and discouraged the Chinese people from boosting economic growth.[23] To mobilize the people's enthusiasm for work, he advocated the slogan: "Go all out, aim high, and achieve greater, faster, better, and more economical results in building socialism."[24] He returned to the theme of class struggle, dividing the population into two kinds of exploiting classes—the remnants of "imperialism, feudalism and bureaucratic capitalism" (landlords, rich peasants, reactionaries, bad elements, and rightists)—the na-

---

[19]Chang Hsing-hsing, "The Reasons Why the Policy Line Set By the CCP's Eighth National Congress Has Not Been Upheld," *Chung-kung-shih yen-chiu* (Studies on the history of the Chinese Communist Party) (Beijing), no. 5(Sept. 25, 1988), p. 34.

[20]Hao Meng-pi and Tuan Hao-jan, "Sixty Years of the Chinese Communist Party," p. 491.

[21]Mao Tse-tung, "*Wen Hui Pao*'s Bourgeois Orientation Should Be Criticized," (July 1, 1957), in *Selected Works of Mao Tse-tung*, vol. 5 (Beijing: Foreign Languages Press, 1977), pp. 451–56.

[22]Mao Tse-tung, "Talks at the Supreme State Conference" (Jan. 28 and 30, 1958), *Mao Tse-tung ssu-hsiang wan-sui*, vol. 1, p. 154.

[23]Mao Tse-tung, "Talks at the Nanning Conference," ibid., p. 146.

[24]Mao Tse-tung, "Talks at the Chengtu Conference," ibid., pp. 166–67.

tional bourgeoisie and intellectuals, and two laboring classes—workers and peasants.[25] Mao succeeded in retrieving power at the Second Plenum of the party's Eighth Central Committee, where he declared that the major contradiction that had to be eliminated before the construction of socialism could be completed was between the proletariat and the bourgeoisie, or between the socialist road and the capitalist road.[26]

During the "Great Leap Forward," Mao called for "high-speed economic development." The mainland news media published slogans such as "The productive capacity of the land can be measured only by boldness of the people who produce; we need not fear the inability to produce—only the inability to imagine how great our productive capacity really is."[27] In August 1958, the party agreed to establish communes, claiming it was the best possible form of organization for building socialism and moving from socialism to communism. That resolution ordered mainland China's 740,000 agricultural cooperatives to be reorganized into some 26,000 people's communes, embracing 120 million households (about 99 percent of the total number).[28]

The "Great Leap" and the people's-commune movement caused serious economic problems and famine. As a result, many Communists began to criticize the "communist wind" (meaning the attempt to realize communism in too short a period of time). After Liu Shao-ch'i was elected state chairman in April 1959, he suggested various measures to save the country from economic collapse, such as restoring peasants' private plots.

At an enlarged meeting of the Politburo held in Lushan on July 2, 1959, Liu Shao-ch'i criticized the "Great Leap" for having caused severe economic problems. Chu Teh said that peasants still had a private-ownership mentality and would not willingly accept a communist system. He also showed his dissatisfaction with communal eating facilities.[29] P'eng Teh-huai, who criticized Mao at the meeting, had earlier written to Mao criticizing the "Three Red Banners" policy for rashly advancing communism, "boasting and exaggeration," "coercion and commandism," and "petty-bourgeois fanaticism."[30] P'eng's opinions received a warm response from Huang K'e-ch'eng,

---

[25]Mao Tse-tung, "Talks at the Hankou Meeting," *Mao Tse-tung ssu-hsiang wan-sui*, vol. 1, pp. 180–81.

[26]"Sixty Years of the Chinese Communist Party," p. 499.

[27]*People's Daily*, Aug. 27, 1958, p. 1.

[28]"Sixty Years of the Chinese Communist Party," pp. 503–5.

[29]Wang Nien-i, "A Study of the Origin of the 'Cultural Revolution,'" *Tang-shih yen-chiu* (Studies on party history) (Beijing; bimonthly), no. 1(Feb. 1985):25.

[30]P'eng Teh-huai, *P'eng teh-huai tzu-shu* (P'eng Teh-huai's autobiography) (Beijing: People's Publishing House, 1981), pp. 266–86.

Chou Hsiao-chou, and Chang Wen-t'ien. Mao was greatly upset. At the Lushan meeting, Mao openly criticized P'eng's letter as a "program of rightist opportunism which had been drafted in a planned and organized way, and with hidden intentions."[31] Mao later was able to purge P'eng. A new movement against "rightist opportunism" gained ground for half a year, and leftist policies succeeded in banning the private-plot system in the countryside. Even the communal canteens were described as a "battlefield for the defense of socialism" and as requiring class struggle.[32]

The economic stagnation and famine caused by "leftist" policies forced Mao to make some changes, however. In his article "A Summary of the Past Ten Years," published on June 18, 1960, Mao had to admit that the socialist revolution and socialist construction had been launched without due consideration. He then presented the principle of "readjustment, consolidation, enhancement, and strengthening" (*t'iao-cheng, kung-ku, t'i-kao, ch'ung-shih*) to promote the rural economy. This new principle allowed commune members to keep some private plots and to engage in limited household sideline production. Markets were organized in rural areas to allow communes, production brigades, and teams to exchange their products. However, some "leftist" tendencies continued. For example, the Central Committee decided to suspend the ration and communal-canteen systems only at the work conference of May 21–June 12, 1961.[33]

Differences within the Chinese Communist leadership over official ideology and economic policies became serious in 1962. At an enlarged, 7,000-person Central Committee work conference held in Beijing from January 11 to February 7 of that year, Liu Shao-ch'i said that a number of mistakes had been committed during the "Three Red Banners" period: overambitious targets for industrial and agricultural production; overexpansion of capital construction; disproportionate development of various sectors of the economy; hasty transition from collective ownership to communism through the people's communes.

After this work conference, Liu Shao-ch'i convoked an enlarged meeting of the party's Central Committee in Chungnanhai on February 21, 1962, to continue the criticism of leftist tendencies. Chou En-lai, Teng Hsiao-p'ing, and Ch'en Yun decided to form a "central financial and economic group"

---

[31]Ibid., p. 276.
[32]Cheng Teh-jung et al., *Hsin chung-kuo chi-shih (1949–84)* (Chronicle of New China, 1949–84) (Kirin: Northeast China Normal University Publishing House, 1986), pp. 263–64.
[33]Ibid., pp. 27–89 and 299.

under Ch'en's leadership.[34] This provoked a counterattack from Mao. At a Central Committee work conference in Peitaiho in August, Mao claimed that classes, class contradictions, and class struggle still existed in socialist countries, and that class struggle would last through the entire historical period of socialism. The "rightist opportunism" advocated by some people within the party, he said, was actually revisionism. Later, at the Tenth Plenary Session of the party's Eighth Central Committee held in September of the same year, Mao reiterated the importance of class struggle and criticized fixing farm-output quotas for each household as a form of capitalism. Meanwhile, he criticized P'eng Teh-huai for having maintained secret relations with foreign countries.[35] From then on, this leftist doctrine became official ideology. Mao's theory of class struggle inspired the socialist-education movement from 1963 to 1965. At one work conference held from December 15, 1964, to January 14, 1965, the Politburo adopted a document entitled "Some Current Questions in the Socialist Education Movement in Rural Areas" (also known as the "Twenty-three Articles"), which stated that the struggle between the bourgeoisie and the proletariat and between capitalism and socialism would exist during the transition from socialism to communism, and that the movement's targets were "power-holders taking the capitalist road." This document not only helped Mao to attack his rivals in the party but also served as the ideological and theoretical basis for the Cultural Revolution.

In November 1965, the Shanghai paper *Wen hui pao* published, with Mao's approval, an article by Yao Wen-yuan criticizing Wu Han's historical drama "Hai Jui's Dismissal from Office" for having linked the sufferings of the Ming Dynasty official Hai Jui with those of party leaders, especially P'eng Teh-huai, in 1962.[36] This criticism raised the curtain on the Cultural Revolution, and official ideology took another sharp turn to the left that would last until 1976.

Mao still believed in utopian socialism, even though he had realized its shortcomings in 1958. In the early 1960s, he claimed that the Soviet Union had failed to establish socialism in the countryside because peasants were given too much freedom and because household sideline production was still heavily emphasized.[37]

---

[34]Cheng Teh-jung, *Hsin chung-kuo chi-shih*, p. 313.

[35]Ibid., p. 323.

[36]Wu Han, a noted scholar of Ming Dynasty history, was at that time vice-mayor of Beijing and vice-chairman of the Democratic League. He died in October 1966 as a result of persecution.

[37]T'an Tsung-chi and Cheng Ch'ien, "A Comment After Ten Years: Collection of

Mao could not tolerate any challenge to his authority. To consolidate his leadership, he cultivated a personality cult. At the Central Committee's meeting in Chengtu in March 1958, Mao said that there were both incorrect and correct personality cults, the correct ones being those of Marx, Engels, and Stalin because they represented the truth. The incorrect kind of cult was the blind worship of any individual. Here, Mao confused reverence for truth with worship of an individual, because reverence for truth should not be interpreted as a personality cult. Mao's comments on personality cults were actually aimed at establishing his absolute power. At the Chengtu meeting, K'e Ch'ing-shih, a member of the Central Committee and the first secretary of the CCP's Shanghai Municipal Committee, flattered Mao by saying that party members should believe in Mao and obey him blindly. Instead of being refuted, his words were relayed to party members. Consequently, at the Fifth Plenary Session of the Eighth Central Committee held two months later, K'e was elected a Politburo member. In the summer of 1958, K'ang Sheng said that Mao Tse-tung's thought was the culmination of Marxism-Leninism. Again, at the end of 1959, he praised Mao's thought as the "last word" in Marxism-Leninism.[38] At the 7,000-person Central Committee work conference in 1962, Lin Piao praised Mao, even though many other party leaders criticized him for the mistakes he had committed during the "Three Red Banners" period.[39] It seems that Mao still held fast to his policy line, despite its having proved disastrous, if only to restore his absolute authority.

Mao also feared that if the party's policies were not leftist enough, anticommunist and antisocialist forces would gather strength. Between September 1956 and the spring of 1957, strikes and student demonstrations erupted in some parts of mainland China, and some peasants asked to leave the people's communes or production brigades. This unrest was sparked by the riots of June 1956 in Poznan, Poland, and the uprising in Hungary in October of the same year. On March 25, 1957, the party issued a directive about how to handle strikes and demonstrations emphasizing the existence

---

Articles on the History of the 'Great Cultural Revolution,'" (Beijing: Publishing House of Materials on the History of the Chinese Communist Party, March 1987), p. 244.

[38]Hsi Hsuan, "An Exploration of the Cause of the 'Great Cultural Revolution,'"*Chung-kung tang-shih yen-chiu*, 1988, no. 5:55.

[39]Chang T'ien-jung, "The Seven Thousand-Person Conference in 1962," *Tang-shih yen-chiu*, 1981, no. 5:29.

of class contradictions and class struggle.[40] The directive was obviously based on opinions Mao had expressed at Beijing's Eleventh Supreme State Conference in February 1957. Mao's speech at the conference was published in June of the same year under the title, "On the Correct Handling of Contradictions Among the People."[41] Mao's class struggle theories now paved the way for the later purge of his political opponents.

Mao's adherence to leftist policies enabled him to safeguard his leadership position by attacking his opponents as revisionists. Mao sharply criticized revisionism on a number of occasions. At a nationwide propaganda conference in March 1957, he said revisionism was more harmful than dogmatism; at a Central Committee work conference in September–October 1965, he even claimed that some people in the Central Committee had engaged in revisionism and attempted to organize a "counterrevolutionary coup." He always worried about the possibility of such a coup.[42] The Chinese Communists responded to Khrushchev's dismissal by saying it signaled the bankruptcy of revisionism.[43] When Chou En-lai and Ho Lung were in Moscow in November 1964 for the celebrations of the October Revolution, the Soviet defense minister R. Ya. Malinovsky allegedly proposed to Ho Lung that Mao should be forced to step down in China as Khrushchev had been in Russia. Chou lodged a protest, and Brezhnev apologized. After that, Mao held his power even tighter to guard against a possible coup by his associates.[44] Mao's fear of that possibility is clear from one of his letters to Chiang Ch'ing in 1966.[45]

The Hua Kuo-feng Period

On October 7, 1976, less than a month after Mao's death, the Politburo chose Hua Kuo-feng to be chairman of the party and its Military Commission. With Hua in power, two political ideas coexisted: Hua Kuo-feng's

---

[40]Hao Meng-pi and Tuan Hao-jan, *Sixty Years of the Chinese Communist Party*, p. 483.

[41]Mao Tse-tung, *Selected Works of Mao Tse-tung*, vol. 5 (Beijing: Foreign Languages Publishing House, 1977), pp. 395–99.

[42]Hsi Hsuan, "An Exploration of the Cause of the 'Cultural Revolution,'" p. 57.

[43]"How Was Khrushchev Thrown Out?" *Hung-ch'i* (Red flag), 1964, no. 22:1–8.

[44]Hsi Hsuan, p. 57.

[45]"Mao Tse-tung's Private Letter to Chiang Ch'ing" (written on July 8, 1966, and published in Sept. 1972), in *Classified Chinese Communist Documents: A Selection* (Taipei: IIR, 1978), pp. 54–57.

"two whatevers" and Teng Hsiao-p'ing's "practice is the sole criterion for testing truth."[46]

On the strength of Mao's note, "With you in charge, I am at ease," Hua assumed power; Mao's prestige had been essential. Teng's attitude to Mao was different, because Mao had purged him twice. He proposed that "practice" be used to evaluate Mao and his theories; ideas, therefore, to be retained, must be proved correct, and incorrect ideas discarded.

While both men might have disagreed on ideology, Hua also did not want Teng back in power because Teng was more prestigious and capable and posed a great threat to his leadership. He continued to criticize Teng after ousting the Gang of Four. Meanwhile, he reiterated the "two whatevers" and Mao's concepts of "class struggle" and "continued revolution under the dictatorship of the proletariat."

Teng feigned meekness and subservience to Hua. Teng's efforts at last bore fruit when the Third Plenary Session of the Tenth Central Committee on July 16, 1977, decided to reappoint him to the Politburo and its Standing Committee, and made him vice-chairman of the Central Committee, vice-premier of the State Council, and chief of the general staff of the People's Liberation Army.[47]

After returning to power, Teng launched reforms in education, cadre training, science and technology, ideology, the army, and the economy. In education, he rejected the assertions that before the Cultural Revolution, education had been dominated by the bourgeoisie, and that intellectuals were basically bourgeois.[48] He insisted that teachers be trusted, and that the government's education departments be reformed, calling for more teaching of general theory and foreign languages, promoting audio-visual education, compiling new unified teaching materials, and introducing teaching materials from abroad. He also proposed that graduate schools reopen, students go abroad to study, and foreign experts come to mainland China; that the entrance examination system be restored; and that, if necessary, schools not advance students or expel them. On September 7, 1977, the Ministry of Education issued a notice ordering that middle and primary schools delete

---

[46]The slogan "Practice is the sole criterion for testing truth" was first advanced by Hu Fu-ming, deputy head of the Department of Philosophy of Nanking University. The slogan of the "two whatevers" derives from an editorial jointly published by the *People's Daily, Red Flag,* and *Liberation Army Daily* on Feb. 7, 1977. It means "Whatever policies Chairman Mao devised, we will resolutely support; and whatever directives Chairman Mao laid down, we will forever observe."

[47]Cheng et al., *Hsin chung-kuo chi-shih,* p. 608.

[48]Teng Hsiao-p'ing, "Setting Things Right in Education" (Sept. 19, 1977), in *Selected Works* (Beijing: Foreign Languages Press, 1984), pp. 80–81.

from their teaching materials speeches and articles published by the Gang of Four and its followers and any favorable references to them.[49] Teng also proposed changes in the regime's cadre policy. He appointed Hu Yao-pang director of the party's Organization Department in 1977 and asked him to investigate previous injustices. Teng also stressed that science and technology were the key to modernization and asserted that "mental workers who serve socialism are part of the working people."[50] To mobilize intellectuals for the modernization program, the Central Committee approved requests by the United-Front Work Department and the Public-Security Ministry to clear the names of those who had been labeled rightists.[51] Concerning ideology, Teng criticized Hua's "two whatevers" concept, arguing to the party's central leadership on May 24, 1977, that no such theory existed in the writings of Marx, Engels, Lenin, Stalin, or Mao Tse-tung.[52] Teng's supporters formulated a rival theory that "practice is the sole criterion for testing truth," and this slogan appeared in Teng's speeches starting from May 11, 1978. To overhaul the armed forces, Teng suggested "ten fighting tasks" and "nine documents"[53] and pledged to clear the army of followers of the Gang of Four. To make economic reforms, Teng convened meetings on agriculture, industry, coal mining, transportation, railways, metallurgy, forestry, aquatic production, and economic planning.

Teng's efforts to reorganize the party and government encountered many obstacles because of ideological conflicts within the party leadership. For example, Hua Kuo-feng refused to drop previous slogans such as "taking class struggle as the key link" and "continuing the revolution under the dictatorship of the proletariat," and the "two whatevers."[54] Injustices of that period still remained. At the party work conference of November 1978, certain senior cadres, including Po I-po, T'ao Chu, Wang Ho-shou, and T'an Chen-lin, were re-admitted to the party. After heated discussion of

---

[49]Cheng et al., *Hsin chung-kuo chi-shih*, pp. 609 and 611–12.

[50]Teng Hsiao-p'ing, "Speech at the Opening Ceremony of the National Conference on Science" (March 18, 1978), in *Selected Works*, pp. 101–5.

[51]*Chung-kung kuang-tung sheng-wei nei-pu wen-chien hui-pien* (Collections of documents issued by the CCP Kwangtung Provincial Committee), pp. 35–39. Also included in that collection were the CCPCC's documents on correcting false verdicts.

[52]Cheng et al., *Hsin chung-kuo chi-shih*, p. 606.

[53]For details see Teng Hsiao-p'ing, "Speech at a Plenary Meeting of the Military Commission of the Central Committee of the CPC," in *Selected Works*, vol. 87, pp. 402–3.

[54]Shao Hua-tse, "Some Questions Concerning the 'Cultural Revolution,'" *Tang-shih hui-i pao-kao chi* (Collection of reports of meetings on party history) (Beijing: Publishing House of the CCPCC Party School, March 1982), p. 348.

some important historical events, Teng closed the conference with a speech about emancipating people's minds, a theme that became the party's dominant ideology at the Third Plenary Session of the CCP's Eleventh Central Committee. Teng said:

> When everything has to be done by the book, when thinking turns rigid and blind faith is the fashion, it is impossible for a party or a nation to make progress. Its life will cease and that party or nation will perish.[55]

He criticized people who followed the "two whatevers" on the pretext of supporting Mao, but in fact merely to peddle the ideas of Lin Piao and the Gang of Four in a new guise.[56]

Teng always took precautions against any possible opening for the leftists to return to power. To suppress the leftists, Teng criticized Hua Kuo-feng by name in the "Resolution on Certain Questions in the History of Our Party Since the Founding of the PRC." He argued that supporters of the Gang of Four and others were "waving the banner of Hua Kuo-feng," and that Hua could not be relieved of his posts if he was not criticized by name.[57]

Teng's tactic of criticizing Hua by name was unanimously accepted by members of the committee in charge of drafting the above-mentioned resolution. The document accused Hua of having committed the following mistakes: (1) "leftist" errors in his capacity as chairman of the Central Committee; (2) promoting the erroneous "two whatevers" policy and refusing to admit the error; (3) suppressing discussions in 1978 on how to judge truth; (4) procrastinating and obstructing reinstatement of veteran cadres and correcting injustices, including those of the Tienanmen Incident of 1976; (5) welcoming and encouraging the personality cult of himself, while continuing the personality cult of Mao; and (6) being responsible for the overambitious economic policies of the past and their disastrous consequences, as well as for other leftist policies. The resolution concluded by saying that under Hua's leadership, the party's leftist errors could not be corrected.[58] Charged with these offenses, Hua lost all his posts, retaining

---

[55]Teng Hsiao-p'ing, "Emancipate the Mind, Seek Truth from Facts, and Unite as One in Looking to the Future," in *Selected Works*, p. 154.

[56]Teng Hsiao-p'ing, "The Organizational Line Guarantees Implementation of the Ideological and Political Lines," ibid., pp. 196–98.

[57]Teng Hsiao-p'ing, "Remarks on Successive Drafts of the 'Resolution on Certain Questions in the History of Our Party Since the Founding of the People's Republic of China,'" ibid., pp. 295–96.

[58]*Beijing Review*, vol. 24, no. 27(1981):26.

only his membership in the Central Committee. Teng had employed the principle that "practice is the sole criterion for testing truth" to eradicate the foremost leftists in the party.

The Teng Hsiao-p'ing Period

Mainland China experienced significant ideological change when the party's new leadership started criticizing Mao Tse-tung and some of his doctrines after Teng Hsiao-p'ing's return to power in late 1978. The close relations between Mao and the Gang of Four would lead one to believe that all criticism of the Gang's ideology during the Cultural Revolution period could also apply to Mao. The party charged the Gang of being responsible for bureaucratism, the personality cult, and rule by individual rather than by law.[59]

The concepts advocated by the Gang of Four now came under fire. These were: (1) continuing the revolution under the dictatorship of the proletariat; (2) taking class struggle as the key link; (3) giving prominence to politics; (4) dictatorship over ideology, and leftist education and literature and art policies; (5) factionalism; (6) "speaking out freely, airing views fully, holding great debates, and writing big-character posters"; and (7) erroneous economic theories and policies. The Gang had criticized any measures to develop productivity introduced by their opponents—including payment according to work and efforts to develop the "forces of production"—as "revisionist" and engendering capitalism. Material incentives and any attempts to improve people's living standards were also frowned upon. Collective enterprise and individual businesses linked to the predominantly state-owned economy were also labeled "remnants" of capitalism. In the rural areas, the Gang and their supporters opposed the reintroduction of private plots, household sideline production, rural markets, and household-based production-responsibility systems. These reforms were regarded as "revisionist" and represented a return to independent farming. Efficient business accounting was labeled as "putting profits before all else" and the development of commodity production and circulation meant developing capitalism. According to the Gang, importing advanced foreign technology and promoting foreign trade was practically a treasonable offense. The Gang also discouraged the professionalization of cadres and any measures to in-

---

[59]An-chia Wu, *Chung-kung shih-hsueh hsin-t'an* (Renewed inquiry into the Chinese Communists' historiography), 2nd ed. (Taipei: The Youth Cultural Service, Oct. 1984), pp. 23–77.

crease the prestige of intellectuals, scientists, and technologists. Any regulations necessary for the efficient running of the economy were labeled "restrictions" and "repression."[60] In the resolution on party history, however, the party evaluated the Cultural Revolution as a disaster, not a revolution, and as not bringing about any significant social progress.[61]

While criticizing the Gang of Four and the Cultural Revolution, Teng re-evaluated Mao and his doctrines according to the principle that "practice is the sole criterion for testing truth." This principle is based on Mao's work "On Practice," published in July 1937,[62] and Teng has always quoted Mao in propounding this theory.[63] Teng's evaluation of Mao and his ideas concluded that Mao's merits are primary and his errors secondary,[64] therefore, some parts of Mao's thought are correct and others incorrect. Mao's thought has been interpreted as the "crystallization of the collective wisdom of the Chinese Communist Party."[65] To justify this judgment, Teng Hsiao-p'ing quoted Mao's statement that no one, including Marx, Engels, Lenin, Stalin, and Mao himself, can avoid making mistakes, and that if one's work is 70 percent achievements and 30 percent mistakes, that is quite all right.[66]

Mao's alleged major mistakes were the following: he broadened the scope of class struggle; attempted to build socialism through political movements; advocated equalitarianism; permitted the growth of a personality cult; advocated the theory of "continuing the revolution under the dictatorship of the proletariat"; and discriminated against intellectuals. Despite all Mao's mistakes and the shortcomings of his ideas, the Chinese Communists

---

[60]Chiang Ssu-i, "Education to Negate Thoroughly the Cultural Revolution Should Be Carried Through," *Kung-fei kuang-po chi-yao* (Mainland radio broadcasts) (Taipei), Sept. 5, 1984, Military 1–10. Chiang was at that time the vice-president of the PLA Political Academy.

[61]*Shih-i-chieh san-chung ch'üan-hui i-lai chung-yao wen-hsien hsuan-tu* (Selection of important documents published since the Third Plenary Session of the CCP's Eleventh Central Committee), vol. 1 (Kirin: People's Publishing House, Aug. 1982), pp. 314–25.

[62]*Selected Works of Mao Tse-tung*, vol. 1 (Beijing: Foreign Languages Press, 1967), p. 296. In the article, Mao emphasized that man's social practice alone is the criterion of truth and of his knowledge of the external world.

[63]Teng Hsiao-p'ing, "Speech at the All-Army Conference on Political Work," in *Selected Works*, p. 130.

[64]Teng Hsiao-p'ing, "On the Reform of the System of Party and State Leadership," ibid., p. 317.

[65]*Beijing Review*, vol. 24, no. 27(1981):29.

[66]Teng Hsiao-p'ing, "The 'Two Whatevers' Do Not Accord with Marxism," in *Selected Works*, p. 51.

still refuse to discard Mao Tse-tung's thought today. They have divided Mao's performance and his ideas into two parts: pre- and post-1957. His leadership before 1957 is considered correct, but he is judged to have committed more and more mistakes after the antirightist movement of 1957.[67] The Teng faction made this distinction in order to criticize Mao while affirming his historical role and continuing to use his ideas.[68] The Chinese Communists continue to revere Mao Tse-tung because of his contribution to the establishment of the Beijing regime. When Teng accepted Ch'en Yun's suggestion that the 60-year history of the Chinese Communist Party should be reviewed and summed up in the "Resolution on Certain Questions in the History of Our Party Since the Founding of the PRC," he hoped this would provide an adequate basis for affirming Mao's historical role and the justification for adhering to and developing Mao's thought.[69] In that resolution, Mao's leadership before 1957 was considered to be correct;[70] repudiating Mao's role before that date would be tantamount to repudiating the entire history of the party. In fact, Teng said that exaggerating Mao's mistakes meant discrediting the CCP and the Chinese Communist regime.[71] Therefore Mao is still lauded as the "chief founder of the People's Liberation Army and the chief founder of the People's Republic of China."[72] Hu Yao-pang even eulogized Mao as the "greatest and most outstanding figure China has had in the past century and more," and said his position and role in the party and the Chinese Communist revolution were unparalleled.[73]

Because Mao's thought served as the guiding principle of the Chinese Communist Party from 1945 to 1979 and then became a core element of the Four Cardinal Principles, any repudiation of Maoist doctrine would invite demands to reject the theoretical system that has long guided the party.[74] In

---

[67]Teng Hsiao-p'ing, "Remarks on Successive Drafts of the 'Resolution on Certain Questions in the History of Our Party Since the Founding of the People's Republic of China,'" ibid., p. 280.

[68]Ibid., p. 276.

[69]Ibid., p. 289.

[70]*Beijing Review*, vol. 24, no. 27(1981):10–26. The same judgment was also made in Liao Kai-lung's report, "Historical Experiences and Our Road of Development," *Issues & Studies*, vol. 17, no. 11(1981):101–2.

[71]*Beijing Review*, vol. 24, no. 27(1981):287.

[72]Editorial, "Mao Tse-tung's Thought Is Radiant Forever," *People's Daily*, Dec. 26, 1983.

[73]Hu Yao-pang, "The Best Way of Recollection," *People's Daily*, Dec. 26, 1983, p. 1.

[74]Teng Hsiao-p'ing, "Uphold the Four Cardinal Principles," in *Selected Works*, pp. 166–91.

the *Selected Work of Deng Xiaoping,* published in July 1983, Teng mentions Mao 521 times; most of these references are positive. In fact, Mao's ideas on "new democracy," the encirclement of cities by villages, people's war, and the united front as strategies instrumental to the Communist unification of mainland China were included in the 1981 resolution on CCP history. At Ch'en Yun's suggestion, party cadres were instructed to study Mao's articles: "On Practice," "On Contradiction," "On Protracted War," "Problems of War and Strategy," and "On Coalition Government."[75]

Finally, the continued adherence to Mao's ideas is advantageous to the senior cadres now in power because those ideas give prominence to their contributions to the party and enable them to escape criticism by pro-Maoists. By making a show of adhering to Mao's thought, the Teng faction has exposed Mao's mistakes. It is interesting to note that Teng has maintained that other leaders should share the blame for Mao's errors.[76] He said that criticizing Mao's personal mistakes alone will not solve any problems, and systems and institutions are more important than individuals. Teng contends that although many of Mao's statements were correct, faulty systems and institutions caused his decisions to be implemented wrongly,[77] implying that something should be done to reform these systems and institutions, in addition to criticizing Mao's mistakes.

Another important change in this accommodation period has been the reinterpretation of Marxism to bring it into line with current policies and practice.

In common with utopian socialists, almost all Marxists share an aversion to private property in the means of production and the exploitation of the poor by the rich, and a belief in Proudhon's idea that "property is theft." They are passionately committed to collectivism—the common ownership of wealth—and regard socialism as the means to extirpate strife, antagonisms, and selfishness. They also strongly believe in "social collectivism," a concept emphasizing the interdependence and solidarity of social life. They also regard communitarianism as the supreme value and detest individualism, competition, and self-interest.[78] Most of the policies adopted by the Chinese Communists in the past were actually guided by these utopian

---

[75] *Shih-i-chieh San-chung-ch'üan-hui i-lai chung-yao wen-hsien hsuan-tu,* p. 829.

[76] Teng Hsiao-p'ing, "Remarks on Successive Drafts of the 'Resolution on Certain Questions in the History of Our Party Since the Founding of the People's Republic of China," in *Selected Works,* pp. 281 and 292.

[77] Ibid., p. 283. Teng meant that the mistakes committed by Mao were the result of one-party dictatorial rule.

[78] Roy C. Macridis, *Contemporary Political Ideologies,* pp. 49–50.

ideas. However, practice has proved that many of these Marxist principles are inapplicable to mainland China, and as a result, people have lost confidence in communism. As early as 1951, the Central Committee launched a mass movement aimed at overcoming people's indifference to politics.[79] In 1957, Mao Tse-tung complained that many intellectuals were reluctant to accept Marxism-Leninism and communism.[80] Later, the Chinese Communists initiated mass movements to strengthen people's belief in communism, including the "never forget class struggle" movement of 1962 and the "socialist education movement" of 1964. Nevertheless, popular antipathy toward communism became more apparent after the Cultural Revolution and the fall of the Gang of Four. Popular opposition manifests itself mainly in a lack of confidence in the regime, its ideology, and the Four Modernizations program. Instead, many now claim that "communism is but a dim illusion" and that "socialist alienation" exists.[81] These new developments suggest that although Marxism was originally designed to serve the people, the Chinese Communists use it to control the people. People now realize that the root cause of such alienation is the communist system itself. Fearing that the idea of "socialist alienation" would bring opposition to socialism, the party eventually decided that it was a form of "spiritual pollution" and should be eliminated.[82]

The party's political and economic movements of the last 30-odd years have been aimed at moving China from socialism to communism. Yet communism is merely a dim illusion.[83] The people have realized that many conditions and problems that now confront them cannot be solved by Marxism-Leninism or Mao Tse-tung's thought.[84] Marx merely suggested that socialism was a transitional stage to communism, but he did not say how this transition was to be carried out. After abolishing private ownership of the means of production by violent means, both the Chinese and the Soviet Communists experimented. From Lenin's "war communism" and "new economic policy," to Stalin's agricultural collectivization and five-

---

[79]*People's Daily*, July 25, 1951, p. 6.

[80]Mao Tse-tung, "On the Correct Handling of Contradictions Among the People," in *Selected Works of Mao Tse-tung*, vol. 5 (Beijing: Foreign Languages Press, 1977), p. 405.

[81]Li Hung-lin, "'What Does the 'Crisis of Faith' Indicate?" *People's Daily*, Nov. 11, 1980, p. 5; Lei Ch'eng, "Confidence and Trust," *People's Daily*, March 13, 1980, p. 5.

[82]*China Daily* (Beijing), Oct. 27, 1983, p. 1.

[83]Lo Kuo-chieh, "Ideals and Realities," *Kwangming Daily*, Oct. 25, 1982, p. 3.

[84]Yü Hao-ch'eng, "Superstition and Belief," *Hsin-hua wen-chai*, 1982, no. 9, p. 5.

year economic plans, to Mao Tse-tung's "Three Red Banners" policy and Teng Hsiao-p'ing's production-responsibility systems, these efforts evolved by trial and error. More people are now distressed that the "dictatorship of the proletariat" (or "people's democratic dictatorship") was nothing more than the autocratic rule of the Chinese Communist Party, whose members only looked after their own interests.[85]

To inspire people's confidence in communism, the party intensifies its propaganda about Communist ideology.[86] People are told that communism is a system and a movement, not an illusory theory,[87] and that it is incorrect to attempt a premature transition to communism. The Chinese Communists now see their main task as developing socialism; communism must wait.

To revive peasants' enthusiasm for work after 1978, the party allowed them to keep private plots for farming activities outside the socialist economy, and they also introduced a household-based production-responsibility system. In his report to the Thirteenth National Congress in October 1987, Chao Tzu-yang announced that individual and private businesses would be allowed to exist. Then, in March 1988, the Seventh National People's Congress decided to amend the state constitution to enable people to transfer their land-use rights and to permit private businesses. If the current policy is continued, Communist ideology will erode.[88]

In addition to separating ideals from practice, the party, after its Twelfth National Congress, claimed that they are building "socialism with Chinese characteristics."[89] This means abandoning certain outdated Marxist doctrines. In March 1983, Chou Yang, chairman of the Joint Association of Literature and Art Workers, said that Marxism is still being developed, and that over the past century or more, this process of development has stagnated, retrogressed, and even degenerated. He also said that the development

---

[85]Yang Erh-lieh et al., "Reform and Perfect the Socialist Political System," *Kwangming Daily*, April 25, 1983, p. 3.

[86]Hu Yao-pang, "Create a New Situation in All Fields of Socialist Modernization," *Beijing Review*, vol. 25, no. 37(1982):21.

[87]Hsing Pen-ssu, "Marxist Philosophy and Communist Ideology," *People's Daily*, Sept. 24, 1982, p. 5.

[88]Stuart R. Schram, "To Utopia and Back: A Cycle in the History of the Chinese Communist Party," *China Quarterly*, 1981, no. 87:407–39. Schram believes that the Chinese Communists will never abandon their utopian ideals, as these are the only grounds for their existence.

[89]Teng Hsiao-p'ing, "Speech at the Opening Ceremony of the CCP's Twelfth National Congress" (Sept. 1, 1982), *Hsin-hua yueh-pao* (Hsinhua monthly) (Beijing), 1982, no. 9:5–6.

of Marxism should depend on the history and current situation of the country in which it is being applied.[90]

While discarding some Marxist doctrines, the Chinese Communists have also criticized the practice of copying foreign experience and foreign models. At the Third Plenary Session of the Twelfth Central Committee held in October 1984, the party openly indicated its determination to abandon the Soviet model. In its place, the market mechanism, a commodity economy, and the separation of government administration from enterprise management were adopted.[91] In December, the Chinese Communists admitted that the writings of Marx and Lenin cannot solve present-day problems, and that quotations from Marxist-Leninist works should not be regarded as a ready-made panacea.[92] In October 1987, a new theory of the "initial stage of socialism" justified such capitalist practices as a commodity economy, hired labor, and unearned income from bonds and stocks, which were imported during the economic reforms.[93] In September 1988, the Chinese Communists published an article urging people to adopt a new understanding of capitalism and to recognize its merits. Capitalism, the article said, ensures fair competition through antimonopoly laws and supports the development of medium-sized and small enterprises. The writer admitted that social welfare and other income-distribution policies in capitalist countries serve to mitigate class conflict, improve labor-management relations, and guarantee social and political stability. This, the article said, enhances the living standards of people with low incomes and protects the rights and interests of working people. Shareholding by workers has also blurred the division between employers and their employees, and many people in capitalist societies feel they can raise their economic and social status by their own efforts.[94]

Although the party refused to admit the existence of two such factions in its ranks, a long-standing ideological feud rages between the conservatives

---

[90]Chou Yang, "A Preliminary Study of Several Theoretical Issues Concerning Marxism," *People's Daily*, March 16, 1983, p. 4.

[91]"The CCPCC's Decision on the Reform of the Economic Structure," *People's Daily*, Oct. 21, 1984, p. 2; "The Third Plenum in the Eyes of an Economist: Our Reporter Interviews Chiang I-wei in Peking," *Ta kung pao* (Hong Kong), Oct. 21, 1984, p. 2.

[92]"Theory and Practice," *People's Daily*, Dec. 7, 1984, p. 1.

[93]Chao Tzu-yang, "Advance Along the Path of Socialism with Chinese Characteristics," *Beijing Review*, vol. 30, no. 45(1987):centerfold.

[94]Hsu Chia-t'un, "Reunderstanding Capitalism," *Beijing Review*, vol. 31, no. 46 (1988):19–21.

and the reformists.[95] When Teng Hsiao-p'ing attributed the Pai Hua incident of 1981 to laxity among cadres in charge of ideology and literature and art,[96] Hu Yao-pang defended himself by saying that the party's general secretary should not have to bear all the responsibility for laxity and weakness in the leadership.[97] Meanwhile, Hu Ch'iao-mu, a leading member of the conservative faction, attacked Hu Yao-pang indirectly by saying that a handful of people within the party had attempted to cover up the tilt toward liberalization. At a forum on ideology sponsored by the Propaganda Department on August 8, 1981, Hu Ch'iao-mu gave a speech which had a great impact on the party's subsequent ideological work. First, he used the term "bourgeois liberalization" to denigrate such democratic practices as parliamentarianism; the two-party system; campaigning for office; the freedoms of speech, the press, assembly, and association; individualism and liberalism; self-seeking; money-grubbing; acquiring literature and art from capitalist countries; and the capitalist way of life. He complained that because a "handful of people" within the party sympathized with and even supported such "liberalization," party organizations should be purged to overcome lax and weak supervision over ideology.[98]

The ideological struggle between the two factions grew more fierce after the opening of the Second Plenary Session of the Twelfth Central Committee in October 1983. On the basis of Teng Hsiao-p'ing's remarks condemning the theory of "socialist alienation" and humanism as examples of "spiritual pollution" which the party must combat, the conservatives launched the movement to eliminate this pollution. They directed their attack at the

---

[95]In the "Decision on the Reform of the Economic Structure" published in 1984, the Chinese Communists admitted that cadres had voiced different opinions about the reform, but they opposed the division of cadres into "reformists" and "conservatives." In "Some Questions Concerning the Guiding Ideology for the Construction of Socialist Spiritual Civilization," P'eng Chen criticized the reformist-conservative division and said that both of these factions support the reform policy and Marxism-Leninism. See *People's Daily*, Jan. 15, 1987, p. 4. Therefore, in distinguishing between the factions, we have to pay attention to two points: (1) both the reformists and the conservatives want to safeguard Communist Party rule and the socialist system; (2) both of them are in favor of the reform and opening-up policy, and the only point at issue is the scope and speed of the reform.
[96]Teng Hsiao-p'ing, "Concerning Problems on the Ideological Front" (July 17, 1981), in *Selected Works*, p. 368.
[97]Hu Yao-pang, "Talks at the Meeting on Issues Concerning the Ideological Front," in *San-chung-ch'u"an-hui i-lai chung-yao wen-hsien hsuan-pien*, pp. 884–97.
[98]Hu Ch'iao-mu, "Some Questions on the Current Ideological Front," ibid., pp. 905–29.

spheres of ideology, literature and the arts, and economics. Many of Hu Yao-pang's followers in charge of literary and propaganda work were adversely affected by that movement.[99]

After the "Decision on the Reform of the Economic Structure" was ratified at the Third Plenary Session of the Twelfth Central Committee on October 20, 1984, Hu Yao-pang asserted that one obstacle to economic reform was that cadres had not been "ideologically emancipated."[100] In December, Hu authorized a series of articles in the *People's Daily*, the most important of which were "The Part and the Whole," "Theory and Practice," and "A Further Discussion on Theory and Practice." These articles criticized the dogmatists for their obstinate adherence to a brand of Marxism hindering the implementation of reform policy.[101]

At the height of this campaign against dogmatism, Hu Yao-pang succeeded in depriving Teng Li-ch'ün of his post as director of the Propaganda Department. Chu Hou-tse, a follower of Hua from Kweichow, replaced Teng. During his tenure, Chu vigorously promoted ideological emancipation. In two of his public speeches in particular, he threw down a number of challenges to conservatives. Arguing that Marxism itself was not indigenous to China, he said it was necessary to absorb other progressive ideas from abroad. He also advocated a period of "introspection" regarding ideological and cultural matters. Chu called for an end to administrative intervention in literary and artistic creation, literary inquisitions, and isolated discussions of ideological concepts. He said that "cultural enterprises" should be managed in accordance with economic principles.[102] Intellectuals were greatly inspired by Chu's speeches. On November 2, 1985, the *Workers' Daily* published an article by Ma Ting (pseudonym of Sung Lung-hsiang, a lecturer in philosophy at Nanking University) which criticized Marxist political economy for its inability to solve current practical problems and advocated the introduction of Western economic theories.[103] Conservatives

---

[99]For details, see An-chia Wu, "The Movement to 'Eliminate Ideological Pollution,'" *Issues & Studies*, vol. 20, no. 3(March 1984):11–24.

[100]Hu Yao-pang, "Important Speeches by Hu Yao-pang on the Reform of the Economic Structure during His Investigation of the Coastal Areas in Shantung," *Hsinhua yueh-pao* (Hsinhua monthly) (Beijing), Nov. 30, 1984, no. 10:39–49.

[101]For details, see An-chia Wu, "Will the Chinese Communists Abandon Marxism-Leninism?" *Issues & Studies*, vol. 21, no. 3(March 1985):42–46.

[102]Chu Hou-tse, "Cultural Atmosphere and Cultural Opening-up," *Hsin-hua wen-chai* (Hsinhua digest) (Beijing), 1986, no. 8:1–3; idem, "An Examination of Some Questions Concerning Ideological and Cultural Matters," ibid., 1986, no. 9:1–4.

[103]Ma Ting, "Ten Major Changes in the Study of Economic Science in Our Party,"

such as Hu Ch'iao-mu and Teng Li-ch'ün accused him of having violated
Marxist principles, deviated from the socialist road, and "having swallowed
Western theories without digesting them."[104] In December, *Wen-hsüeh p'ing-
lun* (Literature commentary) published an article entitled "On the Integrity
of Literature," by Liu Tsai-fu, director of the Institute of Literature of the
Chinese Academy of Social Sciences. Liu pointed out that Beijing's policy
on literature and art had neglected the nature and value of human beings
and substituted politics for art. This provoked fierce criticism from the
conservatives. In an article penned by Ch'en Yung, a research fellow in the
Policy Research Office (whose director is Teng Li-ch'ün), Liu was criticized
for trying to negate Marxism.[105] During the backlash against these two
articles, Chao Tzu-yang and Chu Hou-tse openly defended Ma Ting's academic freedom. Liu Tsai-fu was able to keep his post in the Academy of
Social Sciences at the height of the criticism against dogmatism and was
fired as editor in chief of *Wen-hsüeh p'ing-lun* only in February 1987.

In June 1986, Teng Hsiao-p'ing openly proposed reform of the political
structure. His proposal met with a warm response from Hu Yao-pang, Chao
Tzu-yang, Wan Li, T'ien Chi-yun, Hu Ch'i-li, Wang Chao-kuo, and many
prominent scholars such as Yen Chia-ch'i (director of the Institute of Politics
of the Chinese Academy of Social Sciences), Su Shao-chih (director of the
academy's Institute of Marxism-Leninism and Mao Tse-tung Thought), Li
Hung-lin (president of the Fukien Academy of Social Sciences), Pao Hsin-
chien (director of the Theoretical Research Office of the Shantung Academy
of Social Sciences), and Fang Li-chih (vice-president of the University of
Science and Technology in Hofei, Anhwei Province). These scholars responded to Teng's proposal with speeches on the subject of political reform.
For example, Yen Chia-ch'i advocated the "division of power" and "checking power with power." He also proposed the adoption of a Western-style
parliamentary system.[106] Su Shao-chih emphasized the importance of legislative and judicial independence, the separation of party and government

Workers' Daily, Nov. 2, 1985. Reprinted in *Beijing Review*, 1985, vol. 28, no. 47 (Dec.
9):17–20.
[104]*Ta kung pao* (Hong Kong), April 26, 1986, p. 3.
[105]Ch'en Yung, "Questions Concerning Methodology in Literature and Art," *Red
Flag*, 1986, no. 8:27.
[106]Tai Ch'ing, "On China's Reform of the Political Structure: An Interview with
Yen Chia-ch'i," *Hsin-hua wen-chai*, 1986, no. 9:9; Hsu Hsing, "The Ideological Reform
That Has Emerged Quietly," *Cheng ming* (Contending) (Hong Kong), no. 108(Oct.
1986):21.

functions, and the rule of law.[107] Fang Li-chih maintained that freedom, equality, and fraternity are the products of historical development, and that true democracy can be obtained only through struggle; it is not something that is bestowed by the authorities.[108] In contrast to the old practice of always giving priority to political consciousness, Fang emphasized the importance of respecting knowledge.[109] These views were not acceptable to the conservatives. At the Joint Group Meeting of the Eighteenth Session of the Sixth National People's Congress Standing Committee on November 25, 1986, P'eng Chen maintained that socialist democracy is superior to bourgeois democracy.[110] P'eng's argument was later used in the campaign against bourgeois liberalization.

At the Sixth Plenary Session of the Twelfth Central Committee held on September 28, 1986, a heated debate erupted between the conservatives and the reformists as to whether the phrase "combatting bourgeois liberalization" should be put into the "Resolution on the Guiding Principles for the Construction of Socialist Spiritual Civilization." The reformists called for the exclusion of the phrase on the pretext that it was not clearly defined. The phrase was later included on Teng Hsiao-p'ing's instructions.[111]

According to documents no. 2 and no. 3 issued by the Central Committee in 1987, Teng's speech was pigeonholed by Hu for five months. Hu's speech at the Fourth Congress of the Chinese Writers' Association, held in December 1984, argued that people should no longer talk about the elimination of spiritual pollution and combatting bourgeois liberalization. The conservatives took this as proof that Hu had resisted the drive to eliminate these two "tendencies."[112]

---

[107]Su Shao-chih, "A Preliminary Study on the Reform of the Political Structure," *Hsin-hua wen-chai*, 1986, no. 11:12–15.

[108]Fang Li-chih, "Intellectuals and Chinese Society," *Chung-kuo ta-lu* (Chinese mainland) (Taipei) vol. 20, no. 3(March 15, 1987):57–60. The text of his speech was prepared from a tape of his lecture.

[109]Fang Li-chih, "A Brand New Consciousness Is a Breakthrough in the Reform of the Political Structure," *T-uan-chieh pao* (Unity) (Beijing), no. 780(Sept. 28, 1986).

[110]P'eng Chen, "On Democracy and the Legal System at the Joint Group Meeting of the Eighteenth Session of the NPC Standing Committee" (Nov. 25, 1986), *Hsin-hua yueh-pao*, Jan. 30, 1987, no. 12:40.

[111]Teng Hsiao-ping, "Resolutely Combating Bourgeois Liberalization," *Shih-erh-ta i-lai chung-yao wen-hsien hsuan-pien* (Selection of important documents published since the CCP's Twelfth National Congress), compiled by the Document Research Office of the CCPCC, vol. 3 (Beijing: People's Publishing House, May 1988), pp. 1216–17.

[112]*Pai-shing* (The people), no. 138(Feb. 16, 1987):4.

The party document described the student demonstrations of December 1986 as an inevitable outcome of some cadres' inability to support or even resist the antibourgeois liberalization movement. The Central Committee launched the campaign on January 6, 1987, on Teng's instructions.[113] Hu Yao-pang's opponents at the enlarged Politburo meeting ten days later charged the general secretary with failing to exercise effective leadership in the movement.[114] Hu was forced to resign. As a result of his patron's dismissal, the party replaced Chu Hou-tse, the propaganda chief, with Wang Jen-chih, formerly vice–editor in chief of *Red Flag*.[115]

In early 1988, a heated debate broke out on the question of whether the development of productive forces should be the sole criterion for evaluating the economic reforms. Chao Tzu-yang asked party members to further emancipate people's minds and develop productive forces;[116] in an address via satellite to the World Economic Forum in Switzerland on February 2, 1988, Chao said that whatever is beneficial to the development of mainland China's productive forces should be permitted and encouraged, and anything not promoting a market economy should be rejected.[117] The speed of economic change did not slow until September 1988, when the party responded to Ch'en Yun's demand for economic "readjustment." Ch'en now worried that too rapid a pace of economic reform would destroy socialism.[118]

Disputes continued to exist between Chao Tzu-yang and Li P'eng about reform policy. In his "Government Work Report" delivered to the Second Session of the Seventh National People's Congress, Li criticized Chao indirectly by saying that the problems and predicaments arising from economic reform came from "shortcomings and mistakes in the policy decisions" and from the "tendency of being too eager to make results." The death of ousted CCP general secretary Hu Yao-pang in April 1989 became the pretext for college students to demonstrate and demand freedom of information and more democracy. Within a month, their number had grown from a little

---

[113]"Resolutely Combating Bourgeois Liberalization (editorial), *People's Daily*, Jan. 6, 1987, p. 1.

[114]Teng Hsiao-p'ing, "Strengthen Education on the Four Cardinal Principles, Persist in the Reform and Opening-up Policy," *Wen wei po*, March 20, 1987, p. 3.

[115]Chu Hou-tse was then appointed deputy director of the State Council's Rural Development Research Center (director, Tu Jun-sheng). He was appointed the first secretary of the All China Federation of Trade Unions on Oct. 28, 1988.

[116]*People's Daily*, Feb. 7, 1988, p. 1.

[117]*Ta kung pao*, Feb. 3, 1988, p. 1.

[118]Ho Yuan-cheng, "Ch'en Yun Said That There Should Be a Counterattack in the Ideological Sphere," *Ching pao* (Mirror) (Hong Kong), Jan. 1989, p. 29.

more than one hundred to over a million. The party was divided over how to handle the student movement. Li P'eng and Yang Shang-k'un proposed military suppression, while Chao Tzu-yang favored "consultation and dialogue." Li and Yang won the upper hand in this struggle, and the June 4 massacre at Tienanmen Square followed. The democracy movement caused the replacement of Chao Tzu-yang by Chiang Tse-min as the party's general secretary.[119] At the Fourth Plenum of the Thirteenth Central Committee, Chao was accused of having committed the mistakes of supporting turmoil and splitting the party; he had erred in his formulation of guidelines and in his practical work; adopted a passive approach to the adherence to the Four Cardinal Principles; and opposed bourgeois liberalization. The plenum decided to strengthen political-ideological work.[120] Concrete measures included: theoreticians should write articles and books elaborating the importance of the Four Cardinal Principles and the need to fight against bourgeois liberalization; some cadres must take up the specific duty of political work in enterprises; journalists should observe the party's order in their work; college students should receive more ideological indoctrination; and theoretical studies for party members and the masses should be intensified. The news media in Beijing also propagated the theory that "China's development must depend only on socialism," and that "class struggle still exists." It also criticized Hu Yao-pang's viewpoint that "Marxism is outdated" and Chao Tzu-yang's proposal for changing the public-ownership system.[121] Compared with the 1987 antibourgeois liberalization movement, the current ideological movement is not only larger in scale but might last longer.

Conclusion

In the past decade, drastic changes in ideology have occurred. Two basic principles have been followed by the Chinese Communists in their management of ideological matters: outdated theories and taboos that obstruct reform should be abandoned; and a Marxist rationale to justify reform should be sought. Party leaders have shifted from blind worship of Mao Tse-tung and his thought to a more critical view of his acts and ideas. This approach also enabled them to criticize the Stalinist model and to imitate the economic

---

[119]"Main Points of Comrade Teng Hsiao-p'ing's Talks with Comrades Li P'eng and Yao I-lin" (May 31, 1989), *Tung-fang jih-pao* (Hong Kong), July 14, 1989, p. 5.
[120]*People's Daily*, June 25, 1989, p. 1.
[121]Fang Chueh, "Why the Private-Ownership System Cannot Be Applied in China," *Ching-chi jih-pao* (Beijing), July 4, 1989, p. 4.

practices of Yugoslavia, Romania, and Hungary, which previously had been called "revisionist." Marxism is no longer regarded as a universal truth. This change of attitude toward the Marxist classics has been forced on the party by the pressing need to eradicate persistent poverty in mainland China.

Unlike Mao, who extolled poverty, Teng Hsiao-p'ing has said that "[the purpose of] Socialism is to put an end to poverty. Poverty is not socialism, nor is it communism."[122] Teng has repeatedly criticized such slogans as "It is better to have socialist grass than to have capitalist seedlings," and "Poor socialism and communism is better than rich capitalism."[123] The methods Teng used to raise China from "poverty and blankness" are also different from those used by Mao. In Mao's time, violent political movements aroused people's enthusiasm for work. Instead of achieving that goal, those political movements and calls for "egalitarianism" and "overcoming selfishness and fostering public spirit" only hindered economic development.

Teng also initiated political movements to change people's ideas, but he also tried to make people more productive by offering material incentives. However, while seeking capital, technology, and management methods from capitalist countries, Teng adopted a firm stand against capitalist ideology and politics. This dichotomy between essence (*t'i*) and application (*yung*) might derail mainland China's modernization effort, just as in the late Ch'ing Dynasty. The Western *yung*—capital, technology, and management expertise—is closely connected to the Western *t'i*—freedom, democracy, experimentation, a critical spirit, and open disputes.[124] Democracy and a legal system are necessary if mainland China's reforms are to succeed.

The theory of the "initial stage of socialism" advanced at the Thirteenth National Congress in October 1987 to rationalize the reforms has also failed to solve problems such as inflation, excessive production of some items, party cadres' using their privileges to seek private gain, and many other

---

[122]Teng Hsiao-p'ing, *Chien-she yu chung-kuo t'e-se te she-hui chu-i* (Building socialism with Chinese characteristics) (Beijing: People's Publishing House, 1984), p. 36.

[123]Teng Hsiao-p'ing, "We Have to Cast Away Poverty If We Are to Persist in Socialism," in *Teng Hsiao-p'ing t'ung-chih chung-yao t'an-hua* (Important talks by Comrade Teng Hsiao-p'ing), compiled by the Document Research Office of the CCP Central Committee (Beijing: People's Publishing House, 1987), pp. 21–22. At a meeting with Yugoslav president Radovan Vlajkovic on April 4, 1986, Teng said: "We cannot say that not wanting capitalist riches is incorrect. But the Marxist viewpoint definitely does not equate communism with poverty." See *Ta kung pao*, April 5, 1986, p. 1.

[124]Chalmers Johnson, "The Failures of Socialism in China," in *Proceedings of the Eighth Sino-American Conference on Mainland China* (Columbia, S.C.: University of South Carolina, 1979), pp. 36–38.

problems. Cadres in charge of theoretical research have been asked to discover the root causes of these problems and work out solutions. At a forum on theory held to commemorate the tenth anniversary of the Third Plenary Session of the Eleventh Central Committee on November 18, 1988, Chao Tzu-yang said the realization that Marxism has proved incapable of solving current problems marks a turning point in its development. He asked cadres in charge of theoretical work not to regard Marxism as a dogma, but to study all situations and solve new questions from the Marxist point of view by using Marxist methods.[125]

Following the Four Cardinal Principles, however, has created ideological problems. First, some "ultraleftist" ideas still dominate. Chao Tzu-yang referred to the following remarks by cadres about the reforms as examples of "ultraleftist" ideology: (1) the economic reforms have led to disorder; (2) leasing state enterprises is tantamount to private ownership; (3) making factory managers responsible for profits and losses is tantamount to abolishing the party's leadership; (4) the rural household-responsibility system is undermining the collective economy; (5) the planned economy is socialist, while the commodity economy is capitalist, and the development of the commodity economy is the root of bourgeois liberalization; (6) there is no need to reform the political structure because this would destroy the party's leadership; (7) opening up to the outside world has resulted in "liberalization" and mainland China is now in danger of inclining too far toward the "West" (the United States and Western Europe) rather than the "East" (the Soviet Union) as in the past; and (8) to oppose liberalization in politics, one must oppose economic liberalization because bourgeois liberalization has its roots in the economy.[126] In his report to the Thirteenth Congress, Chao underlined the importance of eliminating these leftist ideas if the reforms were to be successfully carried through. Yet popular resentment against inflation and other economic dislocations increased, so that nostalgia for the halcyon days of Mao was on the rise.[127]

The second ideological problem is to preserve the true spirit of socialism when more and more capitalist elements are introduced by the reforms. Some theoreticians claim that a convergence between capitalism and socialism is likely, because the socialist system has not yet been reached and will

---

[125]Chao Tzu-yang, "To Further Arm the Whole Party with the Theory Advanced at the Thirteenth Congress" (Dec. 18, 1988), *People's Daily*, Dec. 19, 1988, p. 1.
[126]Chao Tzu-yang, "Speech at the Meeting on Propaganda, Theory, Journalism, and Party School Cadres," *Shih-erh-ta i-lai chung-yao wen-hsien hsuan-pien*, vol. 3 (Beijing: People's Publishing House, May 1988), pp. 1405–7.
[127]*South China Morning Post*, March 10, 1989, p. 27.

not be able to transcend the industrialization stage, which, they say, is characterized by industrial civilization and a developed commodity economy. They also claim that socialism will coexist with modern capitalism for some time to come.[128] This theory, however, conflicts with Teng Hsiao-p'ing's view that socialism and capitalism will be forever opposed to each other. Teng has maintained that the purpose of absorbing some capitalist elements is to develop socialist productive forces rather than to establish capitalism.[129] In March 1989, Chao Tzu-yang also said that mainland China does not intend to adopt the capitalist private-ownership system or to privatize the economy. Therefore, socialism and capitalism may coexist for the time being, but it will be difficult to solve the contradictions between them.

The third problem is whether to follow "dogmatism" or "revisionism." Theoretically speaking, the party leaders always found barriers in their way. While upholding the Marxist ideals of communism, public ownership, and the dictatorship of the proletariat, they argued that Marxism was not dogma but a guide to action and that it was impossible to find ready answers in Marxist writings to the new problems of the day. In formulating policies, the party leaders have followed both dogmatist and revisionist lines. Their experiments in building socialism were based on Marxist principles, but these principles have been revised when found to be inapplicable. For example, Marxist theory decrees that commodities, money, and profit are the root cause of exploitation in society and should therefore be abolished. However, after repeated failure to abolish them, commodities, money, and profit have been permitted to exist in both mainland China and the Soviet Union. After the abolition of private ownership and the establishment of the public-ownership system, the party advocated the "dictatorship of the proletariat" in violation of the Marxist principle that this dictatorship should automatically die away after the establishment of a public-ownership system. According to one Marxist principle, private ownership should no longer be allowed to exist after the establishment of public ownership. Yet mainland China's production-responsibility system allows an individual economy. Seen in this light, the recently revived commodity economy has had a great impact on people's lives.

The fourth problem is to balance centralism and localism. The Four

---

[128]Li Chen, "Convergence of Two Systems as Viewed from the Standard of Productive Forces," *Kwangming Daily*, Sept. 12, 1988.
[129]Teng Hsiao-p'ing, "Talks at the Sixth Plenary Session of the Party's Twelfth Central Committee" (Sept. 28, 1986), *Shih-erh-ta i-lai chung-yao wen-hsien hsuan-pien*, vol. 3, p. 1171; Teng Hsiao-p'ing, "We Will Be Able to Get United by Relying on Ideal and Discipline" (March 7, 1985), ibid., pp. 659–60.

Cardinal Principles advocate a highly centralized leadership, but since local governments and departments were granted some autonomy in decision-making, some localities began to resist decisions of the central government. Recently, the party leaders repeatedly emphasized the importance of maintaining the central government's authority and threatened to take back local autonomy to facilitate its economic readjustment. Both Teng Hsiao-p'ing and Chao Tzu-yang have openly supported the "new authoritarianism" advocated by some young scholars because it enhanced the power of the central leadership.[130]

The fifth problem is whether people have more freedom in their daily life. Before the reforms in 1979, no one dared to challenge the party's monolithic leadership or to criticize Marxism-Leninism and Mao Tse-tung thought. However, frequent contact with the outside world in recent years has brought more diverse opinions to mainland China and stimulated a remarkable ideological change. These new ideas have encouraged many people to demand greater freedom of information, greater accountability by those in power for their actions, and better living conditions. These popular aspirations will put the party under great pressure. A publicly owned, planned economy can embrace a democratic political system. Broadly conceived, liberty means that individuals have freedom to engage in trade and to establish businesses to pursue gain, freedom to move about and keep their earnings and assets, and security against arbitrary seizure of their property. These freedoms are obviously not enjoyed by people in a socialist society where private ownership of the means of production is nonexistent, and private ownership of consumer goods is greatly restricted.

---

[130]*Wen wei po* (Hong Kong), April 8, 1989, p. 2.

Current Debates over Marxist Theory in the PRC

In the first part of the last decade, the ideological debates in China shifted from class struggle to the development of productivity, egalitarianism, and other related class policies.[1] Since late 1984, the theoretical discussion has shifted still more to the character of Marxism, the meaning of socialism for China (considered as a preliminary stage of socialism), and the role of the state.

The question of the character of Marxism was first raised by reformists in late 1984 for the purpose of strengthening their position. Discussing the character of Marxism and "socialism with Chinese characteristics" was originally intended to help justify Deng Xiaoping's reform program.

In late 1987, the Chinese Communist Party's (CCP) Thirteenth National Congress adopted a crucial document in which the party attempted a comprehensive ideological justification for the economic reforms based on the concept of the "preliminary stage of socialism" as currently corresponding to China's "backward" economy. Nevertheless, the official theory of the "preliminary stage of socialism" was very different from that presented in

---

[1]On the debates over these issues, see Edward I-hsin Chen, "The Evolution of Post-Mao Class Policy in a Comparative Perspective" (Ph.D. diss., Columbia University, 1986).

1979 by Prof. Su Shaozhi, a leading liberal scholar. How have party intellectuals viewed these new issues?

The discussion on the role of the state involves two concepts: the "new authoritarianism" and democracy. Democracy has been suggested by some liberal theorists as a political solution for the reform program, whereas the "new authoritarianism" was proposed by young, aggressive political thinkers in late 1988 as a means of avoiding the disruptive effects of the economic reforms. How do party theorists view democracy and the "new authoritarianism"?

The Debate over the Character of Marxism

On December 7, 1984, the *Renmin ribao* (People's daily) published a front-page article entitled "Theory and Practice," which asserted Marxism could not solve China's current problems.[2] This unusual statement provoked considerable interest, and some Western commentaries suggested that China was rejecting Marxism. Another article followed with a correction on the front page stating that the article only meant Marxism could not solve "all" of China's problems.[3]

The reformists had focused on the character of Marxism, as it had been shown to pave the way for widespread acceptance of developing a commodity economy with markets and money in China. The follow-up article hinted that Marx was wrong in predicting that commodities and money were unnecessary under socialism.[4] Chinese theorists began to interpret Marxism in different ways.

Some reformist theorists argued that only Marx's idea that socialist countries should not buy and sell the means of production was being rejected. For example, Lin Xili, an economist who helped draft the party's reform proclamation of October 20, 1984, outlined China's shift to a market-oriented economy. He emphasized that the reforms are faithful to Marxism, which is an evolving doctrine based on "seeking truth from facts."

Mr. Lin admitted that China's shift toward a market economy, or a "socialist commodity economy," was never an element of classic Marxism. The nineteenth-century philosopher had envisioned a system in which money was unnecessary; he failed to understand that selling, buying, and the law

---

[2]*Renmin ribao* (hereafter *RMRB*), Dec. 7, 1984, p. 1.
[3]*RMRB*, Dec. 10, 1984, p. 1.
[4]"Talk About Theory and Practice Again," *RMRB*, Dec. 21, 1984, p. 1.

of supply and demand are essential for a socialist economy. Nor should a real Marxist do whatever Marx said, and not whatever Marx did not say. Instead, a real Marxist must constantly test Marx's principles, discarding those that are outdated or that "go against today's reality."[5]

In an interview with a correspondent from *The Christian Science Monitor*, Su Shaozhi, a distinguished political theorist and then director of the Institute of Marxism-Leninism–Mao Zedong Thought at the Chinese Academy of Social Sciences, said that there is nothing new in the *People's Daily* article's view on Marxism because it reflected the policies and statements of Deng Xiaoping since late 1978.

"Creative Marxism," Prof. Su says, means applying Marx's principles and methods to Chinese circumstances, while perfecting the practical application of his theories. The distinction between the Soviet-style orthodoxy and "socialism with Chinese characteristics" is that other socialist countries have misunderstood and misapplied Marxism, whereas the Chinese will follow creative Marxism and will apply it to their country's reality.[6]

Such remarks were consistent with *People's Daily* commentaries in late December 1984 asserting that classical Marxism cannot always provide solutions to Chinese problems.

The reformist theories did not directly challenge Marxism. They merely questioned the applicability of Marxism in today's China. They were emphasizing certain negative parts of Marxism.

Meanwhile, the party's conservatives tried to strike a middle line between unquestioning acceptance of Marxist dogma and a partially negative view of Marxism. The party's journal *Hongqi* (Red flag), which had kept aloof from the debate initiated by the *People's Daily* for nearly two months, spoke out. One article asserted that although the principles Marx envisioned for socialist societies might not apply to contemporary China, the Marxist principles intended to serve to interpret human history and capitalist societies were not wrong. Marxism is a science, not a religion, and that theory does not provide any magic remedies. Instead, one must take an analytical attitude and articulate theory and practice to study Marxism in order to determine which Marxist theories are still applicable to today's China, and which theories are no longer applicable and might require creative development.[7]

Peng Zhen, then chairman of the National People's Congress Standing

---

[5]Lin Xili made these remarks informally at the All-China Journalists Association; see *International Herald Tribune*, Jan. 5–6, 1985, p. 5.

[6]*Christian Science Monitor*, April 17, 1985, pp. 4 and 17.

[7]Editorial Board, "How to Work Better in Our Own Departments," *Hongqi* (hereafter *HQ*), Feb. 1, 1985, pp. 4–5.

Committee, offered a similar view.[8] One should flexibly make good use of the basic principles and methods of Marxism to find solutions for the current problems facing today's China. A real Marxist should distinguish the basic principles of Marxism from simple solutions to problems. Some theorists confuse the two. Such theorists will feel frustration when they try to apply the principles and methods Marx advanced one century ago to today's China.

Although this viewpoint was also in line with the reformist policies, the conservatives wanted to stress the positive side of Marxism.

During this debate, there seemed to be some agreement. Xue Muqiao, a prominent Marxist economist, argued that the studies of a socialist economy should not be confined to Marx's theory on capitalism, a theory denying the necessity of a commodity economy in a socialist society. One should instead combine the scientific principles of Marx's historical materialism and the experience of socialist practice to creatively develop Marxism and to make progress in building a "socialism with Chinese characteristics."[9]

The debate over the character of Marxism did not polarize Chinese leaders, largely because they agreed at least on two points. First, the Chinese leaders wanted to use this debate to test the response of the Soviets, who might still think that the Chinese reforms had gone too far. Less than a month and a half after the release of the *People's Daily* article, Chinese leaders—including then–general secretary Hu Yaobang, Prime Minister Zhao Ziyang, Politburo members Yang Shangkun and Peng Zeng—met to commemorate the 50th anniversary of the historic Zunyi Conference. They reaffirmed that China has once and for all rejected Soviet-style socialism as "ineffective" for China.[10]

Second, they probably wanted to create favorable conditions paving the way for acceptance of the new concept of "socialism with Chinese characteristics." At the commemoration, Yang Shangkun reportedly called for everyone to respect the "Zunyi spirit" by helping to build a "socialism with Chinese characteristics" and contribute to the country's modernization drive.[11]

The debate among Chinese thinkers over the character of Marxism officially ended in late 1985.[12] At the party congress in September 1985,

---

[8]Peng Zhen, "Studying Hard the Basic Theories of Marxism" (key points at a talk with responsible comrades of the National People's Congress Standing Committee on June 7, 1985), *RMRB*, Aug. 16, 1985, pp. 1 and 4.

[9]Xue Muqiao, "To Continuously Push Forward Marxism," *RMRB*," March 20, 1987, p. 5.

[10]*South China Morning Post*, Jan. 19, 1985, p. 7.

[11]Ibid.

[12]Although the discussion on the character of Marxism continued after 1987, nothing

Deng Xiaoping said that Marxist theories are not dogma but guideposts for actions. According to Deng, the Chinese should link the basic principles and methods of Marxism to concrete realities of China to find a separate path and build a "socialism with Chinese characteristics."[13] Deng obviously placed himself once again squarely between the reformists and the conservatives, just as he had in 1979 when he proclaimed the four basic principles of socialism: dictatorship of the proletariat; leadership of the party; following the socialist road; and upholding Marxism, Leninism, and Mao Zedong thought.

The question of what "socialism with Chinese characteristics" precisely means has been a deep mystery since Deng used the formula to justify the reforms he began in 1978. Deng's collected speeches and talks only described what Chinese socialism is not: it is not violent class struggle, not egalitarianism, not shared poverty, not the mechanical copying of other communist countries' experience and models. As for what a "socialism with Chinese characteristics" actually means, Deng did not define the concept.

Chinese reformist leaders and theorists have been unsatisfied with the rigorous definition of Marxism and socialism, a situation they describe as "theory lagging behind practice."

Raising the question of the character of Marxism was the first attempt of the reformist leaders to equip the party with an ideological weapon to push the reform program. But the backlash of the party conservatives and Deng's neutral position produced different reactions from Hu Yaobang and Zhao Ziyang. They had to argue for a dialectical unity between the "four cardinal principles" and the new concepts of "seeking truth from facts" and a "socialist commodity economy."

Although these Chinese leaders failed to provide precise definitions of Marxism and "socialism with Chinese characteristics," the new relevance of

---

new was added beyond debates since late 1984. For example, the theorist Wang Pengling in January 1989 said that, deeply influenced by the theories of Nikolai Lenin, Joseph V. Stalin, and Mao Zedong, the main themes of Marxism had been the proletarian revolution and the class struggle between capitalists and the proletarians. He contended, however, that such themes are no longer suitable for a China undergoing reform. The answers to questions about the role, function, and development rules of commodity economy in socialist society cannot be found in classical Marxism. The main themes of Marxism must be changed so that Marxism will not become obsolete. See Wang Pengling, "Change the Main Themes to Develop Marxism," *RMRB*, Jan. 9, 1989, p. 5.

[13]Deng Xiaoping, a talk at the Party Congress on September 23, 1985, *RMRB*, Sept. 24, 1985, p. 1.

Marx produced strong responses from some theorists. In line with official doctrine, some theorists contended that Marxism should be constantly evolving while presenting advice and policy alternatives they hoped party leaders might consider. Others argued that Marxism was not suitable for China now, but one day it might be. Still others declared that Marxism was out of date and obsolete.

Yan Jiaqi, then director of the Institute of Political Science at the Chinese Academy of Social Sciences, wrote several articles on the character of Marxism to promote his idea of academic freedom. In an early 1986 article in *Illuminating Daily (Guangming ribao)*, Yan wrote that only when Marxism is analyzed in a scientific way and the policy of "letting a hundred schools contend" is correctly put into practice can the leading position of Marxism be established and strengthened in theoretical and ideological fields.[14] He advocated a comprehensive survey of all Western thought and theories and argued that only in this way can the economic and political reforms succeed.[15]

Meanwhile, Su Shaozhi stated there were some new requirements for studying Marxist theories. A real Marxist should not be dogmatic, nor should he be a yes-man who always tries to read his superior's mind. Moreover, he should have a critical attitude toward the socialist bloc so that he can learn from the mistakes and experience of other socialist countries. Last but not least, he should be creative in theoretical development. On academic freedom, Su pointed out that in socialist countries, academic debates should not include class struggle; an individual's academic opinions do not represent his or her political attitudes, and everyone is equal before the truth.[16]

Unlike traditional socialist theorists, Su admitted that socialist societies were in crisis. This crisis in socialist societies, however, did not mean their destruction. Only when the crisis was acknowledged could reforms follow. Furthermore, he argued that respect for human freedom and the liberation of human beings were the most essential components of Marxist theories. In the real socialist world, what Marx had envisioned with regard to human freedom had not materialized, largely because of mechanization and collectivism, developments pushed for reasons of national interests. Su also said

---

[14]Yan Jiaqi, "Discussing the Shift of Theoretical Works," *Guangming ribao* (Illuminating daily; hereafter *GMRB*), Feb. 14, 1986, p. 1.

[15]Yan Jiaqi, "A Comprehensive Openness in Culture," *Wenhu bao* (Hong Kong), Sept. 16, 1986, p. 17; and Sept. 17, 1986, p. 21.

[16]Su Shaozhi, "Several Problems Concerning 'Letting One Hundred Schools of Thought Contend,'" *GMRB*, Oct. 21, 1985, p. 5; and "'Double Hundred' Course for Three Decades," *Wenhui bao* (Shanghai), May 15, 1986, p. 2.

that human freedom and human liberation must be the ultimate goals of socialist societies.[17]

In studying Marxism, Su asserted, there should no longer be any taboos. He took the coastal areas and special economic zones as examples. Those people no longer believe in the traditional ideologies and have become more independent and creative. Su believed that the commodity economy system was an effective weapon with which to destroy bureaucratism, privilege, and feudalism.[18] In a 1988 interview, Prof. Su insisted that the Chinese should redefine socialism with Chinese characteristics not by using dogmatic Marxist theories, but by integrating Marx's viewpoints into Chinese circumstances.[19]

Returning from Europe in late 1986, Prof. Su redefined the term "productivity," saying that productivity should not only refer to the gross national product, but should involve scientific and technological capabilities, the means of production, and the quality of human activity. According to Marx, human beings cannot be treated as means of production; they are the masters of society. If not, people will not devote themselves to economic development. Su argued that education was the best way to improve human activity.[20]

Disagreeing with what many scholars called "theory lagging behind practice," Su charged that the reform program stagnates in both theory and practice. In a speech at a conference on reform theory to commemorate the tenth anniversary of the Third Plenum of the Eleventh Party Congress, he strongly rebuked the party and some officials for failing to provide academic freedom, arguing that it was ridiculous to say that the "stick" was not being used against the intellectuals when that was actually the case. He also stressed that by the end of 1988, Chinese leaders had launched 34 political campaigns against the intellectuals since 1949. Without real academic freedom, it was

---

[17]Su Shaozhi and Wang Yizhou, "A New Understanding of Socialism," *Shijie jingji daobao* (World economic herald) (Shanghai), reprinted in *Wenhui bao* (Hong Kong), Dec. 24, 1986, p. 4; and Dec. 25, 1986, p. 4.

[18]Su Shaozhi and Wang Yizhou, "Several Issues Concerning Political Institutional Reforms That Require Further Studies," *Lixun xinxi bao* (Newspaper of theoretical messages), reprinted in *Wenhui bao* (Hong Kong), March 2, 1988, p. 32; March 3, 1988, p. 7; and March 4, 1988, p. 7.

[19]The text of Prof. Su's interview with a correspondent from the U.S. magazine *Newsweek* was translated into Chinese by *Lilun xinxi bao*, and an abridged version was printed in *Wenhui bao* (Hong Kong), June 24, 1988, p. 7.

[20]Su Shaozhi's interview with a correspondent from *Wenhui bao* (Hong Kong), Dec. 26, 1988, p. 1; Dec. 27, 1988, p. 1; Dec. 28, 1988, p. 4.

no wonder that Marxism had stagnated in theoretical development and was in a crisis.[21]

Su warned that the stagnating reforms in both theory and practice not only had alienated the intellectuals, but that the intellectuals no longer supported the reformist leaders. The most important reason for the lack of theoretical advances was that people could not freely debate and express their own opinions. Moreover, only a few Chinese leaders decided the course of reform. Without new theory, the Chinese reforms ran the risk of wandering in the dark.[22]

For developing Marxism, Li Zehou, a prominent noncommunist theorist of the history of thought, agreed that only when the policy of "letting a hundred schools contend" was thoroughly implemented could Marxism, socialism, and other social sciences fully develop. He stated that intellectuals should be allowed their academic freedom and feel free to express their opinions on politics. According to Li, China had a long way to progress to develop a Western-style democratic and free society. Confucian traditional morality, however, could not provide the motive force to move China toward a modernized, democratic society. Only when the rule of law was institutionalized could China become a democracy.[23] Li argued that establishing laws, applying them, and developing a law-abiding society were the only means by which China could achieve democracy; laws must not be replaced by politics.[24]

Jin Guangtao, a prominent theorist and director of the Institute of Scientific and Technological Policies and Management at the Academy of Sciences, contends that the ruling ideology in China is neither Western Marxism (including neo-Marxism) nor Soviet-style Marxism-Leninism, nor Maoist Marxism characterized by class analysis. It is a Confucianized value

---

[21]Prof. Su's speech was printed in *Shijie jingji daobao*, but other newspapers in mainland China were immediately ordered not to print it. See *Dagong bao* (Hong Kong), Dec. 29, 1989, p. 1; *Xingdao ribao* (Hong Kong), Jan. 24, 1989, p. 2; and *Ming bao* (Hong Kong), Feb. 5, 1989, p. 7. According to him, victims of "political sticks" include theorist Li Shu, economist Yu Guangyuan, and writers Wang Ruoshui and Zhou Yang.

[22]Su Shaozhi's interview with a correspondent from *Wenhui bao* (Hong Kong), Dec. 26, p. 1; Dec. 27, p. 1; Dec. 28, p. 4.

[23]*Ming bao* (Hong Kong), Aug. 19, 1987, p. 9; or *Wenhui bao* (Hong Kong), Aug. 23, 1987, p. 6.

[24]Li Zehou's interview with a correspondent from *Wenhui bao* (Hong Kong), Aug. 19, 1987, p. 12.

system with a Marxist context.[25] In absorbing and sinicizing Marxism, China's own value system remained intact because of what he calls the "super-stable structure" of its culture. China should not overlook Western democracy and science.[26]

Both Li Zehou, a noncommunist, and Su Shaozhi, a party member, assert that Marxism is in a crisis because it stagnates without academic freedom and democracy. Li Zehou even thinks that most Chinese intellectuals no longer believe in Marxism-Leninism.[27]

In a mid-1988 article, Li Honglin, a prominent economist, openly declared that socialism had failed in China. Socialism cannot eliminate competition; the only way out is to confront reality and let competition successfully work in the marketplace.[28]

Having mixed feelings about Marxism and socialism, Jin Guangtao describes himself as a pessimistic optimistic about the open policies in China and an optimist about the prospects of the Chinese as a nation.[29]

On several occasions, Fang Lizhi, a prominent astrophysicist and a leading dissident intellectual, flatly dismissed Marxism as "obsolete." As the most outspoken dissident in China, Fang argued that there can be no economic development without a parallel development of democracy.[30] In an interview in late 1988, he declared that Marxism was "useless"; he had lost faith in Marxism and the party. "Philosophically, it is backward," he points out. "As for socialist theory, experience has proven it a failure." Traveling abroad on scientific exchanges had probably influenced him. Once he said: "Chinese leaders say that without the guidance of Marxism one cannot arrive at correct results. Overseas, I found people achieving striking results, and they were not guided by Marxism."[31]

Renowned as "China's Sakharov," Fang declared that Leninist-Stalinist-

---

[25]Jin Guangtao, "The Confucianized Marxism in the Contemporary China," *China Times* (Taipei), Aug. 30, 1988, p. 18; and Aug. 31, 1988, p. 18.

[26]Jin Guangtao's interviews with correspondents from *Ming bao* (Hong Kong), July 16, 1988, p. 8; and *Wenhui bao* (Hong Kong), July 18, 1988, p. 22; *China Times* (Taipei), May 6, 1988, p. 13; and *United Daily News*, Dec. 22, 1988, p. 9.

[27]Li Zehou's interview with a correspondent from *United Daily News* (Taipei), Dec. 20, 1989, p. 9.

[28]*International Herald Tribune*, June 1, 1988, p. 3.

[29]Jin Guangtao's interview with a correspondent from *Ming bao* (Hong Kong), April 23, 1988, p. 6.

[30]*Washington Post*, May 5, 1988, p. 2.

[31]Fang Lizhi's interview with a correspondent from *The Christian Science Monitor*, Nov. 18, 1988, pp. 1 and 36.

Maoist socialism had lost its credibility. What resonates for him is the May Fourth slogan "Science and Democracy," which Fang believes is still the new hope for Chinese intellectuals. For Fang, China's only hope is that more and more people will no longer blindly believe only the authorities. They must realize that the only way to push social progress is for intellectuals to play a supervisory role for the public; they should have the right to express openly criticisms of the leadership.[32]

Unlike many liberal scholars, Liu Binyan, a writer of reportage literature and a communist already expelled twice from the party, is still optimistic about socialism. "Socialism is the only road that China can pursue," said Liu in a 1988 interview, "because capitalism is characterized by social injustice." He thinks that previous experiments in China were only "pseudo-socialism." A true socialism must be characterized by humanitarianism, respect for human dignity, and freedom of the people to understand their real conditions and to criticize the leadership. When asked what should be pursued in the political reforms, he answered: "The more democracy we have, the better socialism will be."[33] Although he favored the socialist road in China, he seems closer to Western-style democracy than to socialism.

Mr. Liu has lost his confidence in communism. "The communism envisioned by Marx," he says, "is somewhat utopian." Liu is optimistic about China's future for a number of reasons. First, China is undergoing an unprecedented transformation. Only when old systems are destroyed can new ones be established. He believes that China will be chaotic in the post-Deng era. All regions and provinces will then claim more autonomy, causing political and social disorder. But he thinks that this chaos ultimately will help China's progress. Second, ten years of reforms have changed the mentality of the Chinese; they are now much freer from ideological doctrines than before. Third, the social status of the intellectuals has been raised, allowing them to be more outspoken. Fourth, the party's social control is in decline, whereas the spontaneity of the people plays an increasing role in the political arena. Fifth, the relationship between the party and the people has changed. When people within and outside the party are more enlightened and made aware of their rights and freedom, they will strive for their own interests. Sixth, the mass media have played an increasingly important role in monitoring the party and government. Finally, what Mao called the class of the new bourgeoisie has struck back and has formed a coalition with

---

[32]Fang Lizhi, "China's Despair and China's Hope," *Ming bao* (Hong Kong), Feb. 9, 1989, p. 29; and *China Times* (Taipei), Feb. 11, 1989, p. 3.
[33]Liu Binyan's interview with a correspondent from *Wenhui bao* (Hong Kong), Aug. 6, 1988, p. 5.

progressive intellectuals. Liu described the situation in China as like an egg that seems intact although a baby chicken has been hatched inside the eggshell.[34]

The *People's Daily* article of December 1984 did launch a new debate about the character of Marxism and the necessity for a commodity economy. The new concept of "socialism with Chinese characteristics" quickly raised the issue of people's rights within the context of a new commodity economy. The focus on these issues shifted discussion to the rule of law, academic freedom, respect for human freedom, and freedom of the people to understand the facts and criticize the leadership. This new debate was soon followed by discussion of new theory to justify the reforms.

The Preliminary Stage of Socialism

The theory of the "preliminary stage of socialism" was adopted in the political report at the Thirteenth Party Congress in October–November 1987 and soon became official ideology. Six party guidelines were listed in the report: (1) concentrate on the work of modernization; (2) insist on a comprehensive reform program; (3) insist on the open-door policy; (4) resolutely develop a commodity economy based mainly on public ownership; (5) develop democratic policies while maintaining stability and unity; and (6) rely on Marxism to build a spiritual civilization.[35]

Ironically, Su Shaozhi, the theorist who conceived of the "preliminary stage of socialism," was ousted from the Institute of Marxism-Leninism–Mao Zedong Thought because of his unorthodox thinking.[36]

According to official interpretations, the theory of the "preliminary stage of socialism" was adopted because the party had scientifically integrated the basic principles and methods of Marxism with the historical, concrete circumstances of China, thereby providing a comprehensive ideological starting point for developing "socialism with Chinese characteristics."

This theory was supposed to solve the problems facing the reform program. First, it clarifies the nature of Chinese society at its present stage.

---

[34]Liu Binyan's interview with a correspondent from *China Times* (Taipei), Aug. 10, 1988, p. 2; *United Daily News* (Taipei), Aug. 5, 1988, p. 9; *Xingdao ribao* (Hong Kong), Aug. 6, 1988, p. 21; *China Times* (Taipei), Dec. 4, 1988, p. 2; and *United Daily News* (Taipei), Dec. 4, 1988, p. 9.

[35]Zhao Ziyang, "Advance Along Road of Socialism with Chinese Characteristics" (report delivered at the National Congress of the Communist Party of China on Oct. 25, 1987), *RMRB*, Nov. 4, 1987, pp. 1–4.

[36]*Ming bao* (Hong Kong), Aug. 25, 1987; and *Dagong bao* (Hong Kong), March 4, 1988, p. 3.

Chinese society already was a socialist society; therefore, China could not abandon socialism for capitalism. Nor could China become completely Westernized. This theory asserted that China was neither in transition to socialist transformation nor at the stage of advanced socialism. This viewpoint implied that people should not experiment in ways that were currently infeasible.

Second, the preliminary stage of socialism would take almost one hundred years to complete the socialist transformation. That meant that the political system and the commodity economy would be modernized gradually.

Third, this current stage is still characterized by a low level of productivity, backward feudalism, and corruptive influence of the capitalist and bourgeois classes. Therefore, China must raise the level of productivity and develop a commodity economy to improve the socialist system of public ownership.

Fourth, this theory further stressed the shift away from class struggle to raising the level of productivity and developing the commodity economy.

Finally, the theory further clarified the central task at the present stage as the development of productivity. The overall reform program and the open-door policies must be continued and sustained.[37]

These official interpretations show that China will not retreat from socialism to capitalism. Moreover, they strongly suggest that the party is not concerned with other issues such as the rule of law, academic freedom, respect for human freedom and dignity, and freedom of the people to understand the real situation and to criticize the leadership. In this sense, this theory of the "preliminary stage of socialism" only justifies the party's ignoring of the demands made by liberal scholars and intellectuals.

Su Shaozhi was naturally an unorthodox thinker. Su was the first scholar who presented the "preliminary socialist stage" theory in a 1979 *People's Daily* article.[38] In a coauthored 1986 article discussing the future of socialism, he further elaborated why Chinese society was still at the preliminary stage of socialism. Like other socialist countries, China had been deeply influenced by feudalism, semifeudalism, or semicapitalism. Socialist countries cannot bypass capitalism in their transition from a presocialist society to a socialist society. Therefore, China must learn from advanced capitalist countries.[39]

---

[37]Yuan Mu's (then deputy secretary-general of the leading team on finance and economy in the party's Central Committee) interview with a correspondent from *Jingji ribao* (Economic daily), Nov. 30, 1987, p. 1.

[38]Su Shaozhi's interview with *Ming bao* (Hong Kong), April 12, 1988, p. 6.

[39]Su Shaozhi and Wang Yizhou, "A New Understanding of Socialism," *Shijie jingji dabao*, reprinted in *Wenhui bao* (Hong Kong), Dec. 24, 1986, p. 4; and Dec. 25, 1986, p. 4.

Socialism cannot be completely separated from capitalism, as demonstrated by some capitalist theories interpreting the proletariat's role during the French Revolution.[40] As for the commodity economy and market mechanism, Su argued that the central-planning system can be connected with the market mechanism, as demonstrated in some capitalist countries.[41]

Su's basic concept of the "preliminary stage of socialism" conforms to the official line, but the conservatives within the party do not agree with Su's contention that capitalism cannot be bypassed.

Moreover, the official interpretation differs from Su's version with regard to ownership. The party maintains that a central task during the preliminary stage of socialism is to improve the system of public ownership. Su does not think the Chinese should discuss public ownership. He argues that the system of Chinese public ownership is still in transition to socialism. It is important to transform the national ownership into private ownership, allowing the individuals and workers to have their capital and financial shares. Workers also should be encouraged to participate in management and to express their own views.[42]

Few theorists sided with Su when he stated these positions. Hu Sheng, a conservative historian of Marxism and head of the Chinese Academy of Social Sciences, argued that it was mandatory for China to adhere to the socialist road. China had already bypassed capitalism, and socialism had been developed in that poor country largely because historical events before and after 1949 never allowed the country to experience capitalism.[43]

Li Yining, a professor of the Department of Economics at Beijing University, agreed that China had entered the preliminary socialist stage in 1956. However, more than twenty years were wasted because the party made some political and economic mistakes; for example, it accelerated class-struggle campaigns and political movements, expanded public ownership in the economic system, strengthened central planning, and distorted the distribution system.[44]

For Li, the stage of preliminary socialism must be a long process. Only when productivity and living standards are more or less equivalent to those

---

[40]*Dagong bao* (Hong Kong), Sept. 17, 1986, p. 2.

[41]Su Shaozhi and Wang Yizhou, "Two Historical Tasks of Reforms," *RMRB*, March 5, 1988, p. 5.

[42]Su Shaozhi's interview with a correspondent from *Wenhui bao* (Hong Kong), Dec. 26, 1988, p. 1; Dec. 27, 1988, p. 1; and Dec. 28, 1988, p. 4.

[43]*Xingdao ribao* (Hong Kong), March 6, 1987, p. 6.

[44]Li Yining's interview with a correspondent from *Dagong bao* (Hong Kong), Oct. 28, 1987, p. 2.

in the second-tier countries can the preliminary stage of socialism end. China should improve public ownership in accordance with productivity standards suitable for the stage of preliminary socialism. The distribution of income can be made more diversified. In addition to wage income, people should also receive nonwage income such as business proceeds, rent, interest, and dividends. Moreover, China should develop a well-planned commodity economy and allow market forces to determine prices for hundreds of commodities.[45]

Another theorist, Gong Yuzhi, stated that the new line based on the "preliminary stage of socialism" is consistent with the reforms implemented since the Third Plenum of the Eleventh Party Congress in 1978. The present stage of socialism is not utopian socialism, but socialism with economic construction as its central task. With economic construction as a "center," there are "two basic points" that should be realized. The reform program and open-door policies should be sustained; the four basic principles proclaimed by Deng Xiaoping should be upheld.[46] He also argued that theorists may hold different opinions on the meaning of the preliminary stage of socialism but the common people only want to see concrete economic results reflecting rising productivity, modernization, and closing the gaps with capitalist countries.[47]

Despite conservatives' objections to the above views, scholars had provided the party with new viewpoints and concepts. More debate followed. One theorist, Chen Xiankui, said that several factors may produce social, economic, and political instability in the preliminary stage of socialism. First, the new division of labor and the new differentiated consumer demands will intensify conflicts over economic and political interests. Therefore, if these conflicts are not resolved, great instability will erupt. Second, there is still a great gap between society's achievements and the demands of the people in their life, culture, political participation, freedom, and equity. Third, China now faces all sorts of problems that could overwhelm society and produce economic collapse. Fourth, the party and government lack the experience needed to solve these new problems. Finally, leftist thinking, such as "intensifying class struggle," "utopianism," and "premature advance," still is shared by many party members and government officials. As a result, the four basic principles must be upheld if political stability is to be

---

[45]Ibid.

[46]Gong Yuzhi, "One Center, Two Basic Points," *RMRB*, Jan. 11, 1988, p. 5.

[47]Gong Yuzhi, "An Inquiry Concerning the Preliminary Stage of Socialism in Our Country," *RMRB*, June 19, 1988, p. 5; and "How Gong Yuzhi Views a Preliminary Stage of Socialism," *Wenhui bao* (Hong Kong), Aug. 4, 1988, p. 7.

maintained. But Chen argued that while unrealistic "democratic" development could be avoided so that the political stability would not be disturbed,
the party must use open, flexible, democratic methods to assimilate the
demands of political participation and to institutionalize the channels for
assimilating such demands.[48]

In an earlier article, Chen Xiankui noted that the demands of the people
should be translated into the nation's will at the current stage of socialism.
This could be done as follows. First, the people should be organized under
the leadership of the party. Second, the existing channels through which the
people can feel free to express their opinions should be strengthened and
expanded. Finally, the organs such as the National People's Congress, the
Chinese People's Political Consultative Conference, the various political
parties, and the autonomous units should be strengthened.[49]

Another theorist, Wang Guixiu, argued that democracy is by no means
insignificant at the preliminary stage of socialism. Democracy should be
gradually developed at a pace corresponding to that of the development of
the commodity economy. Efficiency cannot be pursued at the expense of
democracy. Both are desirable and cannot be separated at the present stage.
The Chinese should not be deprived of their rights of enjoying democracy
only because they lack a democratic culture. The culture of democracy can
only be cultivated in the process of democratization, just as a swimmer can
only learn to swim if he is in the water.[50]

There was an unusual consensus among Chinese theorists on the study
of capitalism. Many scholars were more than eager to justify their studies
of the experience of capitalist countries. Hong Zhaolong, a Chinese theorist,
pointed out that Marx, Engels, and Lenin obtained many valuable findings
in their studies of capitalism and imperialism. Therefore, the Chinese should
now study capitalism.[51]

Other theorists even advocate that the market mechanism and the stock
market have not been patented by capitalist countries; these capitalist principles and methods can also serve socialist countries in their preliminary
stage of socialism.[52]

---

[48]Chen Xiankui, "On Political Stability at the Preliminary Stage of Socialism,"
GMRB, Aug. 1, 1988, p. 3.
[49]Chen Xiankui, "A Few Opinions on Perfecting Political Institutions at the Preliminary Stage of Socialism," *GMRB*, April 4, 1988, p. 3.
[50]Wang Guixui, "Promoting the Democratical Political Construction of Socialism,"
RMRB, Dec. 9, 1988, p. 5.
[51]Hong Zhaolong, "Learning the Scientific Attitudes of Marx and Engels Toward
the 'Communist Manifesto,'" *GMRB*, Feb. 29, 1988, p. 3.
[52]Zheng Bijian and Jia Chunfeng, "Re-Understanding the Great Change," *RMRB*,

To justify studying capitalism, an imaginative theorist named Lu Congming argued that "contemporary capitalism is at the stage of socialist capitalism." He divides capitalism into three stages: (1) laissez-faire capitalism (late eighteenth century through late nineteenth century); (2) imperialist capitalism (late nineteenth century through the 1950s); and (3) socialist capitalism (1950s to the present). Advanced capitalist societies now at the stage of socialist capitalism will transform themselves into socialism in the long run; the advanced capitalist societies that reflect new achievements in human civilization are the best models for a commodity economy.[53]

Even Hu Sheng says that, although China cannot become capitalist, China must experiment with advanced capitalists' methods of large-scale production, management, and scientific and technological development.[54]

One exception in the discussion of capitalism and the PRC is Rui Yuan, a very conservative theorist, who argues that once China enters the preliminary stage of socialism, it cannot move back to capitalism. If China begins learning capitalist lessons, as some theorists want, China will retreat.[55]

The discussion of studying capitalism seemed to end in late 1988 when the Institute of Socialism at the Academy of Social Sciences in Peking, its counterpart in the provinces of Shandong, Henan and Sichuan, and the theoretical department of *Guangming ribao*, a newspaper for the intellectuals, cosponsored a large conference on contemporary capitalism in Jinan, in Shandong province.[56] An article giving an overview of the conference, written by Yu Guangyuan, a prominent economist, argued that only through exhaustive studies of contemporary capitalism can Marxism and socialism be enriched for the purpose of helping China find its proper road.[57]

The report of the party's Thirteenth National Congress presented more

---

May 20, 1988, p. 3; and Xi Guangqing, "Strengthening the Studies of Contemporary Capitalism," *GMRB*, April 25, 1988, p. 3.

[53]Lu Congming, "On Contemporary Capitalism in the Stage of Socialist Capitalism," *GMRB*, Nov. 21, 1988, p. 3.

[54]*Xingdao ribao* (Hong Kong), March 6, 1987, p. 6. For similar views, see Miao Changfa and Long Pingping, "The Guiding Document Concerning the Construction of a Socialism with Chinese Characteristics," *Jingji ribao* (Economic daily), June 13, 1987, p. 3.

[55]Rui Yuan, "Correctly Understanding the Nature of the Preliminary Stage of Socialism," *GMRB*, May 25, 1987, p. 3.

[56]*GMRB*, Jan. 23, 1989, p. 3.

[57]Yu Guangyuan, "Re-Understanding the Contemporary Capitalism," *GMRB*, Jan. 23, 1989, p. 3; see also "How to Comprehend 'Re-Understanding the Contemporary Capitalism,'" *Wenhui Bao* (Hong Kong), Jan. 17, 1989, p. 4; Jan. 18, 1989, p. 2; and Jan. 19, 1989, p. 2.

sophisticated ideological justification for the reforms. Concepts used in that report gave some new meaning to the cliché of "socialism with Chinese characteristics."

Nevertheless, the party ruled out any debate and action on the issues of the rule of law, academic freedom, and respect for human freedom when advancing its interpretations of the "preliminary stage of socialism." Most reform-minded scholars still believed that the economic reforms could not succeed without corresponding political reforms.

Moreover, the theory of the "preliminary stage of socialism" created ideological confusion. The influential scholar Prof. Su Shaozhi, who originally presented that theory, maintained that capitalism remains an indispensable historical stage that China must pass through, and that the public-ownership system really belongs to the stage of communism as envisioned by Karl Marx.

The theory of the "preliminary stage of socialism" as adopted by the Thirteenth National Congress differs from what Prof. Su presented in 1979. The new official theory merely provides an ideological justification of the party's endorsement of economic reform but not of other reforms.

Democracy or the "New Authoritarianism"

In debates over the meaning of socialism, many Chinese thinkers seemed to have lost their patience and sought political solutions. In doing so, some still used Marxist language, as they recognized the political reality in today's China. Others did not bother to use it and openly advocated democracy and freedom. Still others even favored a more centralized political power to speed up the reforms.

When debates over political, institutional reforms began in 1986, Su Shaozhi presented several suggestions. First, Joseph V. Stalin's monism of interest should be replaced by pluralism of interests in the economic, social, and political fields. Political democratization is possible even though a multiparty system is still not allowed. Second, strengthening the party's leadership means neither the absolute leadership of the party nor the party's intervention in nonpolitical affairs. Third, China must restudy the theories concerning the development of nations, governments, and parties, because there are many phenomena that Karl Marx, Friedrich Engels, and Nikolai Lenin failed to consider.[58]

Being sacked in 1987 did not prevent Su, now a senior associate of the

---

[58]*Dagong bao* (Hong Kong), Sept. 17, 1986, p. 2.

institute, from being an outspoken political theorist. In various coauthored articles discussing political institutional reforms, Su said that open decision-making in the political and economic fields is a capital idea as presented by the party, but that those in power also should be constrained by laws, mass media, scholars and experts, and the public.[59]

Recognizing that political reforms cannot be achieved in one day, he urged a step-by-step method of reform. He warned that such a method did not mean that early political institutional reforms can be postponed, arguing that the existing Chinese political system has not been able to meet the needs of development. After the first step is finished, the second step will be to separate the party and the government with regard to their functions. The major work in the final step will be to institutionalize the socialist democratic system so that democracy will not break down when leaders change. Socialist democracy in China must meet the general requirements for sustaining modern democracy: that is, Chinese socialist democracy must have the electoral system, periodic elections, and separation of powers.[60]

In an interview with a correspondent from the U.S. magazine *Newsweek* in mid-1988, Su said the economic reforms in China will have a great impact on political reforms as the development of a market economy eliminates bureaucratism, privileges, and feudalism. Political reforms are indispensable in the process of economic reform. Only when the people learn that they are masters of their country can they become active and autonomous and so create higher productivity. Acknowledging that China has a long way to go before it moves in the direction of a democratic system, he said that a step-by-step approach was necessary. First, the party must democratize itself and allow the people to have a supervisory role. Second, political life in the country should be democratized. Above all, a variety of people's rights as stipulated in the constitution should be put into practice, including the freedom of speech and publication and free assembly. After these basic rights are granted to the people, more comprehensive elections should be held and a multiparty system established.[61]

In late 1988 and early 1989, Su also pointed out the disorder caused by dogmatic officials and corrupt officials. Prices were out of control in 1988

---

[59]Su Shaozhi and Wang Yizhou, "Several Issues Concerning Political Institutional Reforms That Require Further Studies," *Lilun xinxi bao*, reprinted in *Wenhui bao* (Hong Kong), March 2, 1988, p. 32; March 3, 1988, p. 7; and March 4, 1988, p. 7.
[60]Su Shaozhi and Wang Yizhou, "Two Historical Tasks of Reforms," *RMRB*, March 5, 1988, p. 5.
[61]The text of the interview was translated into Chinese by *Lilun xinxi bao*, and an abridged version was printed in *Wenhui bao* (Hong Kong), June 24, 1988, p. 7.

because commodities were being manipulated by officials with privilege; he proposed more privatization of the economy. Only when people become capitalists and the economy moves toward democratization, he declared, can the economic crisis be eased.[62]

Su thought that inflation had probably become *the* insurmountable barrier for all socialist countries in their process of half-capitalist and half-socialist economic reforms. The only possible remedy is to restrict demand caused by high expectations and raise production through economic reforms. Austerity, however, cannot be expected only from the people. Political leaders should set an example by eliminating all privileges, such as their special supplies and shops. Most important, the political system should be further democratized and the decisionmaking process made more open.[63]

When political reform became a hot topic in 1986, Yan Jiaqi violated the taboos set by the Chinese leaders. According to Yan, reforms of political systems involve the following: (1) perfecting the party and government leadership and its horizontal power distribution among governmental institutions; (2) pushing for vertical decentralization of power; (3) restricting governmental jurisdiction and allowing social institutions to take over some work previously handled by the government; (4) perfecting the National People's Congress; and (5) establishing a system of selecting, dismissing, and supervising party and state cadres. The ultimate goals of the political reforms, as Yan claimed, are to reduce highly centralized power, to establish a socialist democratic political system and a scientific decisionmaking system, and to strengthen and improve the leadership of the party.[64]

In the political arena, Li Yining also argued that China should avoid the class-struggle campaigns and political movements of the past. Most important, China should promote democratization in the polity, economy, and society.[65]

In 1988, Li Zehou presented the concept of "New Democracy" as a theoretical basis for a socialist democracy. The "New Democracy" presented by Prof. Li Zehou differs from Mao's version. According to Mao, the new democracy was a dictatorial coalition of all anti-imperialist and antifeudal

---

[62] *United Daily News*, Dec. 10, 1988, p. 9.
[63] Su Shaozhi's interview with a correspondent from *Wenhui bao* (Hong Kong), Dec. 26, 1988, p. 1; Dec. 27, 1988, p. 1; and Dec. 28, 1988, p. 4.
[64] For Yan Jiaqi's interview with a correspondent from China News Agency, see *Dagong bao* (Hong Kong), June 18, 1986, p. 2; or *Wenhui bao* (Hong Kong), June 18, 1986, p. 2; and Sept. 9, 1986, p. 18.
[65] Li Yining's interview with a correspondent from *Dagong bao* (Hong Kong), Oct. 28, 1987, p. 2.

classes, such as the proletariat, peasants, intellectuals, and other petty bourgeois classes.[66] Li, however, does not classify democratic systems by means
of class analysis, as Mao did.[67]

Second, Li believes that the demand for academic freedom has become
an irresistible trend in China, and that there is no way to suppress the new
ideas presented by young scholars. If intervention in the academic field is to
be reduced, there must be freedom and democracy in society; that can only
be realized through the rule of law and the development of pluralism. He
points out that democracy cannot be supported by slogans, and that democratization can only be maintained by the law. China's economy has
become increasingly pluralistic. Pluralism must now develop in the political
and cultural fields and in daily life.[68]

Third, he strongly opposed ideological monism, saying that there should
not be a unitary ideology in China. Li pointed out that "New Democracy"
is needed in theoretical and cultural development because it is scientific and
democratic.[69]

Fourth, unlike Liu Binyan, Li does not think that the intellectuals can
check and balance the government by means of the mass media. Only when
the judicial branch becomes truly independent can the intellectuals play any
role.[70]

Finally, Li thinks that there must evolve a competitive multiparty system
in China because a dominant party like the CCP tends to become corrupt
without competition.[71]

In response to Li Zehou's "New Democracy," Su Shaozhi pointed out
that he had presented the same view in 1979, and that he was criticized by
his superiors for that view. In an article published in 1979, he said that at
that time China was in the preliminary stage of socialism. In other words,
China was in the transition from what Mao called "New Democracy" to
what Marx called "socialism," but was still locked in the stage of "New

---

[66]Mao Zedong, "On New Democracy," in *Mao Zedong xuanji* (Selected works of
Mao Zedong) (Beijing: Renmin chubanshe, 1953), pp. 668–69.

[67]Li Zehou's objection to Mao's class analysis and his thesis of class struggle can be
found in his interview with a correspondent from *Ming bao* (Hong Kong), March 5,
1988, p. 5.

[68]Li Zehou's interviews with correspondents from *Ming bao* (Hong Kong), March 5,
1988, p. 5; and *United Daily News* (Taipei), Dec. 20, 1988, p. 9.

[69]Li Zehou's interviews with correspondents from *Ming bao* (Hong Kong), March 5,
1988, p. 5; and *United Daily News* (Taipei), Dec. 20, 1988, p. 9.

[70]Li Zehou's interview with a correspondent from *United Daily News* (Taipei), Dec.
20, 1988, p. 9.

[71]Ibid.

Democracy."[72] What Li meant by "New Democracy" is not really different from what Su meant by the "preliminary stage of socialism."

Jin Guangtao, however, thinks that "New Democracy" is a deterministic concept with roots in economic activity. According to Jin, a society should not, in its development, emphasize only political, economic, social, or cultural factors, but should maintain an equilibrium in its development.[73] The ideas presented by Li Zehou are not entirely different from those advocated by Jin Guangtao.

In early 1988, Yan Jiaqi decided to give up his directorship of the Institute of Political Science at the Chinese Academy of Social Sciences, because he thought that writing books was more important. Since then, Yan has become increasingly critical of the political reforms that had stagnated.

Among the problems he identifies with political reforms was that party leaders misunderstood the meaning of democracy. Their misunderstanding of democracy is evident because party leaders asked the military to democratize itself by electing company commanders and platoon leaders through a democratic process, while maintaining the bureaucratic appointment of governors and mayors.[74]

Other problems were: (1) the loss of authority and the ineffectiveness of administrative organizations without laws for administration and economy; (2) worshiping authority; (3) failing to establish the authority of law; (4) no separation between the party and government; (5) arbitrary rule under a patriarchal system; and (6) no free press and speech.[75]

Returning from a visit to the United States in late 1988, Yan took an optimistic attitude toward China's future. "As long as freedom of speech, press freedom, and a sound democratic system are granted to the Chinese," said Yan, "all the difficulties [ahead of China] will be solved."[76] In early 1989, he even advocated abolishing the Politburo because he thought it violated the principle of separation of power between party and government.[77]

---

[72]*Ming bao* (Hong Kong), April 12, 1988, p. 9.

[73]Jin Guangtao's interview with a correspondent from *Ming bao* (Hong Kong), April 23, 1988, p. 9.

[74]*Ming bao* (Hong Kong), May 1, 1988, p. 10.

[75]Yan Jiaqi, "China, No Longer a Dragon," *RMRB* (overseas edition), May 24, 1988, p. 2; "The Spirit of Lao Siguang," *Ming bao* (Hong Kong), June 20, 1988, p. 3; his interview with a correspondent from *Dagong bao* (Hong Kong), June 20, 1988, p. 5; *Xingdao ribao* (Hong Kong), Oct. 18, 1988, p. 19; and *United Daily News* (Taipei), Nov. 17, 1988, p. 19.

[76]*Wenhui bao* (Hong Kong), Nov. 17, 1988, p. 4.

[77]Yan Jiaqi's interview with a correspondent from *Shijie jingji daobao*, "The Eve of the Duel Between the New and Old Systems," and an excerpt from it printed in

Disillusioned by disruptions caused by the economic reforms, many young theorists began to call for a new authoritarianism in China in late 1988. Witnessing the successes of Asia's four little dragons—the Republic of China on Taiwan, the Republic of Korea, Singapore, and Hong Kong—they wanted a new strong man to push economic reform and usher in democracy.

In fact, establishing such a new authority had been discussed in China for some time. As early as 1986, two young theorists, Zhang Bingjiu, then a graduate student, and Chen Huning, a young scholar in Shanghai, emphasized the need for a centralized power to carry out economic reforms.[78] In April 1987, Wen Yuankai, the director of the Chemical Department at the University of Chinese Science and Technology, also suggested in an interview that over time "while political power is more centralized at the top, more autonomy is granted in the economic field."[79]

In late 1988, many aggressive reformists believed a new authority was necessary for the reform program because economic disorder, caused by corrupt officials, had worsened. At an academic conference in September 1988, Dai Qing, a woman writer, argued that a strong man was needed if the economic reforms were to continue.[80] In the same vein, Wu Jiaxiang, a researcher at the party's Political Reform Institute in Beijing, argued that centralized power at the top could coexist with more liberty at the bottom of society, if a traditional society was becoming modernized.[81]

"Without authority," said Wu, "the healthy development of liberty is impossible." He argued that a traditional authoritarian system cannot bypass the stage of a new authoritarianism to achieve a transition to democracy. The reason for that was that the powers lost by the old authorities were not distributed to the people of the society, but recaptured by the so-called middle structure—a group of powerful bureaucrats created by the old authorities. Therefore, new authorities must be established so that the power lost by the old authorities can be distributed to the top and bottom of society simultaneously. Later, the new strong-man despotism would transform

---

Dagong bao (Hong Kong), Nov. 28, 1989, p. 13. See also *Ming bao* (Hong Kong), Feb. 25, 1989, p. 9.

[78]Cited by Hu Shaooan in his article "The Controversies over the New Authoritarianism," *Wenhui bao* (Hong Kong), Feb. 12, 1989, p. 3.

[79]Wen Yuankai's interview with a correspondent from *Ming bao* (Hong Kong), April 14, 1987, p. 2.

[80]Hu Shaooan, "The Controversies over the New Authoritarianism," *Wenhui bao* (Hong Kong), Feb. 12, 1989, p. 3; and *Ming bao* (Hong Kong), March 8, 1989, p. 9.

[81]Ibid.

itself into a democratic system. Wu pointed out that "democracy is the spouse of liberty, whereas despotism is the lover of liberty."[82]

Not all theorists who support the concept of "New Authoritarianism" necessarily share Wu's optimism. Xiao Gongqin says that he is not sure whether the new authoritarianism will lead to democracy or to a more conservative, backward despotism. He argues, however, that the new despotism supported by the military is a "necessary evil" for China, if economic reforms are to be pursued.[83]

Wu's theory of "New Authoritarianism" was strongly supported by his superiors, Chen Yizi and Wang Xiaoqiang, director and deputy director, respectively, of the party's Political Reform Institute in Beijing.[84] This institute is a think tank working for Zhao Ziyang. Zhao apparently discussed the idea of "New Authoritarianism" with Deng Xiaoping on March 6, 1989, and Deng supported the idea in principle.[85] A more widely circulated rumor is that Zhao Ziyang is the theorists' favorite choice as strong man and that promoting Zhao has challenged the party conservatives. The conservatives do not oppose a strong man; rather, Zhao does.[86]

Liberal theorists also harshly criticized the "New Authoritarianism," fearing that it would justify a return to the personality cult and abusive, one-man rule of the Mao era.

"We cannot protect Zhao Ziyang by means of the 'New Authoritarianism,'" said Wang Rousui, former deputy editor in chief of the *People's Daily*. The conservatives, as he puts it, can also take advantage of this theory to seize power. He believes that the only way to prevent reforms from being distorted is to inject more openness and democracy into the political situation.[87]

"It would be a big mistake," said Yan Jiaqi, "for some theorists to say that authoritarianism is to be established only for the time being, while arguing that their real intention is to push democracy." Yan warned that the conservatives would use the concept as a pretext for opposing the reforms.[88]

---

[82]Wu Jiaxiang's article was originally published in *Shijie jingji daobao*, no. 426. An excerpt was reprinted in *RMRB*, March 3, 1989, p. 6, and *GMRB*, March 17, 1989, p. 3.

[83]Xiao Gongqin, "No Easy Choice: The New Authoritarianism," *Wenhui bao* (Hong Kong), Jan. 17, 1989, p. 4. See also *RMRB*, March 3, 1989, p. 6, and *GMRB*, March 17, 1989, p. 3.

[84]*United Daily News* (Taipei), March 13, 1989, p. 9.

[85]*Xingdao ribao* (Hong Kong), April 8, 1989, p. 2.

[86]*United Daily News* (Taipei), March 13, 1989, p. 9.

[87]Ibid.

[88]Ibid.

If some authority must be established in China, it should not be the authority of an individual, a few people, a group, or an ideology, but, as Yan puts it, the authority of constitution and law.[89]

Su Shaozhi, too, disagreed with the "New Authoritarianism." He pointed out that "New Authoritarianism" is a very dangerous concept, especially if it is connected with the idea of nationalism or gains military support. "What would guarantee that this authoritarian leader would use his powers wisely and wouldn't be corrupted by his power?" he asks.[90]

Hu Jiwei, former publisher of the *People's Daily,* noted that the Chinese have always referred to authority in terms of leadership authority. What is needed, however, is not to establish the authority of leaders but the authority of democracy.[91]

In an article written for the *People's Daily,* Fan Zhongxin, a theorist of the Institute of Taiwan Studies at the Chinese Academy of Social Sciences, views advocacy of the "New Authoritarianism" as a big retreat in the contemporary Chinese thought. Fan noted that because the gap between China and the West had widened, some theorists believed only a strong man could lead the country to modernize and close the gap. For these theorists, both democracy and the "New Authoritarianism" were only "means" to modernization. Since, in their view, democracy is not possible in China, they chose the latter.[92]

Another theorist, Wang Wenzhang, believes that the supporters of the "New Authoritarianism" made three mistakes. First, China's problem is not the loss of authority, but how to make good use of authority in a scientific way. Second, these theorists have underestimated the possibility that more authority of leaders could derail reforms. Finally, they have oversimplified how other countries modernized.[93]

---

[89]Yan Jiaqi's interview with a correspondent from *Shijie jingji daobao* was published under the title "The Eve of the Duel Between the New and Old Systems," and an excerpt from it printed in *Dagong bao* (Hong Kong), Nov. 28, 1989, p. 13.

[90]Su Shaozhi's interview with a correspondent from *The Christian Science Monitor* appeared in that newspaper on Feb. 22, 1989, p. 2.

[91]*Ming bao* (Hong Kong), March 9, 1989, p. 8. For details of Hu's suggestions on how to push forward democratization in China, see *Wenhui bao* (Hong Kong), Feb. 11, 1989, p. 4.

[92]Fan Zhongxin's article was originally published in *RMRB*, March 6, 1989; it was cited by *Ming bao* (Hong Kong), March 7, 1989, p. 10.

[93]Zhou Wenzhang's article was originally published in *Gongren ribao* (Workers' daily), Feb. 3, 1989; an excerpt from it was printed in *RMRB*, March 3, 1989, p. 6, and in *GMRB*, March 17, 1989, p. 3.

The theory of the "New Authoritarianism" was not only questioned by many theorists, but was also challenged by some young thinkers. Rong Jian thinks that the "New Authoritarianism" is not suitable for China for the following reasons. First, the problem of ownership has not yet been solved in China, and therefore politics and economy cannot be separated. A centralized political power will not evolve into a decentralized economic power. Second, China's problem is not the loss of traditional authority, but the abuse of that authority, which is the main obstacle blocking economic liberalization. Third, the centralization of power at the top only will increase political intervention in people's economic life. Fourth, as democratization becomes a worldwide trend, China should not resist such a trend. Finally, imposing the "New Authoritarianism" in China will not satisfy the people's demands for political reforms and democratization. Believing that China needs a powerful, effective, and incorruptible government ruled by law, Rong Jian points out that such a government is neither a traditional, highly centralized system nor a system characterized by a "New Authoritarianism," but a product of political democratization.[94]

Wang Yizhou, a young theorist and Su's student, points out that there are at least three defects in the theory of the "New Authoritarianism." First, supporters of the theory expect too much from a strong man and naively believe he will promote democracy. Second, they prefer rapid economic development at the expense of political liberty and liberal values. Finally, they think that an authoritarian system can handle problems caused by the reform more easily than a democratic system.[95]

Several Chinese legal experts have also participated in the debate. Yu Haocheng says that there has been a honeymoon between despotism and liberty in China's history. Chinese leaders always fear that democracy will have a negative impact on political stability and solidarity. He points out that only when a democratic system is institutionalized can political stability and solidarity be guaranteed.[96] Cao Siyuan, a drafter of the Chinese bankruptcy law, does not think that the "New Authoritarianism" is feasible for

---

[94]Rong Jian, "'The New Authoritarianism' Is Not Feasible in China," *Shijie jingji daobao*, Jan. 16, 1989. An abridged version was printed in *Wenhui bao* (Hong Kong), Feb. 15, 1989, p. 34, and in *Dagong bao* (Hong Kong), Feb. 22, 1989, p. 4.

[95]*GMRB*, March 17, 1989, p. 3.

[96]Yu Haocheng's article was originally published in *Shijie jingji daobao*, no. 429. An excerpt from it was printed in *RMRB*, March 3, 1989, p. 6; *Ming bao* (Hong Kong), March 9, 1989, p. 8; and *GMRB*, March 17, 1989, p. 3.

China. What is needed in China, he says, is socialist parliamentary democracy.[97] Zhang Zongyuan believes that an unsound legal system is the major reason political reforms have stagnated. China only needs the absolute authority of a constitution and law, not absolute personal authority.[98]

The debate over whether China should move in the direction of the "New Authoritarianism" or democracy will undoubtedly continue without any resolution. One thing is certain. As of 1989, many liberal, outspoken scholars no longer pay even lip service to Marxism.

Conclusion

The debate on the character of Marxism and "socialism with Chinese characteristics" was originally intended to justify the reform program which Deng Xiaoping began in the late 1970s. The suggestions—academic freedom, rule by law, and respect for human freedom—presented by many theorists were not accepted by the conservative leaders. Major ideological differences emerged between the reformists and the conservatives within and outside the party.

In late 1987, the party's Thirteenth National Congress adopted a crucial document in which the party attempted a comprehensive ideological justification for the economic reforms based on making the concept of the "preliminary stage of socialism" correspond to China's current "backward Chinese economy. However, the official interpretation of this concept was different from the view that Su Shaozhi presented in 1979, which argued for "bypassing capitalism" and having a system of mixed property ownership. Moreover, the new official interpretation implied that academic freedom and respect for human freedom were not realistic, given China's political reality of today. As a result, the ideological gap between liberal reformists and the conservatives widened still more.

Debate on the role of the state produced two concepts: democracy and "New Authoritarianism." Democracy has been described by some other liberal theorists as a political solution for the reform program. The "New Authoritarianism" was viewed in late 1988 as a means to overcome the disruption caused by economic reforms. That approach was rejected by the conservatives because they regarded it as unrealistic; they turned down the latter approach because the theorists' choice of strong man was Zhao Ziyang.

Marxism is being interpreted in an increasingly more complex way. At

---

[97]*Ming bao* (Hong Kong), March 9, 1989, p. 8.
[98]Ibid.

first, many Chinese theorists sided with the party, probably because party leaders had encouraged more debate. With few exceptions, most of these theorists advocated more free discussion and new policies, but in the context of Marxism. The conservatives ignored or criticized discussion advocating the rule of law, respect for human freedom and dignity, and academic freedom when many tried to connect these terms with "socialism with Chinese characteristics" and the "preliminary stage of socialism." The debates became more intense. More theorists advocated democracy, a new authority, and even criticized the leadership, the party, Marxism, and socialism, no longer fearing punishment by the party.

During these debates, most of the liberals and outspoken Chinese theorists seemed to have lost their faith in Marxism or socialism for China. Some theorists showed no interest in a rigorous study of Marxism and the relevance of the socialism of Mao's era for today's China.

The loss of confidence in Marxism and socialism among some Chinese theorists also revealed some pessimism toward the reform program and greater cynicism toward the Chinese leadership. Yet most of them are still optimistic about China's future. For example, Jin Guangtao describes himself as a "pessimistic" optimist on the open-door policies in China, but an optimist about the nation's future. Declaring that Marxism is obsolete and useless, Fang Lizhi takes a totally pessimistic view of the current leadership. He thinks China's hope is to enlighten the people. Yan Jiaqi seems to have an optimistic attitude about China's future only if freedom of speech and of the press and a sound democratic system can evolve. Adhering to his "egg" philosophy, Liu Binyan is optimistic about China's future. While most have lost faith in Marxism and socialism, they have faith in their own nation.

The debate over the character of Marxism in late 1984 marked a watershed in Chinese theoretical discussion. As these debates heated up in the past two or three years, terms such as freedom and democracy discussed by theorists seem to take on the meanings they have in the West, rather than as defined in the Marxist or socialist context. During the debates, Chinese theorists did not seem to disagree very much when discussing humanitarianism, freedom, and democracy. These terms seemed to have universal values in the eyes of many Chinese theorists. In the final analysis, Chinese theorists have not yet found any answers on which most can agree.

Chapter 13:   Stanley Rosen

Youth and Social Change in the PRC

On April 26, 1989, an editorial in the authoritative *People's Daily* described China's most recent student demonstrations—prompted by the death of former Communist Party (CCP) general secretary Hu Yaobang on April 15—as a "planned conspiracy to negate the leadership of the CCP and the socialist system."[1] It was widely known that the editorial closely reflected the views Deng Xiaoping had expressed to Premier Li Peng a day earlier, and that an emergency meeting of the Politburo Standing Committee had authorized the Beijing municipal government to take whatever means necessary to end the student protests.[2] To ensure that this chilling warning would reach a wide audience, the editorial was read on national television and rebroadcast that evening over campus loudspeakers. The student response—and the public support the students received—was a personal rebuff to Deng and revealed the extent of the party's loss of authority and social control. Arguably, it marked a turning point in state-society relations in post-1949 China. A mass demonstration of 150,000 students and their supporters marched through Beijing for fourteen hours, pushing past ineffective police lines and eliciting the vocal encouragement of more than half a million onlookers before peacefully returning to their campuses.

---

[1] *FBIS Daily Report: China*, April 25, 1989, pp. 23–24 (Radio Beijing, April 25). Hereafter cited as *Daily Report*.
[2] *Daily Report*, April 27, 1989, pp. 21–22 (*South China Morning Post*, April 27).

As striking as the student challenge to the party leadership may have been, it was not entirely unexpected. Periodic student demonstrations had become a familiar feature since the suppression of the last large-scale protests in December 1986–January 1987. Indeed, authorities had been expecting further student unrest following the protests against African students in China from late December 1988 into January 1989.[3] What was highly unusual, however, was the bold manner in which student defiance was manifested, and the open support the students received from workers and intellectuals. How are these developments to be explained? This paper will seek preliminary answers in several places. Broadly, we will examine the CCP's changing relationship to the society it governs. The reform process, with its emphasis on the expansion of the market, has created serious contradictions within the party, and in the linkage between the party and society. The CCP has been unable to respond quickly and appropriately to a society in transition, and this inability has affected its leadership capability and even its relevance.

Although our primary emphasis will be on the CCP's relationship with China's youth, it is impossible to understand the boldness of that youth without some examination of the wider social context, of the widespread discontent over the consequences of partial reform. This chapter therefore has two major sections. We will examine the party's attempt to understand university students and to reform its ideological-political work in the aftermath of the demonstrations of 1986–1987. Greatest attention will be devoted to a key survey on the state of ideological work in Beijing universities conducted by party and government authorities in 1986–1987. This will be followed by a discussion of the "social mood," of the political, economic, social, and ideological uncertainties that marked China in the late 1980s. It is first necessary, however, to set the context, to address the important changes in the party's relationship to youth under the impact of the reforms.

The Reform Decade and the Changing Expectations of Youth

Over the last decade, CCP-youth relations have been marked by an increasingly obvious irony, culminating in the tragic events of June 4, 1989. The successful implementation of the party's ambitious modernization program

---

[3]On the demonstrations against the Africans, see Lin Zufen, "Nanjing xuechaode lailong qumai" (The cause and effect of the Nanjing student unrest), *Mingbao yuekan*, Feb. 1989, pp. 11–14 and 26; and the wide coverage in the *Daily Report* from late December through the first half of January.

has required the active participation of China's brightest young people. To encourage such support, the CCP had allowed them greater freedom of expression and association, sought to recruit them into the party, promote their oversees study, and so forth. At that same time, the gradual marketization of social and economic life had rendered the party's blandishments relatively ineffective and contributed to the decline in the party's social control. If Chinese youth faced highly indefinite prospects in 1978, relying on the party to expand educational opportunities, provide jobs, and integrate them into the still uncertain post–Cultural Revolution society, by 1989 their expectations had risen beyond the abilities—not to mention the inclinations—of the CCP to meet them. In the aftermath of June 4, hardline party leaders have reverted to a concentration on control, forsaking, at least for now, their erstwhile strategy of reaching out to youth.

The dramatic change in Chinese youth's expectations was in fact a product of the CCP's success in solving some of the thorniest problems left over from the Cultural Revolution, so that the structure of opportunity in 1989 far exceeded the limited options confronting youth a decade earlier. The restoration of the university entrance examinations in December 1977 marked the end of the Maoist experimentation with educational leveling. A decade ago there was great pressure on young people to squeeze into the small number of university places. Only 178,000 of the 5.7 million candidates (4.87 percent) were able to enter upon university study in 1977. Those who were unsuccessful commonly became "youth waiting for work" (*daiye qingnian*). The job market was overwhelmed by the combination of current and recent high-school graduates competing with older, "sent down" urban youth which had been trickling back from the countryside, particularly since the mid-1970s. In those uncertain times, the young people of China were seeking stability. Entrance into a university virtually guaranteed a state-assigned job in government or with a state enterprise.

Politically as well, opportunities for youth were far from abundant. The CCP, still recovering from the assault of Mao's Cultural Revolution—spearheaded by college and high-school Red Guards—recruited only five million members from 1977 to 1983, far below the rate of recruitment during the Cultural Revolution. University students were almost completely shunned, as many party officials resisted attempts to substitute ability for political loyalty as the main criterion for party membership. Students, for their part, were suspicious of political entanglements and, following ten years of educational minimalism, were eagerly pursuing professional proficiency. As late as the end of 1983, fewer than 1 percent of Chinese undergraduates were party members, the lowest figure since 1956.[4]

---

[4]Stanley Rosen, "The Chinese Communist Party and Chinese Society: Popular

If youth in the immediate post-Mao period had largely been seeking to recover the stability associated with the mid-1950s—represented by a good job in a state enterprise—by the late 1980s it had expectations unimaginable a decade earlier. The pressure to enter a university had eased, particularly in those areas, such as Guangzhou, where a rapidly expanding economy offered a variety of educational alternatives and employment opportunities for those unable to attend a university. By 1987, there were 1,063 regular colleges and universities, with close to 2 million students. Nationally, 2.275 million applicants sat for the university entrance examinations in that year, and 621,000 were admitted (27.13 percent).[5] The national rate of people in cities and towns awaiting employment had fallen from 5.9 percent in 1979 to 2 percent in 1986; moreover, employment difficulties had shifted from large and medium-sized cities down to the lower levels. One survey noted that the proportion of people waiting for employment in the county seats and towns relative to the total number of people waiting for jobs throughout the country had risen from 38 percent in 1980 to 50 percent in 1986.[6]

The creation of an educational system which is bifurcated into elite and mass sectors, and the increasing importance of—and possibilities for—material success have created differing expectations among China's youth. For those unable to enter a "key" junior or senior high school, continuing their schooling may be considered a poor investment, since the likelihood of entry into a good university is quite small. On the other hand, dropping out and finding a well-paying job, or helping one's family prosper, become attractive possibilities.

For those who could enroll in a good university—by and large the youth discussed in this paper—expectations were far higher. Of those graduating from the elite Beijing University in 1985, for example, 55 percent enrolled as graduate students; 13.7 percent were assigned to research institutes; 5.1

Attitudes Toward Party Membership and the Party's Image" (paper prepared for the annual meeting of the American Political Science Association, Atlanta, Georgia, Aug. 31–Sept. 3, 1989).

[5]It should be noted that only 524,000 were recruited from the state plan, and that 41,000 were sponsored by enterprises, 14,000 were self-financed students, and 42,000 were recruited by the low-prestige "irregular" TV and correspondence universities. Nevertheless, the contrast with the late 1970s remains striking. See *Zhongguo baike nianjian 1988* (Beijing, Shanghai: Zhongguo dabaike quanshu chubanshe, Dec. 1988), p. 479.

[6]Yang Guohua, "Accomplishments in Employing Workers in Townships and Cities and the New Situation We Face," *Qingnian yanjiu*, no. 1(Jan. 1988); translated in Stanley Rosen, ed., "Issues in Employment," *Chinese Economic Studies*, vol. 21, no. 4(Summer 1988):69–91.

percent were assigned to colleges and universities; and 13.3 percent went to government institutions. Only 10 percent went to production departments. The large majority of those going on to graduate school had a reasonable expectation that they could cap their climb up the educational ladder by studying abroad.[7] Graduate students with marketable skills—that is, foreign-language or computer-science majors—were increasingly able to benefit from China's more open labor market by transferring from their universities to well-paying jobs at one of China's new high-tech or foreign-trade corporations, albeit at the cost of a transfer fee of several thousand yuan. Recent changes in the job-assignment system, which allowed for more individual initiative in finding employment, had further diminished the state's control over the brightest university students.

Politically, the party had begun to look favorably on young intellectuals beginning in 1984. Whereas only 318 university students in Beijing entered the CCP in 1980, over 6,000 joined in 1985 (see table 13.5 below). Although joining the party represented a calculated risk—what some Chinese referred to as "a game of snakes and ladders"—and many resisted the temptation to join, there is no question that the CCP's major effort to attract the young and the talented had begun to bear fruit prior to the 1989 demonstrations. Still, relatively few students were interested in using party membership to pursue a career in government or politics. One study of 344 graduating students at the elite Qinghua University found that 73.8 percent were committed to pursuing an academic career, including study abroad; 9.3 percent expressed an interest in going into business and becoming rich; and only 5.5 percent sought party membership and a government position.[8] We now turn more specifically to the CCP's efforts to understand the country's youth, focusing on the results of sociological survey data.

Beijing Young in the Late 1980s:
The Evidence from Survey Research

Surveys conducted on the changing values of youth were among the earliest in the post-Mao period, with those in the late 1970s and early 1980s revealing a "crisis of confidence" in the system as China abandoned a discredited Maoist model, officially vilified as "sham socialism." With many young

---

[7]For details on job assignments of undergraduates and master's degree holders at Beijing University and Hangzhou University from 1983–1986, see Stanely Rosen, ed., "Profiles of Beijing University and Hangzhou University," *Chinese Education*, vol. 21, no. 4(Winter 1988/89).

[8]"An Investigation of the Ideology of a Portion of the Students at Four Nationally Prominent Universities," *Qingnian gongzuo yanjiu yu cankao*, Feb. 10, 1989, pp. 16–19. (No author named.)

people apparently viewing the overriding focus on economic development as taking place in an ideological vacuum, opinion polls conducted among university students consistently showed them to be independent in thinking, patriotic, and unwilling to blindly follow the party leadership.[9]

The various leadership factions had acknowledged the socialization problems visible from attitude surveys, but they differed on the appropriate responses.[10] To the young radical reformers engaged in youth work, the surveys indicated that the youth of the 1980s were very different from those of earlier decades, and hence they called for a dismantling of policies based on outdated conceptions, including a substantial decrease in the time allotted for political study, and more student input into affairs affecting young people's future, such as job assignments. Such reforms were in fact implemented on some campuses in 1985, as the Ministry of Education relaxed its powers of setting ideological study requirements for all universities for the first time since 1949, and experimented with a more flexible assignment system.

Conservative voices, however, although often denied access to the open press, found such liberal reforms alarming. They saw the ideological problems of university students as merely one part of a much larger problem. Conducting their own surveys, publishing in their own restricted-circulation journals, Beijing Municipal Youth League authorities, to take one example, examined a variety of negative social phenomena, seeking to refute the "liberal" explanations that were being widely reported in the press. Their surveys purported to trace deviant youth behavior to a laxity in ideological control and a social environment which offered too much freedom and insufficient management and supervision. For example, statistics had shown a rapid increase in the ratio between youth "waiting for work" (*daiye qingnian*) and juvenile delinquency. While "many people" had argued that a "difficult life" and "lack of income" were the best explanations, the Beijing Communist Youth League (CYL) survey of 120 education-through-labor inmates

---

[9]I have discussed these surveys in the following articles: "The Impact of Reform on the Attitudes and Behavior of Chinese Youth: Some Evidence from Survey Research," in Donna Bahry and Joel Moses, eds., *Communist Dialectic: The Political Implications of Economic Reform in Communist Systems* (New York: New York University Press); "The Impact of Reform Policies on Youth Attitudes," in Deborah Davis and Ezra F. Vogel, eds., *Chinese Society on the Eve of Tiananmen* (Cambridge, Mass.: Harvard University Press); "Value Change among Post-Mao Youth: The Evidence from Survey Data," in Perry Link, Richard Madsen, and Paul Pickowicz, *Unofficial China: Popular Culture and Thought in the People's Republic* (Boulder, Colo.: Westview Press).

[10]This argument draws from Stanley Rosen, "Students," in Anthony J. Kane, *China Briefing 1988* (Boulder, Colo.: Westview Press, 1988), pp. 79–105.

who had been youth waiting for work concluded that "the argument that youth waiting for work are forced to turn to crime and delinquency by economic hardship is invalid."[11]

Another survey examined the exodus of young intellectuals from profit-poor state enterprises which offer low salaries and minimal bonuses. Articles in the open press had routinely acknowledged the rationality of labor mobility, noting that 70 percent of young intellectuals feel they are "not currently able to make full use (or any use) of their potential," that scientific and technological personnel are viewed by most units as their own "private property" and are prevented from seeking employment elsewhere, and so forth. The Beijing CYL survey of 137 such intellectuals explicitly rejected this explanation, arguing that the main contributing factors to "the irrational trend of job hopping" are "concern only with money," "ease and comfort," and "personal fame and gain." They concluded that only 13 percent (and even these cases were "unverified") claimed they had left their posts because the lack of fit between job assignment and prior training prevented them from performing to their full potential.[12]

Amidst this "conservative-liberal" contention came the large-scale student demonstrations of September 1985, which started out as anti-Japanese and later brought up problems in the reform program.[13] To the radical reformers, this was further evidence that the old socialization measures had become ineffective, that students left out of the discussions and debates on reform were becoming alienated from the party and its policies. Their proposed solution was to reduce heavy-handed political control and increase consultation, to bring students more directly into the political process, "to provide them with better political treatment than other members of society."[14]

---

[11]Yan Jianxin, "Is 'Life Is Difficult, Without a Source of Income' the Primary Cause for Rising Crime and Delinquency among Young People Awaiting Job Assignment?" *Qingnian gongzuo yanjiu yu cankao,* no. 7(March 19, 1984); translated in Stanley Rosen, ed., "Issues in Employment," *Chinese Economic Studies,* vol. 21, no. 4(Summer 1988):65–68.

[12]Wang Jianshe, "An Investigation into the Exodus of Young Intellectuals," *Qingnian gongzuo yanjiu yu cankao,* no. 9(Sept. 1985); translated in Stanley Rosen, ed., "Survey Data on Educational Personnel and Other Intellectuals," *Chinese Education,* Spring 1987:111–16.

[13]On the 1985 and 1986 demonstrations, see Suzanne Pepper, "Deng Xiaoping's Political and Economic Reforms: China's Students Protest," *UFSI Reports,* no. 30(1986).

[14]Yang Dongping, "Contemporary Chinese University Students: A New Epoch," translated in Stanley Rosen, ed., "Youth Socialization and Political Recruitment in Post-Mao China," *Chinese Law and Government,* Summer 1987:9–17.

For party committees on university campuses, the message was different. They traced the problems to a lack of proper political education, to "fuzzy understanding" (*mohu renshi*) among the students, and to ideological confusion in the post-Mao period.[15] While some party secretaries went further and traced the problems to political cadres who were unhappy in their jobs because of low status, unclear roles, and inadequate material rewards, others felt that most political workers were satisfied, that the problem was student-centered, and required better ideological control and discipline mechanisms. However, their analysis was largely impressionistic.

To seek answers to these and other questions about the state of youth and youth work in Beijing, a series of large-scale surveys were commissioned.[16] The Beijing CYL conducted a survey (20,000 questionnaires distributed; 16,000 returned; and 12,000 analyzed) in the last half of 1986 which asked young people about their sources of information, the news stories they found most and least interesting, the subjects they most enjoyed discussing, and so forth.[17] Forty-nine news stories from the first half of 1986 were listed, and respondents could choose five expressions, ranging from "familiar and concerned" to "I don't know and I don't care," to reflect their opinions. As table 13.1 shows, four of the six news items garnering the most interest concerned foreign events. Youth also showed an interest in sports news, Chinese achievements, and cadre corruption. Table 13.2 shows that youth most enjoyed talking about and frequently discussed livelihood and life-style issues, as well as leisure-time activities. This concern of youth with issues of direct relevance to their own lives was stressed by the author of the survey report, who noted that virtually none of the ten newspaper items of least interest to youth had a direct connection to their lives. Table 13.3 reveals the importance of the mass media as the primary source of information for China's youth.

---

[15]This section is based on internal reports following the demonstrations from party secretaries at Beijing, Qinghua, and Fudan universities. See *A Collection of Some Speeches at the Forum on University Ideological and Political Work* (in Chinese), May 1986.

[16]The move to large-scale surveys stemmed in part from the enormous success of the national surveys conducted in 1985 and 1986 by the Chinese Economic System Reform Research Institute. For translations of these surveys, see Bruce L. Reynolds, ed., *Reform in China: Challenges and Choices* (Armonk, N.Y.: M. E. Sharpe, 1987). For the influence of these surveys, see Stanley Rosen, "Public Opinion and Reform in the People's Republic of China," *Studies in Comparative Communism*, vol. 22, no. 2/3(Summer/Autumn 1989):153–70.

[17]Wang Qun, "Beijing qingniande xinxi yishi" (Beijing youth's consciousness of news), *Qingnian yanjiu*, no. 6(June 1987):18–23.

Table 13.1
The Ten News Items That Youth Are Most Familiar With
and Concerned About

1. The summertime change carried out nationally	88.5%
2. The explosion of the Challenger	85.9%
3. The ascension of Corazon Aquino to the presidency of the Philippines	84.6%
4. The Thirteenth World Cup Soccer Tournament	82.1%
5. China's winning of the Uber Cup and the Thomas Cup (badminton)	78.2%
6. The Chernobyl nuclear accident	76.9%
7. The convictions of Chen Xiaomeng and Ye Zhifeng*	75.6%
8. China's launching of a communications satellite	75.6%
9. Criticism in news organs of Beijing's commercial services	75.4%
10. The big rainstorms in Beijing in July	74.4%

N = 12,000

*Chen Xiaomeng, convicted of raping many women, was the son of Chen Guodeng, the former first secretary of the Shanghai Municipal Party Committee; Ye Zhifeng, guilty of economic corruption, is the daughter of Ye Fei, former minister of communications and former PLA navy commander.

Source: Wang Qun, "Beijing qingniande xinxi yishi" (Beijing youth's consciousness of news), *Qingnian yanjiu*, no. 6(June 1987):20.

There are several points worth noting about this survey. First, we are told that a stratified random sample taken from Beijing's 2,370,000 young people was surveyed, but we are given little information about how the sample was drawn. Thus we cannot ascertain the percentage of workers, university or high-school students, intellectuals, and so forth among those whose questionnaires were analyzed. Second, the author emphasizes that youth rejected a priori authoritative voices in favor of what they themselves considered reasonable. Thus, despite reliance on the mass media for information, only 2.8 percent said that when they encountered something new, their first thought was to consider what the media or other people had said about it, while 66.5 percent said they would make their own judgment, based on objective reality. Likewise, if public opinion was heavily critical of a novel, 98 percent would insist on reading the book before expressing a judgment. Third, the author reflected on the increasing influence of the mass media, particularly television, in shaping the views of youth. Before 1980, the authorities could more easily control the management of information

Table 13.2
Which Topics Do You Most Enjoy and Most Frequently Discuss?

1. One's income and life	62.9%
2. Literary and art works	9.4%
3. Sports	29.6%
4. Personal relationships	30.1%
5. World affairs	27.7%
6. Production and leadership in one's own unit	23.2%
7. Spare-time study	19.3%
8. Politics in China	21.2%
9. The economy and its reform	16.9%
10. Appearance, attire, food and drink, health, and so forth	19.4%
11. Children's entrance into day-care center or school	12.1%
12. Production skills	20.2%
13. Entrance into the CCP or the Youth League, or being chosen an advanced worker	17.3%
14. Love and marriage	6.1%
15. Professional title and evaluation	9.3%
16. Other	7.9%

N = 12,000

NOTE: One's income and life would include such things as wages, bonuses, welfare, prices, housing, and family life.

SOURCE: Wang Qun, "Beijing qingniande xinxi yishi" (Beijing youth's consciousness of news), *Qingnian yanjiu*, no. 6(June 1987):19.

since so much of it was conveyed through direct contact. The decline in importance of meetings, documents, and youth league activities (see table 13.3) as sources of information had strengthened the independence of youth, but posed problems for authorities.

The Survey on Ideological and Political Work at Universities in Beijing

The most ambitious effort undertaken at this time was a large-scale survey on the state of ideological and political work in Beijing universities, conducted from April 1986 to July 1987, under the auspices of the municipal party committee and youth league, various universities, the municipal education union, and other organs. Thirty thousand questionnaires were dis-

Table 13.3
What Are Your Three Most Important Sources of Information?

1.	Newspapers	78.6%
2.	Television	69.4%
3.	Radio	60.5%
4.	Books and magazines	33.3%*
5.	Conversations	34.1%*
6.	Personal observation	6.5%*
7.	Youth League activities	7.6%*
8.	Meetings	5.0%
9.	Documents	4.7%
10.	Other	0.3%

N = 12,000

*Percentages as reported in original.

SOURCE: Wang Qun, "Beijing qingniande xinxi yishi" (Beijing youth's consciousness of news), *Qingnian yanjiu*, no. 6(June 1987):18.

tributed to students, teachers, and political-work cadres.[18] This study is particularly interesting because the even larger student demonstrations of December 1986–January 1987 occurred before the survey was completed, allowing the authorities to incorporate items relating to these events into the survey instrument.

Consistent with previous surveys, the data revealed a student body much more interested in private activities than in overtly political—or even collectivist—undertakings, as table 13.4 reveals. Authorities particularly lamented the condition of CYL organizations, which were said to be "very weak," offering members few activities. For example, 52 percent of league members felt that the work of their league branch had little influence in promoting collectivism in the classroom, while 75 percent had negative impressions regarding the ineffectiveness of branch cadres. Many did not

[18]The results, covering 375 pages, appear in Beijing Municipal Party Committee Research Office, ed., *Xin shiqi daxuesheng sixiang zhengzhi jiaoyu yanjiu* (Beijing: Beijing Normal University Press, 1988). Several chapters appear in translation in Stanley Rosen, ed., "Political Education (I) and (II)," *Chinese Education*, Fall 1989 and Spring 1990. The survey is also discussed in Stanley Rosen, "Political Education and Student Response: Some Background Factors Behind the 1989 Beijing Demonstrations," *Issues and Studies*, vol. 25, no. 10(Oct. 1989):12–39.

Table 13.4
The Interest Expressed by University Students in Beijing
in Participation in Various Kinds of Activities

Activity	Interested	Not interested	Rank
Sports	92.1%	6.5%	1
Social practice and investigation	90.1%	7.7%	2
Various reports and lectures	84.7%	13.2%	3
Work-study program	81.3%	16.4%	4
Art, literature, and entertainment	77.5%	10.2%	5
Work done for public in addition to one's job (*shehui gongzuo*)	73.5%	23.5%	6
Public activities (*shehui huodong*)	67.5%	29.7%	7
Voluntary labor	63.0%	33.5%	8
Activities of the CCP and the Youth League	52.3%	44.4%	9
Political study	35.0%	51.1%	10

SOURCE: Wang Sunyu *et al.*, "Daxueshengzhong dang de jianshe gongzuo chutan" (A preliminary exploration of party construction work among university students), in Beijing Municipal Party Committee Research Office, ed., *Xin shiqi daxuesheng sixiang zhengzhi jiaoyu yanjiu* (Research on ideological and political education of university students in the new period) (Beijing: Beijing Normal University Press, 1988), p. 209.

even want the league to be more active, with 23 percent hoping for as little activity as possible. In addition, 50 percent of the students would not carry out a league resolution with which they disagreed; 47 percent felt it did not matter whether or not one joined; and 60 percent were not even clear on the nature (*xingzhi*) of the league and its differences from other student organizations. The data on league members' attitudes toward the party and socialism showed a similarly "low" level of consciousness.[19]

The findings on student party members were better, but still problematic. In the early 1980s, as table 13.5 shows, few student party members were being recruited. One internal report from the Ministry of Education noted in 1983 that in some Beijing universities there were fewer student party members than the number of underground party members that had been there before 1949.[20] By 1986, 5.5 percent of Beijing undergraduates

[19]Ibid., pp. 18–19.
[20]For additional data, see "The Impact of Reform on the Attitudes and Behavior of Chinese Youth."

Table 13.5

University Students in Beijing and Party Membership

Year	New members recruited	Total number of university students	Total number of student party members	Percentage of student party members	Undergraduate student party members	Party members as percentage of all undergraduates	Graduate student party members	Party members as percentage of all graduate students	Party members among cadres taking specialized courses	Party members as percentage of such cadres
1980	318	83,032*	n/a	n/a	n/a	n/a	n/a	n/a	n/a	n/a
1981	803	98,103*	n/a	n/a	n/a	n/a	n/a	n/a	n/a	n/a
1982	1,420	94,864*	n/a	n/a	n/a	n/a	n/a	n/a	n/a	n/a
1983	1,455	90,894*	n/a	n/a	n/a	n/a	n/a	n/a	n/a	n/a
1984	3,096	105,307	8,678	8.25%	2,221	2.5%	2,097	23.05%	4,369	48.09%
1985	6,072	125,861	13,562	10.78%	4,410	4.4%	4,011	27.68%	5,141	45.99%
1986	5,879	137,282	15,833	11.50%	5,678	5.5%	5,507	32.00%	4,648	31.30%

*Achievement of Education in China (Beijing: People's Education Press, 1984), p. 263. The 1980–1983 figures for the total number of university students apply only to undergraduates.

SOURCE: Wang Sunyu et al., "Daxueshengzhong dangde jianshe gongzuo chutan" (A preliminary exploration of party construction work among university students), in Xin shiqi daxuesheng sixiang zhengzhi jiaoyu yanjiu (Beijing: Beijing Shifan daxue chubanshe, 1988), pp. 186–87.

Table 13.6
Question: Some of your friends have joined the party, others are striving
to do so. What is your observation and understanding of this?

Responses	Percent
They believe in communism and want to make a contribution.	4%
They think the party is good and are joining in order to be further educated.	10%
In reality they want a "party card," which they can use as capital to receive future benefits.	59%
Other responses	Omitted

N = 2,063

SOURCE: Zhao Yicheng, "Jiazhide chongtu" (Value conflict), *Weidinggao*, no. 8(April 25, 1988):19.

had joined the party but, as the survey showed, some nevertheless held unacceptable political ideas about the party and communism. It was also acknowledged that a minority had joined out of "impure motives." In fact, this was the widespread perception among students in general, as table 13.6, from a recent survey conducted among more than 2,000 students at eighteen Shanghai universities, reveals. Such skepticism over motives appears to be part of a larger suspicion that the party cannot improve its workstyle in the near future. In the Beijing survey, as table 13.7 shows, less than 10 percent were confident such improvement would occur in the next few years.

In separate chapters on graduate students and young teachers, it was clear that the official party line on the demonstrations of 1986–1987 had failed to convince a majority of them. For example, as table 13.8 shows, despite Fang Lizhi's expulsion from the party on Deng Xiaoping's direct orders in January 1987, and the subsequent vilification of his views in the press, apparently not a single respondent in the sample of more than 1,800 was willing to disdain (*tuoqi*) Fang's ideas. About 50 percent either could not understand the significance of the campaign against bourgeois liberalization, or felt it was unnecessary. In addition, 60 percent of the graduate students saw no improvement in party workstyle after the three-and-a-half-year rectification campaign, with some suggesting it had gotten worse. "A considerable portion" (*xiangdang yi bufen*) were also "strongly dissatisfied" (*qiangliede buman*) with the system of choosing cadres, with about 20 percent suggesting that the result of the reform was to allow the children of cadres to climb up the hierarchy, and a much larger number criticizing the use of "connections" (*guanxi*) or simple "blindness" (*mangmuxing*) as the main basis

Table 13.7
Views of University Students in Beijing About the CCP's Workstyle

Very confident	9.7%
Believe that it will basically improve, but not confident the improvement will take place in the next few years	44.6%
As for the improvement in party workstyle, one can only move a step at a time and see the results	26.1%
Lack confidence in any basic improvement	12.2%
No confidence	6.5%

N = 2,723

SOURCE: Wang Dianqing et al., "Daxuesheng sixiang zhuangkuang de diaocha fenxi" (An investigation and analysis of the ideology of university students), in Beijing Municipal Party Committee Research Office, ed., *Xinshiqi daxuesheng sixiang zhengzhi jiaoyu yanjiu* (Research on ideological and political education of university students in the new period) (Beijing: Beijing Normal University Press, 1988), p. 65.

Table 13.8
Views of Graduate Students in Beijing Regarding the Main Ideas
and Thought of Fang Lizhi

Should be praised highly	11.6%
Should be disdained	0%
Worthy of serious study	79.0%
Don't know	9.4%

N = 1,812

SOURCE: Yu Zerong, Wu Yanxi, et al., "Gaijin he jiaqiang yanjiusheng sixiang zhengzhi gong-zuode jianyi" (A proposal for improving and strengthening ideological and political work among graduate students" in *Xin Shiqi daxuesheng sixiang zhengzhi jiaoyu yanjiu* (Research on ideological and political education of university students in the new period) (Beijing: Beijing Normal University Press, 1988), p. 111.

for promotions.[21] Given these views, it is not surprising that graduate students played an important leadership role in the 1989 demonstrations.

The responses of young teachers 35 years old and under—who make up about one-third of the teaching staff in Beijing universities—were also worrisome to the leadership. For example, between 30.7 and 40.7 percent

---

[21]*Xin shiqi*, pp. 84–115.

expressed doubt about the necessity for the "Four Basic Principles" (Adherence to Socialism; the Dictatorship of the Proletariat; Rule by the Communist Party; and Marxism-Leninism–Mao Zedong Thought). Those who were either unclear about what constituted bourgeois liberalization, or felt it had nothing to do with them, or that criticism against it was unnecessary, constituted over 45 percent of the sample. Perhaps most ominously for the future was that "about two-thirds of the young teachers had differing levels of sympathy for the demonstrations," with the majority understanding the feeling that something was needed to speed up reform and democratization, even if they did not necessarily approve of the methods adopted.[22]

Nor did the students absorb the "proper" lessons from the fate of the demonstrations. In surveys done after things had quieted down, 62 percent of the undergraduates and 92 percent of the graduates saw the root cause of the demonstrations as either the corrupt party workstyle or the lack of democracy; moreover, 76 percent of the undergraduates and 71 percent of the graduates either felt that the demonstrations had promoted democratization, or at least had positive aspects as well as negative ones.[23]

Since the survey had been conducted to examine the state of ideological-political work in the universities, a key target group to be investigated were the 3,092 political-work cadres—only 37.6 percent of whom were full-time—at the 68 universities. Investigation of them would also help clear up some ambiguities stemming from the analysis of the 1985 demonstrations. At that time, some party committees had traced the problems, in part, to improper ideological work. For example, Wang Xuezhen, the party secretary at Beijing University (Beida), had noted the low pay and low status given political workers, "so that many people with ability didn't want to do this work."[24] On the other hand, Huang Shenglun, the deputy secretary of the party committee at Qinghua University, had felt that political workers on his campus were at ease in their work and were rather successful. For example, he pointed to the 7.2 percent of Qinghua undergraduates and the 31.9 percent of the graduate students who had joined the party.[25]

The survey results indicated the accuracy of the Beida assessment. Tables 13.9 and 13.10 reveal the demoralization of political-work cadres. For ex-

---

[22]Ibid., pp. 170–85.
[23]Ibid., p. 290.
[24]Wang Xuezhen, "Sigeyue gongzuode huigu" (Looking back on four months of work), in *A Collection of Some Speeches*, pp. 1–18.
[25]Huang Shenglun, "Gonggu he fazhan makesi zhuyi zhendi, jiji zuohao xuesheng sixiang zhengzhi gongzuo" (Consolidate and develop the ranks of Marxism, actively do a good job of student ideological and political work), in ibid., pp. 32–49.

Table 13.9
Desire of Political-Work Cadres in Universities in Beijing
to Continue in Their Work

University (College)	Want to continue in this work over a long period of time	Do not want to continue in this work over a long period of time	Do not want to engage in this work; hope to immediately transfer out of political work
Qinghua University	0%	73.3%	20.0%
Beijing University	12.5%	50.0%	37.5%
Beijing Normal University	7.7%	51.3%	25.6%
Beijing Engineering College	41.2%	23.5%	29.4%
Beijing Teachers' College	37.5%	37.5%	17.5%
Beijing Steel Institute	12.8%	79.5%	23.1%
China Capital Medical	50.0%	6.3%	27.6%
Beijing Forestry University	27.8%	55.6%	44.5%
Northern Communications University	37.5%	37.5%	25.0%

NOTE: Since some respondents opted for two categories, the totals may exceed 100% in some cases.

SOURCE: Li Zhixiang et al., "Daxuesheng sixiang zhengzhi jiaoyu gongzuo duiwude xianzhuang ji jianyi" (The current situation of ideological and political education workers and a proposal), in *Xin shiqi daxuesheng sixiang zhengzhi jiaoyu yanjiu* (Research on ideological and political education of university students in the new period) (Beijing: Beijing Normal University Press, 1988), p. 138.

ample, not a single individual engaged in such work at Qinghua University was willing to continue in the job over the long term, a situation common at the best universities. At Beijing Normal University, only 7.7 percent, and at Beida, only 12.5 percent expressed an interest in such work. Among the nine universities surveyed, the percentage of political-work cadres who requested immediate transfer to other kinds of work ranged from 17.5 to 44.5 percent. The most common reason given by those seeking a transfer was the low—and "inaccurate"—evaluation society gave to such work.[26]

The problem was not limited to political-work cadres at the university

---

[26]*Xin shiqi*, pp. 134–50.

Table 13.10

Reasons Why Respondents Do Not Want to Spend Their Lives Engaged in Political Work

University (College)	Does not receive a correct evaluation from society	Fear of future policy change	Cannot develop one's future	Material benefits low	Not suited to this work	Political work is meaningless; one is merely busy wasting time	Fear of making a political mistake	You cannot use what you've studied
Qinghua University	100 %	53.3%	6.7%	6.7%	26.7%	0%	0%	0%
Beijing University	43.8%	37.5%	31.3%	25.0%	31.3%	6.3%	0%	12.5%
Beijing Normal University	60.0%	56.4%	28.2%	10.3%	20.5%	5.1%	0%	15.4%
Beijing Engineering	64.7%	52.3%	23.5%	5.8%	29.4%	5.9%	5.8%	0%
Beijing Teachers'	55.0%	35.0%	30.0%	15.0%	32.0%	5.0%	10.0%	0%
Beijing Steel Institute	15.4%	46.2%	7.7%	15.4%	59.0%	41.0%	7.7%	0%
Capital Medical	25.0%	62.5%	25.0%	12.5%	25.0%	0%	0%	0%
Beijing Forestry	22.2%	50.0%	11.1%	11.1%	50.0%	50.0%	5.6%	0%
Northern Communications	87.5%	75.0%	25.0%	12.5%	25.0%	0%	12.5%	0%

SOURCE: Same as table 13.9.

level, however. An extensive survey of middle-school political workers conducted from April to June 1987 in Beijing turned up equally discouraging results. Not only was there a shortage of young workers, but those that were there did not really want to work in this field, with many leaving if they could.[27]

To deal with these problems, a number of policy changes were announced by mid-1987. Political standards were to be reintroduced for university enrollment, labor education was stepped up, and military training time was doubled and made compulsory. The much-maligned and demoralized political-work cadres had their status and benefits upgraded. Instructors responsible for political and ideological work, including CYL secretaries, were to be given the same titles, from assistant lecturer to full professor, as their academic counterparts. Moreover, their ranks were to be expanded, with the State Education Commission suggesting that one instructor of ideological and political education would be needed for every 150 college students.[28] Although it is clear that Deng Xiaoping set the tone for the conservative backlash in his remarks to leading officials on December 30, 1986, blaming the student unrest on "weakness in opposing bourgeois liberalization," some of the specific changes may be seen as responses to problems brought out in the Beijing survey.

According to interviewees, official policy toward the students was also shaped by a series of surveys conducted for the State Council by the State Commission for Restructuring the Economic System and its survey arm, the China Social Survey System. They recommended that the authorities improve the democratic atmosphere of the campuses. With more freedom inside, they argued, the students would be less willing to engage in off-campus demonstrations. Moreover, the authorities should seek to prevent the students from leaving the campuses in pursuit of their demands, warning the students that a clear distinction would be made between activities on and off the campus. This distinction should be backed up by a large contingent of off-campus police, when necessary, to discourage demonstrators from leaving the university grounds. These recommendations were largely adopted and, until April 1989, appear to have been reasonably successful. However, given the rising discontent, the pressure to move off campus became increasingly difficult to contain. For example, the number of applications for street demonstrations, mostly from students, swelled in 1988—there were more than 1,000 in the first half of the year alone—but very few were

---

[27]*Gaojiao yanjiu* (Beijing Normal Institute), no. 1(1988):74–80.
[28]For more details on the changes, see Rosen, "Students."

approved. One official admitted at the time that regardless of party efforts, another student movement was probably inevitable.[29]

Despite the conservative backlash, the policy changes of 1987 appear to have had little lasting effect on ideological-political work, at least to this point. For a time, interviewees report, students felt a necessity to attend their courses on politics. However, as the campaign against bourgeois liberalization wound down, attendance gradually petered out. Indeed, attendance of all classes began to decline, according to some, right after the 1986–1987 demonstrations, with an absentee rate above 30 percent for any course with political content and 20 percent for courses in the student's specialization.[30] "Business fever" and materialism began to "infect" the campuses, with more students typically showing up to hear a lecture on the making of pickled vegetables than for lectures on current events.[31] The "dropout fever," already serious at the primary- and high-school levels, began to claim graduate students as well. Some students deliberately created the conditions necessary to guarantee their expulsion from the university, thus enabling them to pursue business opportunities or study abroad.[32]

This widely reported decline in the academic environment of Chinese universities helped mask a contrary and even more significant development, one fostered by the decision to improve the democratic atmosphere on the campuses. With university authorities exercising tolerance and restraint during much of 1988 and the early part of 1989, democratic "salons" and discussion groups began to emerge on the campuses of Beijing. This brought distinguished intellectuals, including those critical of regime policies and priorities, into contact with the students. A wide variety of Western and heterodox ideas were introduced. Students now under arrest as leaders in the street demonstrations, such as Beijing University's Wang Dan, could trace their rise to their role in organizing these salons. In a sense, as the Chinese press noted after June 4, the authorities were losing control of the campuses.

The crisis in ideology—indeed, the deeper "moral crisis"—was a common theme, openly discussed, in the Chinese press throughout 1988 and

---

[29]*Daily Report*, Oct. 31, 1988, p. 33 (*Ming Pao*, Oct. 28).

[30]Zhu Wentao, "Ling ren shenside xiaoyuan 'xin chao': guanyu daxuesheng yanxuede xianzhuang he sikao" (A 'new tide' on campus that causes one to ponder: Thinking about the new situation in which students despise studies), *Shehui*, no. 8(Aug. 1988):8–11.

[31]*Daily Report*, Dec. 2, 1988, pp. 21–24 (*Liaowang Overseas Edition*, Nov. 21).

[32]Cheng Ying, "Dalu yanjiusheng zhengqu bei 'taotai'" (Mainland graduate students strive to "be eliminated through competition"), *Jiushi niandai*, Jan. 1989, pp. 27–29.

continuing into 1989. When Hu Qili met with four university presidents and party secretaries, one told him: "Nowadays, the whole classroom rocks with laughter whenever communism and Marxism-Leninism are mentioned . . ." [33] Political-economy instructors complained that their textbooks "had been the same for 40 years" and were now unrelated to reality.[34] Visitors noted the increasing similarities between the "dens of debauchery" in Hong Kong and Guangzhou and the ineffectiveness of periodic crackdowns.[35] Many reports in the press referred to the "grim" public-security situation, with the vice-minister of public security warning that things would remain grim for the next few years. The graduate-student unions at twelve Beijing universities submitted a petition to the Chinese People's Political Consultative Conference detailing the declining moral climate in the country, and asking the authorities to take action.[36] As a partial response, a national meeting on moral education recommended an increase in China's 5.28 million moral educators and, on December 25, 1988, the Party Central Committee issued a "Circular on Reforming and Strengthening Moral Education for Primary- and Secondary-School Students."[37]

Increasing the ideological work force and drafting documents was likely to be of little use, however. While everyone agreed that a problem existed, and that a new approach was needed, there was no consensus on how to instill moral and political values that would be appropriate to a developing commodity economy in the primary stage of socialism. The difficulties of such a task—and the clash between old and new concepts of politics and morality—was brought home most forcefully in the wide coverage given to the "Shekou Storm."[38]

In January 1988, invited by the local CYL branch, three well-known "professors" of propaganda from the Research Center on Ideological Education for Chinese Youth addressed 70 young workers in Shekou, in the

---

[33] *Daily Report,* Aug. 12, 1988, pp. 28–29 (*Zhejiang ribao,* July 31).

[34]*Daily Report,* Nov. 7, 1988, p. 3 (*Gongren ribao,* July 15).

[35]*Daily Report,* Dec. 6, 1988, pp. 26–27 (*Hong Kong Standard,* Dec. 5).

[36]*Daily Report,* Jan. 27, 1989, pp. 13–14 (Hong Kong, *Wen wei po,* Jan. 26); *Daily Report,* April 10, 1989, pp. 33–34 (*Zhongguo tongxun she,* April 5).

[37]*Daily Report,* Jan. 24, 1989, pp. 20–24 (*Renmin ribao,* Jan. 17); *Daily Report,* June 10, 1988, p. 23 (Xinhua, June 1).

[38]The following discussion draws from *Daily Report,* Sept. 21, 1988, pp. 53–60 (*Renmin ribao,* Aug. 6 and 29, and Sept. 14); *Daily Report,* Sept. 28, 1988, pp. 68–70 (*Renmin ribao,* Sept. 3); *Daily Report,* Oct. 26, 1988, pp. 19–21 (*Jingjixue zhoubao,* Oct. 2); *China News Analysis,* no. 1374(Dec. 15, 1988); Chang Tianyu, "'Shekou fengbo' shuomingle shenma?" (What does the 'Shekou Storm' signify?), *Guangjiaojing,* Sept. 1988, pp. 94–95.

Shenzhen special economic zone (SEZ). What made the symposium news-worthy was the unexpected attack on the content and form of traditional ideological work by members of the audience. Two cultures had collided. Youth in Shekou had no patience with what one called "empty sermons," preferring "a discussion of concrete questions." The propagandists were used to neither dialogue nor discourtesy. They could not have expected to be challenged on positions they considered unassailable. For example, one professor had earlier criticized as "gold diggers" those who came to the SEZs to make money; rather, they "should contribute a large portion of their income to the state to be spent on public welfare." This smacked of "leftism" to some youth, who pointed out that making money was fine, and, in fact, gold diggers had developed the American West.

Confronted with what they took to be the familiar sanctimonious, self-righteous style of the propagandists, the youth seemed to enjoy flaunting their freedom and Shekou's "foreignness." One reportedly noted that "the central government is far away. Even if I swear at you, no one will come to interfere, and my Hong Kong boss will not fire me because of this." Another stated: "We find newspaper propaganda disgusting. It says Shenzhen takes the socialist road with Chinese characteristics. What Chinese characteristics are actually there? The characteristics of Shenzhen are foreign characteristics!" One propagandist asked whether the troublesome youth challenging him dared to reveal his name. To the audience's great amusement, the young man presented his business card.

Between August 15 and September 16, 1988, the *People's Daily* published 35 letters—out of the thousands received—commenting on the Shekou Storm. The propagandists were given a chance to reiterate and defend their style and their views. They also noted their own personal health, family difficulties, and lack of interest in financial remuneration. In comments that could have been made by any political-work cadre, one noted: "When ideological and political work is difficult, we who work on the front line have given so much and yet have not been properly assessed." Most poignantly, he ended with a plea, saying, "We admit that we need to improve. However, even if there are weaknesses and mistakes in our work, shouldn't people help in a positive way and as comrades?"

The "Social Mood": A Rising Tide of Discontent

If Chinese authorities were reconciled to the likelihood of periodic student unrest—indeed, their surveys indicated that they should be—their greater concern has always been with the spread of such unrest from the campuses to the streets, factories, and office buildings. This concern escalated from June 1988 to June 1989, as city dwellers have voiced increasing dissatisfaction with official corruption and inflation. Thus, after students from Beida took to the streets in June 1988, with some, including children of senior cadres, entering factories to "educate" the workers on party corruption, an extraordinary warning broadcast on national television urged university authorities to control their campuses and severely punish those who violated school discipline.[39]

The rising tide of public discontent has been well documented in a series of fourteen longitudinal social surveys conducted by the Chinese Economic System Reform Research Institute.[40] During the course of the surveys, the researchers noted an increasing "pluralism" in both discontent and desire. In addition to dissatisfaction over rising prices, there was also a rising tide of opposition to abuses of power to make private gains, giving jobs only to relatives, inequality in pay, and so forth. Similarly, reform wishes were no longer limited to rising income, but covered a wide variety of political, social, and economic issues. Throughout 1986, inequality of opportunity registered as the public's leading complaint, intensifying with each survey. For example, a survey carried out in February 1986 revealed that only 29.3 percent felt that the reforms offered equal opportunities to all. At the same time, the surveys revealed a steadily increasing disparity among different social groups with regard to aspirations and attitudes toward the reforms.

More recent studies of urban residents show a continuation of these trends. For example, in November 1986, 73.8 percent of those surveyed expressed dissatisfaction with inflation, rising to 79.9 percent in May 1987, to 83.2 percent in October, and to 92.1 percent in May 1988. Moreover, the perception of inequality of opportunity exacerbated social contradictions and convinced people that society was unjust. For example, as the surveyors noted, individual entrepreneurs could pass increased costs on to consumers or shift to more lucrative trades; government cadres could use their authority to profiteer in the sale of goods and materials, enjoy preferential rights in contracting to run or in leasing enterprises, establish profit-making companies, and so forth. Workers, particularly those in state enterprises, and most intellectuals, had no such opportunities.

The public not only saw an unjust society being created, but one in which winners and losers were being designated in a seemingly arbitrary manner. Workers doing similar kinds of work might be rewarded very differently, depending on governmental deregulation. This often led to

---

[39]*Washington Post*, June 12, 1988.
[40]The following two paragraphs draw from Rosen, "Public Opinion."

slowdowns, with the state commonly compelled to respond, eventually, with wage increases. For example, following the 1984 urban reforms, a taxi driver in Beijing could earn 500–600 yuan a month. Bus drivers, limited to around 100 yuan, were upset, and many tried to shift to driving taxis. The bus company, however, would only let them leave if they paid a 2,000 yuan "training fee." Those unable or unwilling to pay started a slowdown. Eventually, they were given a 30 yuan increase, and the pay of taxi drivers was reduced. In response, taxi drivers organized their own work stoppage. Similar slowdowns affected postal and market workers, among others.[41] For the past few years, public dissatisfaction with the "unfair" system of income distribution has been widely addressed in the press.[42]

Mass discontent over unclear and changeable government policies has also produced, as in the past, evocative popular ballads (*koutou wenxue*) to describe the inequalities. The following stanza is an example of such a song.[43]

Dangde luxian xiang taiyang
Zhaodao nali nali liang
Dangde zhengce xiang yueliang
Chuyi shiwu bu yiyang

The party line is like the sun
Wherever it shines will be bright
The party's policies are like the moon
The fifteenth of the month will be different from the first

The public perception that party leaders lack the answers to China's problems has been documented in many surveys. One recent poll showed that 58.3 percent of respondents had "very little confidence" in the success of the plan to reduce this year's price increase to a level markedly lower than

---

[41]Fang Lizhi, "Reform and Intellectuals," *China Spring Digest,* March/April 1987, p. 31. On problems with taxis in Beijing, see Hu Shilong, "Beijing chuzuche weihe gao buhao?" (How is it that the Beijing taxi situation is in a mess?), *Guangjiaojing,* March 1988, pp. 52–55; on recent protests by taxi drivers in Xian and Chongqing, see *Daily Report,* June 30, 1988, p. 66 (*Zhongguo xinwen she,* June 29) and Jan. 3, 1989, p. 64 (*Zhongguo xinwen she,* Dec. 29, 1988).
[42]*Daily Report,* March 3, 1989, pp. 40–44 (*Jingji yanjiu,* Jan. 1989); Dec. 8, 1988, pp. 45–47 (*Ban yue tan,* Nov. 10); Nov. 8, 1988, pp. 41–42 (*China Daily,* Nov. 5); Nov. 7, 1988, pp. 3–4 (*Gongren ribao,* July 15).
[43]As reported by a Beijing informant. On this general subject, see Wang Hailun, "Koutou wenxue re yu quanmin laosaochao" (Ballad fever and the tide of mass discontent), *Jiushi niandai,* Feb. 1989:62–64.

last year's and are "very deeply worried" about the plan's prospects.[44] At the same time, there is no shortage of suggested solutions to political or economic reform. One recent visitor distinguished five groups of political reformers: (1) idealists promoting Western liberal democracy; (2) conservatives, or "economic determinist realists"; (3) "political system determinist realists"; (4) "cultural enlightenmentists"; and (5) "new authoritarians."[45]

Leaving aside the threat of inflation, recent opinion polls show that the absence of ideological orientation, leading to confused social values, is the issue of most concern to Chinese citizens. Those conducting the polls argue that the public wants to be "grasped" by a new, authoritative set of ideas and values, that they are confused by all the new Western ideas and economic reforms of the last ten years, and are finding it difficult to adjust to a relatively free society.[46] The ideological confusion also comes through in the controversies appearing in the press, as the Shekou Storm showed. The ideological ironies can even be amusing. In Liaoning province, the millionaire who runs the largest private enterprise in the northeast, employing 240 workers, has applied to join the Communist Party. Since no one has dared to make a decision, the provincial party committee's Organization Department has thrown the matter open for general discussion.[47] The perennial hero, Lei Feng, has been modernized and transformed into a proponent of capitalist-style reform by the news agency Xinhua. One report on Lei, the investor, noted that the $27 he deposited in an interest-bearing bank account in 1961 would have nearly doubled by now.[48]

The lack of appeal of a recycled Lei Feng to an audience of skeptical youth is, of course, neither new nor particularly significant. Far more ominous, however, is the decline in the party's key transmission belts—notably the CYL and the trade unions—which are expected to channel, as well as contain, demands to the leadership. Even the open press has discussed the failure of the league and the unions. One recent report, addressing the failure of the league as a mass organization, noted that "the fatal weakness of CYL organizations is their being unable to represent the specific interests of young people, thus losing their attractiveness and appeal."[49] League cadres, as well,

---

[44]*Daily Report*, Feb. 23, 1989, pp. 34–35 (*Zhongguo xinwen she*, Feb. 20).

[45]Qiu Chuiliang, "Dalu Zhishijie zhenggai wupai" (The five schools of political reform among mainland intellectual circles), *Jiushi niandai*, Feb. 1989:22–23.

[46]*Daily Report*, Dec. 16, 1988, pp. 45–46 (*South China Morning Post*, Dec. 16).

[47]*Daily Report*, April 6, 1989, pp. 34–35 (*Zhongguo xinwen she*, March 31).

[48]*Wall Street Journal*, April 5, 1988; Huang Mingsong and Yang Minqing, "Jiaru Lei Feng huo dao jintian" (If Lei Feng had lived until today), *Rencai kaifa*, no. 5(1988):22–23.

[49]*Daily Report*, Jan. 11, 1989, pp. 31–32 (*Ban yue tan*, Dec. 10, 1988).

noting that fewer CYL and political cadres have been promoted in an era when economic work and management is stressed, say "there is no future for a CYL cadre." In the demonstrations of April–May 1989, of course, a key issue dividing the students and the leadership was the latter's insistence that any dialogue be conducted through officially sanctioned youth organizations, while the students sought official recognition for their own, independent organization.

A similar—if less visible—fate has befallen the trade unions. Official reports admit that "there remain many problems in trade-union work and resentment has been widespread among workers."[50] An investigation in Shenyang found that fewer than 20 percent of the workers willingly attended union-sponsored political-study meetings; over 80 percent gritted their teeth and participated out of fear of losing their bonuses.[51] One top official noted that the unions are tinted with "a strong official and administrative color" and have long been "a party and government subsidary" owing to leftist influence.[52] His final comment that "the trade unions have not fulfilled their social functions very well and have more or less become separated from the masses" reflected the results of a large-scale national survey conducted by the unions in 1986.[53] Table 13.11, based on that survey, reveals the generally low opinion workers held of the unions. Only 9 percent gave the unions a strongly positive assessment. The large size of the sample—647,112 valid returned questionnaires out of 770,000 that were distributed (84.04 percent)—compels attention.

Conclusion

Chinese authorities have come to expect periodic student unrest, particularly around the anniversaries of politically significant events in which youth had been active, when the party leadership is divided over policy direction, and

---

[50]*Daily Report,* Jan. 23, 1989, pp. 26–29 (*Gongren ribao,* Dec. 28); Li Fen, "Zhongguo gonghuide wenti" (Problems of China's trade unions), *Guangjiaojing,* no. 12(Dec. 1988):52–55.
[51]*Ban yue tan,* Aug. 25, 1988, pp. 22–23.
[52]*Daily Report,* Nov. 2, 1988, pp. 24–25 (Xinhua, Nov. 2).
[53]The report has been published for internal circulation under the title *Zhongguo zhigong duiwu zhuangkuang diaocha* (An investigation into the situation of China's workers and staff) (Beijing: Gongren chubanshe, 1987). The report runs to 596 pages; selected chapters are translated in Stanley Rosen, ed., "The General Trade Union Survey of China's Workers and Staff," *Chinese Economic Studies,* Summer 1989.

Table 13.11
What Do You Think of the Work Done by Trade Unions?

Responses	Percentage
They are able to speak for workers and do things for their interests.	9.1%
They have done some good things, some solid things for the workers.	30.2%
They make a lot of appeals but do few solid things.	17.5%
Except for collecting dues, and some cultural and sports activities, we cannot see any function of the trade unions.	24.8%
Trade unions rarely listen to workers' opinions or appeals.	8.9%
Trade unions don't resemble mass organizations; rather, they are more like government organs.	8.6%

N = 647,112

SOURCE: Wu Shouhui and Guo Jinhua, "Zhigong dui gonghuide pingjia he qiwang" (Workers' evaluation of and hopes for trade unions), *Weidinggao*, no. 3(Feb. 10, 1987):10.

after some extraordinary, unexpected event.[54] The sudden death of Hu Yaobang amidst preparations for the impending 70th anniversary of the May Fourth Movement thus created the ideal opportunity for the students. Since Hu had been deposed in part because his alleged policies of "bourgeois liberalization" had led to the demonstrations of 1986–1987, and since he nevertheless retained a seat on the Politburo, the students could make a symbolic political statement while mourning a top party official.

But the atmosphere on the campuses was already volatile in the months prior to Hu's death, with tension at its height around the thirteenth anniversary of the April Fifth Tiananmen Square Incident. Ding Shisun, then president of Beida, had suggested to an interviewer in February that campus unrest was perhaps inevitable and also had a positive aspect, showing that college students were concerned about national affairs. He urged that such students not be excessively reproached.[55]

As the 70th anniversary of the May Fourth Movement drew closer, the Chinese leadership vied with liberal intellectuals and students to set the agenda for the anniversary celebrations. On several occasions, students at

---

[54]Milton D. Yeh, "Student Unrest in Mainland China," *Issues and Studies*, July 1988:9–11.

[55]*Daily Report*, Feb. 21, 1989, p. 26 (*Zhongguo xinwen she*, Feb. 16).

Beida tested the limits of official tolerance by participating in "unauthorized" meetings, putting up a big-character poster, and submitting a petition to the university's president, all part of their appeal for an improved democratic atmosphere on and off campus.[56]

The CCP sought to monopolize the anniversary celebrations by organizing a marathon series of commemorative events on the "orthodox theme" of patriotism and the party's role in carrying forward the May Fourth spirit. Aware that the issue of democratization could not be completely avoided, the CCP attempted to funnel all such discussion and activities through "legitimate" channels, such as the CYL and mass organizations.[57]

In the end, the party failed because of its increasing estrangement from society and its loss of moral authority. The change in the public mood from 1987–1989 had been dramatic. Deng Xiaoping, hailed as a great reformer only several years earlier, was now considered a key obstacle to further political change. The impending visit of the 57-year-old Mikhail Gorbachev for the first Sino-Soviet summit in 30 years highlighted the differences between what students saw as a dynamic regime unafraid to experiment with daring democratic reforms, and a Chinese leadership under siege, whose highest value was stability, and which feared its own people. Indeed, Deng's reputed comments to Li Peng on April 25 seemed to confirm that assessment. He ended the meeting with a tragically prophetic assurance, insisting that the student demonstrations could be brought under control, and noting that "the students may be acting out of line, but the broad masses of workers and peasants are on our [the party's] side. Even if the workers and peasants were to join the students, we can still rely on more than three million soldiers to maintain law and order.[58] Chairman Mao could not have said it better.

---

[56]*Daily Report*, April 3, 1989, pp. 38–39 (*Hong Kong Standard*, April 3); April 4, 1989, pp. 33–34 (*Ming pao*, April 4); April 6, 1989, pp. 20–21 (*South China Morning Post*, April 6); March 8, 1989, pp. 3–5 (*Ching pao*, Jan. 1989); *Cheng ming*, April 1989, pp. 9–10.

[57]*Daily Report*, April 6, 1989, p. 23 (*South China Morning Post*, April 6).

[58]*Daily Report*, April 27, 1989, pp. 21–22 (*South China Morning Post*, April 27). For an account of how senior Communist Party leaders defied Deng's orders for a crackdown, see the *Asian Wall Street Journal*, May 15, 1989, p. 10.

The Evolution of Chinese Politics, 1949–1989

Even without the tragedy in Tiananmen Square, 1989 would have been a time for a reconsideration of the issue of change and continuity in Chinese politics. The 40th anniversary of the establishment of the People's Republic, and the 70th anniversary of the May Fourth Movement of 1919, would inevitably have stimulated a re-examination of the areas in which China's political life has remained rather constant under Communist rule, and the ways in which it has changed.

But the mass movement that swept across urban China in April and May of 1989, and its bloody suppression in Beijing in early June, have given these questions even greater urgency. Much of what happened in the streets of Beijing, Shanghai, and other major cities was unprecedented since the establishment of the People's Republic in 1949: the scale of the protests, the tactics and demands of the demonstrators, the degree of public support for the student movement, and the imposition of martial law. In other respects, however, the events of 1989 had an all-too-familiar ring to them. Mass demonstrations calling for the ouster or rehabilitation of various party and government leaders, intense factional struggle within Chinese Communist leadership, the intervention of the People's Liberation Army in civilian politics, the forcible suppression of popular protest, the denunciation of heterodox ideas as "bourgeois liberalism" and the labeling of political opposition as "counterrevolutionary conspiracy"—all these are echoes of earlier developments in Chinese politics. The blend of old and new in China at the end of the Tengist era underlines the need for a consideration of change and continuity in the country's political life.

This essay is a broad review of the major trends in Chinese politics since 1949. It is organized not chronologically, but around some of the principal structural features of the Chinese political system that emerged in the early postrevolutionary period. Identifying the defining characteristics of Chinese politics is always an arbitrary exercise, and features that may appear to be distinct analytically are often intertwined in reality. Still, I have selected five dimensions that I believe to be the most critical to an understanding of the Chinese political system since 1949:

- the promulgation of an official ideology and the regular criticism of heterodox ideas and those who have advanced them;
- the mobilization of mass support for regime policies, coupled with the suppression of dissent and the absence of mechanisms for the independent articulation of political demands;
- a highly politicized bureaucracy with low levels of technical competence or formal procedures;
- a relatively decentralized political system, with substantial power delegated to, or arrogated by, provincial and regional units of governance; and
- frequent struggle among factions within the leadership of the Chinese Communist Party, largely as the result of the lack of institutionalized procedures for political succession.

In each of these five areas, we will discuss the evolution of the Chinese political system from the establishment of Communist rule in 1949 to the death of Mao Tse-tung in 1976. We will then examine the process of political reform in the post-Mao era, asking whether China has experienced fundamental change along any of these dimensions. We will conclude with a periodization of Chinese politics since 1949 and a consideration of the prospects for the future.

Tutelary Politics

The first defining feature of Chinese Communist politics has been its tutelary quality. Like earlier Chinese governments before it, the Chinese Communist Party has regarded the promulgation of an official ideology and the criticism of any heterodox tendencies as critical instruments of national political rule.

The key elements of tutelary politics were put into place soon after the establishment of the People's Republic in 1949. The most basic element was Marxism-Leninism-Mao Tse-tung Thought, established as the guiding ideology of both the Chinese Communist Party and the new Chinese state. Although drawing on the works of Marx, Engels, Lenin, and Stalin, Chinese Communist leaders had asserted from the 1930s and 1940s their intention to determine the tenets of party doctrine independently of Moscow. Chinese ideology always had, therefore, a distinctively Chinese tone, with a more populist, egalitarian, and agrarian flavor than its Soviet counterpart.[1]

To transmit this official ideology to all sectors of society and to secure understanding and acceptance of its principle components, a nationwide network of propaganda and political education was created in the early 1950s. This network included central organs for the formulation and explanation of ideology, such as the party propaganda department, the Higher Party School and the theoretical journals of party committees at various levels. It also comprised the national and local media—first print and then increasingly electronic—all of which served as mouthpieces of the party. Perhaps most important, the party established a network of political study groups in mass organizations, places of employment, and even urban residential neighborhoods, so that ideological messages could be conveyed to virtually all of China's adult citizens directly and individually.[2]

The promulgation of official ideology was accompanied by the creation of controls to prevent and sanctions against heterodox ideas. Press censorship was instituted, with a ban against independent media and postpublication review of official party and government organs. Laws were enacted against counterrevolutionary speech, as well as counterrevolutionary behavior. Periodic "thought-reform" campaigns were launched throughout the 1950s and early 1960s, directed in the early 1950s against officials remaining from the Nationalist government, then in 1957–1958 against intellectuals and

---

[1]On the doctrine of the Chinese Communist Party in the early years of the People's Republic, see Arthur Cohen, *The Communism of Mao Tse-Tung* (Chicago, Ill.: University of Chicago Press, 1964); John Wilson Lewis, *Leadership in Communist China* (Ithaca, N.Y.: Cornell University Press, 1963); Stuart Schram, *The Political Thought of Mao Tse-tung* (New York: Praeger, 1963); and some of the essays in Benjamin I. Schwartz, *Communism and China: Ideology in Flux* (New York: Atheneum, 1970).

[2]The propaganda network of the Mao Tse-tung Communist Party is discussed in Franklin Houn, *To Change a Nation: Propaganda and Indoctrination in Communist China* (New York: The Free Press, 1961); Alan P.L. Liu, *Communications and National Integration in Communist China* (Berkeley: University of California Press, 1971); Martin King Whyte, *Small Groups and Political Rituals in China* (Berkeley: University of California Press, 1974); and Franklin T.C. Yu, *Mass Persuasion in Communist China* (New York: Praeger, 1964).

students who had participated in the Hundred Flowers Movement, and then, during the Socialist Education Movement of the early 1960s, against ordinary peasants, workers, and bureaucrats as well.[3]

In the 25 years between the establishment of this tutelary system in the early 1950s and the death of Mao Tse-tung in 1976, there were times—such as the Hundred Flowers Movement of 1956–1957 and the so-called Second Hundred Flowers period of the early 1960s—during which restrictions on intellectual inquiry were relaxed, and during which the party asked both for new ideas on matters of public policy and for criticism of the party's performance. This reflected some awareness that tight controls on political discussion and on intellectual activity dampened the enthusiasm of the nation's intellectuals, prevented the identification of pressing national problems, and hampered the development of effective solutions to major national issues.

However, both of these experiments with political liberalization produced criticism of prevailing policies, institutions, and doctrines that was more intense than party leaders could bear. Each of these two periods was followed by renewed political purge and ideological rectification. And, viewing the quarter-century of Maoist rule as a whole, the broad tendency was for an intensification of the tutelary character of the Chinese political system, particularly during the Cultural Revolution.

One area of pronounced change concerned the content of official doctrine. In the mid-1950s, once the nationalization of industry and the collectivization of agriculture had been completed, it appeared that Chinese Communist doctrine might become an ideology of modernization, rather than one of revolution. After the Hundred Flowers period of 1956–1957, however, Mao Tse-tung began to place emphasis on continued struggle against "class enemies," both within the intellectual community and within the party itself. At the same time, party doctrine began to take on a more utopian cast, emphasizing egalitarianism and hard struggle, disparaging material incentives and consumerism, and negating both markets and private entrepreneurship. The need for continued struggle against class enemies, to prevent the emergence of revisionist tendencies in the economy, became the principal feature of later Maoist ideology.[4]

---

[3]The classic treatment of thought reform remains Robert Lifton, *Thought Reform and the Psychology of Totalism: A Study of "Brainwashing" in China* (New York: Norton, 1961).

[4]On the evolution of Maoist doctrine, see Maurice Meisner, *Marxism, Maoism, and Utopianism: Eight Essays* (Madison: University of Wisconsin Press, 1982); Stuart R. Schram, "From the 'Great Union of the Popular Masses' to the 'Great Alliance,'"

To Mao Tse-tung and the ideologues surrounding him in the 1960s and 1970s, these tendencies toward revisionism were endemic in virtually all sectors of society, from the bureaucracy to the peasantry. To combat those tendencies, ideological considerations had to be taken into account in all decisions. No sphere of activity—not economic management, nor scientific research, nor artistic endeavor—was held to be exempt from ideological restrictions. The compilation in the early 1960s of the *Quotations* from Mao's works, and its publication as a pocket-sized volume bound in durable red plastic, produced a compact and comprehensible summary of doctrinal considerations, suitable for constant reference by all members of society. In this sense, the late Maoist period witnessed an expansion of the scope of doctrine, as well as a redefinition of its content.

The more militant tone in official doctrine in the later Maoist period, and the insistence that politics be placed "in command" of all areas of life, were accompanied by a tightening of the controls inherent in the tutelary system. Those intellectuals and officials labeled as "rightists" or "reactionaries" during the party's various rectification campaigns were dismissed from their positions and, during the Cultural Revolution, were often subjected to physical persecution. Restrictions on the mass media were intensified to the point that, in the 1970s, only a few national newspapers or journals were being published, and those that remained in operation were printing banal exegeses of official doctrine. The amount of time devoted to political education steadily increased and, in the early 1970s, university curricula were rewritten to stress ideological rather than academic content. Tens of thousands of intellectuals and officials, and millions of students, were sent to the countryside to engage in "education through labor" at the grass-roots.

Paradoxically, the exacerbation of the tutelary features of Chinese politics produced not greater commitment to the party's doctrine, but rather a thoroughgoing crisis of faith in official ideology. To the extent that, using Karl Mannheim's terms, doctrine remained "utopian," setting forth a vision of a new society that the party was struggling to achieve, the calamities of the Great Leap Forward and the Cultural Revolution suggested that that vision was more a nightmare than an attractive set of "wish-images." Con-

---

China Quarterly, no. 49(Jan.–March 1972):88–105; Schram, "Mao Tse-tung and the Theory of the Permanent Revolution," *China Quarterly*, no. 46(April–June 1971):221–44; Schram, "Introduction: The Cultural Revolution in Historical Perspective," in Stuart R. Schram, ed., *Authority, Participation, and Cultural Change in China* (Cambridge, Eng.: Cambridge University Press, 1973), pp. 1–108; and John Bryan Starr, *Continuing the Revolution: The Political Thought of Mao* (Princeton, N.J.: Princeton University Press, 1977).

versely, to the extent that doctrine had become an "ideology," rationalizing the prevailing distribution of power in China, it was increasingly unable to legitimate the economic stagnation and political persecution characteristic of the late Maoist period. Over time, commitment to doctrine was giving way to skepticism, and conviction was yielding to cant.[5]

In the post-Mao era, in an effort to resolve this crisis, the Chinese tutelary system was significantly liberalized along several dimensions. First, the content of ideology was revised to stress modernization over class struggle and socialist democracy over proletarian dictatorship. The economic role of markets, material incentives, private and collective ownership, foreign trade, and foreign investment was reaffirmed, while virtually all the doctrinal concepts associated with the later years of Maoism were explicitly repudiated. Second, the role of doctrine was attenuated. The party acknowleged that a wider range of policy decisions could be taken on pragmatic grounds, and artistic creation, scientific investigation, and intellectual inquiry were less constrained by ideological considerations than they had been during the Maoist era.[6]

Third, the official monopoly over communication was relaxed. Political study sessions were held less frequently and affected fewer sectors of society. A wider range of books and periodicals was published, and these were subject to less stringent censorship than had been the case in the 1970s. Chinese— especially those knowledgeable in a foreign language—were able to get more ready access to news and information from abroad, from both foreign broadcasts and the Western press. And, finally, the sanctions against heterodoxy were also reduced. Those criticized for unorthodox political ideas could still be dismissed from administrative positions or party membership,

---

[5]On the distinction between "ideology" and "utopia," see Karl Mannheim, *Ideology and Utopia: An Introduction to the Sociology of Knowledge* (New York: Harcourt, Brace and World, 1966). On the transformation of political attitudes in China from commitment to cant, see Richard H. Solomon, "From Commitment to Cant: The Evolving Functions of Ideology in the Revolutionary Process," in Chalmers Johnson, ed., *Ideology and Politics in Contemporary China* (Seattle: University of Washington Press, 1973), pp. 47–77.

[6]On the evolution of Chinese Communist doctrine since the death of Mao, see Bill Brugger, ed., *Chinese Marxism in Flux, 1978–84* (White Plains, N.Y.: M. E. Sharpe, 1985); William A. Joseph, *The Critique of Ultra-Leftism in China, 1958–1981* (Stanford: Stanford University Press, 1984); Stuart R. Schram, "'Economics in Command?' Ideology and Policy Since the Third Plenum, 1978–84," *China Quarterly*, no. 99(Sept. 1984):417–61; and An-chia Wu, "The Theory of the 'Initial Stage of Socialism': Background, Tasks, and Impact," *Issues and Studies*, vol. 24, no. 7(July 1988):12–32.

but in general were not subject to more serious punishment. The political labels imposed before 1976 were, in most cases, removed in the late 1970s and early 1980s.

As the events of 1989 demonstrated, China's tutelary system remains largely in place despite the changes of the post-Mao era. To begin with, there is still no tolerance of ideological diversity. The content of official doctrine may have been revised, and the scope of activities subject to ideological restriction may have been reduced, but the political system still attempts to maintain the vestiges of ideological orthodoxy. The "four cardinal principles"—commitment to Marxism, acceptance of party leadership, maintenance of the existing state structure, and pursuit of socialism—continue to place limits on permissible political discourse. Although political education has been relaxed, and although there are fewer attempts to secure active support for official ideology, citizens are still forbidden to publicly advocate any alternative systems of political belief. There is, to use Thomas Metzger's phrase, no concept of the "autonomous self" in Chinese Communist political philosophy. Rather, the cultivation of "correct" ways of thinking is still regarded as a fundamental prerogative of the party.

Relatedly, there have been continuing campaigns against ideological heterodoxy, including the campaign against liberalism in 1979, the campaign against spiritual pollution in 1983–1984, and the campaigns against bourgeois liberalization in 1987 and again in 1989. To be sure, compared with the rectification movements of the Maoist years, the campaigns in the post-Mao era have encountered increasing resistance and evasion within the academic and intellectual communities, have imposed relatively light sanctions on most dissidents, and have generally been of short duration and limited impact. But they reflect the determination of the Chinese Communist Party to maintain at least the vestiges of a tutelary system.[7] The wave of political suppression in 1989 also revealed that the mechanisms of ideological control—censorship of the mass media, political study sessions organized by local party committees, military training of students, and "education through labor" in the countryside—may have been relaxed or deactivated earlier in the 1980s, but had not been completely dismantled.

Perhaps the most important continuity with the recent past is that the

---

[7]The continuing rectification campaigns in the post-Mao era are discussed in Perry Link, "Introduction: On the Mechanics of the Control of Literature in China," in Link, ed., *Stubborn Weeds: Popular and Controversial Chinese Literature After the Cultural Revolution* (Bloomington: Indiana University Press, 1983), pp. 1–28; and Judith Shapiro and Liang Heng, *Cold Winds, Warm Winds: Intellectual Life in China Today* (Middletown, Conn.: Wesleyan University Press, 1986).

crisis of confidence which characterized the country in the late 1970s and early 1980s had not at all been overcome. The revised official doctrine—variously described as "socialism with Chinese characteristics" or the ideology to carry China through the "primary stage of socialism"—has generated little popular interest, let alone enthusiasm. Instead, China is characterized by an absence of a compelling or attractive public political philosophy. A sense that the government and people of China have been cast morally adrift is widely believed to be one of the causes of the corruption that has become endemic in the country, which in turn was one of the roots of the demonstrations that swept across so many major cities earlier this year. The suppression of that movement, in turn, has only served to intensify the party's lack of legitimacy in the eyes of much of the population.[8]

Mobilizational Politics

A second characteristic of Chinese politics under Communist rule has been a mobilizational relationship between the Chinese people and their government. Citizens have been treated as subjects, rather than active participants; their responsibility has been to give active support to government policy, not to issue demands that would shape government action.

The mechanism of ideological education described above obviously supported and reinforced the mobilizational features of Chinese politics. Beyond this, the mobilization of support and the suppression of demands were conducted through a further set of political institutions that were put in place during the consolidation of political power by the Chinese Communist Party in the early 1950s. Drawing heavily on the Leninist model of political organization, the party demanded near-universal membership of adult Chinese in a network of officially sanctioned mass organizations and professional associations, all under the leadership of the Chinese Communist Party.[9] Similarly, the collectivization of agriculture and the nationalization of industry facilitated the penetration of virtually every workplace by branches and committees of the party and made each unit dependent on the central-

---

[8]On the crisis of confidence in post-Mao China, see Peter R. Moody, Jr., "Spiritual Crisis in Contemporary China: Some Preliminary Explorations," *Issues and Studies*, vol. 23, no. 6(June 1987):34–66; and Orville Schell, *To Get Rich Is Glorious* (New York: Pantheon, 1984).

[9]The opportunities for political participation in the pre–Cultural Revolution period are reviewed in James Townsend, *Political Participation in Communist China* (Berkeley: University of California Press, 1967).

planning apparatus of the state. The expansion of the public-security and internal-intelligence apparatus—the details of which remain inadequately understood—provided yet another channel of political control.

However, the mechanisms of political control in Communist China went beyond those envisioned in the purely Leninist model of political mobilization. As recent scholarship has persuasively demonstrated, the reorganization of the economy gave the state and the collective control not only over an individual's income, but also over housing, welfare, leisure activities, and access to rationed commodities. The ultimate dependence on the state for the essentials of life, with few alternative sources for satisfying basic needs, has been a crucial element of political control in China since the 1950s.[10]

At the same time as the party strengthened the levels used for political control, it weakened the channels for the articulation of political interests. The party itself was a hierarchical institution, with key decisions made by a small number of leaders at the center and merely ratified by the party's representative bodies. The government, too, had a weak legislative system, featuring noncompetitive indirect elections to powerless assemblies, which were composed primarily of party leaders and model workers rather than of independent professional legislators, and which met infrequently and irregularly in short sessions to give symbolic approval to party decisions. Perhaps most important, just as the party forbade the formulation and expression of any independent bodies of political belief, so too did it prevent the formation of any independent political organizations. Except for a brief period at the height of the Cultural Revolution, the party banned the existence of independent unions, associations, or political parties. Participation in sanctioned organizations was mandatory; participation in independent organizations was prohibited.

Through these mechanisms, political participation in Communist China was intended to express support for the policies of the party and government. The network of mass organizations and state-controlled workplaces was mobilized in a continuing series of political and economic campaigns designed not only to impart understanding of official doctrine and to stimulate criticism of deviant behavior, but also to tap popular energies to undertake ambitious economic construction programs, to promote emulation of model

---

[10]On the dependence of the ordinary citizen on his work unit, see Andrew Walder, *Communist Neo-Traditionalism: Work and Authority in Chinese Industry* (Berkeley: University of California Press, 1986); and Jean C. Oi, *State and Peasant in Contemporary China: The Political Economy of Village Government* (Berkeley: University of California Press, 1989).

units and to ensure the implementation of social and economic policies.[11] In contrast, the channels for the expression of political interests were stunted and atrophied. Reports on the popular mood were supposedly provided through the party apparatus and the mass organizations; individual citizens could petition local officials and send letters to newspapers; and, in extreme circumstances, workers and peasants could take the risk of engaging in strikes, demonstrations, slowdowns, and other forms of protest. But, as elections were meaningless and independent political organizations were banned, there were few institutions for the effective articulation or aggregation of political interests.

The weaknesses of such a system were apparent as early as the mid-1950s. The lack of accountability of the government to its people gave rise to the danger of widespread popular alienation, especially as the legitimacy and goodwill acquired during the revolution were gradually dissipated. The uprisings in Poland and Hungary in 1956 gave Chinese Communist leaders a graphic illustration of the grave potential consequences of a divorce between the state and society.

At first, during the Hundred Flowers period of 1956–1957, the Chinese Communist Party adopted a relatively liberal approach to the problem of popular alienation. Ideological constraints on political discourse were relaxed, and intellectuals were encouraged to use the meetings convened by various professional associations, the "democratic parties," and the party's United Front Work Department to express their views on the work of the party and on various issues of public policy. In the course of the Hundred Flowers period, a number of high-ranking officials and intellectuals, including some in the Commnist Party itself, proposed significant changes in national political institutions, including more active roles for the national legislature, the mass organizations, and the news media in articulating popular concerns. None of these proposals would have made China a pluralistic state, but they would have moved it away from a mobilizational style of politics toward a more consultative one.[12]

---

[11]On campaigns, see Gordon Bennett, *Yundong: Mass Campaigns in Chinese Communist Leadership*, China Research Monographs, no. 12(Berkeley: Center for Chinese Studies, University of California, 1975); and Charles Cell, *Revolution at Work: Mass Campaigns in China* (New York: Academic Press, 1977).

[12]The experimentation with political liberalization in 1956–1957 is addressed in Harry Harding, *Organizing China: The Problem of Bureaucracy, 1949–1976* (Stanford: Stanford University Press, 1981), chapter 5; Roderick MacFarquhar, *The Origins of the Cultural Revolution*, vol. 1, *Contradictions Among the People, 1956–1957* (New York: Columbia University Press, 1974); and Richard Solomon, *Mao's Revolution and the*

The outpouring of grievances during the Hundred Flowers period— much of which was directed against the perquisites and power of the Communist Party itself—demonstrated how serious the crisis of confidence in the political system had already become. At the same time, however, it discredited the liberal structural solution in the eyes of most of the party's senior leaders. The party was simply not prepared to sanction demands for sweeping political change. The immediate response, therefore, was to return to mobilizational politics, as reflected in the great mass campaigns to implement the new agricultural and industrial policies associated with the Great Leap Forward.

But the problem of mass alienation from party leadership had not been solved. Indeed, the economic disaster of the Great Leap Forward served only to intensify it. In the early 1960s, therefore, Mao Tse-tung began to formulate an alternative, more radical approach to the question. Essentially, it involved the mobilization of grass-roots criticism of various sectors of the party through relatively uninstitutionalized channels: the criticism of rural corruption by Poor and Lower-Middle Peasant Associations during the Social Education Movement in the early 1960s, the criticism of basic-level urban officials by the Cultural Revolution Committees in 1966, then the attacks on higher-level party leaders by Red Guard and revolutionary rebel organizations during the high tide of the Cultural Revolution between late 1966 and mid-1968, and finally the periodic instances of "revolutionary criticism" of allegedly revisionist officials during the early and mid-1970s.

These new forms of participation were intended to express the intensified "class struggle" against the revisionists in the party that Mao had demanded after the debacle of the Great Leap Forward. Mao's intention was that one segment of society, believed to be particularly loyal to his utopian version of ideology, would be mobilized to criticize, and even overthrow, those "party persons in authority taking the capitalist road." In reality, however, the mass movement itself split into innumerable factions, some of which were loyal to competing party leaders; and the uninstitutionalized forms of protest sanctioned during the Cultural Revolution soon degenerated into violence, turmoil, and persecution. The result, again, was to intensify, rather than to remedy, popular alienation from the leadership of the Chinese Communist Party. By the time of Mao's death in 1976, the crisis of confidence in the party had become more acute than ever before.[13]

Chinese Political Culture (Berkeley: University of California Press, 1971), chapter 17.

[13]On the Maoist approach to political participation, see Harding, *Organizing China*, chapter 8.

In the post-Mao era, China's reformers have attempted to address this problem by returning to the liberal alternative that had been considered so briefly during the Hundred Flowers movement of 1956–1957. Since 1978, they have undertaken a number of measures to relax political controls and to allow more opportunities for political participation. The use of mass campaigns to implement party policy, particularly in the economic realm, has been virtually eliminated. The growing number of private and collective enterprises, the dismantling of the communes and the decollectivization of agriculture, and the use of market forces to allocate goods and services to consumers have all helped reduce the control that the workplace previously exercised over individual workers and peasants. The legal system has become somewhat less intrusive and somewhat less arbitrary.

At the same time as political controls have been relaxed, opportunities for political participation have been increased. Contested elections have been held for some government and party positions, and the role of legislative bodies, particularly at the national level, has been expanded. The National People's Congress now meets more frequently and engages in more lively debate, and some government decisions have actually been postponed or modified as a result of legislative opposition.[14] Drafts of the party's policy documents are reviewed and revised after consultation with interested professional associations and knowledgeable specialists, and major social and economic issues are discussed more freely in the national press.[15] To assess the public mood, leaders have begun to turn to public opinion polls and to mass organizations.

Although there has been some limited expansion of the channels for

---

[14]The experiments with contested elections in the post-Mao period are analyzed in Barrett L. McCormick, "Leninist Implementation: The Election Campaign," in David M. Lampton, ed., *Policy Implementation in Post-Mao China* (Berkeley: University of California Press, 1987), pp. 383–413; Andrew Nathan, *Chinese Democracy* (New York: Alfred A. Knopf, 1985), chapter 10; and Brantly Womack, "The 1980 County-Level Elections in China: Experiment in Democratic Modernization," *Asian Survey*, vol. 22, no. 2(March 1982):261–77. On the expanded role of legislatures in the post-Mao political reforms, see Kevin J. O'Brien, "China's National People's Congress: Reform and Its Limits," *Legislative Studies Quarterly*, vol. 13, no.3(Aug. 1988):343–74; and O'Brien, "Legislative Development and Chinese Political Change," *Studies in Comparative Communism,* vol. 13, no. 1(Spring 1989):57–75.

[15]The methods for consultation in policymaking are analyzed in Nina Halpern, "Making Economic Policy: The Influence of Economists," in Joint Economic Committee, *China's Economy Looks Toward the Year 2000*, vol. 1, *The Four Modernizations,* 99th Cong., 2d sess., pp. 132–46; and James Seymour, *China's Satellite Parties* (Armonk, N.Y.: M. E. Sharpe, 1987).

political participation and consultation, genuine political pluralism has not been tolerated. Direct elections are still conducted only at the county level and below, with representatives to higher-level legislatures selected by their counterparts at lower levels. Most nominees for contested elections are still nominated by the Chinese Communist Party. Although the press has been given somewhat greater freedom of expression, it remains controlled by the party and subject to postpublication censorship. As the political crisis of 1989 demonstrated, autonomous interest groups and mass organizations have remain banned, with severe sanctions against those who attempt to create them. Nor have Chinese leaders indicated any willingness to consider the creation of a truly multiparty system or the emergence of political associations independent of Communist Party leadership. Indeed, one of the charges leveled against Chao Tzu-yang after his dismissal in June 1989 was that he had favored a degree of political pluralism that more senior leaders were unwilling to accept.

The problem is that the limited political reforms of the post-Mao era have lagged far behind the transformation of the economic system. Economic reform has produced new grievances over inflation, inequality, and corruption; has introduced new ideas about politics through greater access to the outside world; and has created new centers of economic power that are relatively independent of the state. But the political system has not been reformed to accommodate these new demands. As a result, the crisis of confidence in China has become worse, not better, since 1976. The explosion of popular protest in the spring of 1989, and the leaders' decision to respond by repression rather than reconciliation, suggest that the gap between political institutions and political demands will become even wider in the years ahead.

Politicized Bureaucracy

The third principal feature of Chinese politics since 1949—indeed, for many centuries before 1949—has been its essentially bureaucratic character. The Chinese have long experience with the maintenance of a national bureaucracy to exercise effective control over a huge population and a large territory. Given the relative weakness of representative or participatory institutions after 1949, the party and state bureaucracies have understandably been the dominant institutions in the Chinese political system.

And yet, drawing on its Leninist heritage and on its own national traditions, what the Chinese Communist Party created in the early 1950s was not a purely bureaucratic apparatus in the Weberian sense, but a quasi-bureaucracy, with the party maintaining control over the appointment of key government officials, assigning the most important positions to party members, and arrogating to party factions within the bureaucracy the power to make the most crucial administrative and policy decisions. The party conducted regular political education campaigns within the government bureaucracy, including periodic rectification movements, purges of disloyal officials, and programs of physical labor designed to maintain political commitment.[16]

The party also obstructed the regularization and routinization of bureaucratic performance. Few rules or regulations were established to define the division of labor within the bureaucracy, the limits of administrative power, or the recruitment, promotion, rotation, or retirement of party and state officials. Moreover, the party tended to favor the use of mass campaigns rather than administrative measures in the implementation of national policies. A mobilizational style of politics was applied to the management of the state bureaucracy as well as to the relationship between the government and the people.

In the mid-1950s, with the inauguration of central economic planning, there was brief acknowledgment that such a politicized bureaucratic structure might not be fully suitable for a sustained program of rapid economic modernization. There was, therefore, a short-lived experiment with more rational forms of bureaucratic organization. Rules and regulations were promulgated, particularly with regard to personnel matters. Procuratorial, supervisory, and party control bodies were established to monitor the performance of party and state officials. As the role of the government in regulating and planning economic activity grew, the role of the party appeared somewhat to shrink.[17]

Just as the liberal interlude in Chinese politics in the mid-1950s was brief, so too was the experiment with bureaucratic rationalization a transitory phenomenon. Leaders of the party apparatus were probably concerned that organizational rationalization would limit the prerogatives and powers of the party. Mao Tse-tung, for his part, came to the conclusion, first, that bureaucratic organizations were inevitably conservative in drawing up plans

---

[16]The classic treatment of China's politicized bureaucracy remains Ezra F. Vogel, "Politicized Bureaucracy: Communist China," in Fred W. Riggs, ed., *Frontiers of Development Administration* (Durham, N.C.: Duke University Press, 1970), pp. 556–68. See also A. Doak Barnett, *Cadres, Bureaucracy, and Political Power in Communist China* (New York: Columbia University Press, 1967); and Franz Schurmann, *Ideology and Organization in Communist China*, 2d ed. (Berkeley: University of California Press, 1968).

[17]On the attempts at organizational rationalization in the mid-1950s, see Harding, *Organizing China*, chapter 3.

for economic development, and second, that they were one of the natural origins of revisionist thinking within a socialist state.

As a result, the prevailing tendency during the later Maoist period was to intensify, rather than to moderate, the key features of politicized bureaucracy outlined above. There was little attention paid to the establishment of rules or regulations to guide the performance of the bureaucracy. One by one, the control mechanisms established to monitor bureaucratic activities in the mid-1950s were deactivated or abolished. Recruitment and promotion continued to be based more on political than on professional criteria, and there were still no mechanisms for the retirement of the highest-level officials at each layer of government. And, throughout the Maoist era, the party and government were periodically admonished to adopt a more "revolutionary" style of decisionmaking and policy implementation, involving regular participation in physical labor, frequent study of ideological materials, inflated goals and targets for government activity, and mass mobilization to implement national policies. Policymaking became less systematic and professionalized and became subject to the whim of ranking party leaders.

Moreover, party penetration and control of the government bureaucracy was increased, rather than decreased, during the later Maoist period. Functional party departments, rather than the equivalent governmental agencies, became the centers of decisionmaking at all levels, especially the center. During the Cultural Revolution, party and government administrative staffs were actually merged, at the provincial levels and below, into streamlined "revolutionary committees," with the state bureaucracy denounced as an unnecessary and duplicative administrative apparatus.[18]

The organizational crisis produced by these policies was perhaps less acute than the crisis of popular confidence that we have discussed earlier, but it was serious nonetheless. As China's priorities shifted in the post-Mao era from continuous revolution to sustained economic modernization and reform, it became increasingly apparent that the administrative institutions of the past were poorly designed and staffed to meet their new responsibilities.

Characteristically, the first approach to reshaping the Chinese bureaucracy to satisfy the demands of modernization was to undertake a rectification campaign—a program of political study and personnel reshuffling designed to increase commitment to the principles of economic reform. But this relatively ineffective rectification campaign was not the principal element

---

[18]The Maoist approach to organizational restructuring is detailed in Harding, *Organizing China*, chapter 9; and Martin King Whyte, "Bureaucracy and Modernization: The Maoist Critique," *American Sociological Review*, vol. 38, no. 2(April 1973):149–63.

of organizational policy during the post-Mao era. Instead, for the first time since the mid-1950s, Chinese leaders have adopted bureaucratic rationalization as the cornerstone of their organizational program.

The administrative reforms of the 1980s have modified the operation of the bureaucracy in four principal ways. First, there has been gradual movement toward the institutionalization of personnel procedures, including the development of a civil-service system to manage the recruitment, assignment, evaluation, promotion, and retirement of government officials. Second, the role of the party has been reduced relative to the state by limiting the party's control over the *nomenklatura*, eliminating leading party groups within bureaucratic agencies, reducing the number of functional party departments at various levels, and restricting the concurrent posting of party officials to government responsibilities. Third, the structure and role of the state bureaucracy has been redefined by gradually streamlining or eliminating government agencies responsible for the direct administration of the economy, and by expanding or adding bureaus responsible for economic regulation. And finally, the policymaking system has become somewhat more professionalized, with greater attention to technical competence and educational background in the selection of high-level officials, and the development of primitive mechanisms for research and analysis on major national issues.[19]

Although many of these reforms are still in the preliminary or experimental stages, they have already had a noticeable impact—not always positive—on the operation of the Chinese bureaucracy. The relaxation of party controls over the government apparatus has resulted in a resurgence of bureaucratic influence over national policy. Recent studies of policymaking in the energy and water conservancy sectors, for example, report a policymaking process in which bureaucratic agencies develop programs based on their organizational perspectives and interests, bargain among themselves in an attempt to reach consensus, and report any remaining issues to higher-level leaders for mediation or resolution.[20] The impact of such a process on

---

[19]On the administrative reforms of the post-Mao period, see John P. Burns, "Reforming China's Bureaucracy, 1979–82," *Asian Survey*, vol. 23, no. 6(June 1983):692–72; Burns, "Civil Service Reform in Post-Mao China," *Australian Journal of Chinese Studies*, no. 18(July 1987):47–84; Christopher M. Clarke, "Rejuvenation, Reorganization, and the Dilemmas of Modernization in Post-Deng China," *Journal of International Affairs*, vol. 39, no. 2(Winter 1986):119–32; Harry Harding, *China's Second Revolution: Reform After Mao* (Washington, D.C.: The Brookings Institution, 1987), chapter 8; and James Kuo-hsiung Lee, "An Assessment of Teng's Bureaucratic Reform, 1979–1984," *Issues and Studies*, vol. 23, no. 5(May 1987):12–31.

[20]The resurgence of bureaucratic interests in post-Mao policy making is documented

the content of policy has not been adequately studied, but it is likely that the implications include long delays in reaching decisions, relatively uncoordinated policies, difficulties in altering budgetary allocations, and a continuing bias in favor of central planning and the sectors of the economy that were the beneficiaries of the Soviet model of economic development.

Similarly, the post-Mao bureaucratic reforms have also unintentionally contributed to an increase in corruption, given that the new administrative and legal controls associated with a more formal civil-service system have not been put in place as rapidly as the previous political and ideological constraints have been relaxed. The extent and scope of corruption are not yet clear, but anecdotal evidence suggests widespread abuse of power by both high- and low-level officials in both urban and rural areas. That the children of some leading party and government officials have reportedly engaged in much corrupt behavior has certainly contributed to the general crisis of confidence that plagues post-Mao China.

A Decentralized System

China has, for most periods since 1949, been governed by a relatively decentralized political system, with considerable administrative authority devolved to the provinces or to supraprovincial regions, and with a substantial number of positions in the central elite occupied by provincial representatives. There have been efforts from time to time to gain greater central control over the provinces, and there has never been a significant danger of fragmentation along provincial lines. But the general trend has been toward the consolidation of a political system in which provincial leaders exercise considerable autonomy.

In the mid-1950s, during the brief flirtation with bureaucratic rationalization, there was also an attempt to design a relatively centralized political system. In drafting the state constitution of 1954, Chinese leaders rejected the Soviet model of a nominally federal government and insisted on a unitary state. With the initiation of central planning, the administration of the economy was placed under a high degree of central control. Memories of the centrifugal tendencies of the warlord period, and awareness of the regionalist

---

in David M. Lampton, "The Implementation Problem in Post-Mao China," in Lampton, ed., *Policy Implementation in Post-Mao China*, pp. 3–24; Lampton, "Chinese Politics: The Bargaining Treadmill," *Issues and Studies*, vol. 23, no. 3(March 1987):11–41; and Kenneth G. Lieberthal and Michel C. Oksenberg, *Policy Making in China: Leaders, Structures, and Processes* (Princeton, N.J.: Princeton University Press, 1988).

tendencies during the early years of the People's Republic, may have helped persuade Chinese Communist leaders to construct a rather centralized national government.[21]

Within a few years, however, the party and its members came to the conclusion that their country could not be ruled effectively from a single political center. Different sets of leaders may have reached this decision from different perspectives. Those responsible for economic planning, such as Ch'en Yun and Hsüeh Mu-ch'iao, insisted that an increasingly complex economy of China's size could not be administered through rigid central planning, and advocated various formulas for the decentralization of economic management to the provinces and to individual enterprises. Mao Tse-tung, for his part, concluded that central planning was inherently conservative in nature, and that only a decentralized system could fully mobilize the enthusiasm he believed to be inherent in the Chinese populace. In addition, Mao came increasingly to conclude that only a cellular economy governed by relatively autonomous provinces could attain an egalitarian distribution of productive capacity and could enable China to survive an all-out invasion by a major foreign power.

Thus, much administrative power was delegated to the provinces during the Great Leap Forward in the late 1950s, creating what several observers have described as a "cellular" political economy. Provinces became highly self-sufficient, trading relatively small quantities of agricultural or industrial commodities with one another. Interprovincial commerce occurred mainly among centrally controlled state enterprises, which formed a small national industrial system resting on top of the much larger provincial base.[22]

Although the cellular political economy was formed out of a combination of strategic, administrative, and ideological considerations, it soon became self-perpetuating. Any one province's attempts to achieve self-sufficiency yielded fewer surpluses for sale to other provinces. Fewer tradable surpluses then encouraged, even required, other provinces to aim at self-sufficiency as well. Moreover, the adoption of a cellular development strategy discouraged investment in a nationwide transportation network; and

---

[21]On the efforts at centralization in the mid-1950s, see Harding, *Organizing China*, chapter 3.

[22]The origins and consequences of decentralization are traced in Nicholas R. Lardy, *Economic Growth and Distribution in China* (Cambridge, Eng.: Cambridge University Press, 1978); Thomas P. Lyons, *Economic Integration and Planning in Maoist China* (New York: Columbia University Press, 1987); and Barry Naughton, "The Third Front: Defense Industrialization in the Chinese Interior," *China Quarterly*, no. 115(Sept. 1988):351–86.

the resulting rail and highway bottlenecks hampered the expansion of the interprovincial trade that might have eroded cellularity.

An attempt at recentralization in the early 1960s transferred some authority to large supraprovincial regions, but the six regional party bureaus soon appeared to reflect local interests as much as to implement central directives. With the chaos of the Cultural Revolution, even more authority flowed to provincial governments, which had the responsibility for restoring order. To a degree unprecedented since the mid-1950s, provincial military and civilian representatives occupied a large share of seats on the Central Committee and other central party organs.[23]

In the post-Mao era, some attempts were again made to reassert central political control. The share of seats on the Central Committee occupied by provincial representatives, for example, fell precipitously by the Twelfth Party Congress in 1982. In the main, however, the economic reforms since 1978 have served to strengthen the authority of the provinces. Not only has there been a reassertion of the general principle that a complex economy requires decentralized government. Even more important, one of the principal economic reforms—allowing provincial governments to retain a larger share of the revenues and profits generated within their jurisdictions—has given provincial leaders unprecedented financial independence from the central authorities.[24]

The tendencies toward provincial cellularity have been echoed at lower levels in the countryside. Research by Vivienne Shue has vividly portrayed the relative autonomy of grass-roots rural society. Communes and collective farms were economically self-reliant, with few commercial links with the outside world and few opportunities for peasants to migrate to urban centers or even to other rural areas. Local officials, although appointed by the party apparatus, were recruited form local residents and paid from local funds. This meant that grass-roots political leaders were as responsive to local pressures and demands as they were to central or provincial directives.[25]

---

[23]On the relationship between central and provincial authorities during the Cultural Revolution, see Parris H. Chang, "Peking and the Provinces: Decentralization of Power," *Problems of Communism,* vol. 21, no. 4(July–Aug. 1972):67–74; and Victor C. Falkenheim, "Peking and the Provinces: Continuing Central Predominance," ibid., pp. 75–83.

[24]On financial decentralization in the post-Mao era, see Barry Naughton, "The Decline of Central Control Over Investment in Post-Mao China," in Lampton, ed., *Policy Implementation in Post-Mao China,* pp. 51–80; and Naughton, "Finance and Planning Reforms in Industry," in Joint Economic Committee, *China's Economy Looks Toward the Year 2000,* vol. 1, *The Four Modernizations,* pp. 604–29.

[25]Vivienne Shue, *The Reach of the State: Sketches of the Chinese Body Politic* (Stanford, Calif.: Stanford University Press, 1988).

The effect of the post-Mao economic reforms on rural society is more ambivalent than the effect on the provinces. On the one hand, the decollectivization of agriculture is further weakening the power of the national administrative apparatus over the countryside. On the other, the rapid growth of rural industry and the greater specialization of agricultural production is eroding the economic cellularity of the rural areas by forging economic links to a wider world. On balance, it may be that the post-Mao reforms have reinforced the political autonomy of the countryside while reducing its economic self-sufficiency.

The growing autonomy of the provinces, like the growing power of the state bureaucracy at the national level, has had a clearly distortive effect on policy in post-Mao China. Provincial party and state leaders, local managers, and local workers have had a common interest in ensuring rapid economic growth for their localities, protection against competition from other provinces, high levels of job security, and steady increases in wages and bonuses. The ability of the provinces to pursue such a high-growth, high-wage economic policy has contributed much to the chronic overheating of the Chinese economy that has been apparent since the mid-1980s. At the same time, the center's assignment of a growing share of state revenues to the provinces has reduced Beijing's ability to use fiscal mechanisms to guide the country's economic development or to undertake new social programs.

This is not to ignore the constraints on local autonomy that have existed both during and after the Maoist period. The national government has maintained the ability to transfer economic resources, including both commodities and capital, from one province to another in order to promote interprovincial equity or to undertake national construction programs. Central party leaders have retained power over personnel appointments at the provincial levels and have periodically dismissed local officials in order to reassert their control over provincial decisions. During the Cultural Revolution and again during the political crisis of 1989, national leaders demonstrated that they could maintain effective central control over the armed forces and forestall tendencies toward military regionalism. And provincial and central authorities have regularly mobilized work teams to penetrate the countryside to implement central policies.

National leaders, however, have had to husband their political resources and use them judiciously to secure compliance on issues of paramount importance. In other areas, or on issues on which the central political elite was divided, provincial and local leaders have been able to thwart unpopular decisions and directives. They have also been able to negotiate for more benefits and fewer exactions from the central government. In the complex balance between central power and local autonomy, open defiance of national decisions has been rare, but evasion, delay, and other forms of subtle resistance have been commonplace.

Uninstitutionalized Succession

Several of the structural features of Chinese politics mentioned earlier—particularly the relatively weak influence of either representative institutions or the national bureaucracy—have contributed to the concentration of power in the hands of a single paramount leader, first Mao Tse-tung and then Teng Hsiao-p'ing. Since that leader has served without a fixed term of office, without any provisions for retirement, and without formal mechanisms for selecting his replacement, he has been responsible for arranging his own succession. Under these circumstances, would-be successors have continuously jockeyed for position, and paramount leaders have constantly been concerned about signs of disloyalty or independence among their subordinates. Ever since the 1950s, Chinese politics has therefore been plagued by a string of crises over political succession.

The struggle over succession has played a central role in Chinese political life from the very earliest years of the People's Republic. The first major turnover within the top party leadership, the Kao Kang–Jao Shu-shih purge of the early 1950s, was the result of competition for positions just subordinate to Mao Tse-tung between two wings of the Communist movement: on the one hand, those leaders who had served in the "red" areas during the revolution and, on the other, those who had served in the "white" areas behind enemy lines. Later in the decade, Mao became concerned with arranging his own succession and attempted to identify candidates to follow him as chairman of the party. But he turned successively against no fewer than four heirs apparent—Liu Shao-ch'i, Lin Piao, Teng Hsiao-p'ing, and his own wife, Chiang Ch'ing—as he suspected each in turn of personal disloyalty, unseemly ambition, or ideological deviation. Ultimately, the succession of Mao Tse-tung culminated in a spasm of conflict within the elite. Within one month of Mao's death, Chiang Ch'ing fell victim to a quick military coup d'état authorized by another contender, Hua Kuo-feng, who was in turn removed from power within two years by a reformist coalition organized by Teng Hsiao-p'ing.[26]

The intensity of the succession struggle increased markedly during the

---

[26]Reviews of the succession struggles in China from 1949 onward include Parris H. Chang, *Power and Policy in China*, 2d ed. (University Park: Pennsylvania State University Press, 1978); Frederick C. Teiwes, *Leadership, Legitimacy, and Conflict in China: From a Charismatic Mao to the Politics of Succession* (Armonk, N.Y.: M. E. Sharpe, 1984); Michael Y.M. Kau, ed., *The Lin Piao Affair: Power Politics and Military Coup* (White Plains, N.Y.: International Arts and Sciences Press, 1975); and Ann Fenwick, *The Gang of Four and the Politics of Opposition: China, 1971–1976* (Ph.D. diss., Stanford University, 1983).

Maoist era. Especially during the decade of the Cultural Revolution, the succession fight was not simply a competition for political advantage, but a fight for political (if not physical) survival. This had four principal consequences for China's political dynamics. First, the succession struggles were conducted in Manichaean terms, as confrontations between good and evil, between forces of revolution and of counterrevolution, between proletarian and bourgeois tendencies within the party. Viewing politics in these terms led to a second phenomenon: it encouraged the contenders to form strong personalistic factions to assist them in their contention for power. Political recruitment revolved more around loyalty than competence, and policymaking was influenced more strongly by factional considerations than by technocratic criteria. Third, the contenders for political succession periodically sought mass support for their causes, thus contributing to high levels of uninstitutionalized popular participation in politics, and consequently a high degree of social instability and political unrest. And finally, as might be expected in a situation where struggle was intense and political institutions were weak, the military played a crucial role in determining the outcome of political succession. This perpetuated the involvement of the People's Liberation Army in civilian politics and greatly hindered the evolution of the military into a professional armed force.

In the post-Mao period, it initially appeared that Teng Hsiao-p'ing, aware of the turmoil that had followed the death of Mao Tse-tung, intended to design and implement a more institutionalized succession process. Between 1982 (when he consolidated his own position as paramount leader of the party) and 1987 (when his succession arrangements began to unravel), Teng seemed to be systematically creating a new mechanism for political succession. By introducing fixed terms of office and mandatory retirement ages, Teng was attempting to develop more regular procedures for the recruitment, rotation, and retirement of the national political elite. By narrowing the range of views on the Central Committee over economic and political reform and by allowing the losers in political battles to retire with their honor intact, Teng was trying to reduce the stakes of political conflict. And by reducing the number of military officers on the Central Committee and by returning the military to the barracks, Teng was signaling the elimination of the role of armed force in political competition.[27]

Since 1987, however, China has experienced two leadership crises that have reduced Teng's plans for the succession to tatters and demonstrated how fragile his succession arrangements actually were. In 1986–1987, Teng

---

[27]On Teng Hsiao-p'ing's efforts to arrange his own succession, see Harding, *China's Second Revolution*, chapter 8.

turned against his first heir apparent, Hu Yao-pang, accusing him of excessive tolerance of student demands for democratization. Although Hu was treated relatively leniently, and although few of his supporters were purged along with him, Hu's purge showed that the succession to Teng Hsiao-p'ing would be determined not by the collective deliberation of the Central Committee or by any other formal institutional mechanism, but rather by the arbitrary decisions of Teng and a few other senior party leaders, most of whom had supposedly retired from office.

The purge of Chao Tzu-yang in mid-1989 has further reversed the progress toward the institutionalization of political succession. Chao's political difficulties stemmed, in large part, from the same issue that had led to the downfall of Hu Yao-pang: tolerance of mass protests for political reform that Teng Hsiao-p'ing and other senior leaders considered unacceptable. But Chao's removal represented an even greater degree of political retrogression than did Hu Yao-pang's, in that it resurrected all four of the maladies that had accompanied the uninstitutionalized succession arrangements of the Maoist era. Once again, the military was reintroduced into a central role in civilian politics, with several hundred thousand troops mobilized to ensure the defeat of Chao Tzu-yang. In turn, Chao—or at least some of his closest advisers—may well have attempted to make use of the mass protests sweeping Beijing to strengthen his position against his rivals inside the party. Once Chao was purged, his dismissal was justified by inflammatory rhetoric accusing him of having fomented a "counterrevolutionary rebellion" against the established party leadership. And, in such a poisonous political climate, the resurrection of personal factions in the struggle for succession is a virtual certainty. Indeed, the political crisis of mid-1989 guarantees that the succession to Teng Hsiao-p'ing will be tumultuous, with political instability and maneuvering within the elite persisting at least until the death of the paramount leader.

Conclusion

This review of the five key structural features of Chinese politics since 1949 suggests the following simple periodization of the evolution of the Chinese political system under Communist rule.

The first seventeen years of the People's Republic, from 1949 until the initiation of the Cultural Revolution in 1966, can be described as a period of *cellular totalitarianism*. In those years China possessed all the defining characteristics of a totalitarian system. Political life was guided by a transformational ideology, which defined the principal task of politics as conducting revolutionary struggle to reshape the country's socioeconomic system, first against the forces defending the ancien régime and then against those seeking to restore it. Politics was conducted through a mobilizational structure comprising a vanguard political party and a network of mass organizations that penetrated the state, the economy, and grass-roots society. That mobilizational network suppressed dissent, exercised effective political control, and channeled all possible resources in support of the socioeconomic programs of the national leadership. In turn, the exercise of power by this tutelary and mobilizational apparatus was not effectively constrained by any legal or institutional mechanisms, but was undertaken by a highly politicized and poorly professionalized bureaucracy headed by a single paramount leader with enormous personal authority.

But, in several important respects, totalitarianism in Maoist China departed from the ideal type. It was partly but significantly limited by the cellularity of the Chinese political and economic system, in which the growing autonomy of the localities and the provinces buffered the population against the whims of the central leaders. The autonomy of the localities was, in turn, reinforced by the emerging divisions within the central elite over social and economic policy, particularly in the late 1950s and early 1960s. And the resolution of those divisions was complicated by the fact that they were increasingly intertwined with a bitter struggle over the looming succession to Mao Tse-tung. It is for these reasons that Chinese politics between 1949 and 1966 are better described as cellular totalitarianism than as totalitarianism in its pure form.

During the decade of the Cultural Revolution, from 1966 to 1976, Chinese totalitarianism simultaneously developed and degenerated. On the one hand, Chinese politics became more doctrinal, more mobilizational, less rational, and less institutionalized. The growing penetration of political life by a tutelary and mobilizational state exacerbated the totalitarian features of the Chinese political system, as did the increasing arbitrariness and irrationality with which political power was exercised. But within the intensification of totalitarianism lay the seeds of its own decay. By the time of Mao's death in 1976, the Chinese political system was in serious disarray. The main characteristics of this crisis were a lack of faith in official doctrine, the alienation of broad segments of the Chinese population from their government, the decay of the Chinese Communist Party under Mao's assault on its authority, increasing provincial autonomy, and intense conflict and instability within the Chinese elite. On balance, the decade of the Cultural Revolution can therefore be described as a period of *decayed totalitarianism*.

After the death of Mao Tse-tung in 1976, there were some efforts to restructure Chinese politics to resolve the country's political crisis. But the limits to political reform have been as apparent as its accomplishments. Although ideological constraints have been relaxed and the content of official doctrine has been redefined, the Chinese system remains a tutelary polity, and the crisis of faith in ideology has not been overcome. Although there are now more channels for political participation than in the past, this aspect of political reform has lagged behind the demands of much of the urban population for political change, and the alienation of the people from their government has not been relieved. Administrative reform has not yet produced a more rational bureaucracy or a clear division of authority between the center and the provinces. And, perhaps most tragically, the events of mid-1989 reveal that the process of political succession remains as uninstitutionalized as it was during the latter years of Mao's life. The political system in the post-Mao era might, therefore, be described as a *post-totalitarian* order, in which the mobilizational and tutelary mechanisms have been deactivated but not dismantled, and in which political discourse and political participation remain highly constrained rather than truly autonomous.

Having been faced with unprecedented popular protest in the spring of 1989, the Chinese Communist Party will be tempted to reactivate the mechanism of totalitarianism in order to regain political control over Chinese society. This will prove to be an extremely difficult undertaking. The crisis of confidence in ideology will make it impossible to resurrect an effective tutelary system capable of generating enthusiastic support for any official doctrine. The rise of market forces and the emergence of private and collective enterprise in both city and countryside will make it hard to restore a mobilizational political system. The coastal provinces, which now have a stake in continuing economic relations with the outside world, will use their greater financial independence to resist or evade a tightening of political controls from the center.

The immediate prospects, therefore, are for a relatively weak central government alienated from large segments of its own society, with limited control over the provinces, and with deep cleavages within its own ranks. Beneath a continued veneer of reform, there is likely to be a mixture of repression of dissent, conflict within the elite, and instability at the grassroots. Only after the most senior generation of Chinese Communist leaders leaves the political stage will a decisive break from the totalitarian legacy of the past and a resumption of meaningful political reform be possible. Even then, the transition from post-totalitarianism to a system that is first more consultative, and ultimately more pluralistic, will inevitably be protracted and arduous.

Social Structure and Political Authority

China's Evolving Polity

China's 1989 political demonstrations, remarkable for their size, duration, and broad popular support, dramatize a widely noted transformation of political authority over the past decade. It has often been said that in China the relationship between "state and society" is being remade, or that the boundaries between the two have been decisively redrawn.[1] Some, borrowing a usage currently popular among students of eastern Europe, find in China today the seeds for a "rebirth of civil society."[2] However apt these characterizations may be, we still have a limited understanding of the nature and scope of this transformation.

Most would agree that this change was set in motion shortly after the death of Mao, as the Chinese Communist Party changed its political course.

---

[1]See, for example, David Stark and Victor Nee, "Toward an Institutional Analysis of State Socialism," in Victor Nee and David Stark, eds., *Remaking the Economic Institutions of Socialism: China and Eastern Europe* (Stanford, Calif.: Stanford University Press, 1989), pp. 1–31; and the contrasting speculations in Vivienne Shue, *The Reach of the State: Sketches of the Chinese Body Politic* (Stanford, Calif.: Stanford University Press, 1984).

[2]See Ivan Szelenyi, "Eastern Europe in an Epoch of Transition: Toward a Socialist Mixed Economy?" in Nee and Stark, *Remaking the Economic Institutions*, pp. 209–32, especially pp. 222–32, for a discussion of these ideas in Eastern Europe; and Thomas B. Gold, "Urban Private Business and Social Chinese Change," in Deborah Davis and Ezra F. Vogel, eds., *Chinese Society on the Eve of Tiananmen: The Impact of Reform* (Cambridge, Mass.: Council on East Asian Studies, Harvard University, 1990).

Spurred by the evident failures of past practice, the party reduced its reliance on political intimidation, mass mobilization, and militant indoctrination as tools of social control and work motivation. It accepted private interest and profit motivations. It reopened the country to the outside world. Reversing three decades of persecution and suspicion, it sought to recruit and reward the skilled and educated into the party and leadership positions. Within shifting boundaries defined vaguely by top leaders, it permitted for the first time significant debate about economic policy and the reform of political institutions.

Most observers would agree, moreover, that the changes initiated by the party's strategic shift were intensified, sometimes in unintended ways, by the reform of China's economic institutions. The earliest and most profound changes were in the countryside. The reversion to household agriculture and the attendant rise of rural incomes, the weakening of state monopolies and the re-emergence of local private-market activity and long-distance trade, and the growth in many areas of a large sector of private enterprise, have all served to alter the framework of rural governance. In urban areas, reformers sought to give enterprise managers heightened efficiency incentives with new forms of profit retention and taxation. They sought to give managers increased ability to hire and fire at their discretion, and they sought also to give some workers greater discretion in choosing their jobs. Extreme austerity gave way to relative abundance: nominal wages increased rapidly, and widespread rationing ended as the supply of foodstuffs and consumer goods improved. A growing petty private sector was legalized. These economic changes have served to alter even further past patterns of political authority. But their effects have been complex, in many ways obscure, prompting much speculation and debate.

Given the current state of our knowledge, broad generalizations about the "boundary between state and society" are very difficult to substantiate. Unless we specify such statements carefully, we will provide labels for certain obvious trends, while leaving unattended difficult questions about the impact of changes in social structure on the exercise of political authority. Our field has developed some very clear and widely accepted propositions about local social structures and political authority in China under Mao. They provide us with clear benchmarks for assessing social and political change. How precisely have these social structures been altered, and how has political authority been transformed? It has now been well over a decade since the end of the Mao era, and while there is still much that we do not understand, we have accumulated a large body of detailed research on subsequent social and economic changes. It is time to review what we know (and just as importantly, specify what we do not know), and offer some specific propositions about changes in political authority.

We shall examine, in turn, four features of China's social structure—the cohesiveness of rural communities and urban workplaces, the politicization of social stratification, material scarcity and administrative allocation, and the suppression of market allocation—and examine the ways that they have changed in the 1980s. Then we shall consider the evidence of change in two features of political authority under Mao: dependence upon authority figures and the system of party-clientelism.

We shall find that the heralded re-emergence of "civil society" in China is fraught with difficulties and ambiguities. While in many ways the extent of change over the past decade is impressive, in just as many ways, China remains mired in the authority patterns of the past. The spread of markets has taken many powers away from rural cadres and has transformed the village economy. But their spread has also given many new regulative powers to cadres. We can observe heightened cadre dependence on their subordinates, as economic reform progresses, and this brings greater balance to certain authority relationships. But the basic form of authority remains the same throughout the system: vertical, personal, and based on loyalty and exchange of benefits. Just as the Chinese economy is caught between the old planned and the new market economy, China's grass-roots polity is caught between the old patterns of personal dependence and the as-yet-undeveloped legal institutions that sanction bargaining, consultation, and enforcement of economic rights. The result is a polity eroded but not yet transformed; the instability of old institutions has created new tensions and conflicts that still await the formation of new institutions which will resolve them.

The Cohesiveness of the Local Community

In both rural and urban areas, local communities and workplaces under Mao were noteworthy for their tightly controlled boundaries and extensive corporate organization. The systems of grain rationing and workpoint allocation in rural areas, and housing registration and rationing in urban areas, effectively controlled the movement of the population.[3] In rural areas, vil-

---

[3]See Martin K. Whyte and William L. Parish, *Urban Life in Contemporary China* (Chicago, Ill.: University of Chicago Press, 1984), chapters 2–4; William L. Parish and Martin K. Whyte, *Village and Family in Contemporary China* (Chicago, Ill.: University of Chicago Press, 1978); Lynn T. White, III, *Careers in Shanghai: The Social Guidance of Personal Energies in a Developing Chinese City* (Berkeley: University

lagers had to obtain the permission of cadres to work outside the village. In urban areas, labor mobility in the state and large-collective sector was almost nonexistent after the 1950s. Permanent jobs in the state sector were highly coveted; the alternatives were transfer to the countryside or temporary employment in a marginal sector at low wages and with poor benefits. Villages and urban workplaces provided the majority of available social services and insurance, to the extent they were available.[4] Economic transactions between units that did not receive the sanction of the state plan were suppressed, though carried out illicitly on a restricted scale. Incomes were redistributed and leveled within these communities, while income disparities between social units grew large by international standards.[5] Within villages and to a considerable extent even in urban workplaces, the local community merged work, residence, and political administration.[6]

At the time of Mao's death, China's social structure was noteworthy for the insularity of its local work communities, the dependence of citizens on them for the satisfaction of a wide array of their needs, and for the extensive intervention of these units in the everyday life of their members. The decollectivization of agriculture transformed these characteristics in the countryside: no longer was the village run as a single agricultural enterprise. In urban areas, a small private-employment sector emerged, and state policies sought to permit greater flexibility in labor allocation, suggesting that the boundaries of the urban work unit might become more permeable as well. These changes raise two questions. First, to what extent have the

---

of California Press, 1978); and Thomas P. Bernstein, *Up to the Mountains and Down to the Villages: The Transfer of Youth from Urban to Rural China* (New Haven, Conn.: Yale University Press, 1977).

[4]White, *Careers in Shanghai*; Andrew G. Walder, *Communist Neo-Traditionalism: Work and Authority in Chinese Industry* (Berkeley: University of California Press, 1986), chapter 2; and Deborah Davis-Friedmann, *Long Lives: The Chinese Elderly and the Communist Revolution* (Cambridge, Mass.: Harvard University Press, 1983).

[5]See the studies reviewed in Andrew G. Walder, "Social Change in Post-Revolution China," *Annual Review of Sociology*, vol. 15(1989):405–24, and idem, "Economic Reform and Income Distribution in Tianjin, 1976–1986," in Davis and Vogel, *Chinese Society*.

[6]In addition to the studies cited above, several others stress this theme: Gail E. Henderson and Myron S. Cohen, *The Chinese Hospital: A Socialist Work Unit* (New Haven, Conn.: Yale University Press, 1985); Jean C. Oi, *State and Peasant in Contemporary China: The Political Economy of Village Government* (Berkeley: University of California Press, 1989), especially chapters 2–4; and Mayfair Yang, "Between State and Society: The Construction of Corporateness in a Chinese Socialist Factory," *Australian Journal of Chinese Affairs*, vol. 22(July 1989):31–60.

boundaries of local communities become more permeable and community control over individuals weakened? Second, to the extent that these communities have become more permeable and have lost their control over members, how has this served to alter patterns of political authority?

The Cellular Village Economy

It now appears that in many areas of the countryside, the cellular village economy and polity have been opened wide by economic changes, effectively undercutting many of the powers formerly exercised by team and brigade cadres. There is little disagreement among researchers that cadres have lost a wide range of powers formerly exercised within the framework of collective agriculture. In the past, production team cadres determined who would get higher-paying agricultural jobs; they allocated coveted opportunities to work in rural collective enterprises or as contract laborers in the cities, and by denying grain rations and work points, could prevent peasants from engaging in outside economic activities. By suppressing private garden plots and containing sideline production within a collective framework, they prevented independent economic activities.[7]

Household agriculture has eroded all of these bases of power. No longer are individual earnings funneled through collective coffers before being paid to households. No longer do peasants receive basic grain rations from the collective: families are to be self-sufficient. No longer can cadres forbid peasants to slaughter their pigs, market their produce, or engage in employment elsewhere. In rural areas, the dismantling of collective agricultural organization, the legalization of free markets for foodstuffs, and the growth of opportunities for temporary employment in urban areas have greatly opened up the boundaries of the village community.[8] This, in turn, has weakened the ability of village officials to control the movement of the village population, or to obstruct economic activities outside of villages.

---

[7]See Jean C. Oi, "Communism and Clientelism: Rural Politics in China," *World Politics,* vol. 37(Jan. 1985):238–66.
[8]Oi, *State and Peasant,* chapters 8–9; Vivienne Shue, "The New Course in Chinese Agriculture," *Annals of the American Academy of Political and Social Science,* vol. 476(Nov. 1984):74–88; Andrew Watson, "The Reform of Agricultural Marketing in China Since 1978," *China Quarterly,* vol. 113(Dec. 1988):1–28; Jonathan Unger, "The Decollectivization of the Chinese Countryside: A Survey of Twenty-Eight Villages," *Pacific Affairs,* vol. 58(Winter 1985/86):585–606.

Millions of rural residents now make up a "floating population" that circulates among urban and rural areas in search of employment.[9]

Many rural cadres recognized this threat to their power at the outset of the reforms, and the early 1980s saw concerted resistance and a variety of strategies to subvert implementation of the reforms.[10] It is generally conceded now that this struggle to resist the reforms was lost: in fact, the early 1980s saw the elimination of the entire class of team cadres, formerly the lowest level of administration in rural areas.[11] Brigade (now village) and commune (now township) cadres have had to adapt to the new situation in a variety of ways.[12] One would logically conclude that these changes have significantly altered political authority in the countryside.[13]

[9]Helen F. Siu describes this in great detail for a county of suburban Guangzhou in "The Politics of Migration in a Market Town," in Davis and Vogel, *Chinese Society*.

[10]Richard Latham, "The Implications of Rural Reforms for Grass-Roots Cadres," in Elizabeth J. Perry and Christine Wong, eds., *The Political Economy of Reform in Post-Mao China* (Cambridge, Mass.: Council of East Asian Studies, Harvard University, 1985), pp. 157–74; David Zweig, "Opposition to Change in Rural China: The System of Responsibility and People's Communes," *Asian Survey*, vol. 23(July 1983):879–900.

[11]Oi, *State and Peasant*, chapter 9; Vivienne Shue, "The Fate of the Commune," *Modern China*, vol. 10(July 1984)::259–83.

[12]John P. Burns, "Local Cadre Accommodation to the Responsibility System in Rural China," *Pacific Affairs*, vol. 58(Winter 1985/86):607–25; and David Zweig, "Prosperity and Conflict in Post-Mao Rural China," *China Quarterly*, vol. 105(March 1986):1–18.

[13]In *The Reach of the State* Shue argues that the reforms may strengthen central state power in rural areas. Her argument rests on the accurate observation that team and brigade cadres were able to resist and subvert many unpopular policies during the Mao era—a finding elaborated upon in great detail by David Zweig in his *Agrarian Radicalism in China, 1968–1981* (Cambridge, Mass.: Harvard University Press, 1989), and by Jean Oi, *State and Peasant*. She argues that the "cellular" nature of villages is what afforded villages this degree of self-protection, and that the evident erosion of village boundaries will now make them more vulnerable to state policies than before. Unfortunately, virtually all of the examples she cites of effective village resistance under Mao were to state policies that have now been abandoned, and she does not specify what types of policies villages will now be unable to resist. In light of the research cited here, we need to know what these newly intrusive state policies might be, and how they will be enforced.

The Corporate Village Economy

Despite the erosion of cadre control over the economic activities of peasant households, the corporate village has not disappeared. With some notable exceptions, collective economic enterprise continues to thrive in most of rural China, and village governments are still major actors in the rural economy.

Researchers have found repeatedly that while most agricultural activities are now contracted to households, rural industry is still predominantly under village and township management.[14] Rural industry has grown rapidly over the past decade, providing a resource base for the maintenance of village corporate structures. Profits from collectively owned and managed enterprises provide the basis for the continued viability of collective institutions. This provides the village government with capital for further investment, and with revenues for public works and collective benefits. Villages with a substantial industrial base have been found to provide a wide array of services and benefits: maintenance of local infrastructure, health insurance, support for schools, scholarships for successful middle-school and university candidates, public theaters, and other community benefits.[15]

Even when they do not directly manage enterprises, villages still formally own property that is contracted to specialized households, and cadres allocate contracts and set the terms of revenue division. The fees from leased collective property are another important source of revenues for village coffers. To manage collective property, oversee lease contracts, and reallocate land as peasants leave agriculture, many villages have formed various kinds of "companies," or management offices.[16]

---

[14]Two documented exceptions are Wenzhou, Zhejiang, and Zhongshan County, Guangdong, where private enterprises now outnumber and outcompete collectively owned ones. On the former, see the fieldwork reported in Helen F. Siu, *Agents and Victims in South China* (New Haven, Conn.: Yale University Press, 1989); on the latter, see Liu Yia-ling, "The Reform from Below: The Private Economy and Local Politics in Rural Industrialization: The Case of Wenzhou" (unpublished paper, University of Chicago, 1988).

[15]Jean C. Oi, "The Fate of the Collective after the Commune," in Davis and Vogel, *Chinese Reform*; and Victor Nee and Su Sijin, "Institutional Change and Economic Growth in China: The View from the Villages" *Journal of Asian Studies* 49(February 1990):3–25; Gordon White, "The Impact of Economic Reform on the Chinese Countryside: Toward the Politics of Social Capitalism?" *Modern China*, vol. 13(Oct. 1987):379–410.

[16]Jean C. Oi, "Commercializing China's Rural Cadres," *Problems of Communism*, vol. 35(Sept./Oct. 1986):1–15; and Tyrene White, "Political Reform and Rural Government," in Davis and Vogel, *Chinese Society*.

The degree to which the village maintains a significant redistributive economy and corporate organization has been found to vary considerably. In the poorer villages in Victor Nee's Fujian sample, the lack of a village industrial base was found to weaken greatly the power of village governments and their ability to provide collective benefits.[17] On the other hand, the wealthier villages had a thriving corporate structure and collective benefits. In studies of villages ranging from average to prosperous in widely separated areas of Liaoning, Tianjin, Shandong, and Sichuan, Jean Oi has found a generally strong corporate village structure.[18] Graham Johnson has noted the same phenomenon in his research in rural Guangdong, as has Tyrene White in her fieldwork in Hubei.[19] There appears to be a growing realization that an industrial base helps strengthen village corporate institutions; Nee and Su in fact predict that with further economic growth, the moribund governments of their poorer villages will revive. To document the pattern of variation in village corporate structures, and specify the variables that affect their strength, is one of the most important subjects of current research.

The Urban Work Unit System

In urban areas, the cellular and cohesive character of work units has changed little. Urban work units still provide a broad array of benefits, services, and goods to their employees, and there is little evidence of significantly increased labor mobility in the dominant public sector. The urban private sector still employs well under 10 percent of urban residents, and has been primarily a phenomenon of urban youths and a transient rural population. Despite the fact that money wages in the private sector are often much higher than in public enterprises, there is strong evidence that urban citizens still vastly prefer the benefits that public enterprises bestow, and there is little evidence of significant mobility between private and public enterprises.[20] Additionally, there have been at most only slight increases in

---

[17]Nee and Su, "Institutional Change."

[18]See "The Fate of the Collective."

[19]Graham Johnson, "The Fate of the Communal Economy: Some Contrary Evidence from the Pearl River Delta," paper presented at the Annual Meeting of the Association for Asian Studies, Chicago, Ill., March 1986; and Tyrene B. White, "Political Reform and Rural Government."

[20]A 1986 survey of 2500 people in 38 cities found that 82.7 percent of the population still preferred jobs in the state sector: see *Jingji Yanjiu*, December 1987. A 1985 survey of Tianjin residents found that state-sector employment was generally considered to be the ultimate object of mobility aspirations: Nan Lin and Yanjie Bian,

the movement of employees between workplaces in the public sector, and some researchers have found that there is even less than before. In short, the private and temporary labor markets of cities are still sharply segmented from the public-sector work force, and the barriers to mobility between public workplaces are still largely intact.[21]

Urban work units, moreover, still maintain a high degree of corporate organization. Firms in the state and collective sectors have added aggressively to their stock of housing, services, and benefits, to the extent that their retained profits permit. Illicit funneling of profit into collective benefits has been a widespread practice in public enterprises.[22] Some Chinese observers single out the resilience of the urban work-unit structure as a major barrier to economic and political reform.[23] While the party places much less stress on intimidation and indoctrination than in the past, there has nonetheless been no documented change in the formal structure of political institutions within the workplace. In sum, if changes have taken place in the exercise of political authority in urban areas, this is not due to an erosion of the traditional work-unit cohesiveness. However, the new marginal sectors, while small, do represent significant sectors of urban society that escape the web of organization in which political authority in China has heretofore been exercised.

Politics and Social Stratification

In the Mao era, political loyalty was a requirement for upward social mobility and material privilege. Educational credentials were denigrated, even penalized, and did not generally lead to high status and privilege. Admission to

---

"Status Attainment in a Chinese Labor Structure" (unpublished, State University of New York at Albany, 1989).

[21]See Deborah Davis, "Urban Job Mobility,"in Davis and Vogel, *Chinese Society*; Ezra F. Vogel, "Early Stage Commodity Society," ibid.; Gordon White, "The Politics of Economic Reform in Chinese Industry: The Introduction of the Labour Contract System," *China Quarterly*, vol. 111(Sept. 1987):379–410; Linda Hershkovitz, "The Fruits of Ambivalence: China's Urban Individual Economy," *Pacific Affairs*, vol. 58(Fall 1985):427–50.

[22]Andrew G. Walder, "Factory and Manager in an Era of Reform," *China Quarterly*, vol. 118(June 1989):242–64; Xia Xiaoxun and Li Jun, "Consumption Expansion: A Grave Challenge to Reform and Development," in Bruce L. Reynolds, ed., *Reform in China: Challenges and Choices* (Armonk, N.Y.: M. E. Sharpe, 1987), pp. 89–107.

[23]Lu Feng, "Danwei: yi zhong teshu de shehui zuzhi xingshi," *Zhongguo shehui kexue*, vol. 1(Jan. 1989):71–88; Xia and Li, "Consumption Expansion."

high-quality middle schools and universities was highly politicized, engendering political competition and activist behavior in youth-league organizations and to significant party participation among university students.[24] Promotion to cadre positions in villages and urban workplaces presupposed party membership or at least a consistent record of loyalty and activism. Party, youth-league, and trade-union organizations provided separate infrastructures to be staffed by party loyalists, creating a separate political-career line.[25] The suppression of private economic activities deprived the ambitious of alternative sources of income and mobility, reinforcing the party's control over the individual's life chances.

With its decision to curtail its intensive efforts at mobilization and indoctrination, and its decision to court intellectuals and the technically skilled, the party seemingly changed many of the past rules of the game. Political campaigns had been the primary opportunity for loyal activists of the past to distinguish themselves. In the late 1970s, the party unilaterally modified the intrusive mobilizational and ideological stance of the Mao era. In so doing, it ended formal ideological grading of candidates for school admission and job promotions, and greatly de-emphasized the political labels and class backgrounds given such strong emphasis in prior years. The new emphasis on education, training, and production radically reduced the time available for purely political activities, greatly devaluing them, and created an apolitical path to success. Moreover, the household economy in rural areas and the private economy in the cities seem to offer lucrative alternative career paths. It would appear, then, that the party's control over career opportunities, so important in its past efforts to control and mobilize the population, may have been relinquished to a large degree.

How far-reaching are these changes, though, and what impact have they had on the exercise of political authority in schools and workplaces?

Politics in Reward Systems

The significant depoliticization of education and career advancement has greatly weakened the party's ability to maintain a party-dominated "political life" within schools and workplaces. The party has not had the ability to

---

[24]Susan L. Shirk, *Competitive Comrades: Career Incentives and Student Strategies in China* (Berkeley: University of California Press, 1982); Jonathan Unger, *Education Under Mao: Class and Competition in Canton Schools, 1960–1980* (New York: Columbia University Press, 1982); Anita Chan, *Children of Mao: Personality Development and Political Activism in the Red Guard Generation* (Seattle: University of Washington Press, 1985).

[25]Walder, *Communist Neo-Traditionalism*, chapter 3.

intimidate and enforce discipline among nonmembers that it had in the Mao era. The importance of performance on standard examinations and of evaluation of skill, educational credentials, and job performance has been greatly elevated. This does not mean, however, that political certification, in the form of party membership, is no longer a requisite for career promotion. This characteristic of political authority in China has not changed: the higher one rises in one's career in state enterprises and public institutions, the more important political certification is for further success. This does mean, however, that the ideological and family-background requirements for party membership have been greatly relaxed, and that the party has made a concerted effort to absorb and promote competence.[26]

But the party's new stress on skill and education has served to weaken the party's ability to discipline nonactivists who have no current interests or immediate prospects of career advancement. The erosion of party influence and control has been especially pronounced among middle-school and university students. The incentives for active and committed participation in Youth League organizations have been greatly undercut, and this organization is reportedly only a shell of its former self. The ability of the party to recruit university students while these are still in college has also dropped dramatically.[27] Political activists in these organizations have become more isolated from the rest of the school community, and their status and reputation have greatly declined.[28] As a result, the party can no longer exert effective control over student populations from which it is now largely estranged.

In urban work units, party organizations have not suffered the serious declines of the universities. Once they have graduated from universities and become concerned with career advancement, young people are more willing to consider party membership.[29] This badge of political certification remains important for upward mobility within state organizations and enterprises. However, political campaigns have not been a feature of work life in the 1980s, and group study and political indoctrination have been neglected for almost a decade. This has reduced the potential cost of subordinates' political

---

[26]Susan L. Shirk, "The Decline of Virtuocracy in China," in James L. Watson, ed., *Class and Social Stratification in Post-Revolution China* (Cambridge, Eng.: Cambridge University Press, 1984), pp. 56–83.

[27]Stanley Rosen, "Prosperity, Privatization and Chinese Youth," *Problems of Communism*, vol. 34(March 1985):1–28; and Stanley Rosen, "Youth Socialization and Political Recruitment in Post-Mao China," *Chinese Law and Government*, Summer 1987.

[28]Stanley Rosen, "The Impact of Reform Policies on Youth Attitudes," in Davis and Vogel, *Chinese Society*.

[29]Rosen, ibid.

indifference and resistance, and has allowed significantly higher levels of contention in the workplace.[30]

Scarcity and Administrative Allocation

Poverty, scarcity, and bureaucratic allocation of goods reinforced the authority of cadres in Mao's China. An emphasis on local self-sufficiency with respect to grain forced most of China's countryside into subsistence agriculture; and low state-procurement prices for grain helped to ensure low rural incomes.[31] The dictates of collective agriculture made peasant households dependent on village leaders for access to the grain they grew, and even for permission to slaughter pigs and chickens.[32] A policy of low wages in urban areas similarly depressed cash incomes for two decades, while the characteristic neglect of nonproductive investment and consumers' preferences led to acute shortages of housing and consumer goods in urban areas. New urban housing was built and allocated primarily through workplaces.[33] Consumer goods were rationed extensively through workplaces. Cadres derived considerable power from their ability to allocate goods and thereby alter the consumption and living standards of their subordinates.

As material scarcity has been alleviated over the past decade, one would expect the allocative power of cadres to decline. Incomes and living standards in both rural and urban areas have undergone unprecedented growth. Rural cadres no longer make cropping and consumption decisions for village households. Urban housing investment and consumer-oriented industry have also grown rapidly. A virtual consumer revolution has improved supplies of all manner of goods—even though certain high-quality brands are still scarce—and the old rationing system has been largely dismantled. It would appear that this important source of the cadres, authority may have been eroded quite deeply. How extensive has been the change, and what has been the impact on the exercise of political authority?

---

[30]See Andrew G. Walder, "Wage Reform and the Web of Factory Interest," *China Quarterly*, vol. 109(March 1987):22–41; and Walder, "Factory and Manager."

[31]Nicholas R. Lardy, *Agriculture in China's Modern Economic Development* (Cambridge, Eng.: Cambridge University Press, 1983).

[32]Oi, *State and Peasant in Contemporary China*, chapter 2.

[33]Whyte and Parish, *Urban Life*, chapters 2–4; Walder, *Communist Neo-Traditionalism*, chapter 2.

Rural Cadre Allocative Power

Village cadres no longer monopolize income opportunities as they did in the past. But they commonly retain the ability to allocate lucrative contracts, distribute agricultural inputs at low state prices, and provide access to capital. The extent and significance of cadres' remaining power, however, is a matter of scholarly dispute.

In villages that retain a healthy collective sector and retain management over the collective economy, village cadres still derive considerable power from their ability to allocate capital and job opportunities in collectively managed enterprises. Moreover, village cadres, some claim, still derive power from their ability to allocate lucrative leases for collective enterprises, and to allocate cheap agricultural inputs.[34] It has also been found that some coercion is still commonly exercised in the imposition of grain contracts at low state procurement prices.[35] Where there is a sizeable sector of individual peasant enterprises, cadres have been found to exert considerable influence over the allocation of credit and the setting of taxation rates.[36] Even in areas where private enterprise predominates, such as Wenzhou, researchers have found that enterprises still depend on local cadres for political protection, for which cadres extract a corrupt "rent."[37]

Scholars have been unable to come to agreement about how much power local cadres currently exercise. Some see them as dominant, sometimes corrupt local figures in their research locales.[38] Others, such as Nee and Su, find in the poorer villages they studied a much humbled and demoralized local officialdom. Debate centers primarily on township (the former commune) and village (the former brigade) officials. More research is needed to clarify the lines of variation already evident. At present, we cannot estimate the predominance of different models of rural government.

---

[34]Oi, *State and Peasant*, chapter 9; and Oi, "Peasant Households Between Plan and Market: Cadre Control over Agricultural Inputs," *Modern China*, vol. 12(April 1986):230–51.

[35]Jean Oi, "Peasant Grain Marketing and State Procurements: China's Grain Contracting System" *China Quarterly*, vol. 106(June 1986):272–90.

[36]Jean C. Oi, "Preliminary Research Report on the Role of Local Government in the Development of Rural Industry in Zouping County" (unpublished paper, Harvard University, 1988); Tyrene White, "Political Reform and Rural Government."

[37]A rich Chinese research literature on Wenzhou is mined effectively in Liu Yia-ling, "The Reform from Below."

[38]William Hinton, "Dazhai Revisited," *Monthly Review*, March 1988, pp. 34–50.

Work-Unit Allocations in Cities

In cities, work-unit allocation of goods and benefits has not declined enough to have a significant independent effect on the exercise of authority. However, because of other changes, work-unit allocation of housing and other benefits has become a source of chronic and open conflict within work units.

In cities, rationing of consumer goods through workplaces has largely been curtailed, as shortages of consumer items have declined. However, the larger workplaces still commonly attempt to procure high-quality brands of color television sets and bicycles that are still hard to purchase in stores, and the larger workplaces are still the main source of new housing, which continues to be very scarce and hotly sought after, and are still an important source of employment for the children of employees.[39]

Since many key goods and services are still allocated through workplaces, declines in scarcity and of the role of the workplace in direct rationing of goods probably has not, in itself, significantly weakened political authority. However, the overall relaxation of party control in factories has made the continued workplace allocation of benefits, especially housing and bonuses, a source of constant contention and sometimes open conflict. Today's factory managers must be prepared to maintain and improve current levels of benefits if they hope to enjoy the cooperation of their work force, and they must devise ways to distribute these benefits in a way that will not stimulate conflict. Evidence of such work-unit conflict has abounded in the 1980s, and has been a major cause of managerial concern.[40] Although there

---

[39]Yok-shiu F. Lee, "The Urban Housing Problem," *China Quarterly*, vol. 115(Sept. 1988):387–407. In a 1986 survey of 1011 households in Tianjin, I and my collaborators found that over 85 percent of the workplaces offered meal halls, shower facilities, and health clinics; over 65 percent offered loans for employees and maintained a nursery; over 50 percent arranged jobs for children of employees, and over 45 percent maintained retail stores, provided relief payments for families, and assisted in the purchase of name-brand bicycles. Respondents reported having used an average of over 75 percent of the benefits offered at the workplace. One-third of the respondents lived in work-unit housing, while of those who thought it possible to get larger housing quarters, two-thirds said it would most likely be from their work units. For a description of the survey, see Andrew G. Walder, Zhou Lu, Peter M. Blau, Danching Ruan, and Zhang Yuchun, "The 1986 Survey of Work and Social Life in Tianjin, China: Aims, Methods and Documentation," Working Paper no. 26, Center for Research on Politics and Social Organization, Harvard University Department of Sociology, 1989.

[40]See Walder, "Wage Reform and the Web of Factory Interest," *China Quarterly*, vol. 109(March 1987):22–41; and Walder, "Factory and Manager."

are no factory-level studies to document such changes, it appears plausible that real and anticipated conflicts over workplace distributions have served to alter the exercise of authority.

Markets and Hierarchies

Under Mao, China's social structure was remarkable for the absence of market allocation. Direct exchange between producing communities, enterprises, households, or individuals was technically a punishable offense if it did not submit to planned state allocation. Many have already pointed out that the suppression of market mechanisms doomed Maoist antibureaucratism to failure by precluding the only logical alternative to bureacratic allocation.[41] And it has become axiomatic among outside observers, and a virtual slogan in China, that the economic reforms seek to increase the role of the market within a planned economy.

According to one influential characterization of Communist societies, centrally planned economies are essentially redistributive, and power and privilege are accorded to the social class of redistributors.[42] Victor Nee builds on this insight in his theory of market transition: to the extent that market allocation replaces bureaucratic redistribution in planned economies, the power and privilege of the officials will decline.[43] In this perspective, markets act as a political solvent, eroding the basis of cadre power and privilege as resources shift from the redistributive (planned) to the market sector.

This line of thinking challenges us to sharpen our ideas about the relationship between markets and hierarchies. What are the features of "markets" in these settings? Monopolies and oligopolies may serve to modify and reinforce, rather than erode pre-existing patterns of authority. Small private sectors with high earnings and profits may easily come to an accommodation (sometimes corrupt) with local cadres, and by providing employment, services, and products that the public sector cannot, may serve primarily to buttress the existing political system. The characteristics of specific

---

[41] Andrew G. Walder, "Some Ironies of the Maoist Legacy in Industry," in Mark Selden and Victor Lippit, eds., *The Transition to Socialism in China* (Armonk, N.Y.: M. E. Sharpe, 1982), pp. 215–37; and Martin K. Whyte, "Who Hates Bureaucracy? A Chinese Puzzle," in Nee and Stark, *Remaking the Economic Institutions of Socialism*, pp. 233–54.

[42] Ivan Szelenyi, "Social Inequalities in State Socialist Redistributive Economies," *International Journal of Comparative Sociology*, vol. 19(1978):63–87.

[43] Victor Nee, "A Theory of Market Transition: From Redistribution to Markets in State Socialism," *American Sociological Review*, 54(October 1989):663–81.

product and labor markets would appear to be a crucial problem in any contrast posited between markets and hierarchies. How extensive is market allocation and how extensive must it be before it significantly influences patterns of authority?

These considerations turn the theorized conflict between markets and hierarchies into a subject for further research. It may well be that market mechanisms of a certain type and extensiveness actually serve to reinforce cadre power. It should therefore be taken as problematic whether markets will erode China's political hierarchies, or whether the political hierarchies will distort and manipulate the workings of market mechanisms.

The Urban Industrial Economy

In urban areas, hierarchies have served to obstruct and distort markets much more than markets have served to break down hierarchies. For reasons specified in an earlier section, the extension of private markets for consumer goods has not in itself greatly affected the exercise of authority in urban institutions. Similarly, the potential effect of the growth of private and temporary labor markets has been undermined by the continuing segmentation of these sectors from the core labor force in the state and large-collective sectors. The urban work-unit structure, especially the common provision of housing and other important benefits, along with the lack of urban welfare and relief services other than those administered through workplaces, have served to obstruct the development of a general labor market. It appears that the growth of markets is being obstructed and distorted by urban institutions. These urban institutions must be reshaped by political intervention before market mechanisms can gain solid footing.

The Rural Household Economy

In rural areas, the effect of markets has been mixed. These markets have served to alter political hierarchies more fundamentally than in urban areas. However, in many areas, rural political hierarchies appear to have adapted well to market forces. There is no simple antithetical relationship between markets and hierarchies; and the growth of the former does not translate in an invariant fashion into an erosion of the latter. Nor are the two completely independent; hierarchies can significantly shape the workings of markets. The relationship, it appears, is contingent and variable. In some villages, political institutions have been virtually destroyed by the spread of markets. In others, cadres have developed a symbiotic relationship with a dominant and thriving private economic sector.[44] In others, cadres have been able to restrict the growth of private enterprise, instead funneling growth into collective enterprises over which they exert control, and from which they derive considerable benefit. In much of rural China, it appears that local cadres, as managers of collective property, are among the most active and powerful participants in rural markets for labor and industrial products.

The relationship between markets and hierarchies in China's villages remains to be clarified conceptually, as do the causes of variation in the relationship. These will be major subjects for future research. The key research question is whether the local political machines based upon the remaining economic powers of government are firmly established and self-sustaining, or whether one can expect the continued spread of market allocation to further erode cadre power.

Political Dependence

Cadre power in the Mao era was characterized by a marked dependence of Chinese citizens on local cadres. Urban and rural residents were heavily dependent on their work units or production teams for the satisfaction of a wide array of their needs, and there were very few alternatives outside of this framework. While local cadres therefore held considerable power over the livelihoods and careers of their subordinates, the party's mobilizational and repressive approach to rule placed potentially arbitrary discretion in the hands of cadres, personalizing this dependence. Finally, political mobilization of activists, coupled with systematic repression of independent activity and thought, served to split the population and make it strikingly dependent politically.[45] It is evident that this degree of dependence on cadres has been eroded significantly over the past decade. How has this change affected the exercise of authority?

Mutual Dependence of Leaders and Led

Economic reforms have heightened cadres' dependence on their subordinates. The result is an intensified mutual dependence between leaders and led that has led to more routinely contested decisions and a pattern of rule characterized by informal bargaining and deadlock in decisionmaking.

---

[44]This is the lesson of Wenzhou as described in Liu, "The Reform from Below."

[45]See Walder, *Communist Neo-Traditionalism*, chapters 2–4; Oi, *State and Peasant*, chapter 7.

We need hardly repeat here the evidence presented already that the dependence of citizens on cadres has declined in rural and urban areas. The economic reforms, more importantly, have heightened the dependence of cadres on their subordinates. Officials are more dependent now on the highly educated and industrious in the increasingly performance-oriented economy that developed in the 1980s. Rural cadres depend on peasants to whom they lease collective property to manage it well and turn over the assigned fees to the collective coffers. They rely upon peasant farmers, who now have alternative sources of livelihood, to fulfill state-procurement contracts that higher levels of government often force upon villages. In areas where private industries are widespread, rural cadres rely on their entrepreneurs for revenues for public use and—a reportedly common corrupt practice—for personal income as well.[46] The occasional temptation of cadres to resort to coercion to enforce peasant fulfillment of contracts can be viewed as an expression of the cadres' weakness and frustration. They now must go to independent peasant households to obtain the funds and grain that their superiors demand of them, whereas in the past peasants had to go to them for grain and funds.[47]

A similar pattern has been reported in urban industry. New fiscal mechanisms have made available for the first time large sums for incentive pay, while responsibility systems place blame for declining labor productivity directly on the factory manager. This provides an increased incentive for workers to bargain with managers, since, in contrast with before, there is now something over which to bargain. And especially in light of the fact that managers are still unable to fire workers for poor labor discipline, workers are given a virtual monopoly of the supply of labor. The reforms have made managers more dependent on their labor forces, and given workers increased bargaining leverage.[48]

Party-Clientelism

Despite its totalitarian pretensions, local political rule in the Mao era was in practice a clientelist system. The local party and its representatives selected loyal supporters on political grounds, provided them with careers and privileges, and relied on these loyal subordinates to push through party policies.

---

[46]E.g., Liu, "The Reform from Below."

[47]Tyrene White, "Political Reform and Village Government," describes the dilemmas of rural officials in this situation.

[48]See Walder, "Factory and Manager."

Cadres inevitably used the economic resources at their disposal to reward the loyal, and through time the mutual support of cadres and activists grew into a web of personal loyalties radiating out from party branches.[49] In retrospect, the harsh repression of independent activity and thought, coupled with the fusion of political with economic power, made these clientelist networks the most prominent feature of political authority of that era. But the era of Mao lies behind us. Since its end what changes have occurred in the party's tradition of rule through patronage?

Clientelism and Conflict

Local party organizations persist in their traditional practice of dispensing patronage to loyal subordinates. This style of rule is less effective than before, however, and has itself become a major source of grass-roots conflict.

Despite the reduced dependence of the subject population, local cadres persist in the well-established party practice of rewarding the loyal with economic and career advantages. Political reform has not yet advanced to the point of implementing, much less articulating, a clear alternative to past practices. Persisting as it does as a permanent network of loyalists with a monopoly of formal government powers, and extending into all major institutions, it is hard to imagine how the party could act differently. Just as in the past, the party must use the resources at its disposal to reward those who help it in its effort to enforce its often unpopular policies at the grass-roots level.

The economic reforms have, however, created new problems for the party. The dependence of the subject population is much reduced, making the enforcement of compliance much more complicated. More important, the reforms have created new expectations and norms that have highlighted party patronage as a source of conflict and discontent. The rural reforms, while maintaining the legal pretenses of collectivism, have in fact created new property rights and conceptions of personal economic rights in villages. Peasants are more likely to view their earnings as something earned through their family's holdings, enterprise, and hard work, and cadre interference or rake-offs are likely to be much more deeply resented than when village cadres were the managers of a unitary agricultural enterprise, disposing of proceeds as they saw fit. This kind of activity is now more likely to be seen

---

[49]Oi and Walder, ibid.

as self-regarding and corrupt.[50] Similarly, party attempts to influence promotions and job assignments—especially when this takes the form of influence exercised on behalf of the relatives of ranking officials—is likely to provoke much deeper public reaction now that competition and merit are more deeply entrenched. The party and its system, weakened but still intact, is itself increasingly becoming a political issue and a target of public opprobrium.

Many observers have seen evidence of increased contestation of cadres' exercise of power when it is seen to arbitrarily abrogate these newly realized rights. Some have seen a nascent tendency of peasant entrepreneurs to resort to the legal system to enforce their rights.[51] Others have described pressures for legal rationalization caused by conflict over regulation of economic activities by rural cadres.[52] As Tyrene White found in her Hubei field site, "peasants who delighted in the immediate benefits of the agricultural reforms now complain bitterly of unreasonable and arbitrary decisions that nullify their contract rights or escalate their tax burdens . . . and favoritism by cadres for those with connections." "[P]easants continue to blame local cadres for their grievances . . . [and] have become the scapegoats for the painful consequences of rural development."[53] This is ultimately the most important impact that the uneven structural changes of the 1980s have had on the exercise of political authority in China. Attempts by cadres to exercise the kinds of prerogatives that they have always exercised are now more likely to be viewed as intolerable and illegitimate; and citizens are more willing, and better able, to resist.

Conclusions

If my observations on recent research are correct, then China has moved from a closed and tightly controlled local pattern of clientelist rule to a more fluid and contested pattern of clientelism (and its correlate, corruption). It appears that political authority in China has evolved into a more unstable

---

[50]Jean C. Oi, "Market Reforms and Corruption in Rural China," *Studies in Comparative Communism*, vol. 22(Spring/Fall 1989).

[51]See David Zweig et al., "Law, Contracts and Economic Modernization: Lessons from the Recent Chinese Rural Reforms," *Stanford Journal of International Law*, vol. 23(1988):319–64.

[52]Victor Nee, "Entrepreneurship and the Politics of Regulation in Rural China," in Nee and Stark, *Remaking the Economic Institutions of Socialism*, pp. 169–207.

[53]White, "Political Reform and Rural Government."

shadow of its former self but not into a qualitatively new type of system. One can only speculate whether the further spread of market mechanisms will eventually bring about a shift to a new pattern of authority—but the experience of the countryside so far would suggest that this is not enough. One may also speculate that greater stability can be achieved only if political reforms of some kind do bring about qualitative changes that break more decisively with the past. The regime's response to the popular protest of April–May 1989, however, indicates that intelligent political reform is not now on the agenda. The current reversion to coercion and political intimidation can treat only the symptoms of eroded political authority; it postpones reforms that will reconstitute authority on a new basis. Because this instability is the structurally rooted outcome of a decade of social change, we can expect that for the foreseeable future China will continue to experience grassroots conflict and ferment.

Index